SWAN

By Kyoko Ariyoshi

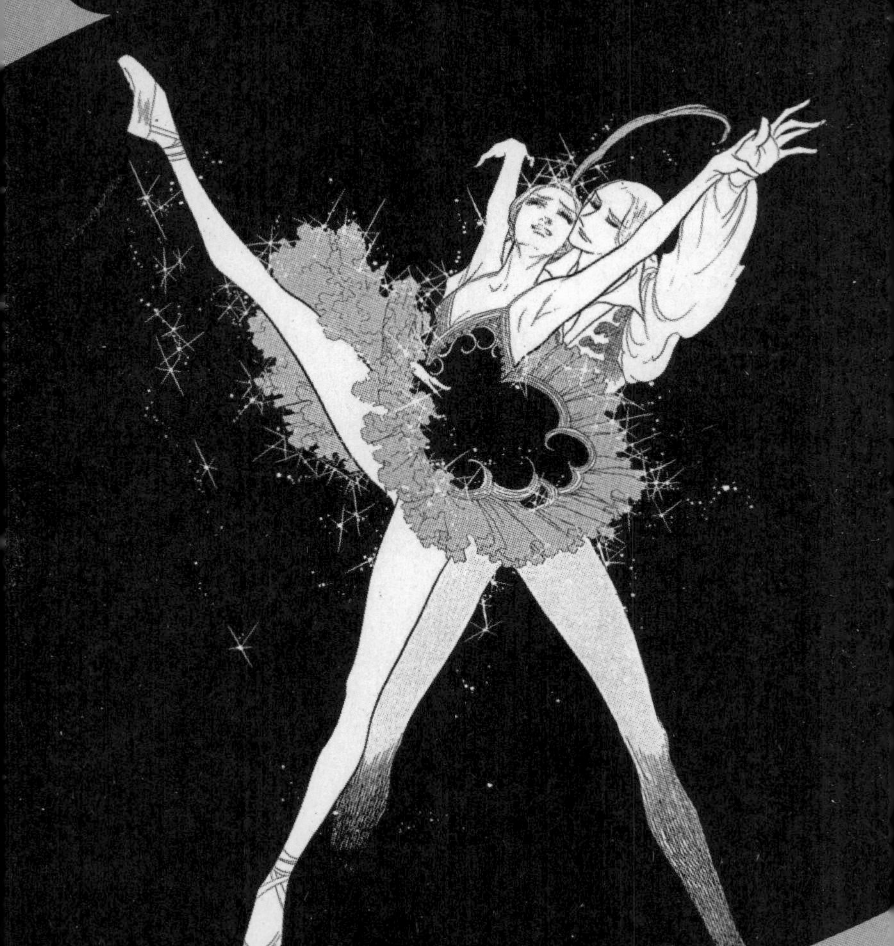

Volume 6

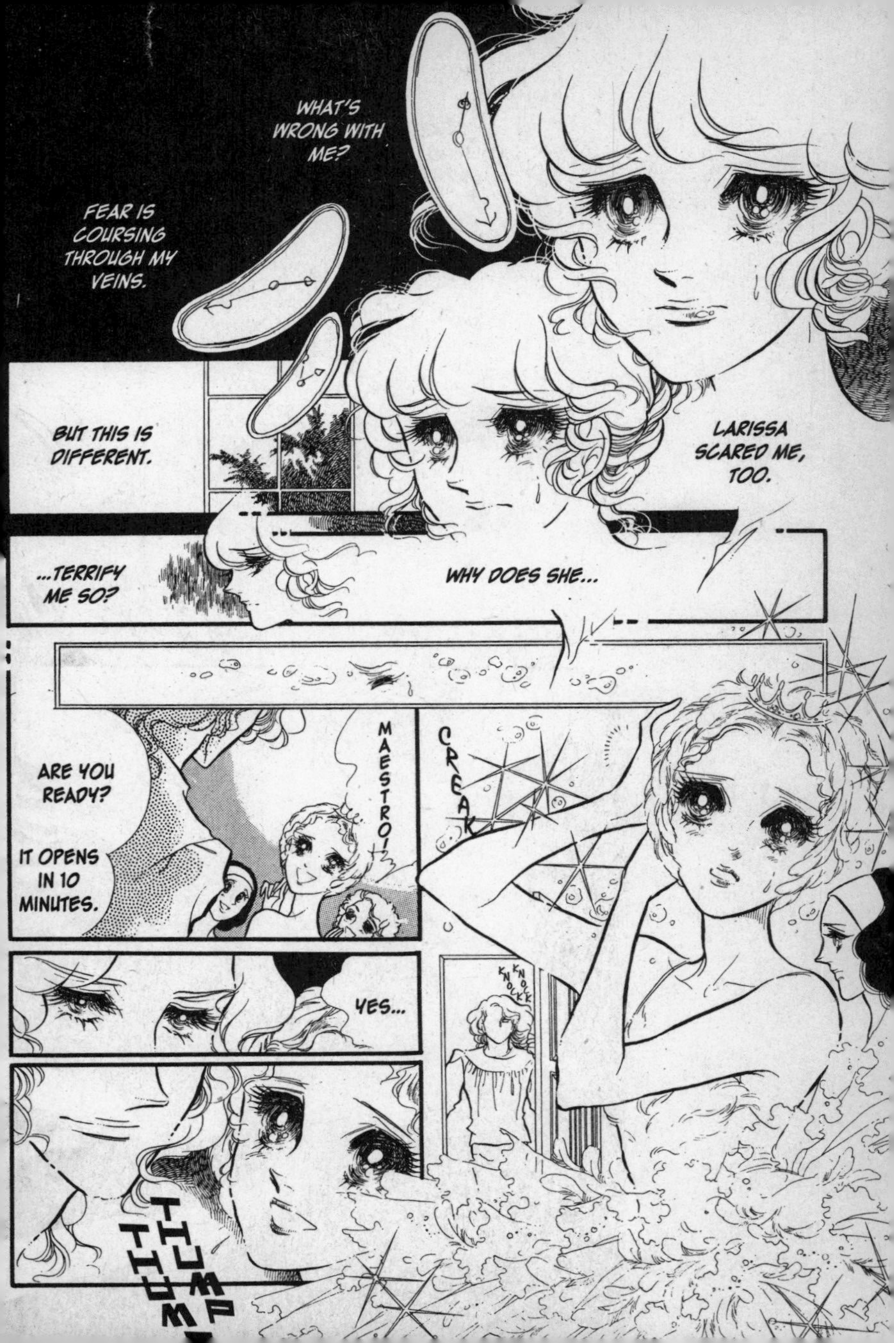
WHAT'S WRONG WITH ME?
FEAR IS COURSING THROUGH MY VEINS.
LARISSA SCARED ME, TOO.
BUT THIS IS DIFFERENT.
WHY DOES SHE...
...TERRIFY ME SO?
CREAK
KNOCK KNOCK
MAESTRO!
ARE YOU READY?
IT OPENS IN 10 MINUTES.
YES...
THUMP THUMP

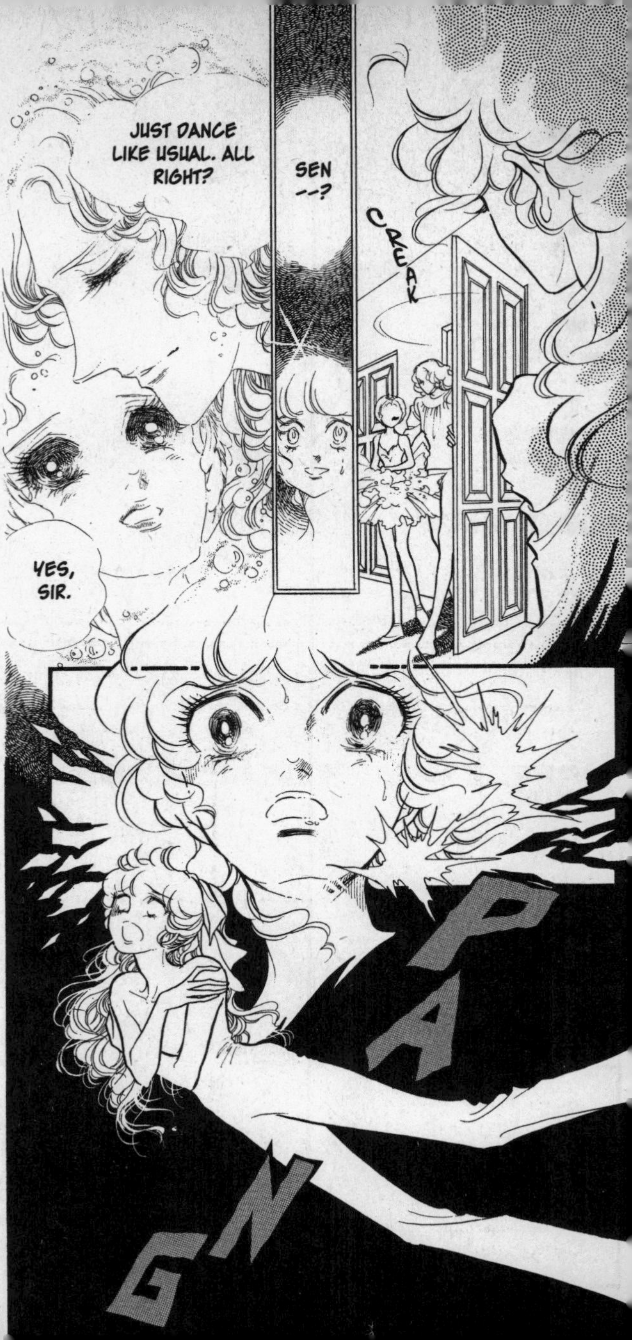
CREAK
SEN --?
JUST DANCE LIKE USUAL. ALL RIGHT?
YES, SIR.
PANG

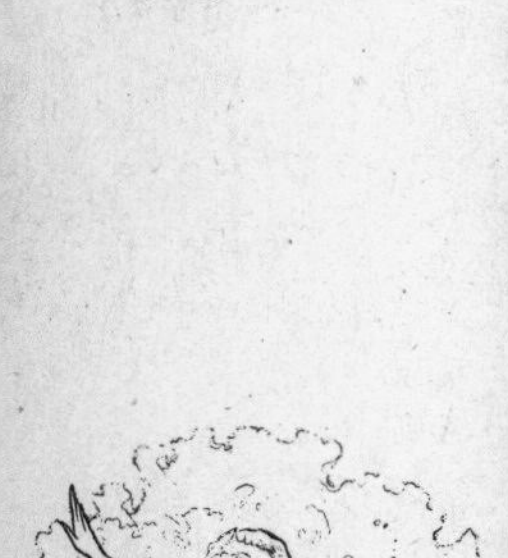

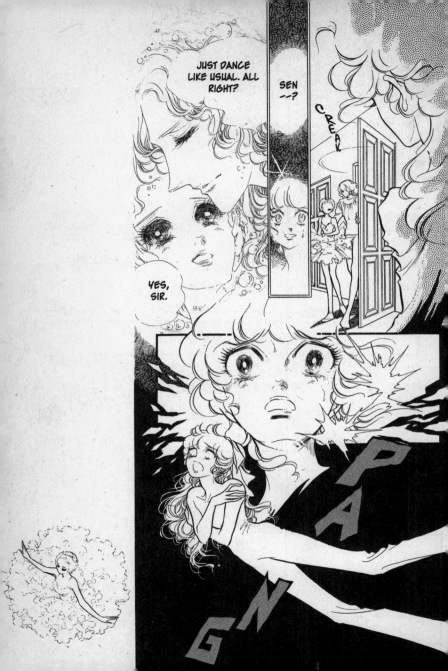

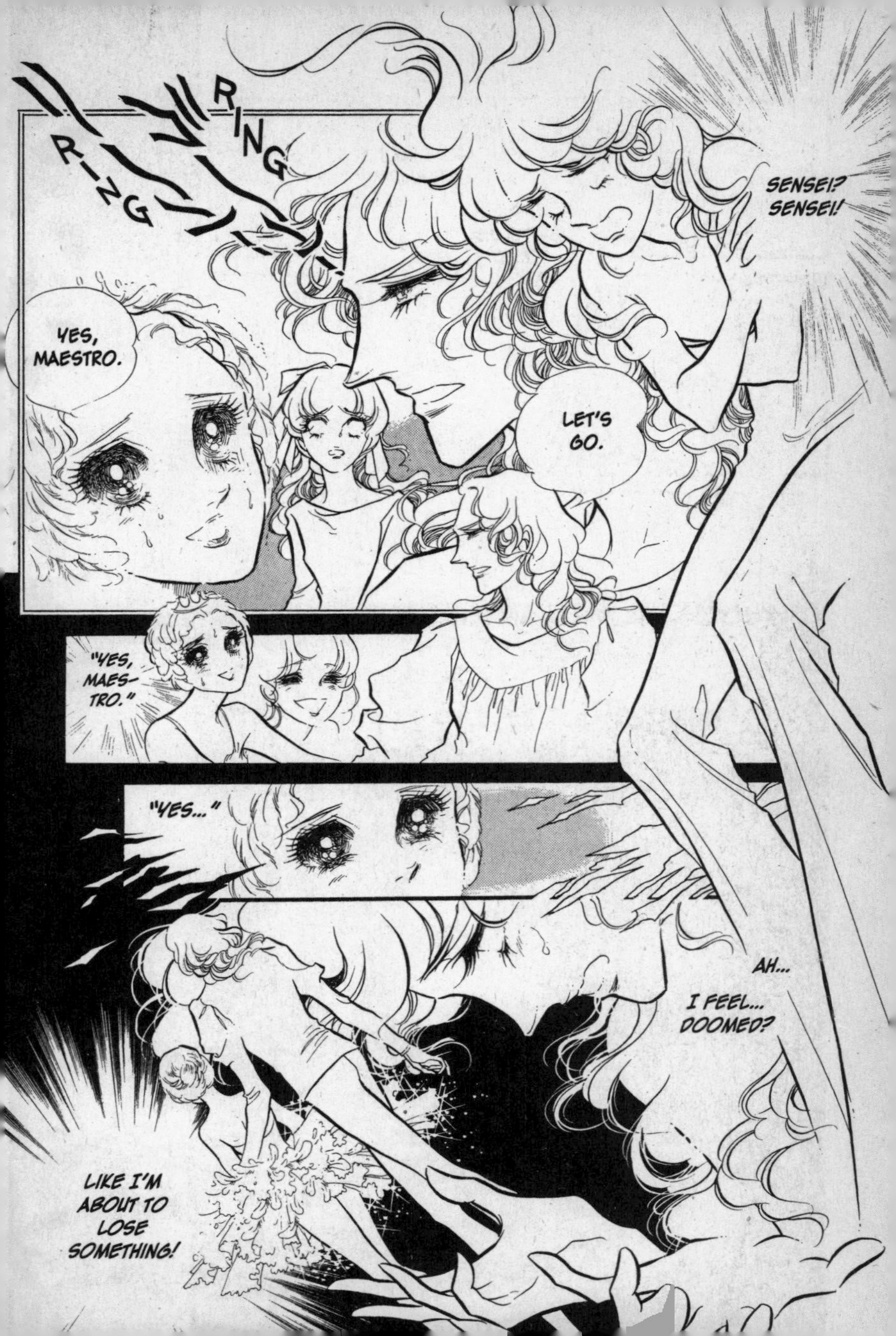
RING
RING
SENSEI? SENSEI!
LET'S GO.
YES, MAESTRO.
"YES, MAES-TRO."
"YES..."
AH...
I FEEL... DOOMED?
LIKE I'M ABOUT TO LOSE SOMETHING!

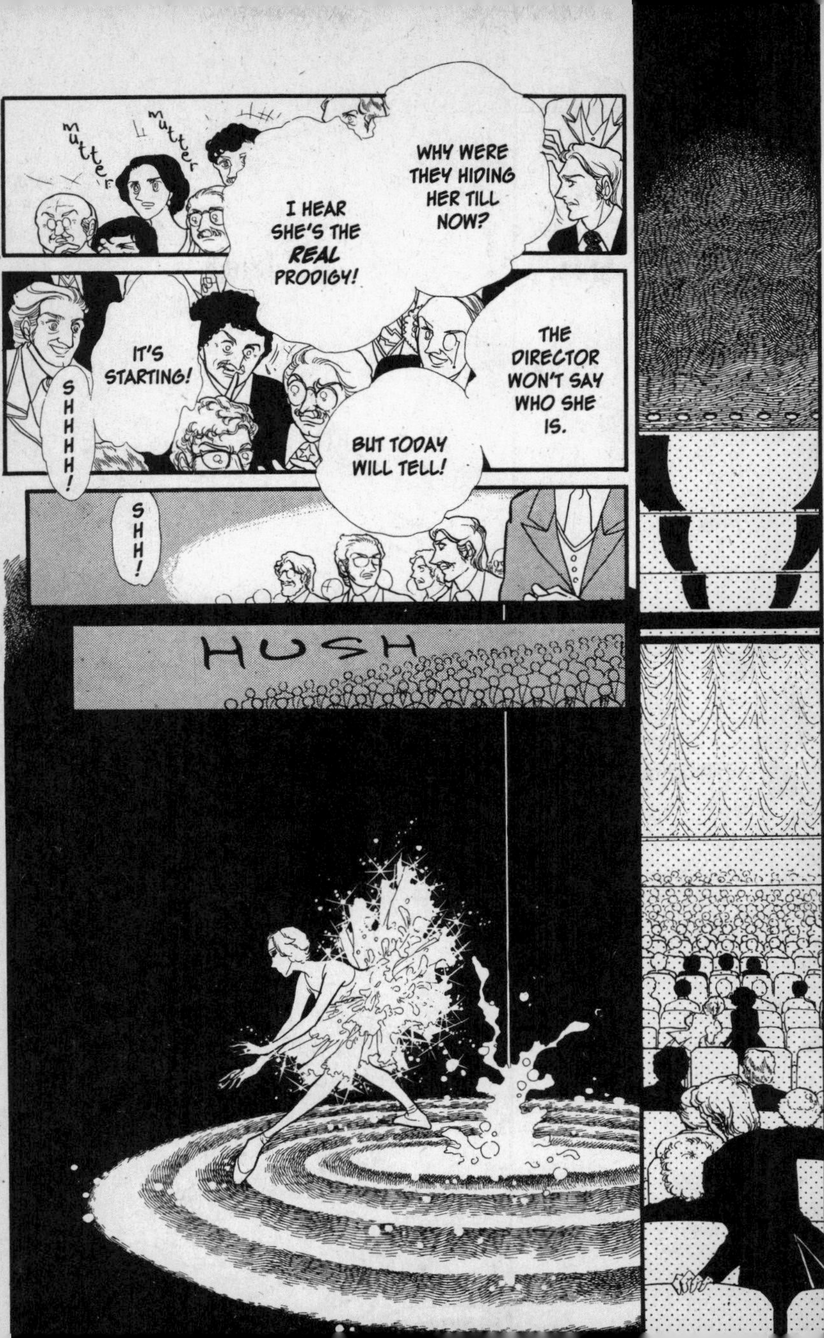
WHY WERE THEY HIDING HER TILL NOW?
I HEAR SHE'S THE *REAL* PRODIGY!
mutter mutter
THE DIRECTOR WON'T SAY WHO SHE IS.
BUT TODAY WILL TELL!
IT'S STARTING!
SHHHHH!
SHH!
HUSH

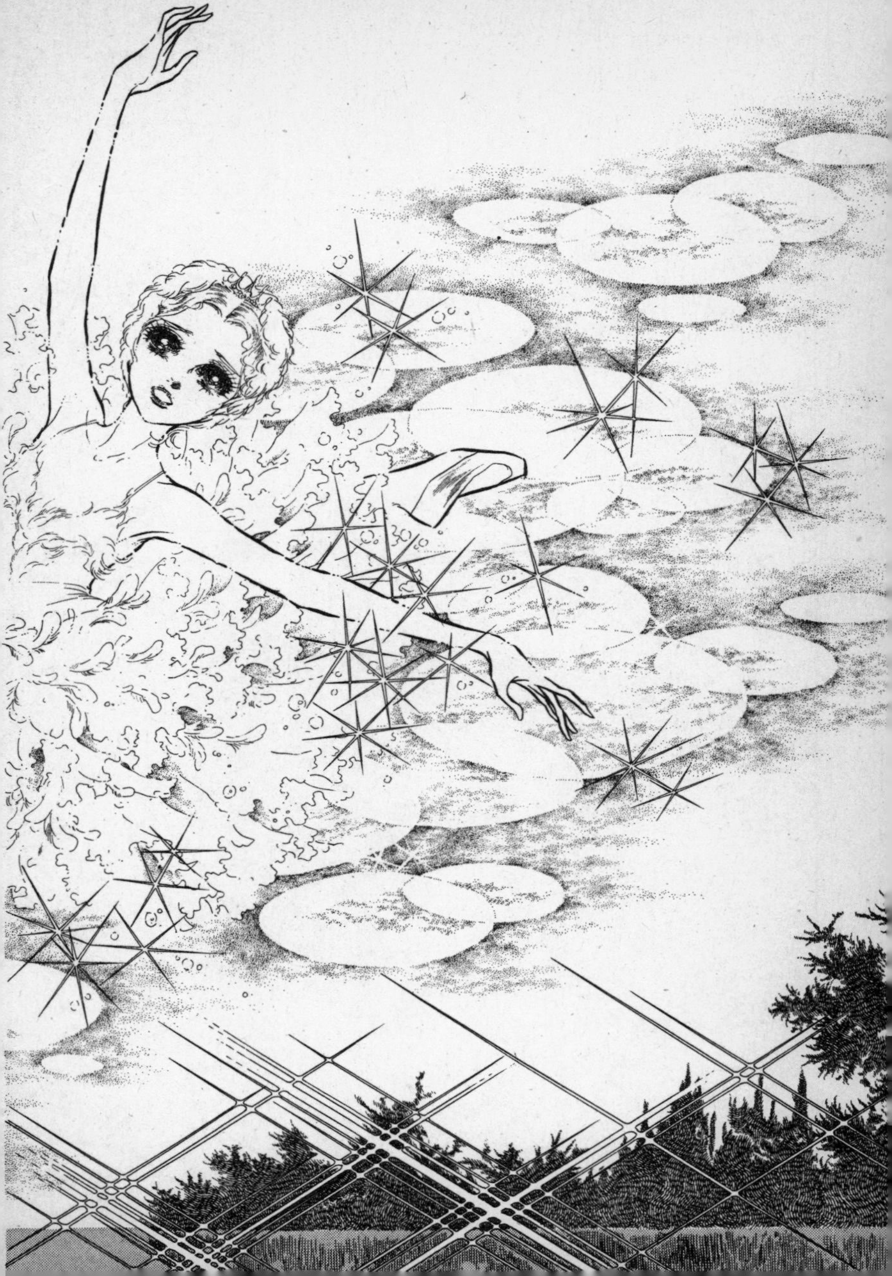

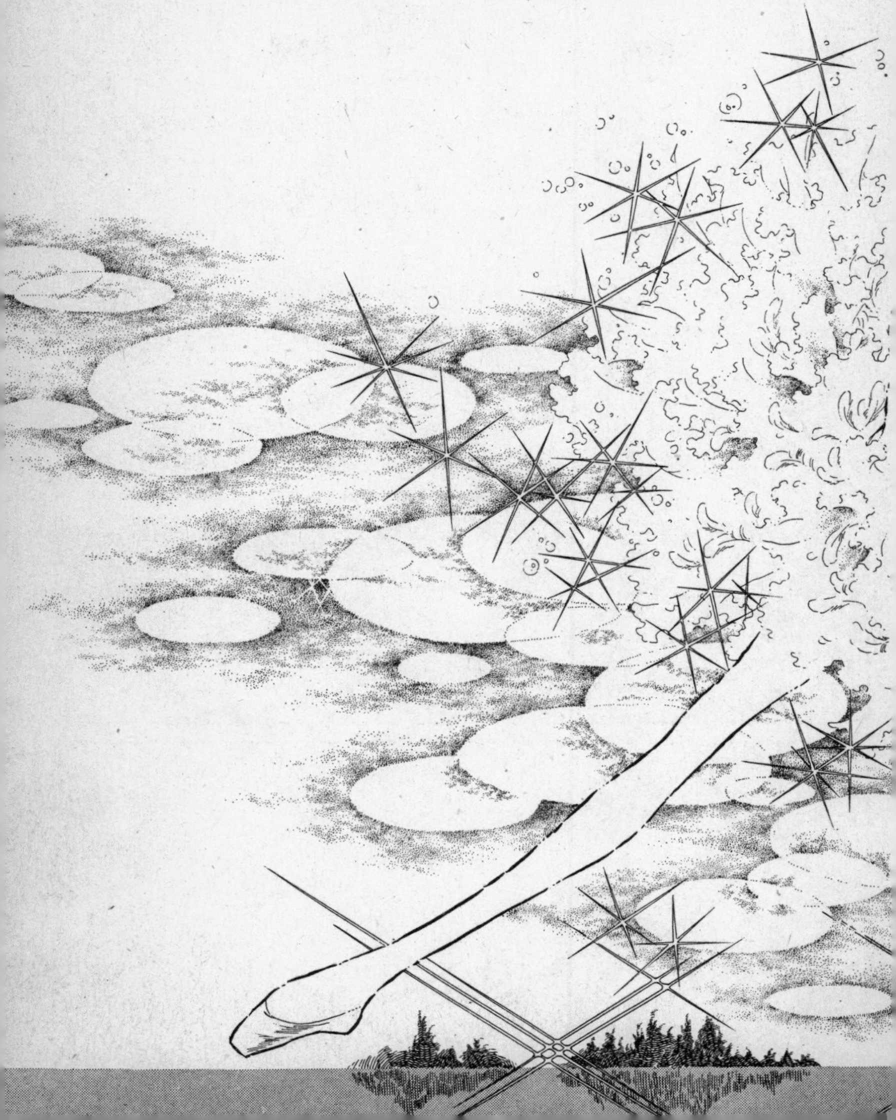

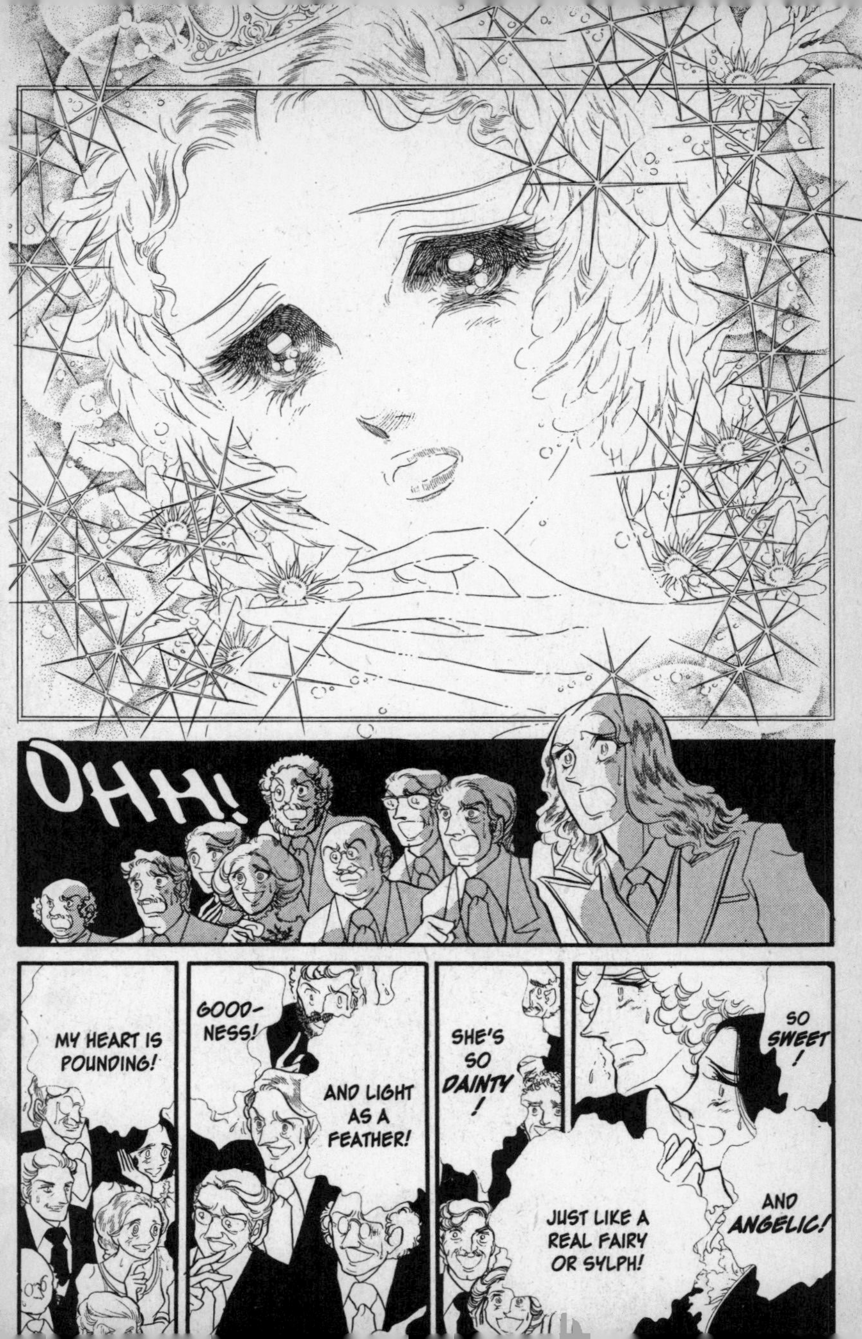
OHH!
SO SWEET!
AND ANGELIC!
JUST LIKE A REAL FAIRY OR SYLPH!
SHE'S SO DAINTY!
GOOD-NESS!
AND LIGHT AS A FEATHER!
MY HEART IS POUNDING!

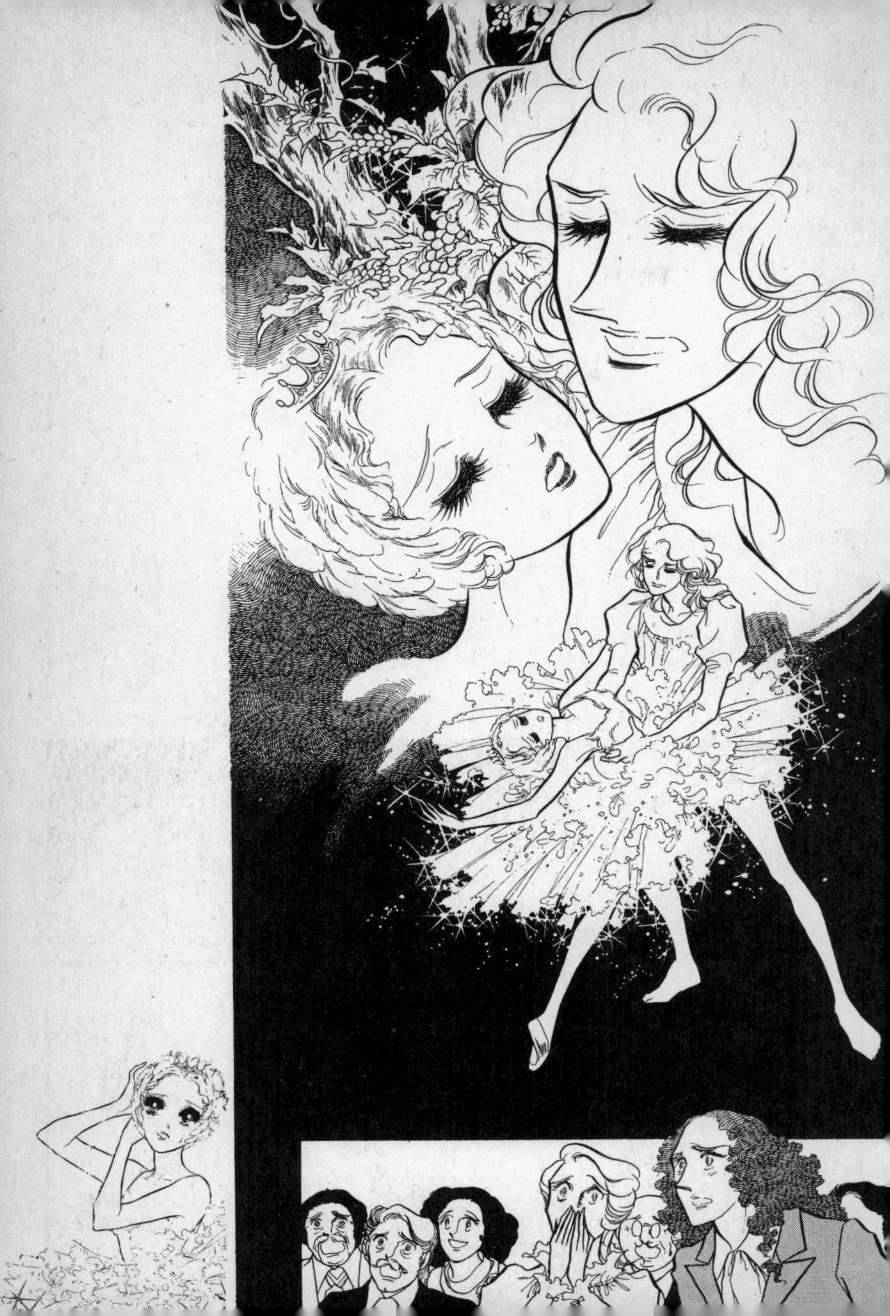

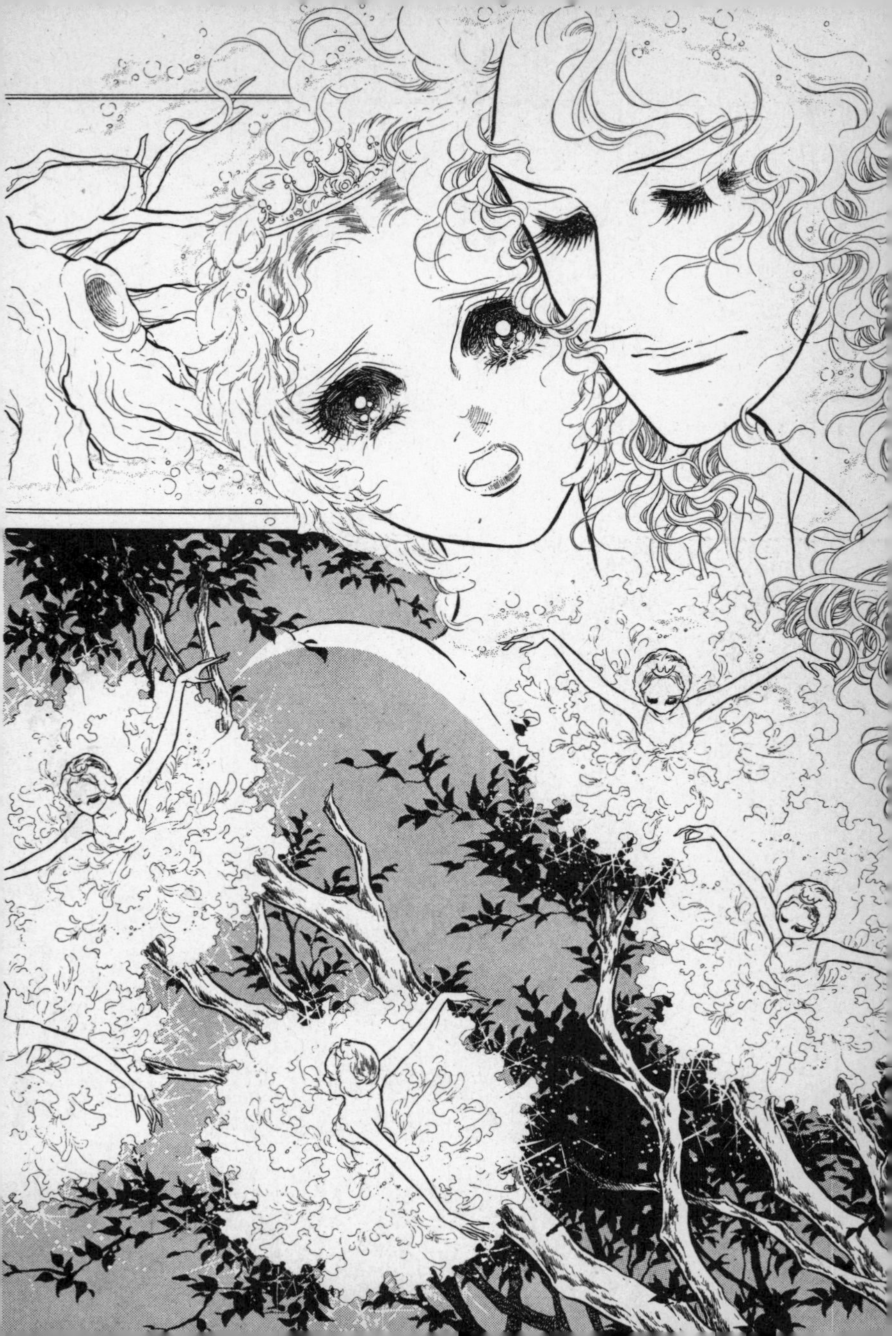

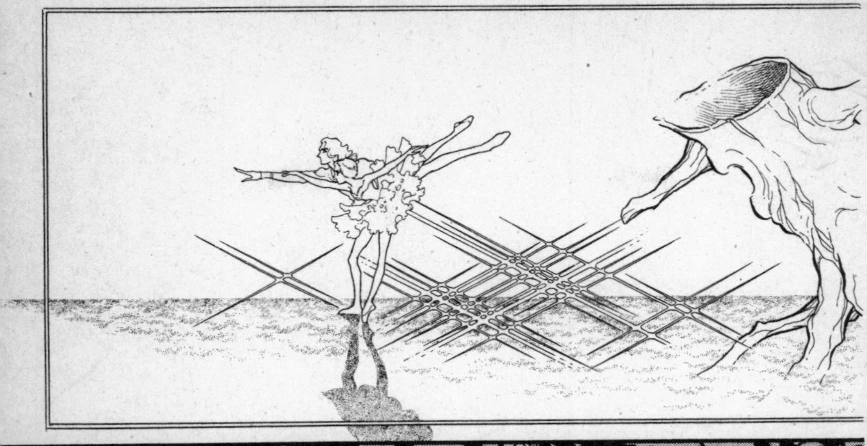
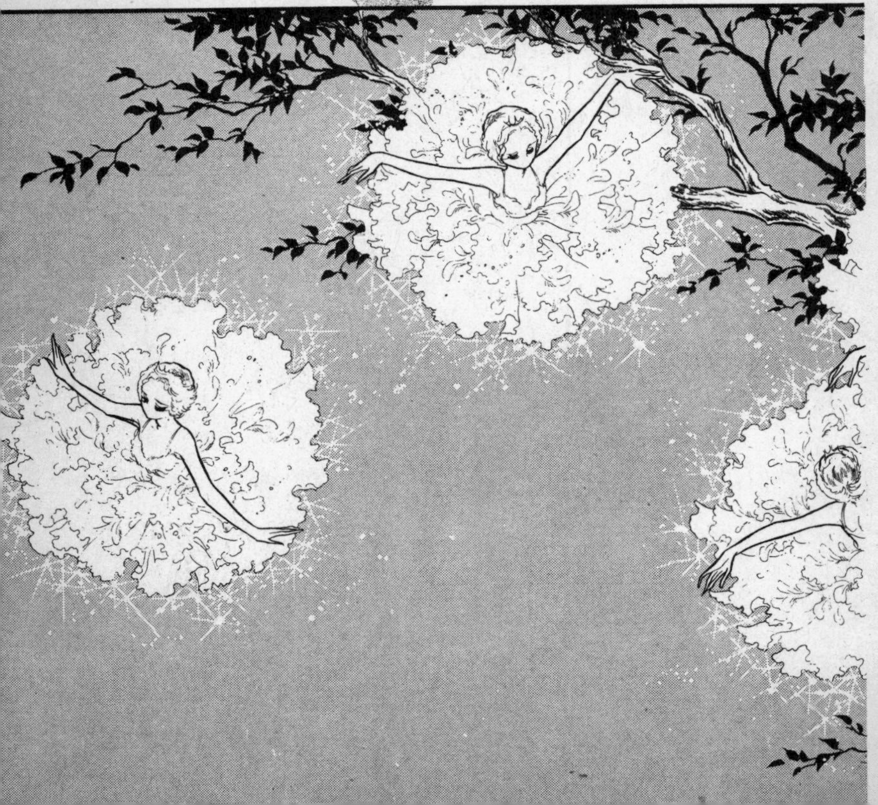

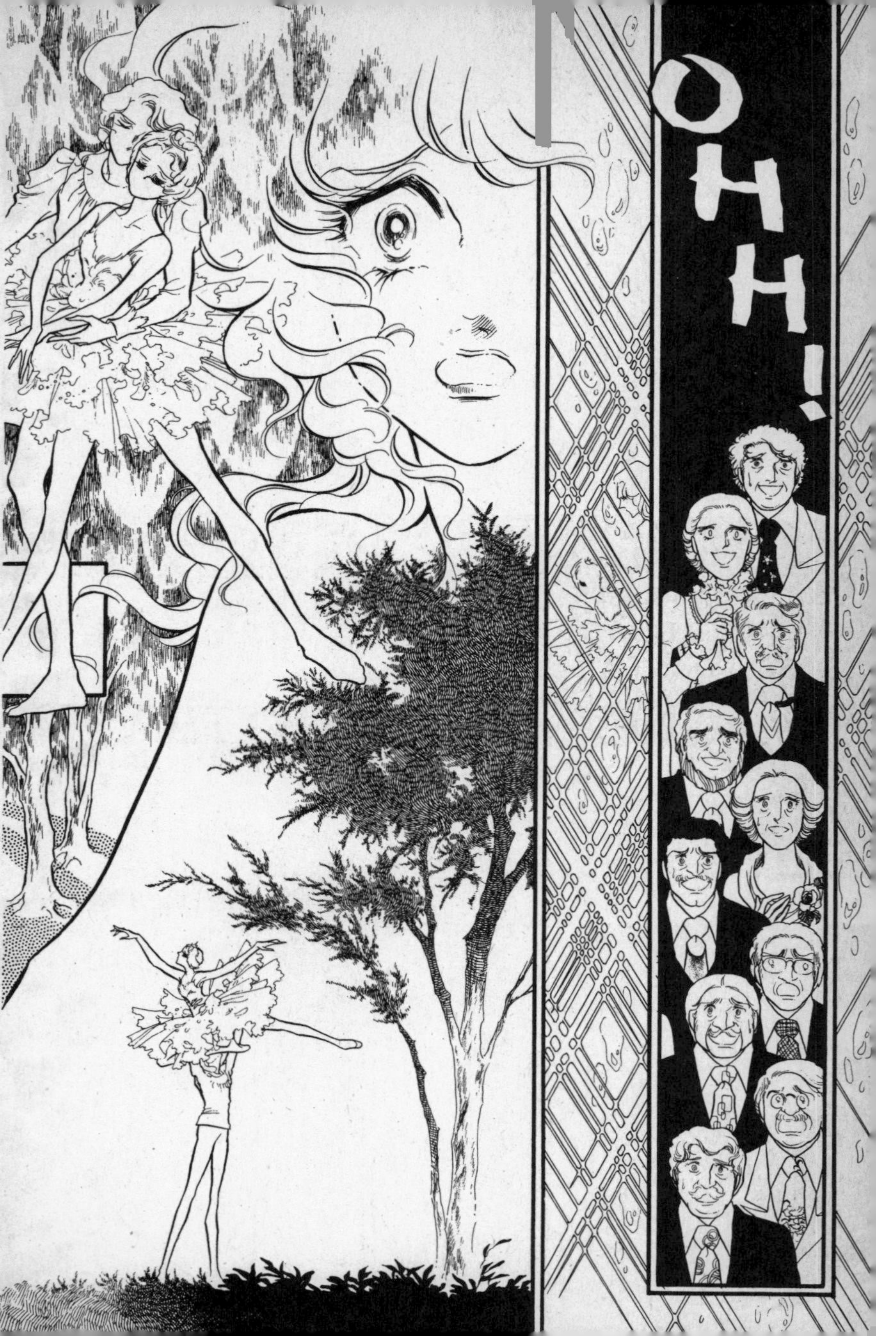
OHH!!

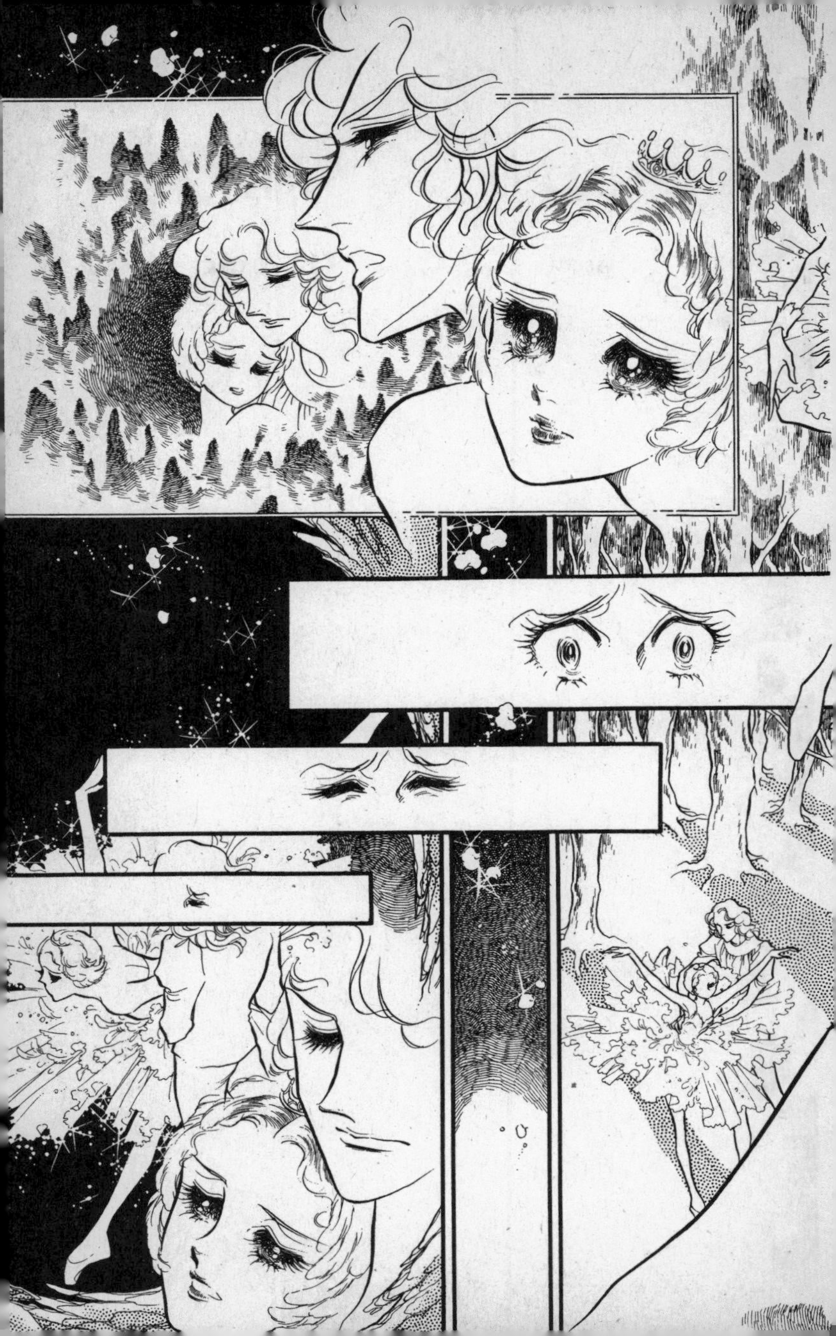

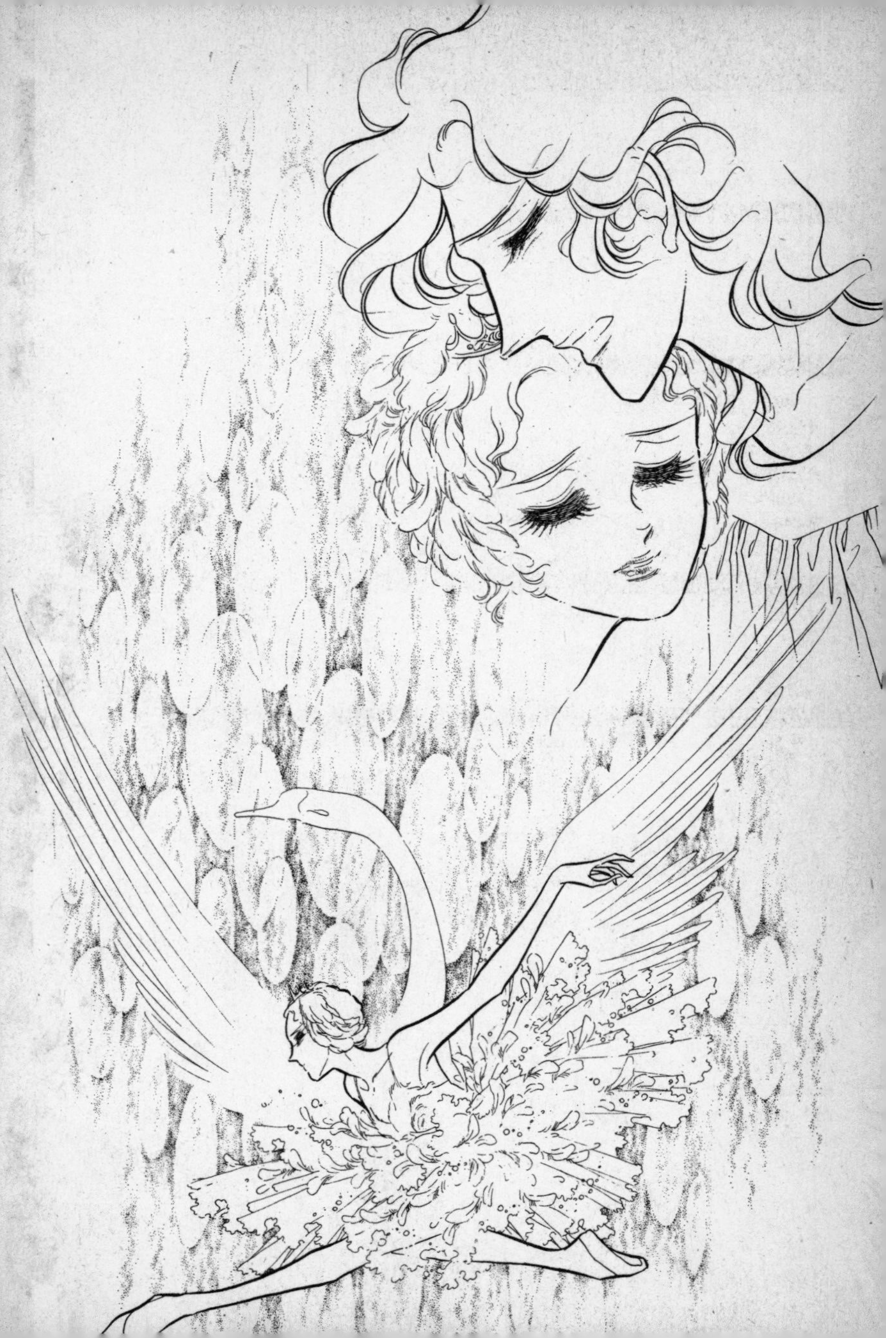

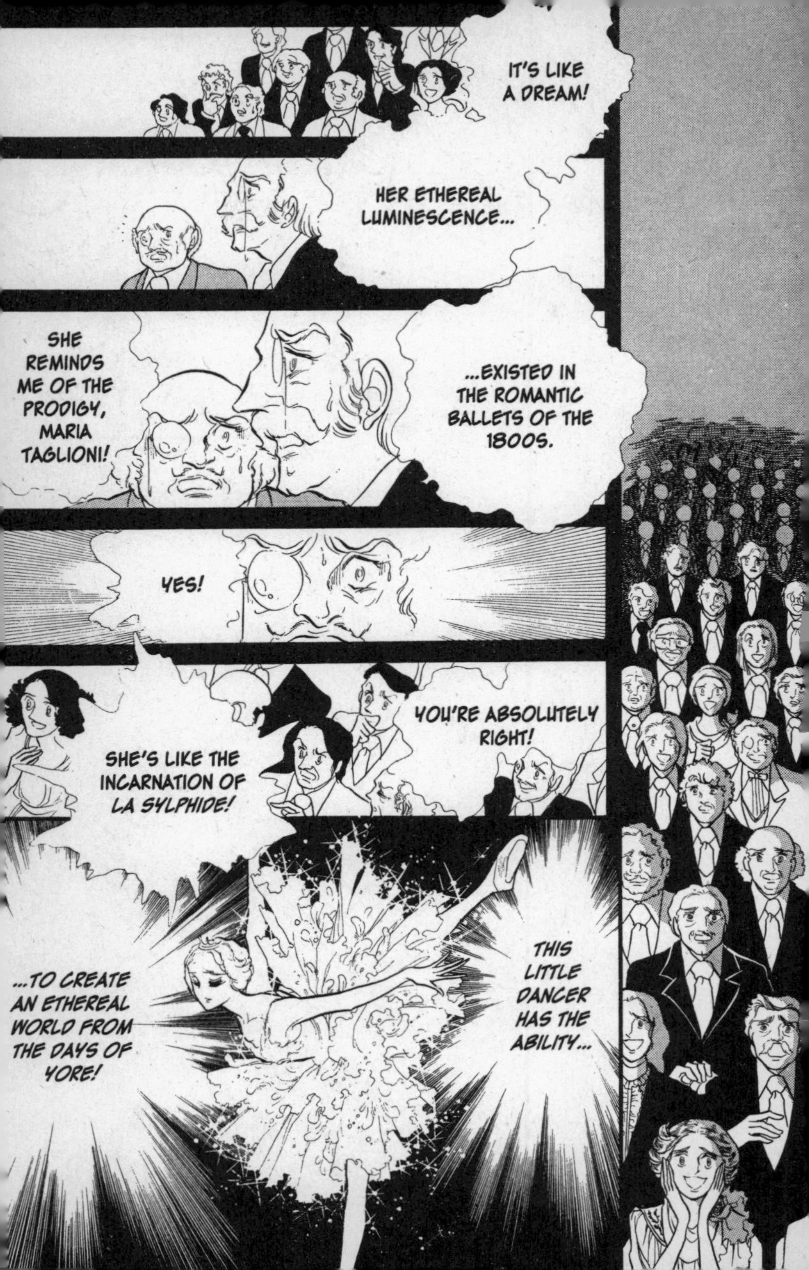
IT'S LIKE A DREAM!
HER ETHEREAL LUMINESCENCE...
...EXISTED IN THE ROMANTIC BALLETS OF THE 1800S.
SHE REMINDS ME OF THE PRODIGY, MARIA TAGLIONI!
YES!
YOU'RE ABSOLUTELY RIGHT!
SHE'S LIKE THE INCARNATION OF LA SYLPHIDE!
THIS LITTLE DANCER HAS THE ABILITY...
...TO CREATE AN ETHEREAL WORLD FROM THE DAYS OF YORE!

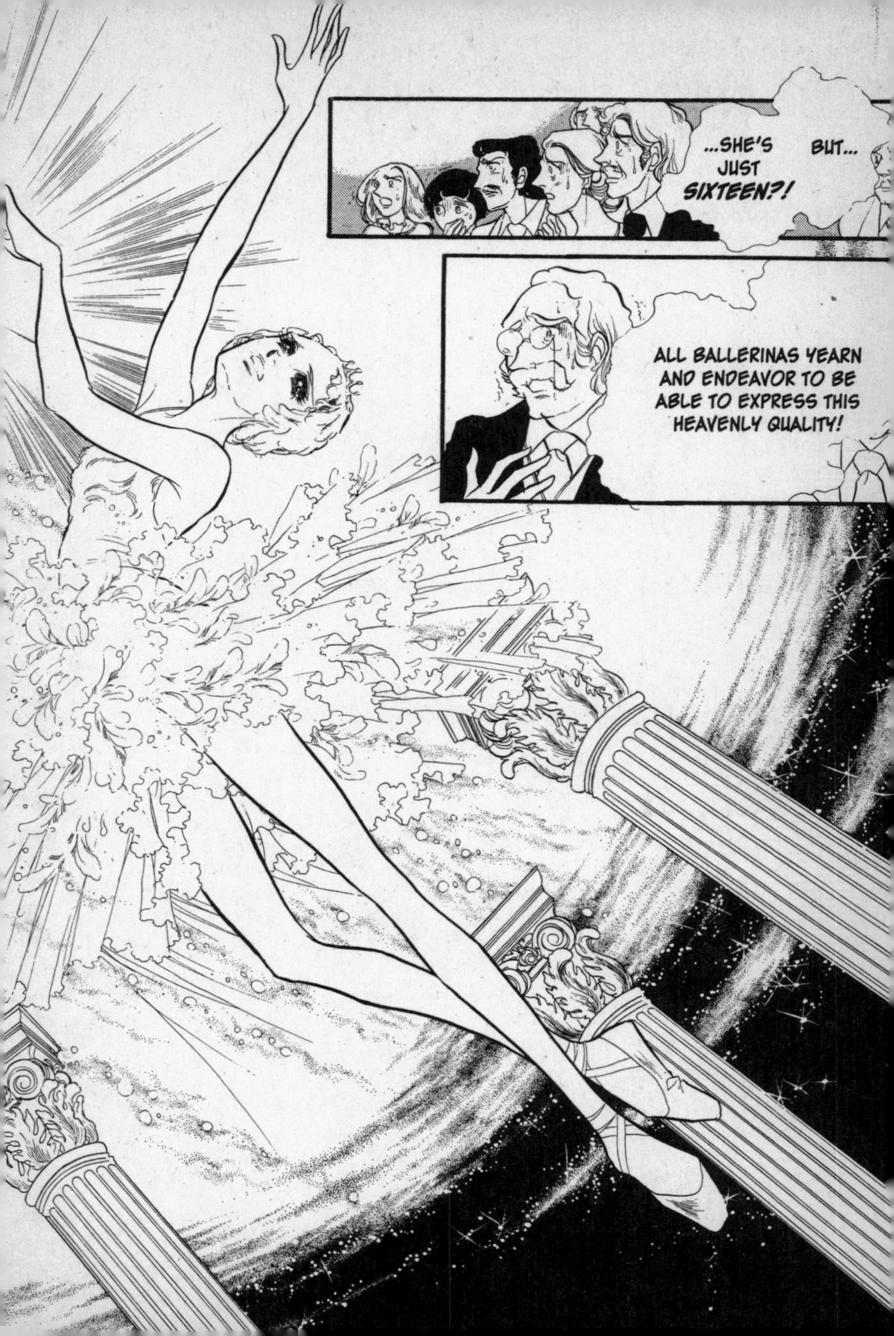
BUT...
...SHE'S JUST SIXTEEN?!
ALL BALLERINAS YEARN AND ENDEAVOR TO BE ABLE TO EXPRESS THIS HEAVENLY QUALITY!

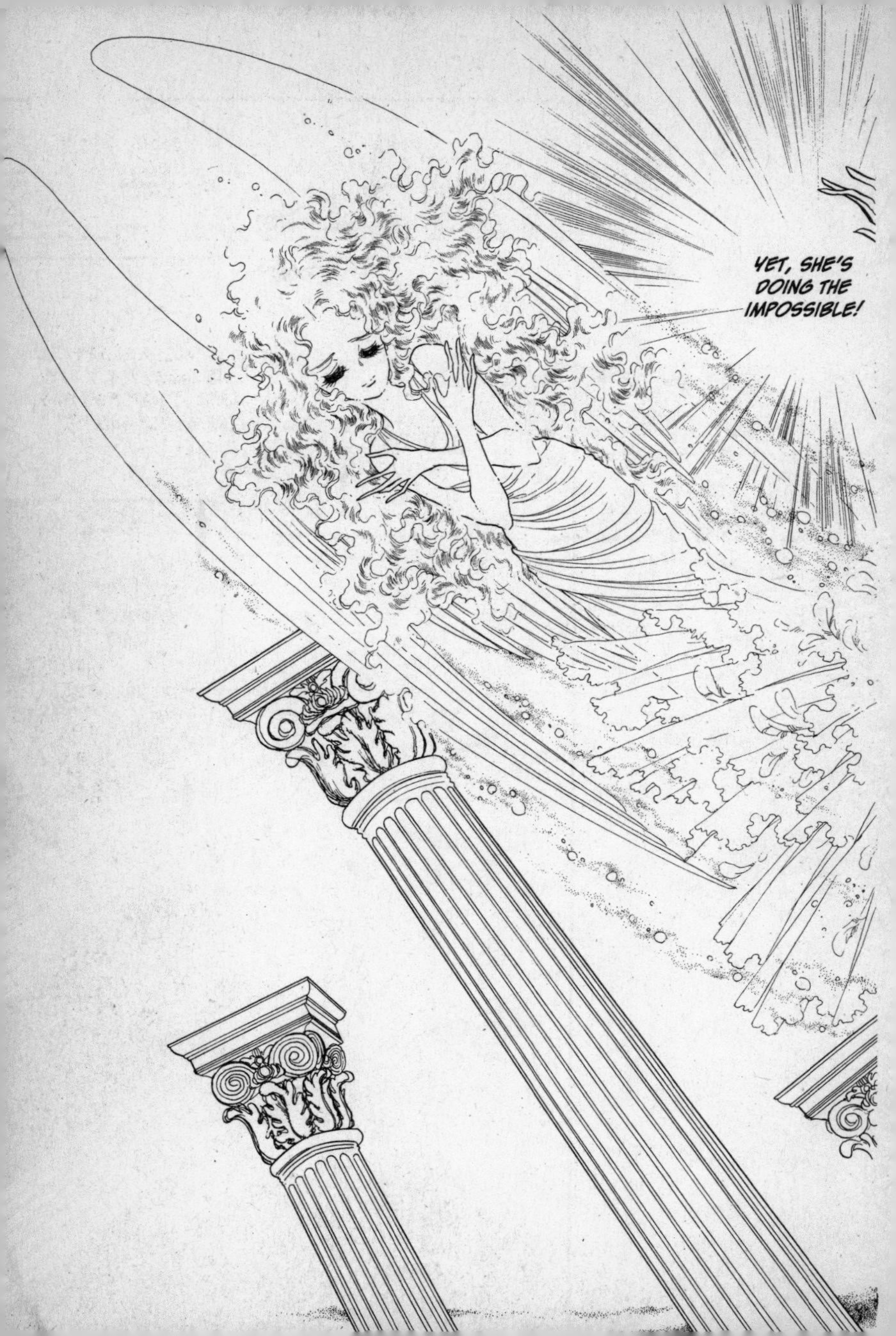
YET, SHE'S DOING THE IMPOSSIBLE!

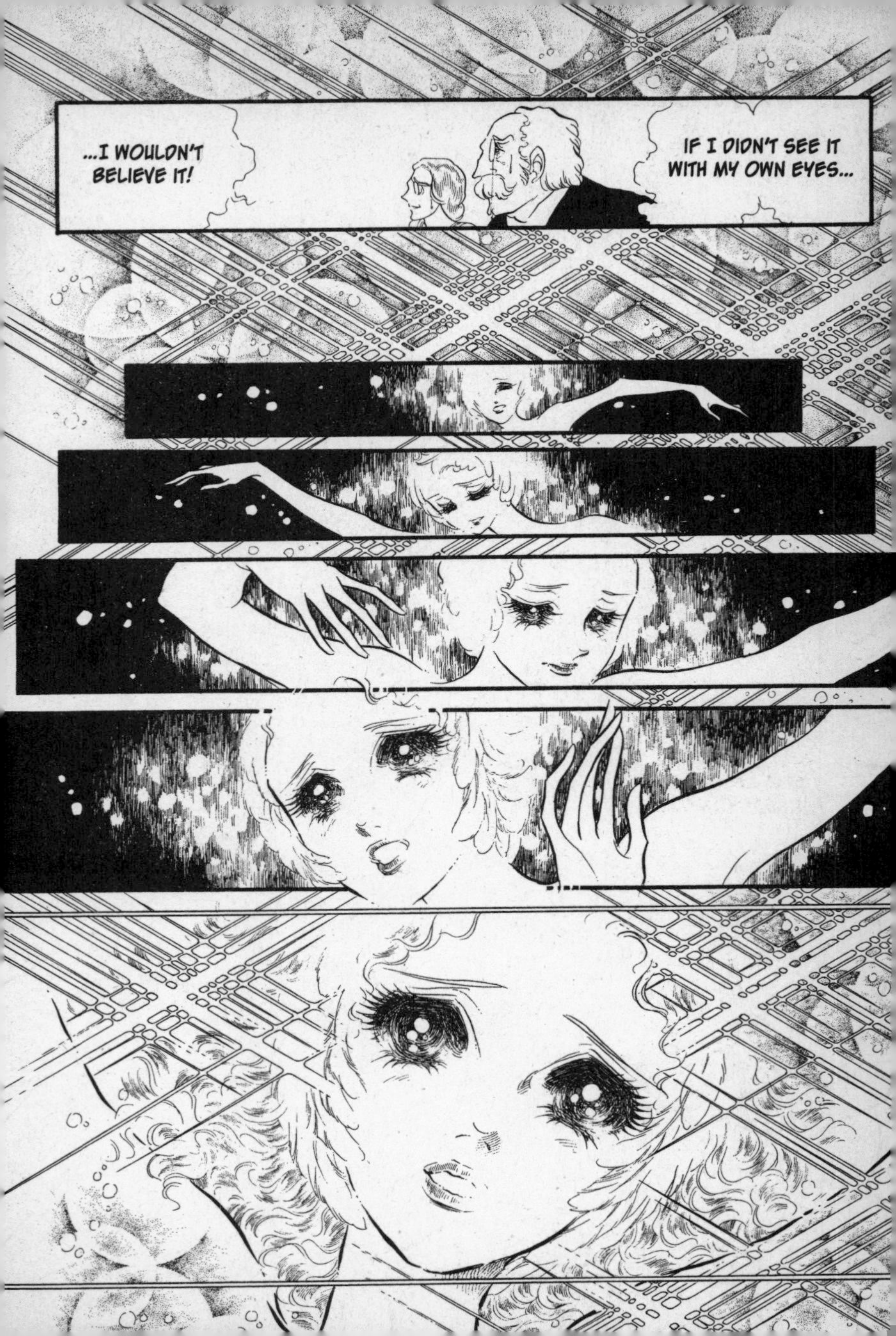
IF I DIDN'T SEE IT WITH MY OWN EYES...
...I WOULDN'T BELIEVE IT!

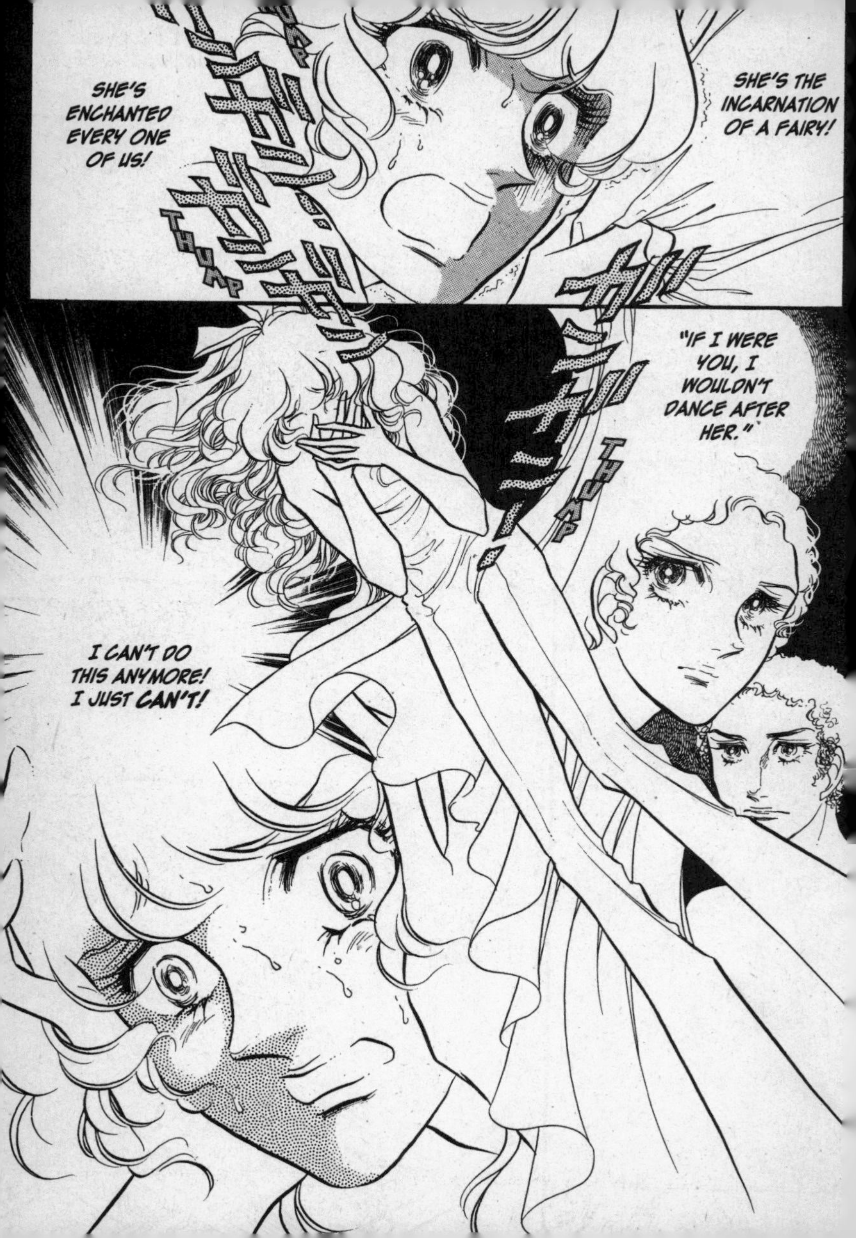
SHE'S THE INCARNATION OF A FAIRY!
SHE'S ENCHANTED EVERY ONE OF US!
THUMP
THUMP
"IF I WERE YOU, I WOULDN'T DANCE AFTER HER."
THUMP
I CAN'T DO THIS ANYMORE! I JUST CAN'T!

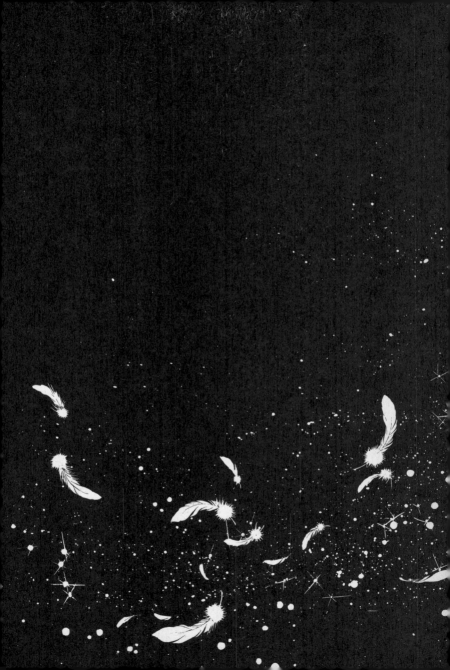

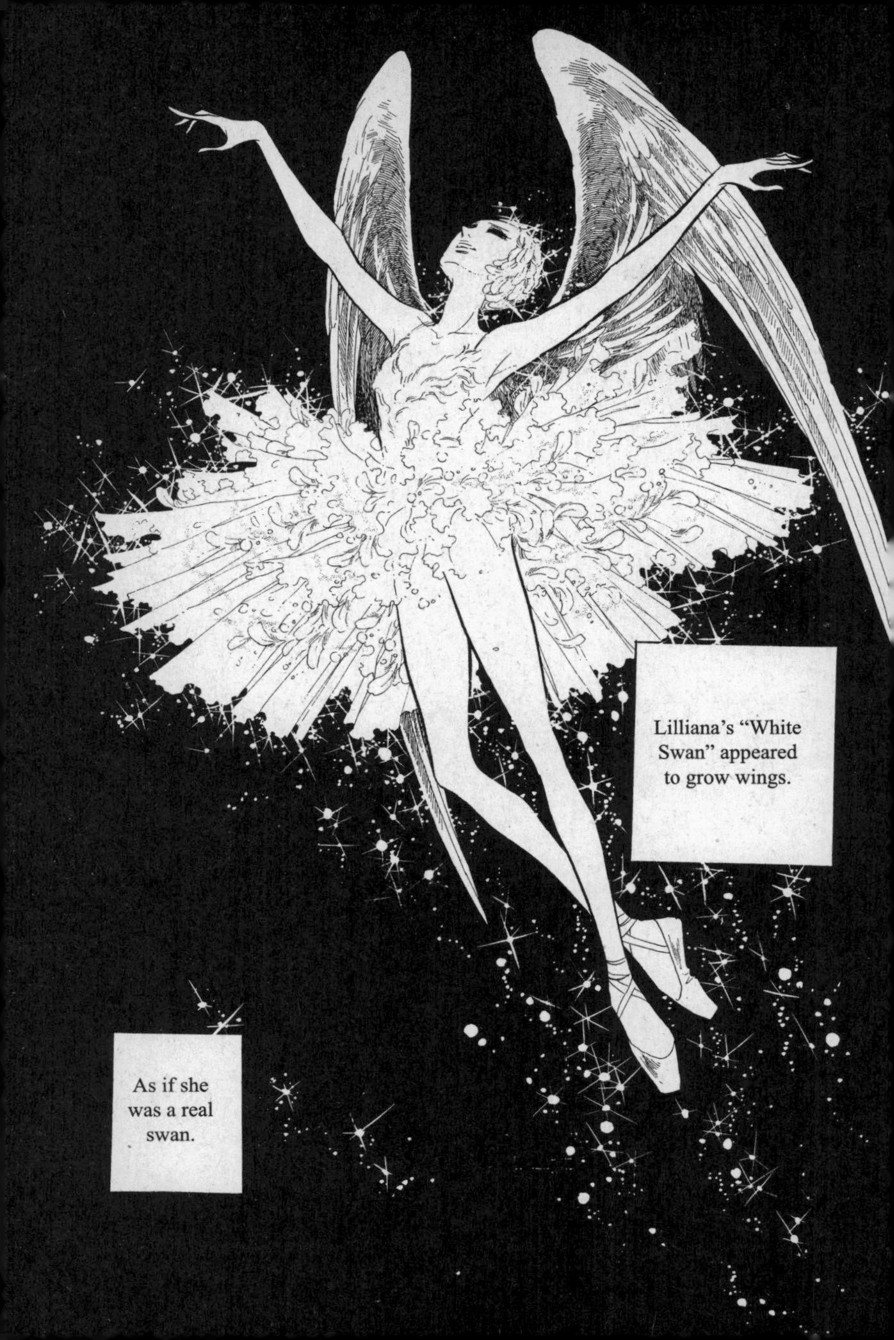
Lilliana's "White Swan" appeared to grow wings.
As if she was a real swan.

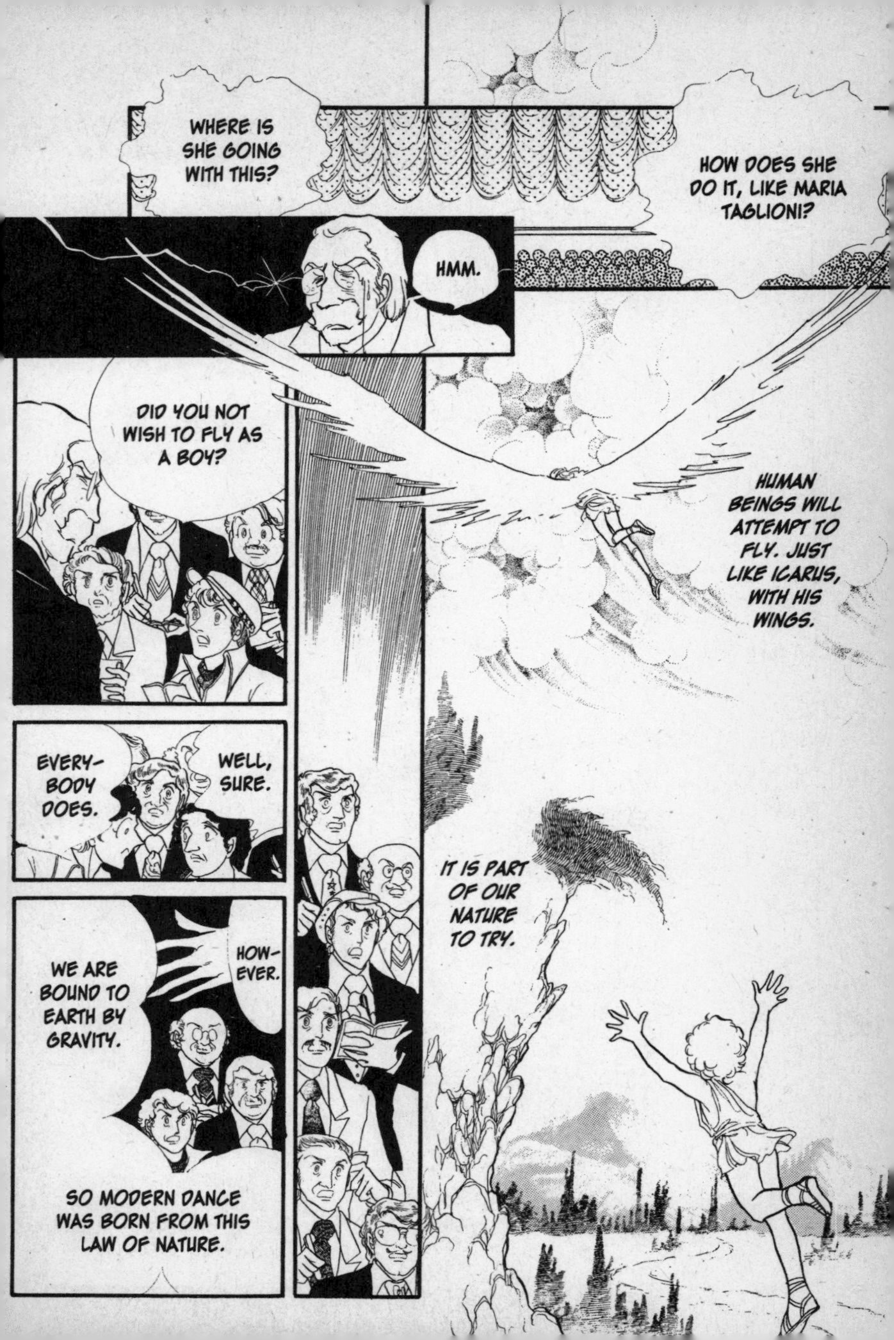

HOW DOES SHE DO IT, LIKE MARIA TAGLIONI?
WHERE IS SHE GOING WITH THIS?
HMM.
HUMAN BEINGS WILL ATTEMPT TO FLY. JUST LIKE ICARUS, WITH HIS WINGS.
IT IS PART OF OUR NATURE TO TRY.
DID YOU NOT WISH TO FLY AS A BOY?
WELL, SURE.
EVERY-BODY DOES.
HOW-EVER.
WE ARE BOUND TO EARTH BY GRAVITY.
SO MODERN DANCE WAS BORN FROM THIS LAW OF NATURE.

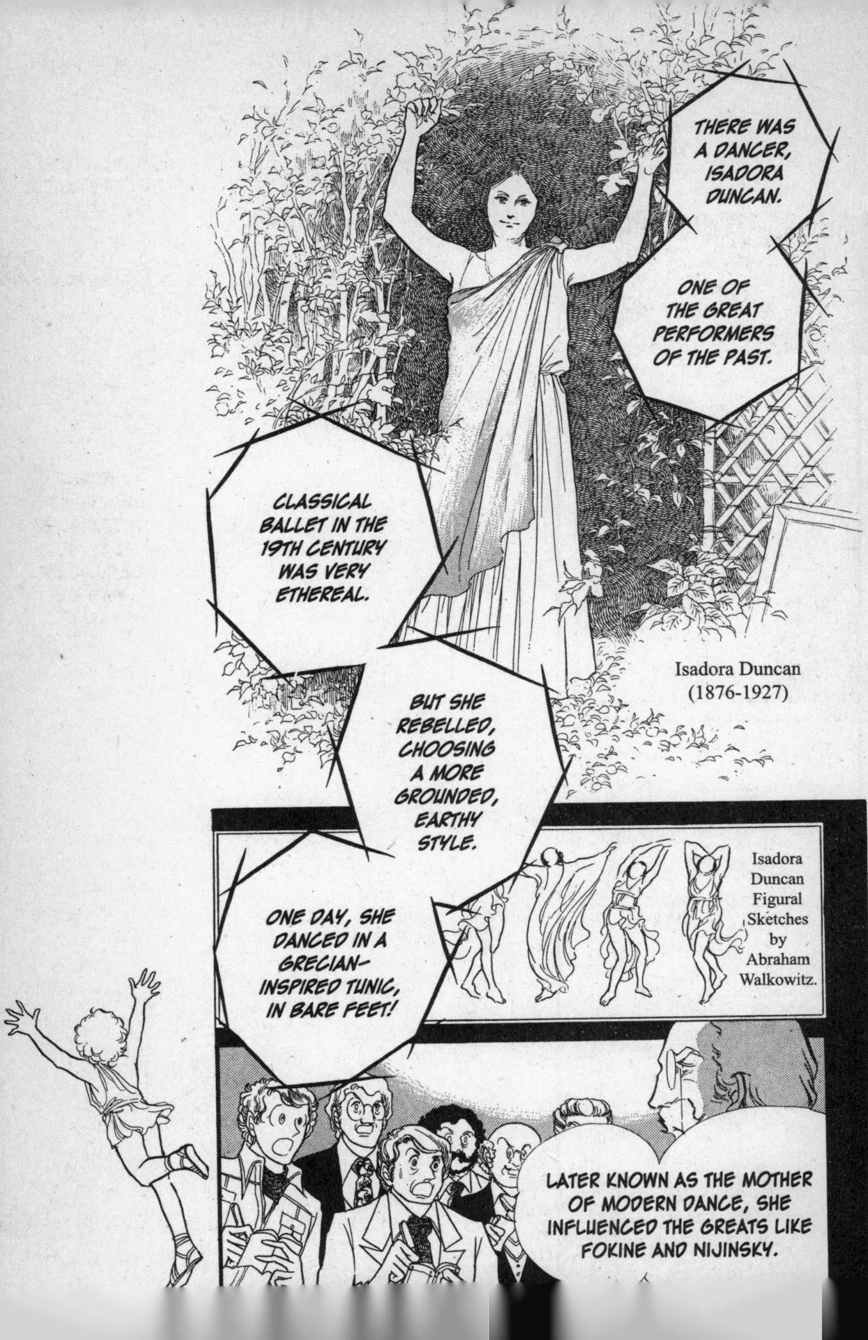
THERE WAS A DANCER, ISADORA DUNCAN.
ONE OF THE GREAT PERFORMERS OF THE PAST.
CLASSICAL BALLET IN THE 19TH CENTURY WAS VERY ETHEREAL.
BUT SHE REBELLED, CHOOSING A MORE GROUNDED, EARTHY STYLE.
ONE DAY, SHE DANCED IN A GRECIAN-INSPIRED TUNIC, IN BARE FEET!
LATER KNOWN AS THE MOTHER OF MODERN DANCE, SHE INFLUENCED THE GREATS LIKE FOKINE AND NIJINSKY.
Isadora Duncan (1876-1927)

Isadora Duncan Figural Sketches by Abraham Walkowitz.

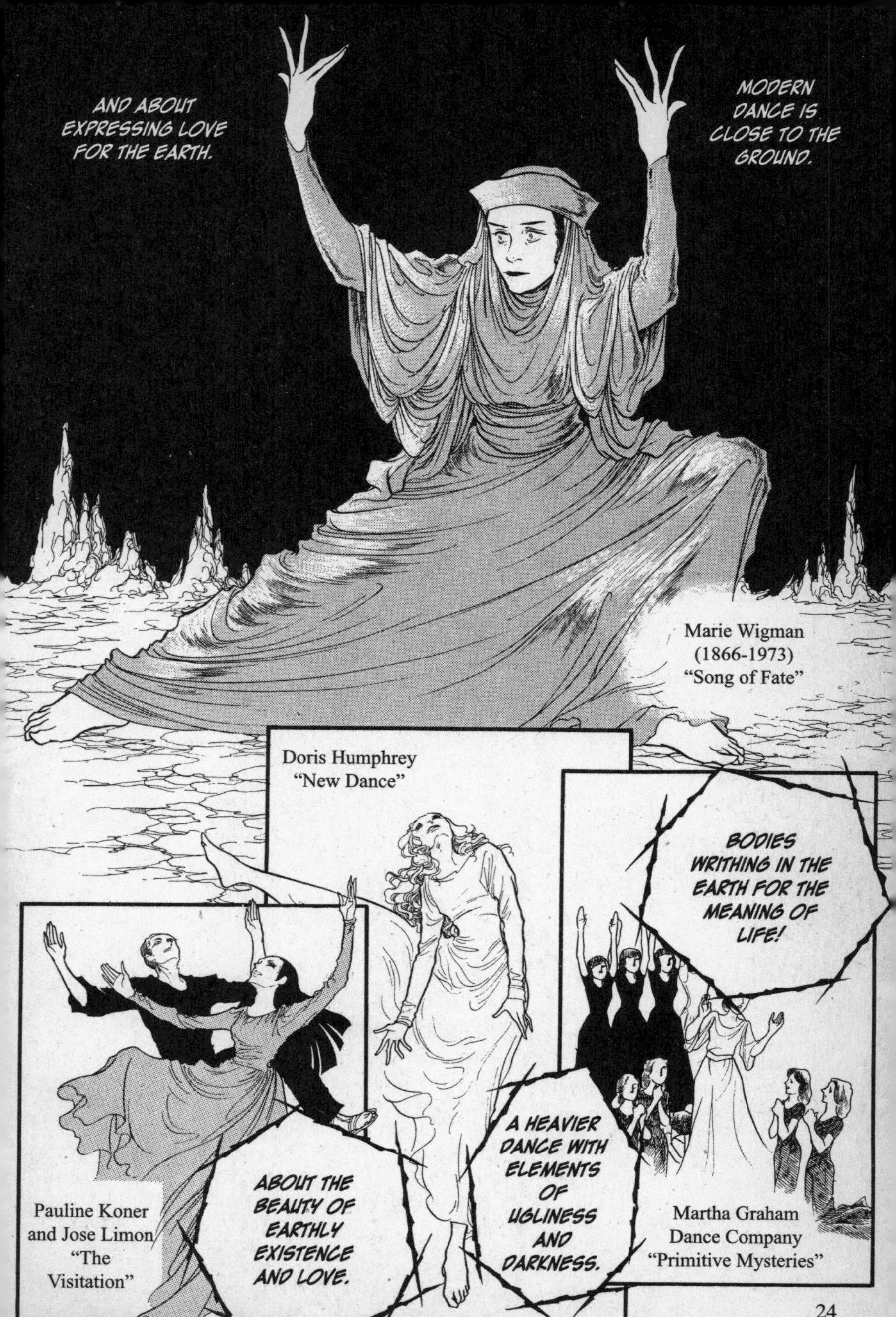
MODERN DANCE IS CLOSE TO THE GROUND.
AND ABOUT EXPRESSING LOVE FOR THE EARTH.
Marie Wigman (1866-1973) "Song of Fate"
BODIES WRITHING IN THE EARTH FOR THE MEANING OF LIFE!
A HEAVIER DANCE WITH ELEMENTS OF UGLINESS AND DARKNESS.
Martha Graham Dance Company "Primitive Mysteries"
Doris Humphrey "New Dance"
ABOUT THE BEAUTY OF EARTHLY EXISTENCE AND LOVE.
Pauline Koner and Jose Limon "The Visitation"

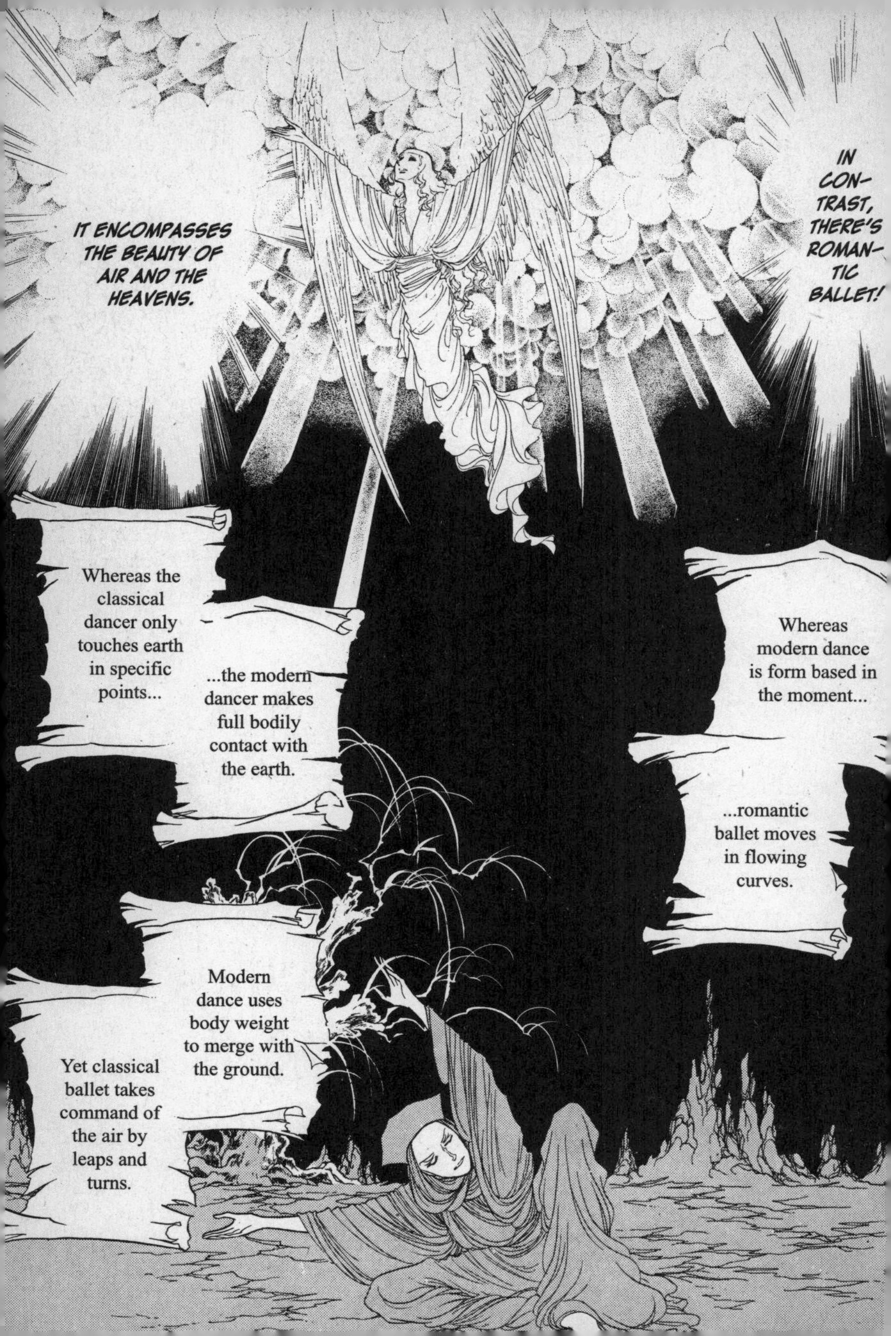
IN CONTRAST, THERE'S ROMANTIC BALLET!
IT ENCOMPASSES THE BEAUTY OF AIR AND THE HEAVENS.
Whereas modern dance is form based in the moment...
...romantic ballet moves in flowing curves.
Whereas the classical dancer only touches earth in specific points...
...the modern dancer makes full bodily contact with the earth.
Modern dance uses body weight to merge with the ground.
Yet classical ballet takes command of the air by leaps and turns.

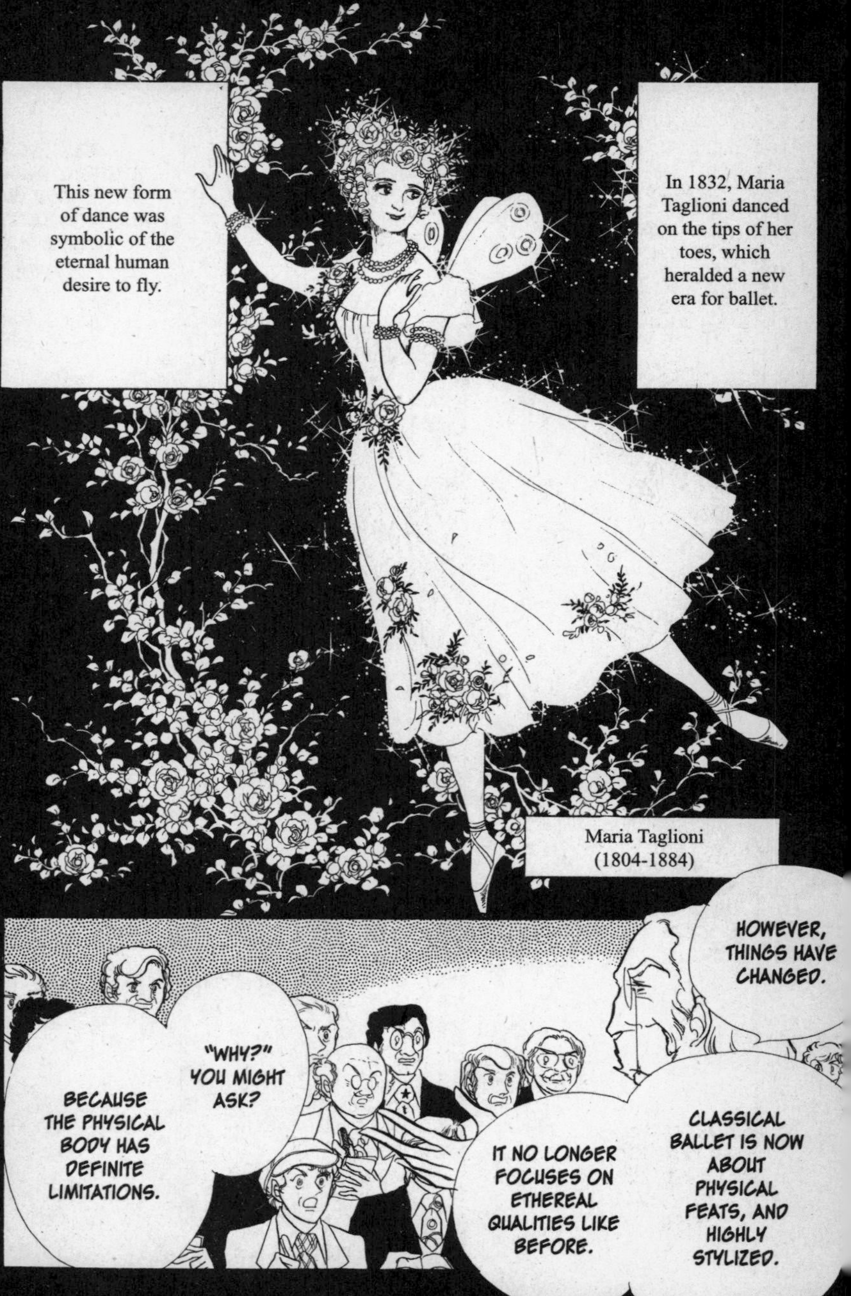
In 1832, Maria Taglioni danced on the tips of her toes, which heralded a new era for ballet.
This new form of dance was symbolic of the eternal human desire to fly.
Maria Taglioni (1804-1884)
HOWEVER, THINGS HAVE CHANGED.
CLASSICAL BALLET IS NOW ABOUT PHYSICAL FEATS, AND HIGHLY STYLIZED.
IT NO LONGER FOCUSES ON ETHEREAL QUALITIES LIKE BEFORE.
"WHY?" YOU MIGHT ASK?
BECAUSE THE PHYSICAL BODY HAS DEFINITE LIMITATIONS.

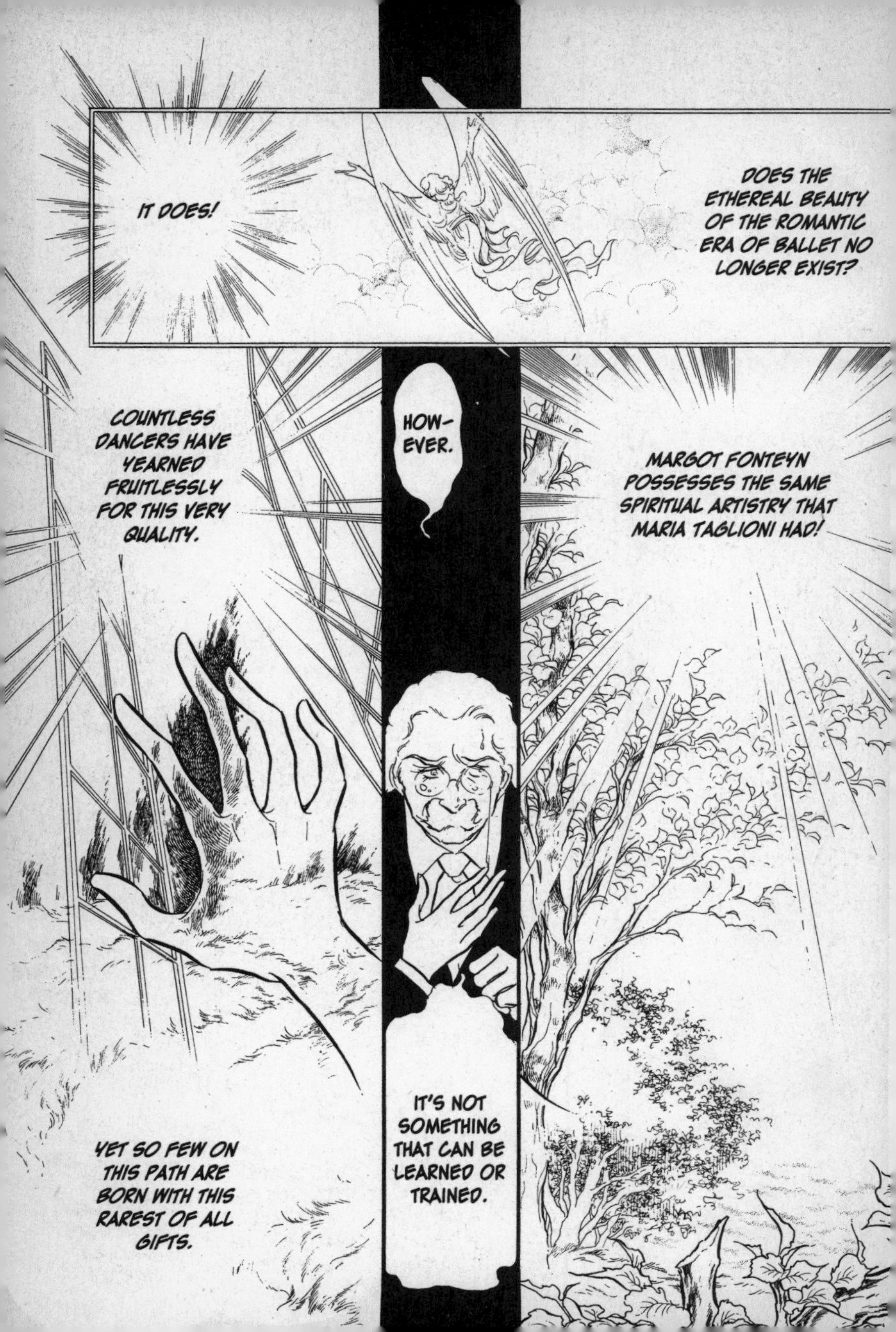
DOES THE ETHEREAL BEAUTY OF THE ROMANTIC ERA OF BALLET NO LONGER EXIST?
IT DOES!
MARGOT FONTEYN POSSESSES THE SAME SPIRITUAL ARTISTRY THAT MARIA TAGLIONI HAD!
HOW-EVER.
IT'S NOT SOMETHING THAT CAN BE LEARNED OR TRAINED.
COUNTLESS DANCERS HAVE YEARNED FRUITLESSLY FOR THIS VERY QUALITY.
YET SO FEW ON THIS PATH ARE BORN WITH THIS RAREST OF ALL GIFTS.

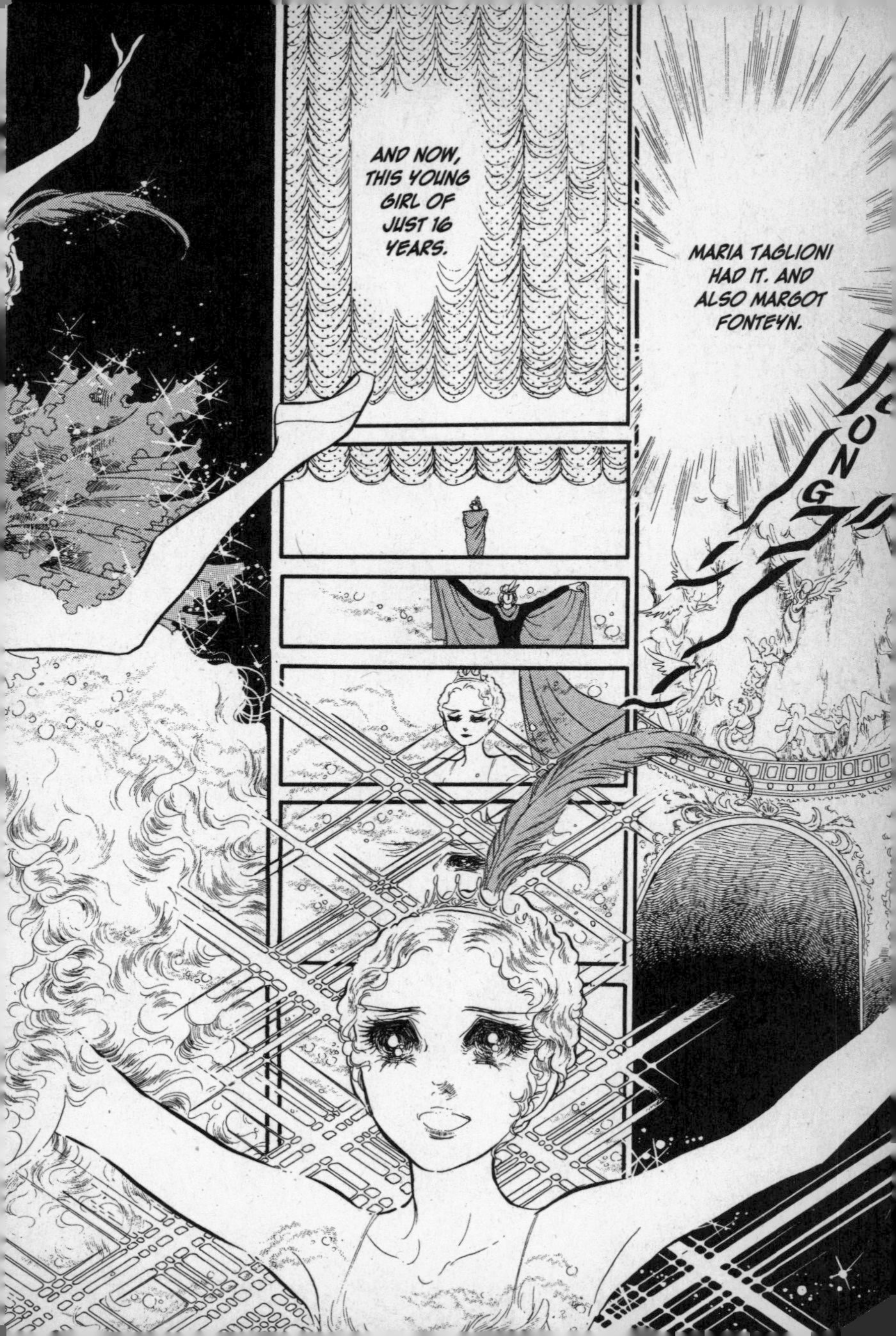
MARIA TAGLIONI HAD IT. AND ALSO MARGOT FONTEYN.
ONG
AND NOW, THIS YOUNG GIRL OF JUST 16 YEARS.

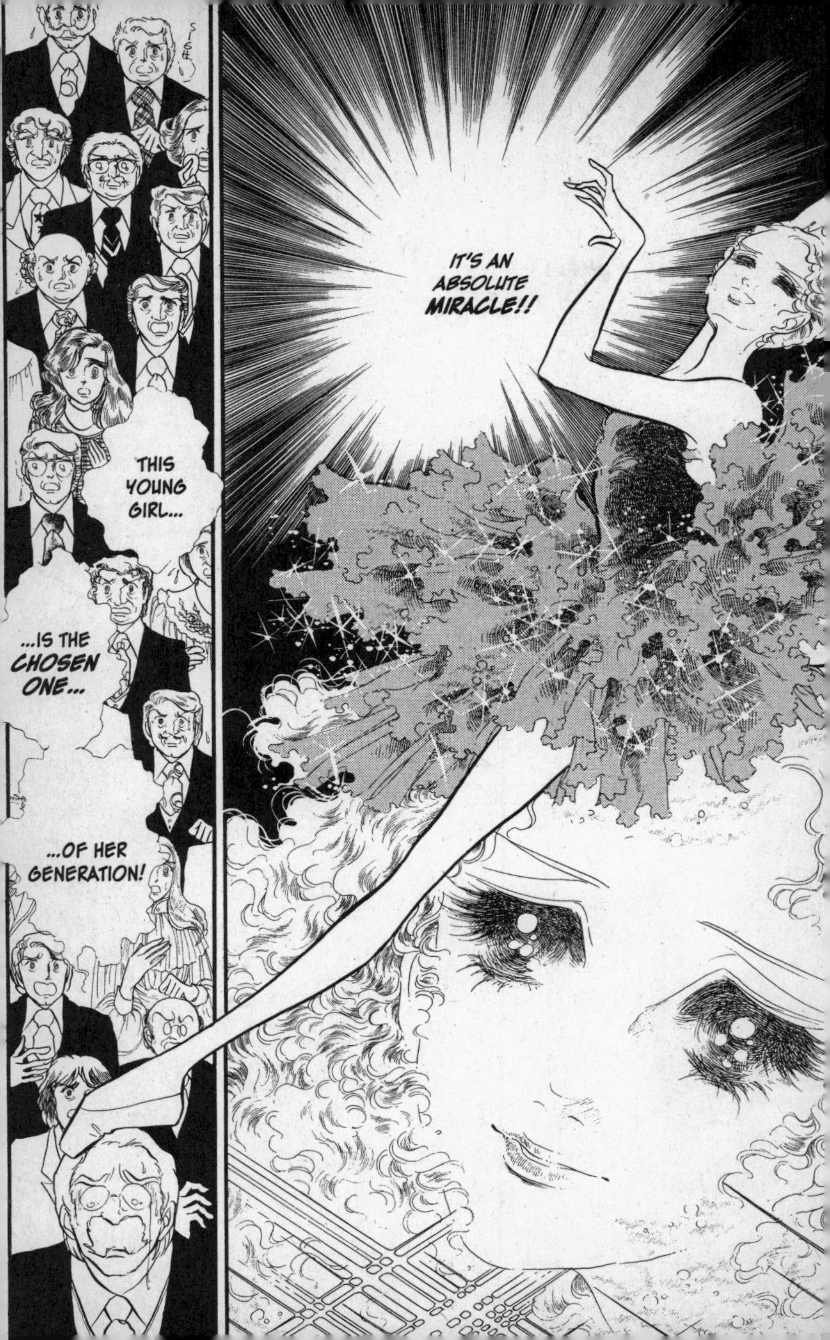
IT'S AN ABSOLUTE MIRACLE!!
SIGH
THIS YOUNG GIRL...
...IS THE CHOSEN ONE...
...OF HER GENERATION!

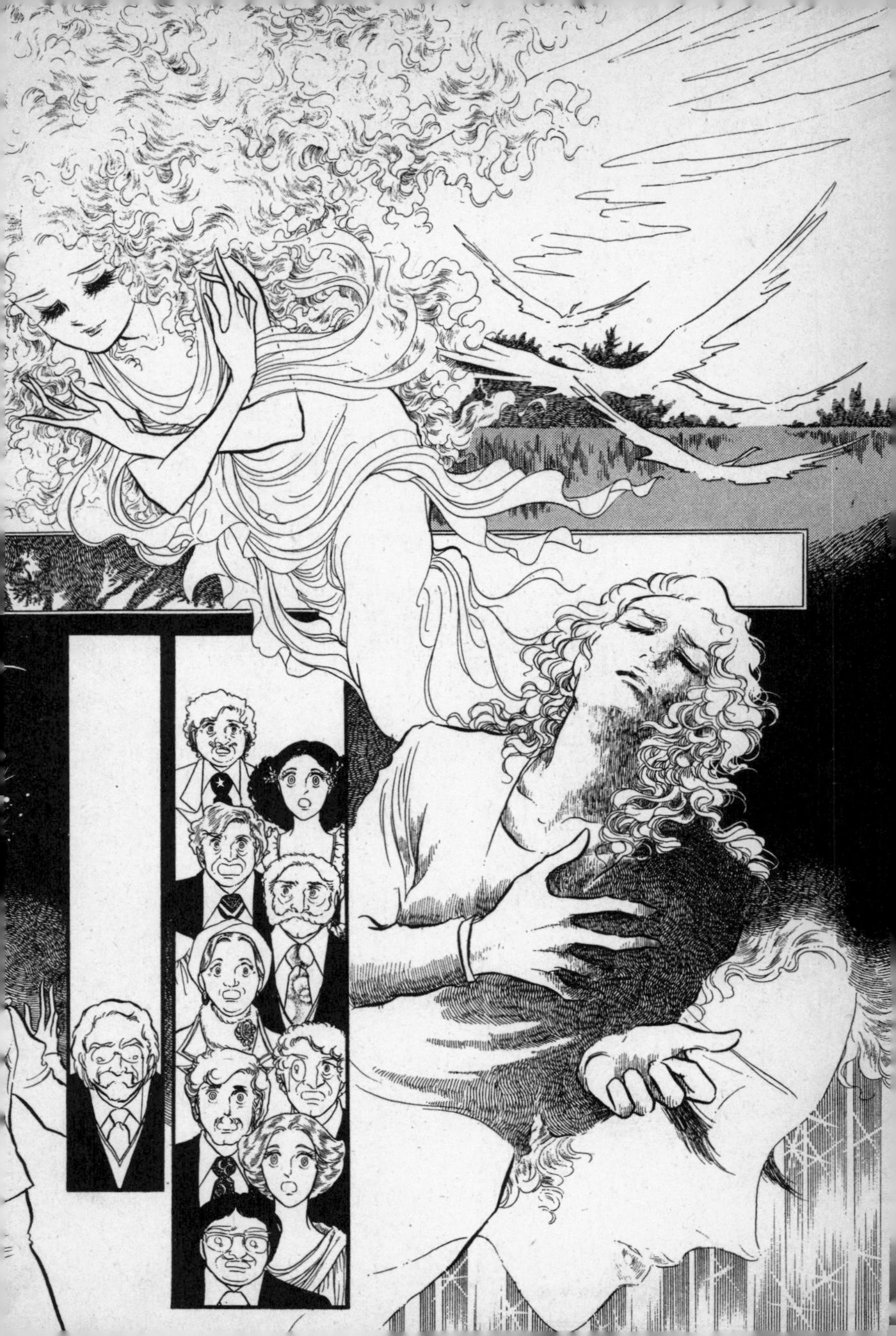

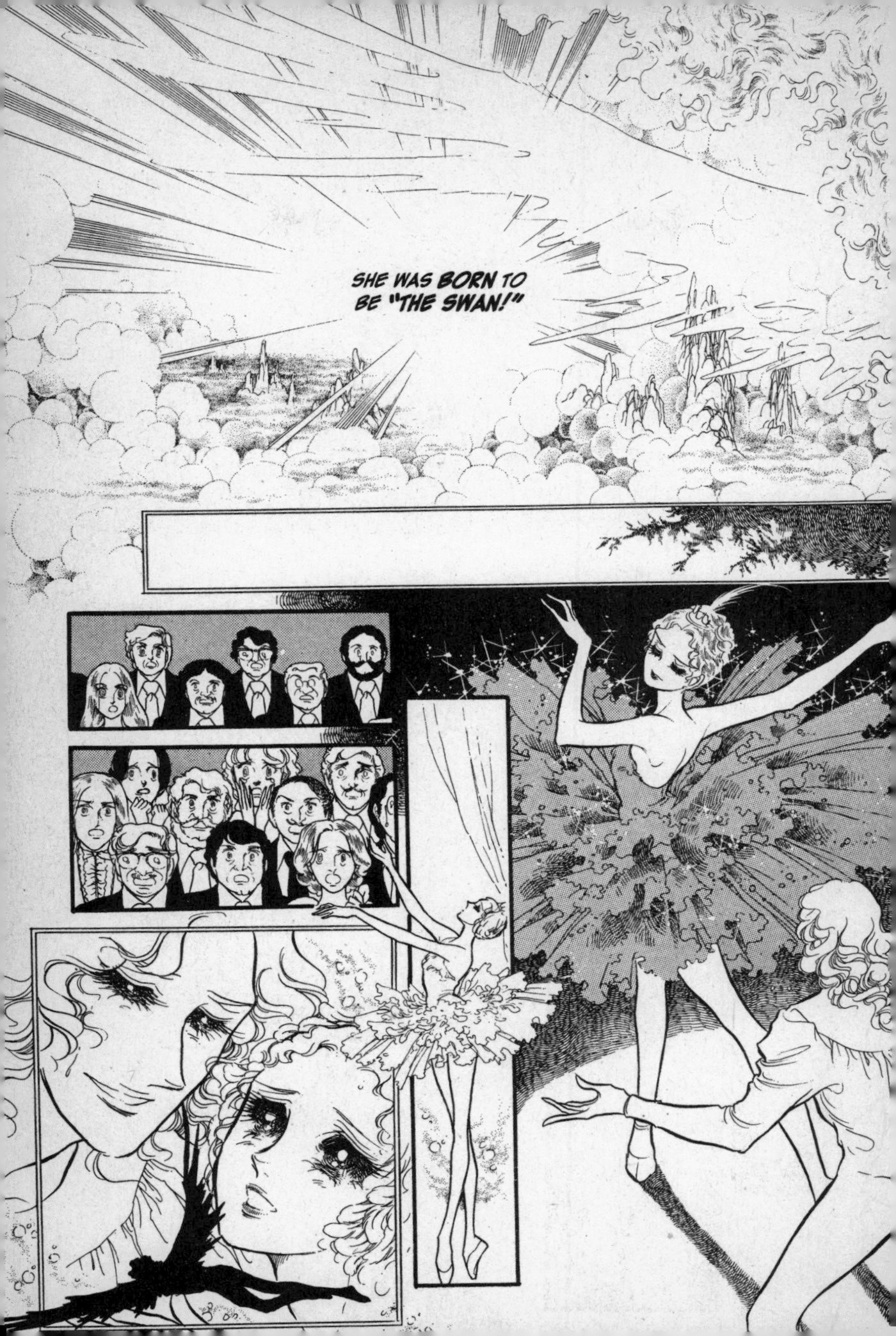
SHE WAS BORN TO BE "THE SWAN!"

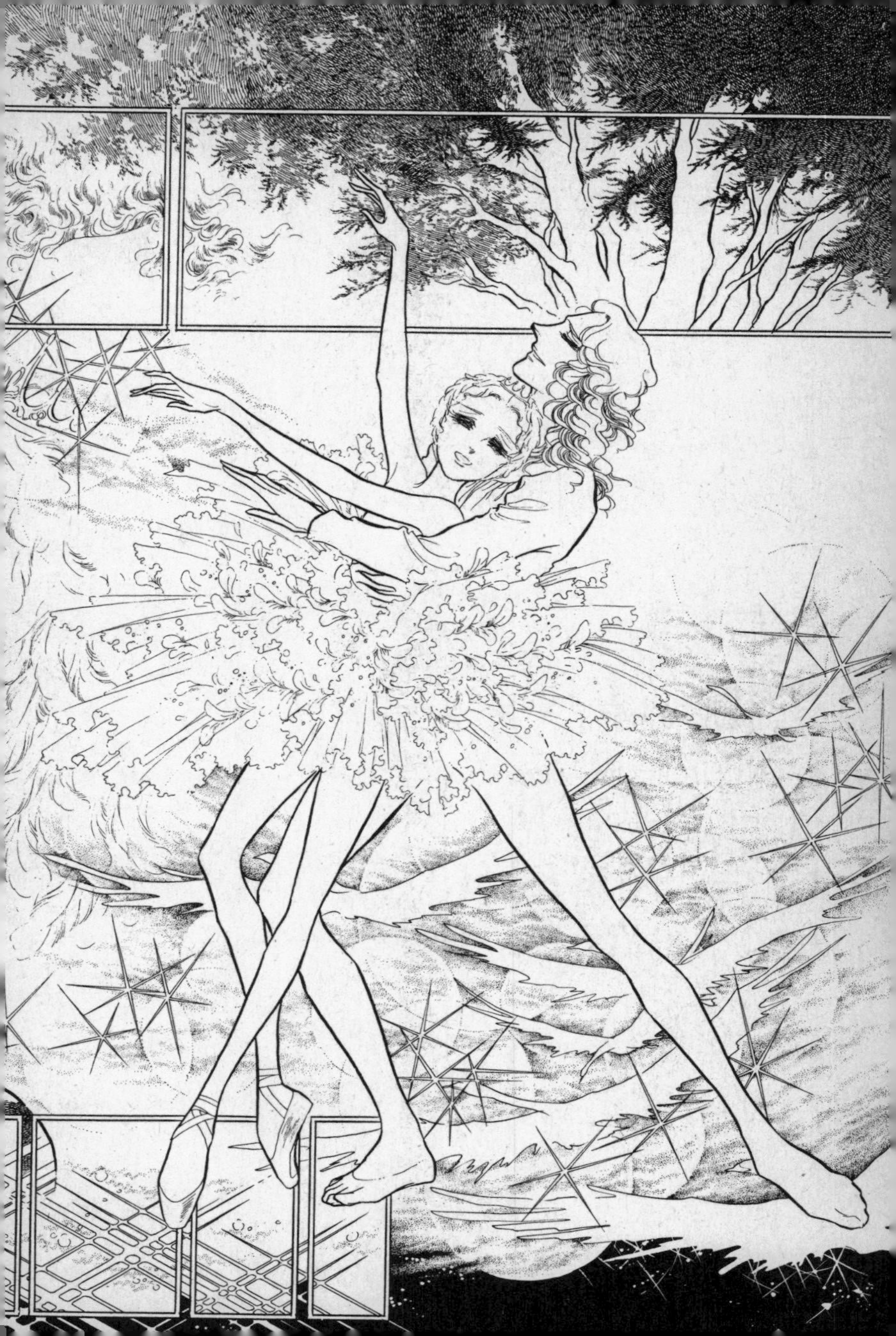

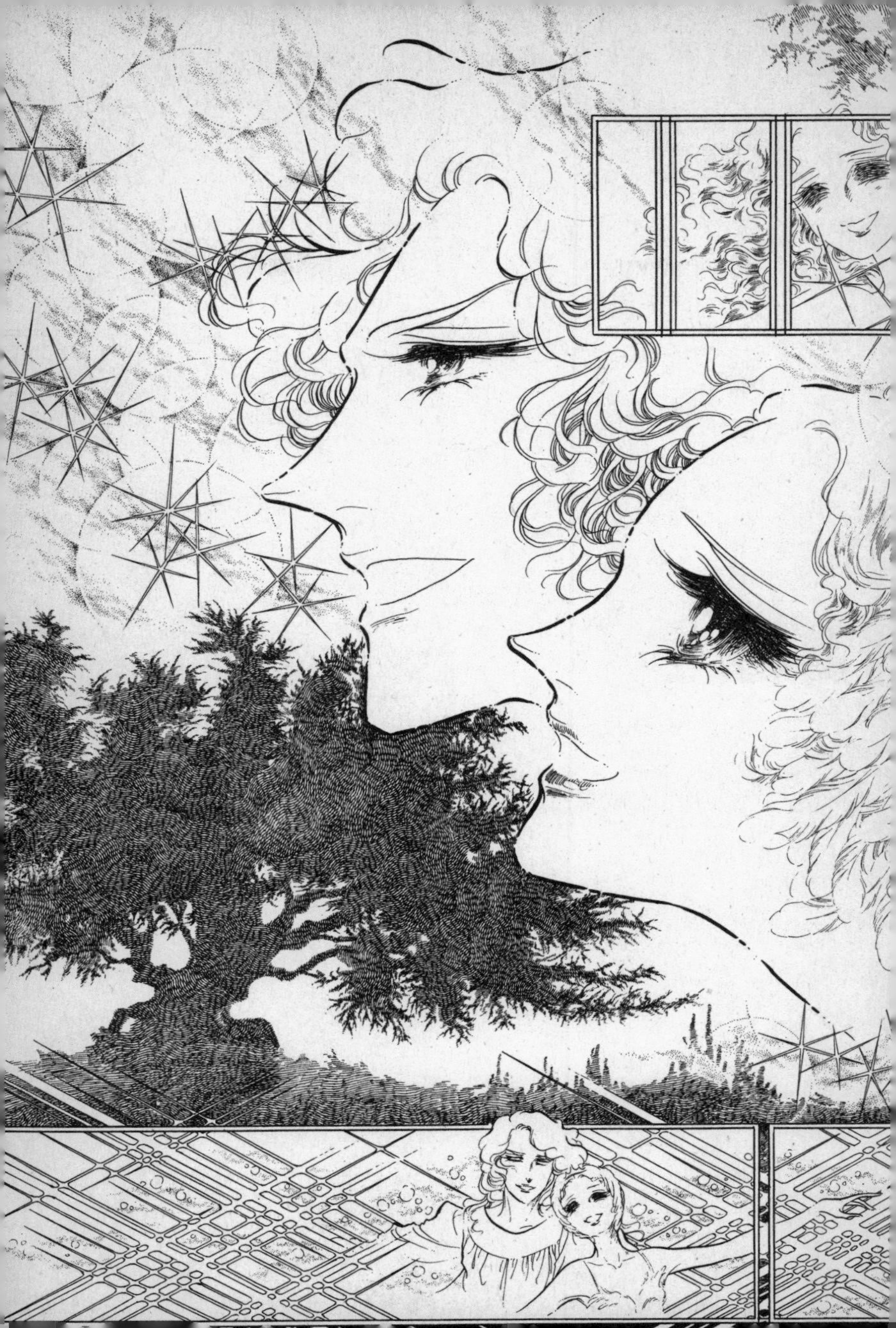

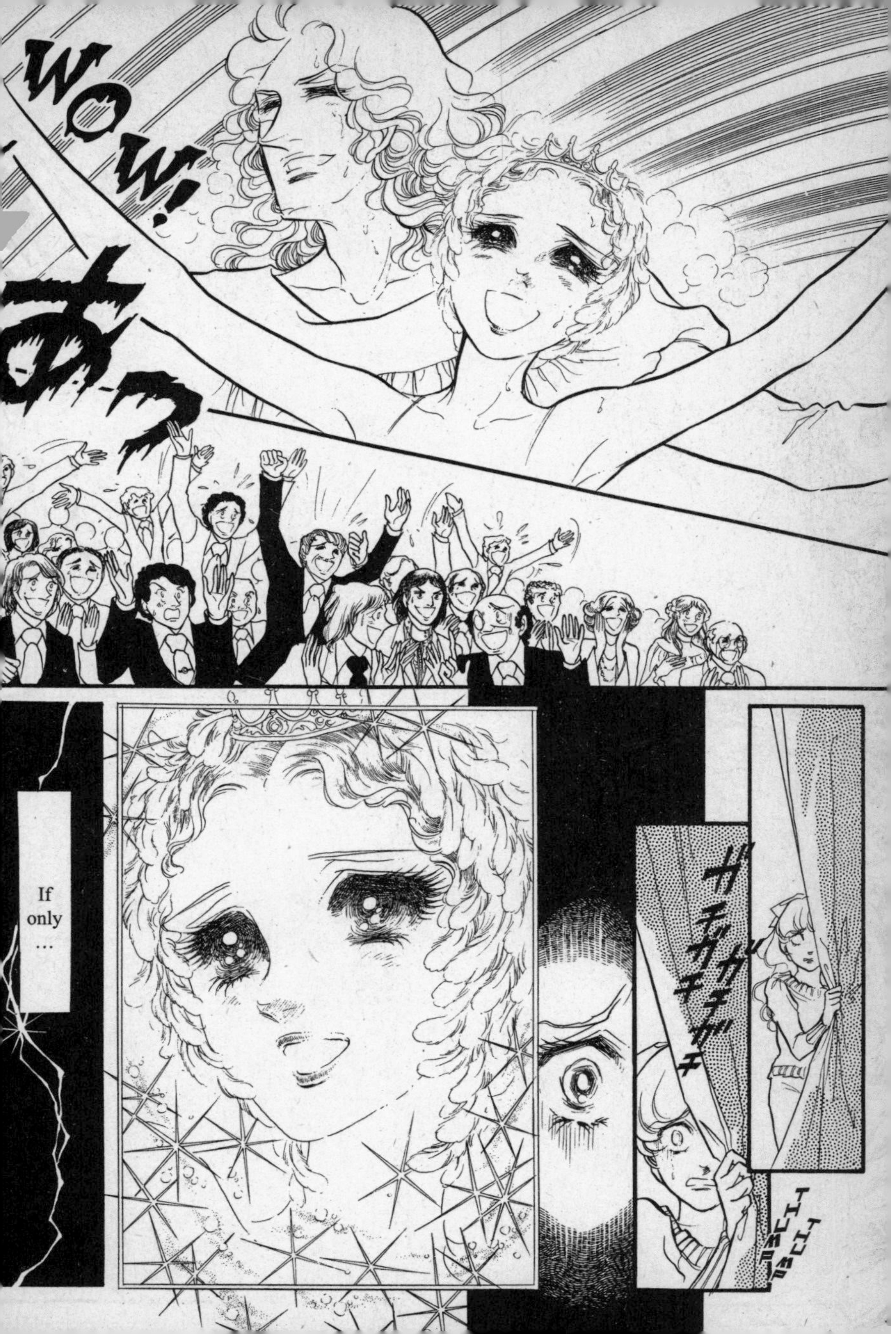
WOW!
わーっ
ガチャガチャガチャ
THUMP THUMP
If only …

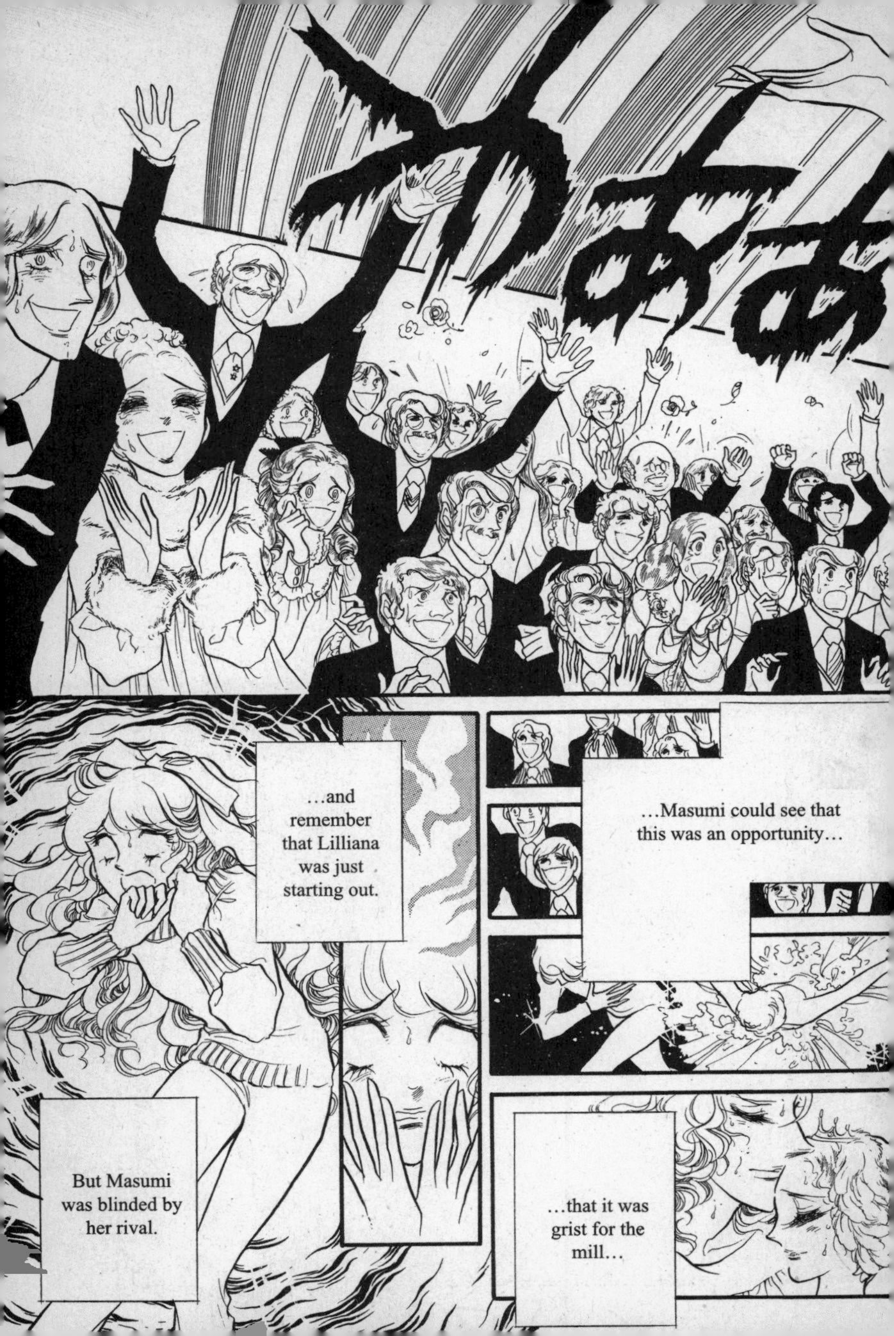
…Masumi could see that this was an opportunity…
…that it was grist for the mill…
…and remember that Lilliana was just starting out.
But Masumi was blinded by her rival.

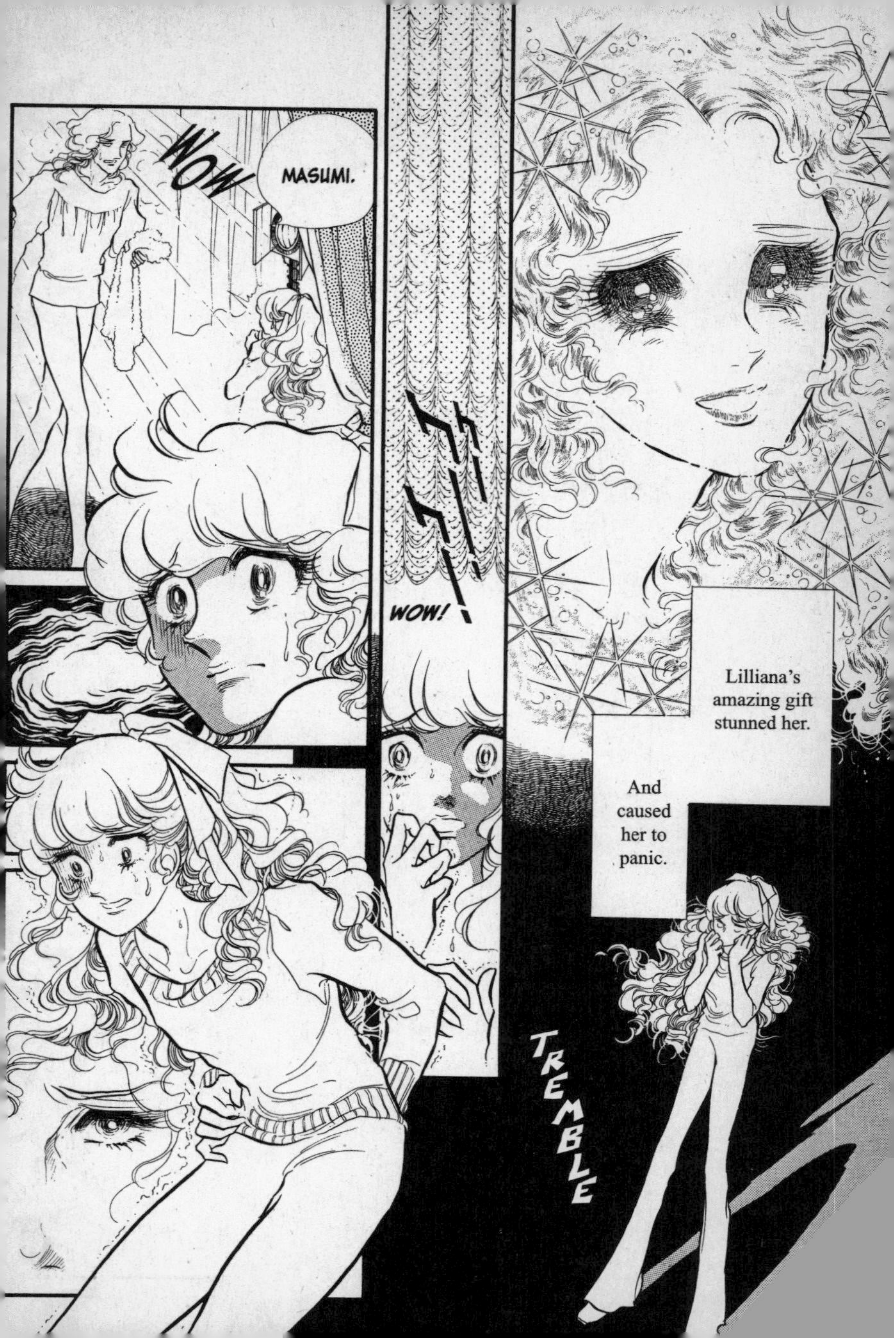
Lilliana's amazing gift stunned her.
And caused her to panic.
TREMBLE
WOW!
MASUMI.
WOW

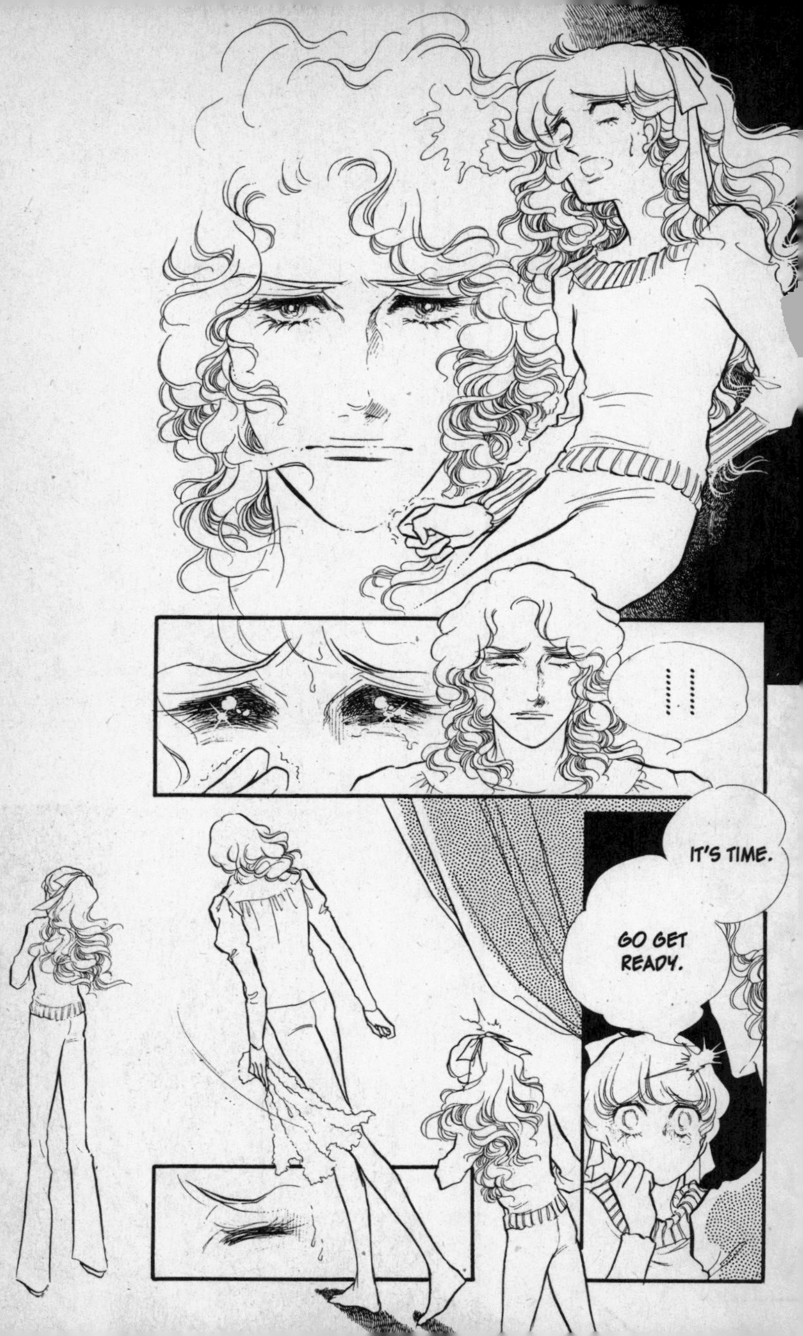

!!
IT'S TIME.
GO GET READY.

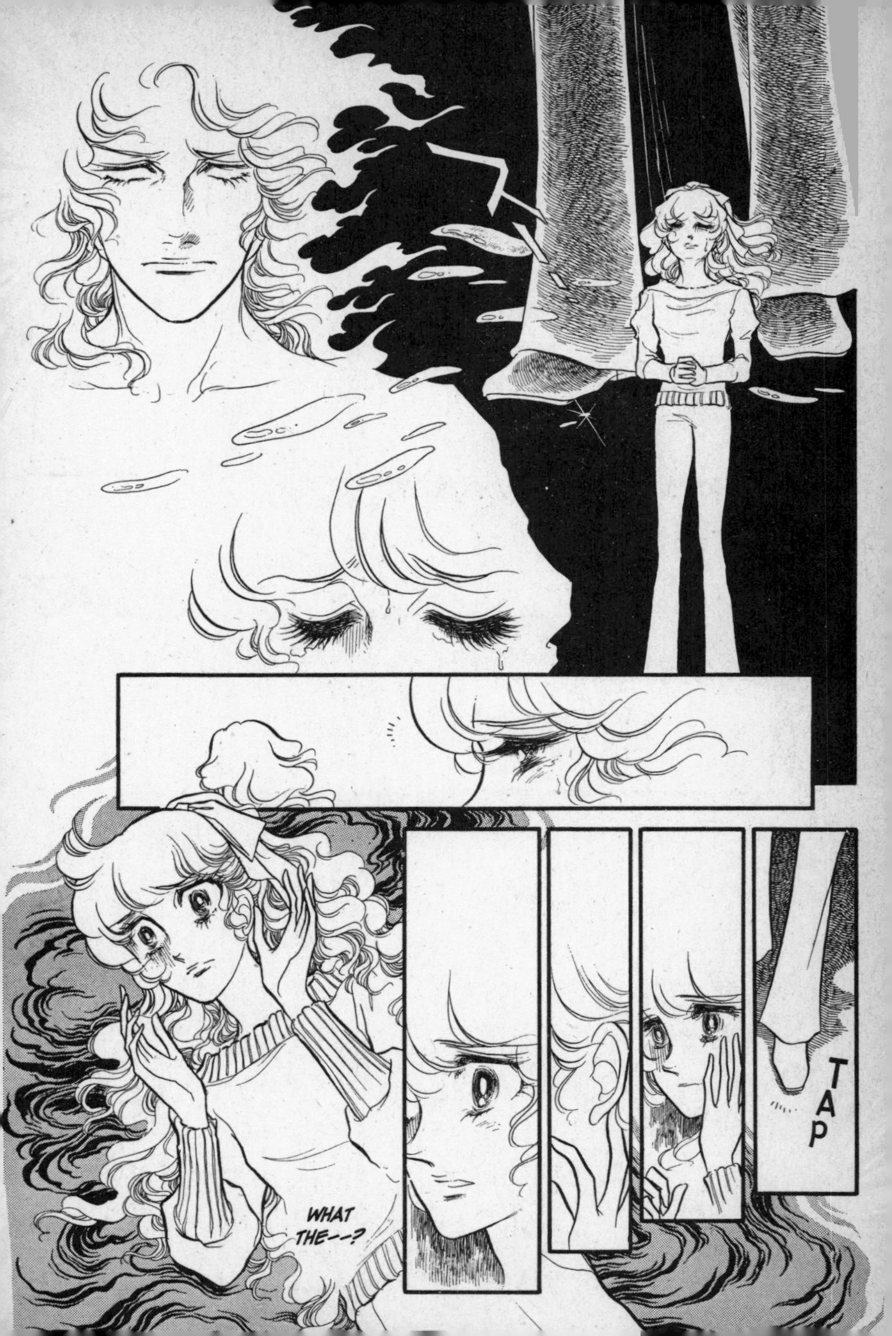
TAP
WHAT THE--?

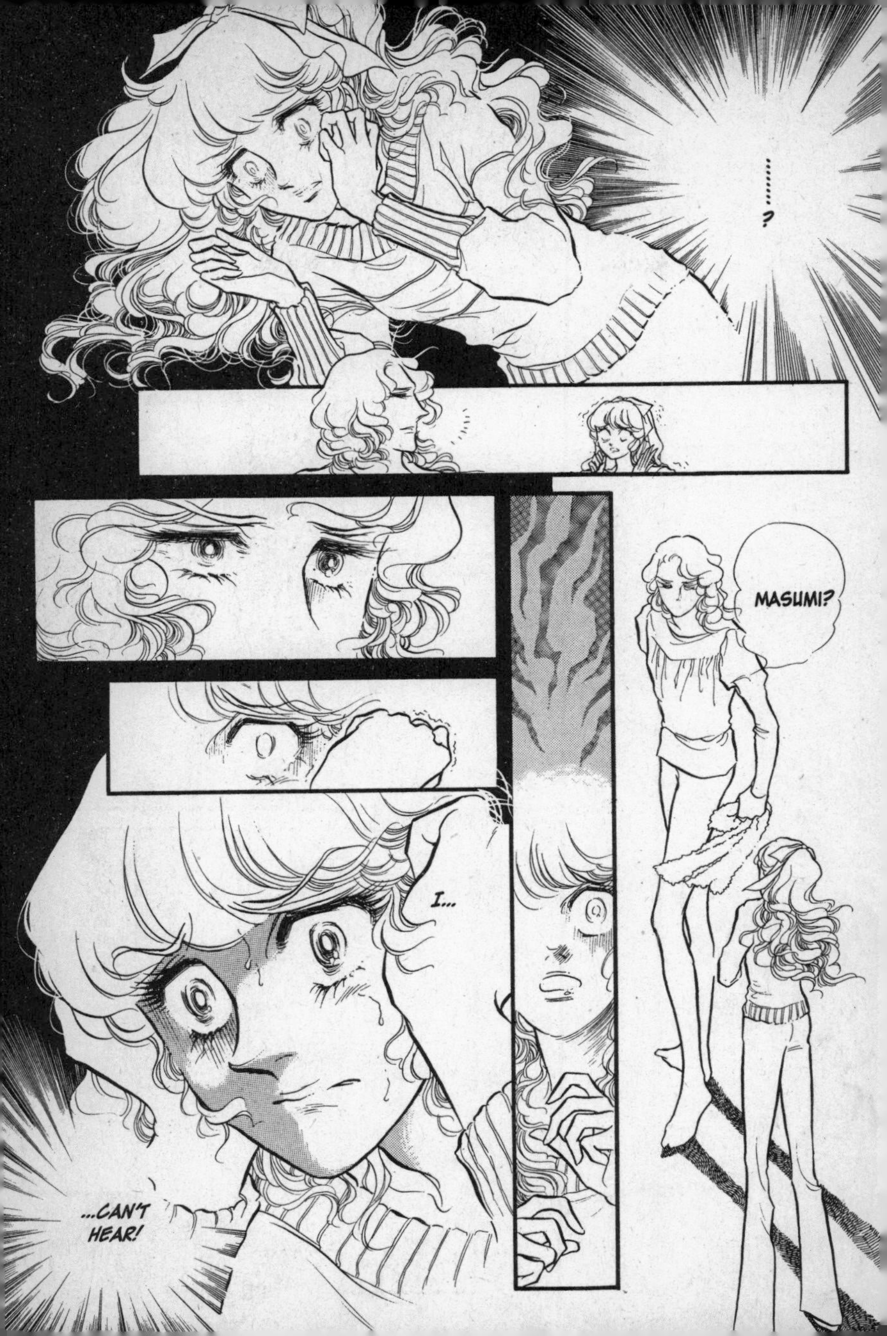
......?
MASUMI?
I...
...CAN'T HEAR!

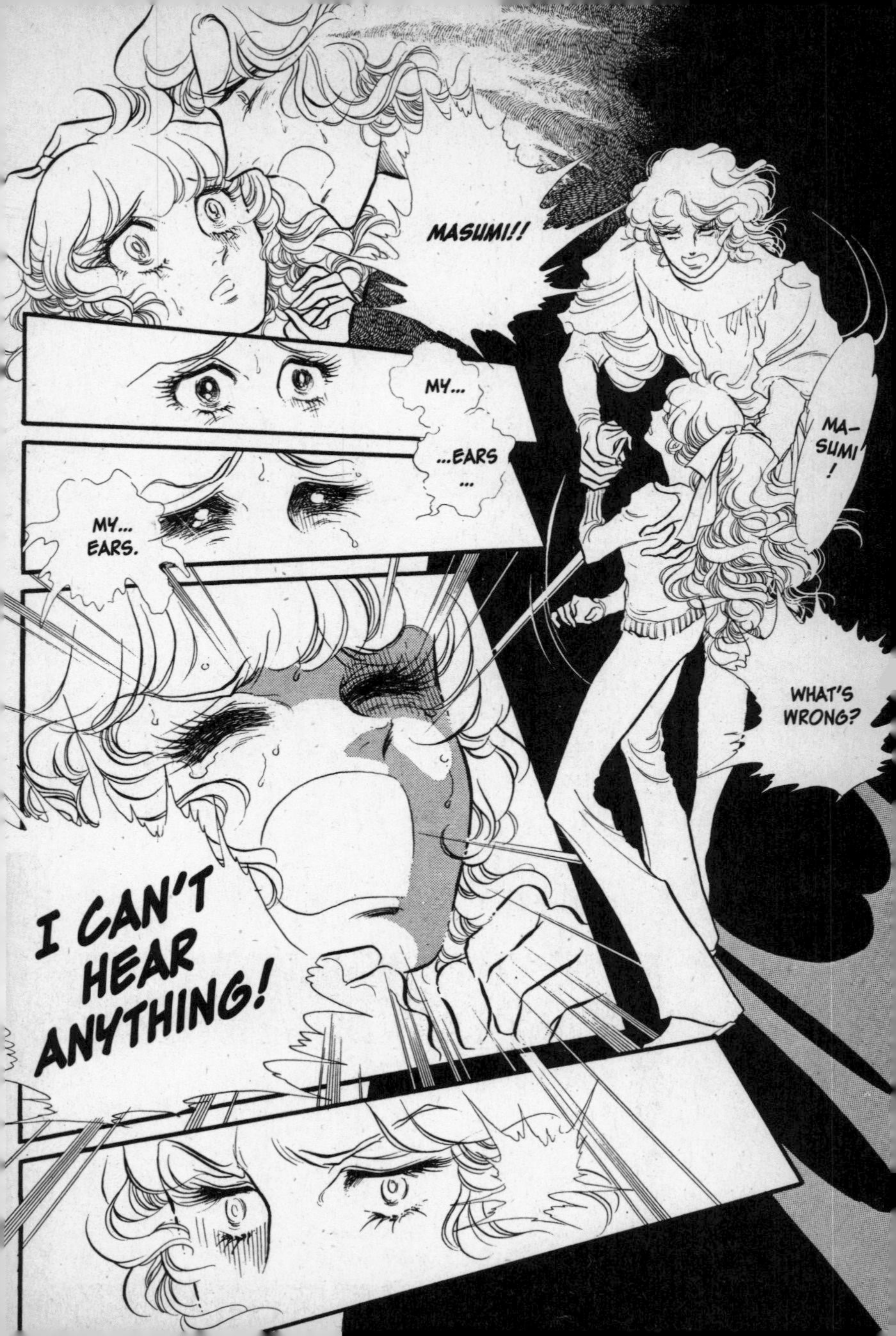
MASUMI!!
MA-SUMI!
WHAT'S WRONG?
MY...
...EARS...
MY... EARS.
I CAN'T HEAR ANYTHING!

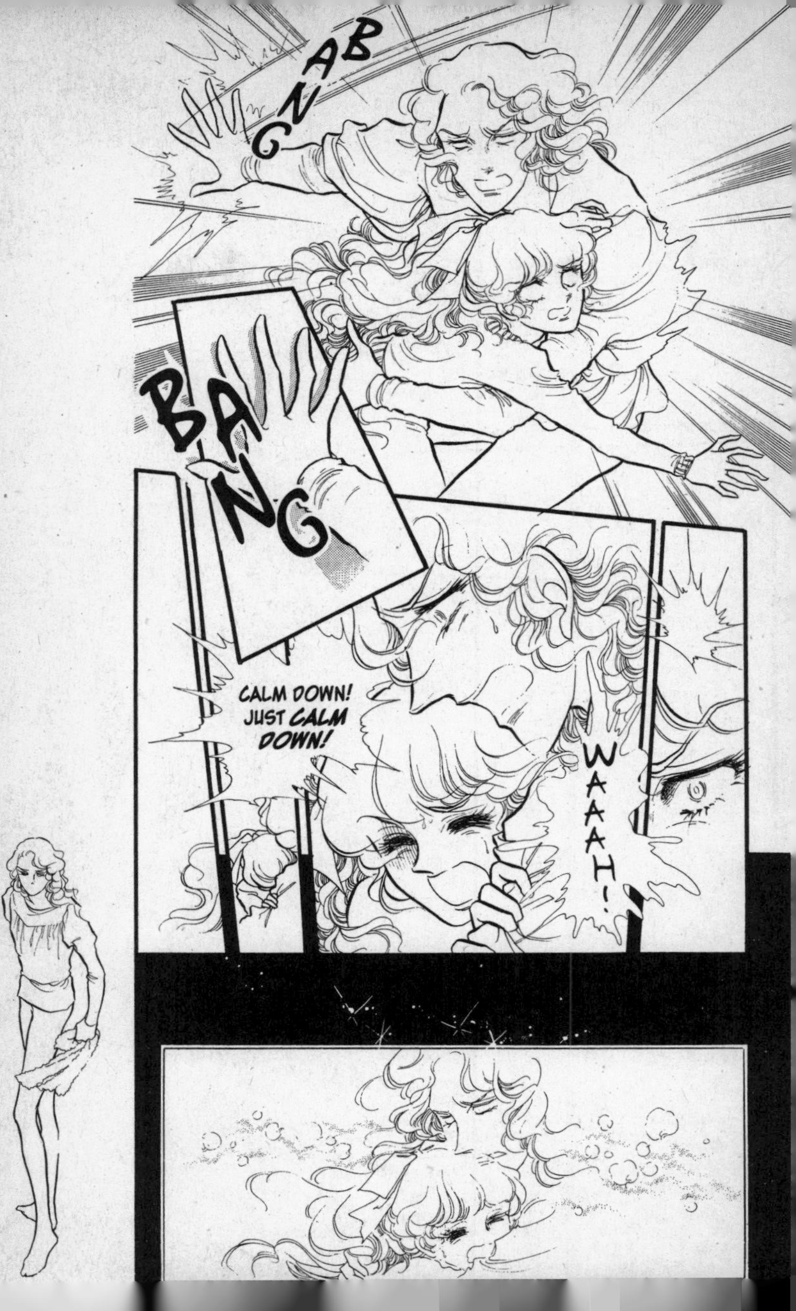
BANG
BANG
CALM DOWN! JUST CALM DOWN!
WAAAH!

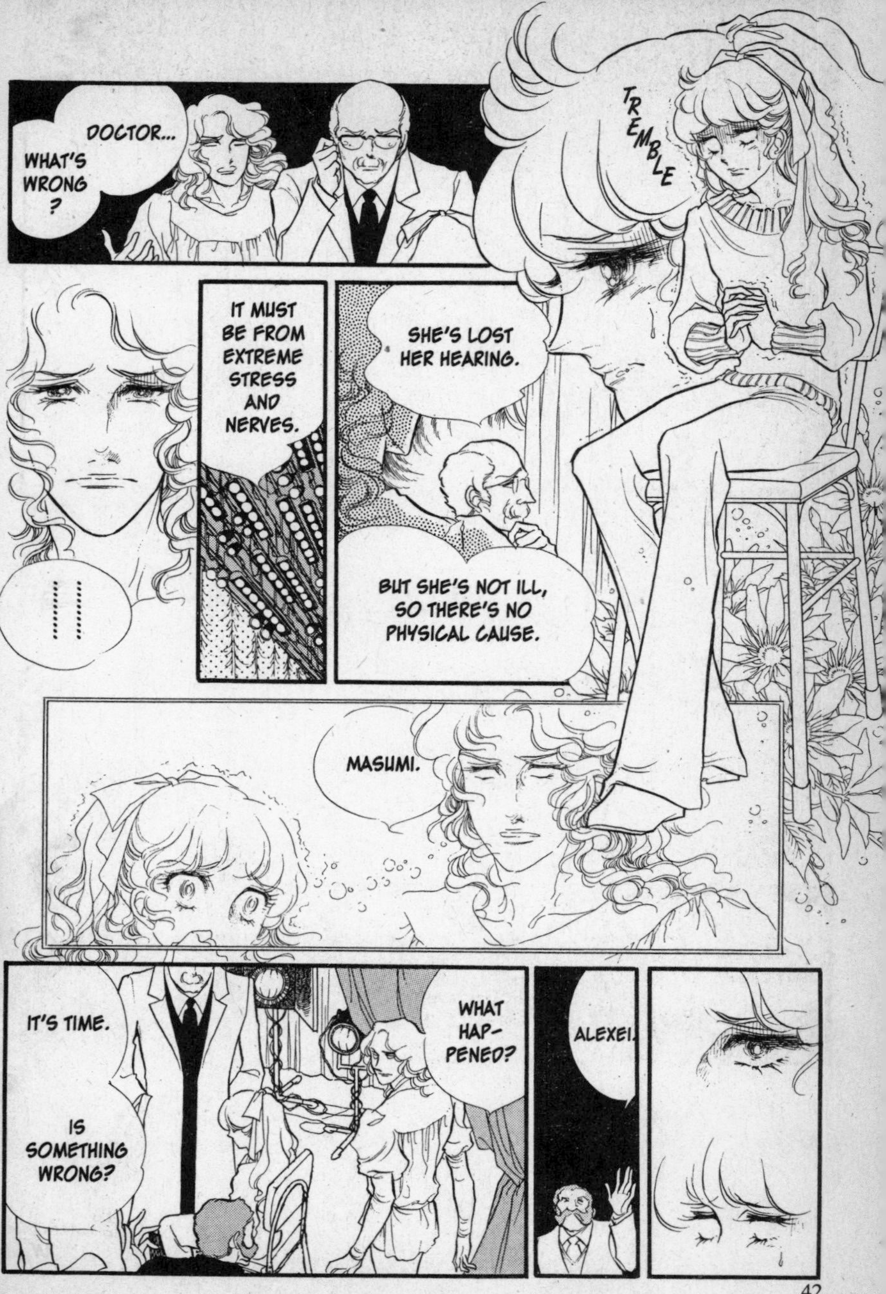
TREMBLE
DOCTOR... WHAT'S WRONG?
SHE'S LOST HER HEARING.
BUT SHE'S NOT ILL, SO THERE'S NO PHYSICAL CAUSE.
IT MUST BE FROM EXTREME STRESS AND NERVES.
......
MASUMI.
ALEXEI!
WHAT HAP-PENED?
IT'S TIME.
IS SOMETHING WRONG?

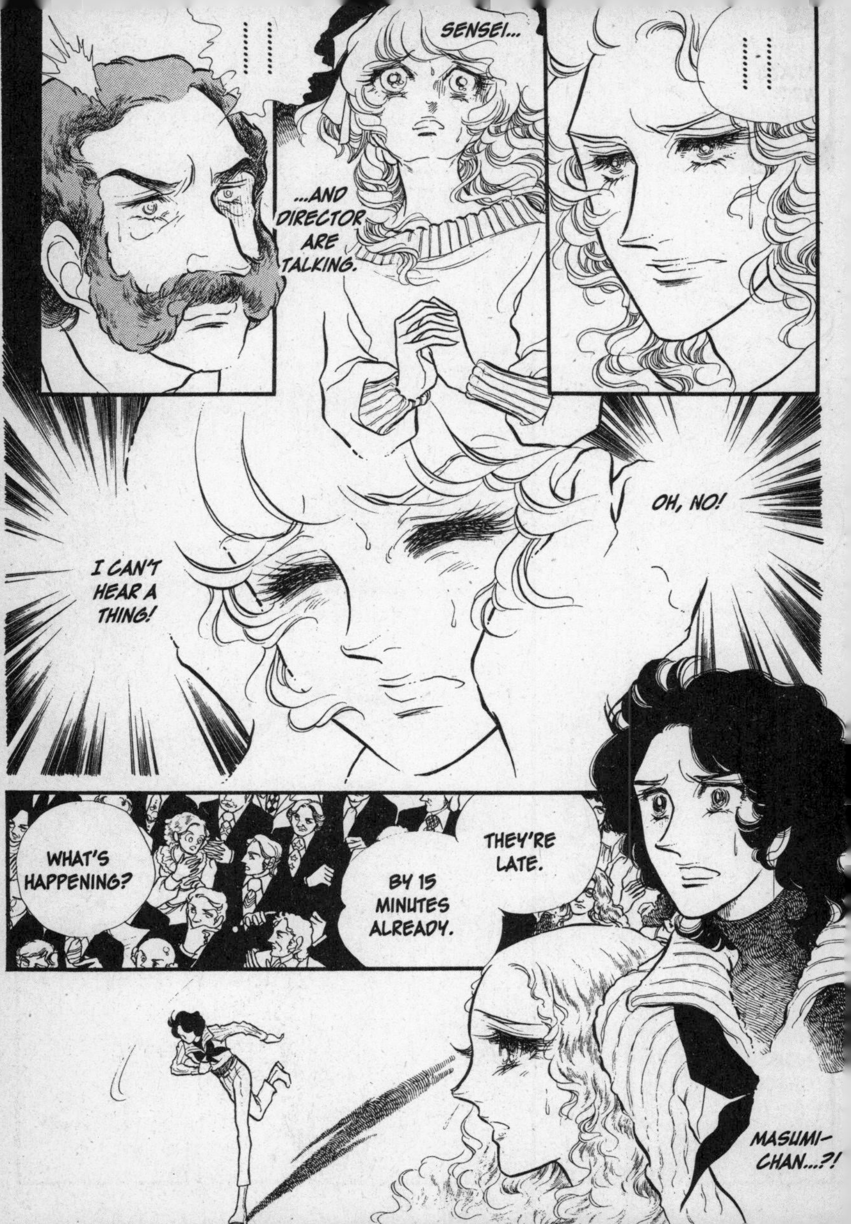
SENSEI...
...AND DIRECTOR ARE TALKING.
OH, NO!
I CAN'T HEAR A THING!
THEY'RE LATE.
BY 15 MINUTES ALREADY.
WHAT'S HAPPENING?
MASUMI-CHAN...?!

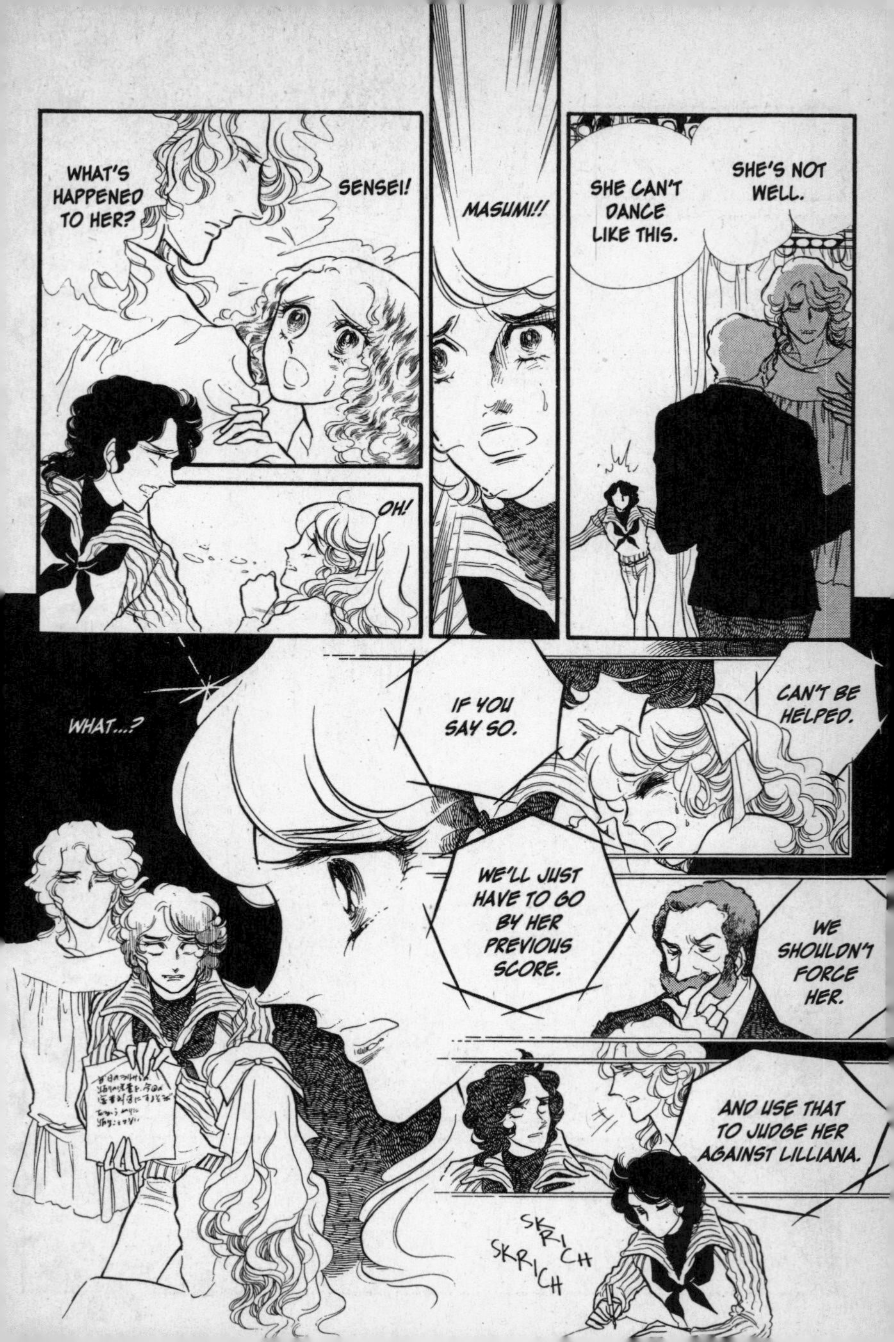

SHE'S NOT WELL.
SHE CAN'T DANCE LIKE THIS.
MASUMI!!
SENSEI!
WHAT'S HAPPENED TO HER?
OH!
CAN'T BE HELPED.
IF YOU SAY SO.
WHAT...?
WE SHOULDN'T FORCE HER.
WE'LL JUST HAVE TO GO BY HER PREVIOUS SCORE.
AND USE THAT TO JUDGE HER AGAINST LILLIANA.
SKRICH SKRICH

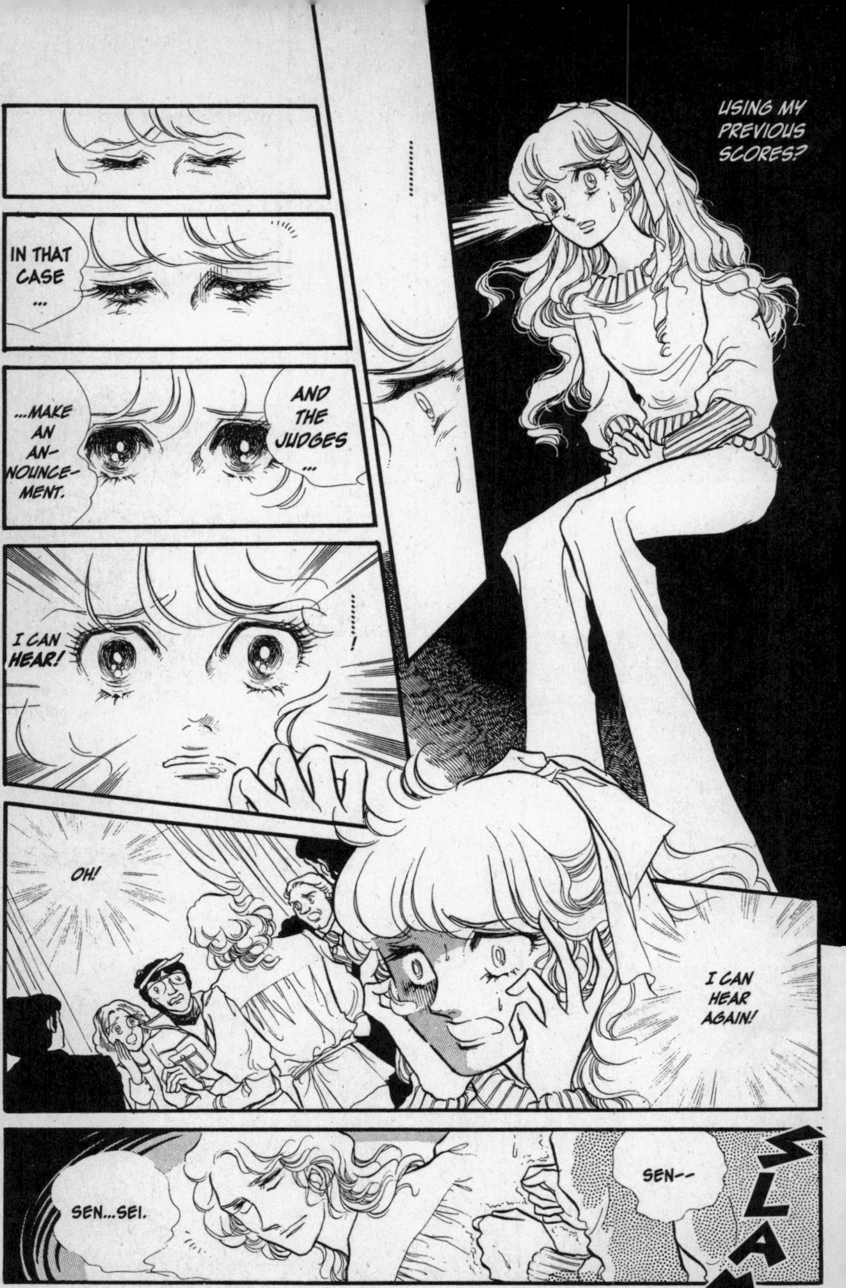
USING MY PREVIOUS SCORES?
......
IN THAT CASE ...
AND THE JUDGES ...
...MAKE AN AN-NOUNCE-MENT.
......!
I CAN HEAR!
I CAN HEAR AGAIN!
OH!
SLAM
SEN--
SEN...SEI.

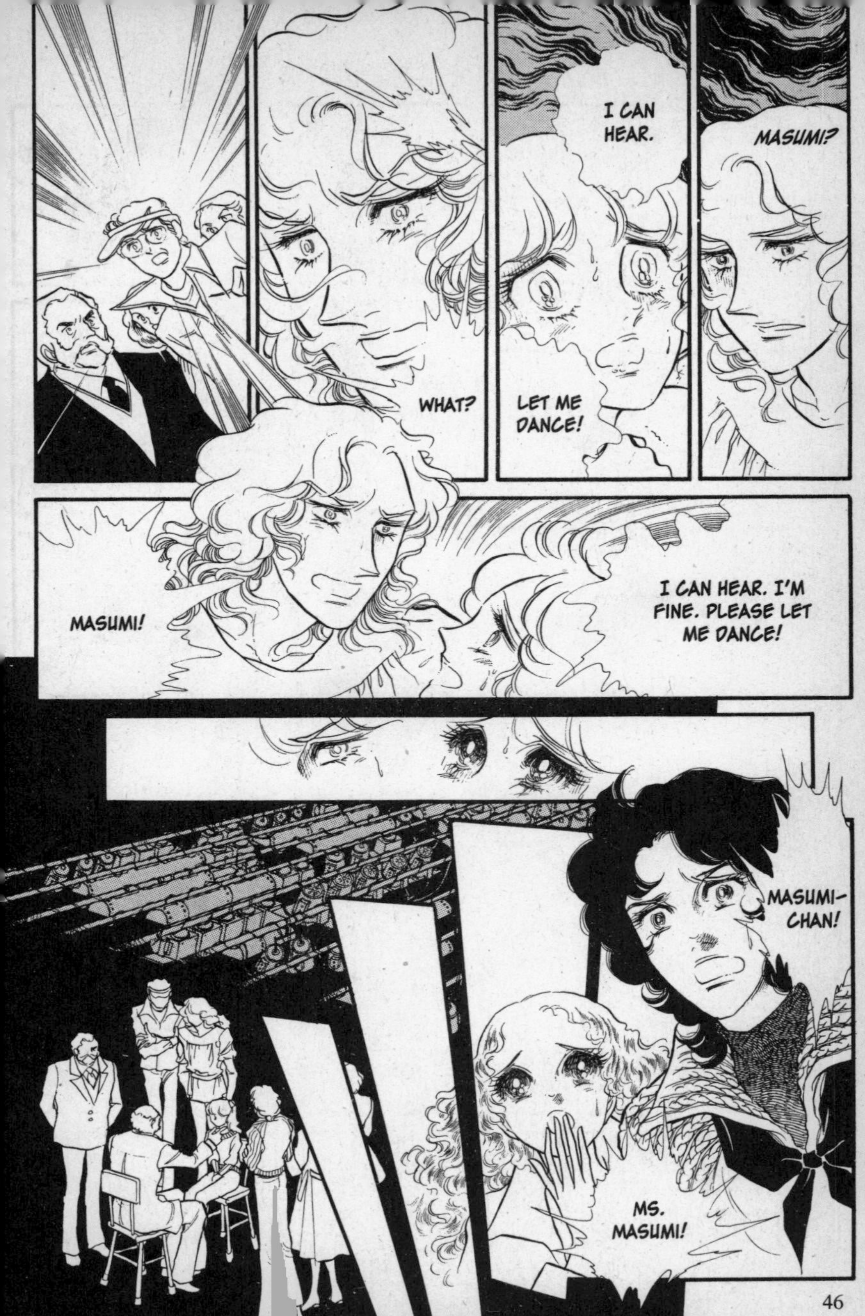
MASUMI?
I CAN HEAR.
LET ME DANCE!
WHAT?
I CAN HEAR. I'M FINE. PLEASE LET ME DANCE!
MASUMI!
MASUMI-CHAN!
MS. MASUMI!

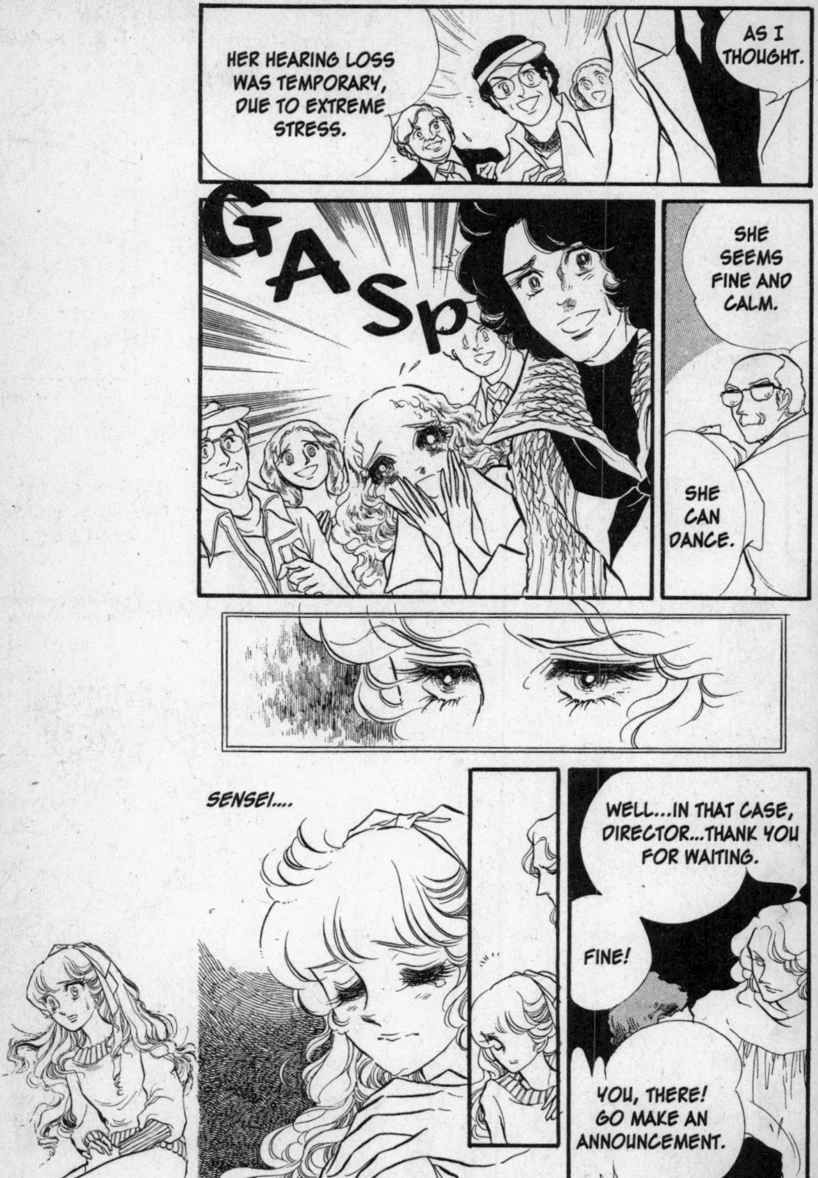
AS I THOUGHT.
HER HEARING LOSS WAS TEMPORARY, DUE TO EXTREME STRESS.
SHE SEEMS FINE AND CALM.
SHE CAN DANCE.
GASP
WELL...IN THAT CASE, DIRECTOR...THANK YOU FOR WAITING.
FINE!
YOU, THERE! GO MAKE AN ANNOUNCEMENT.
SENSEI....

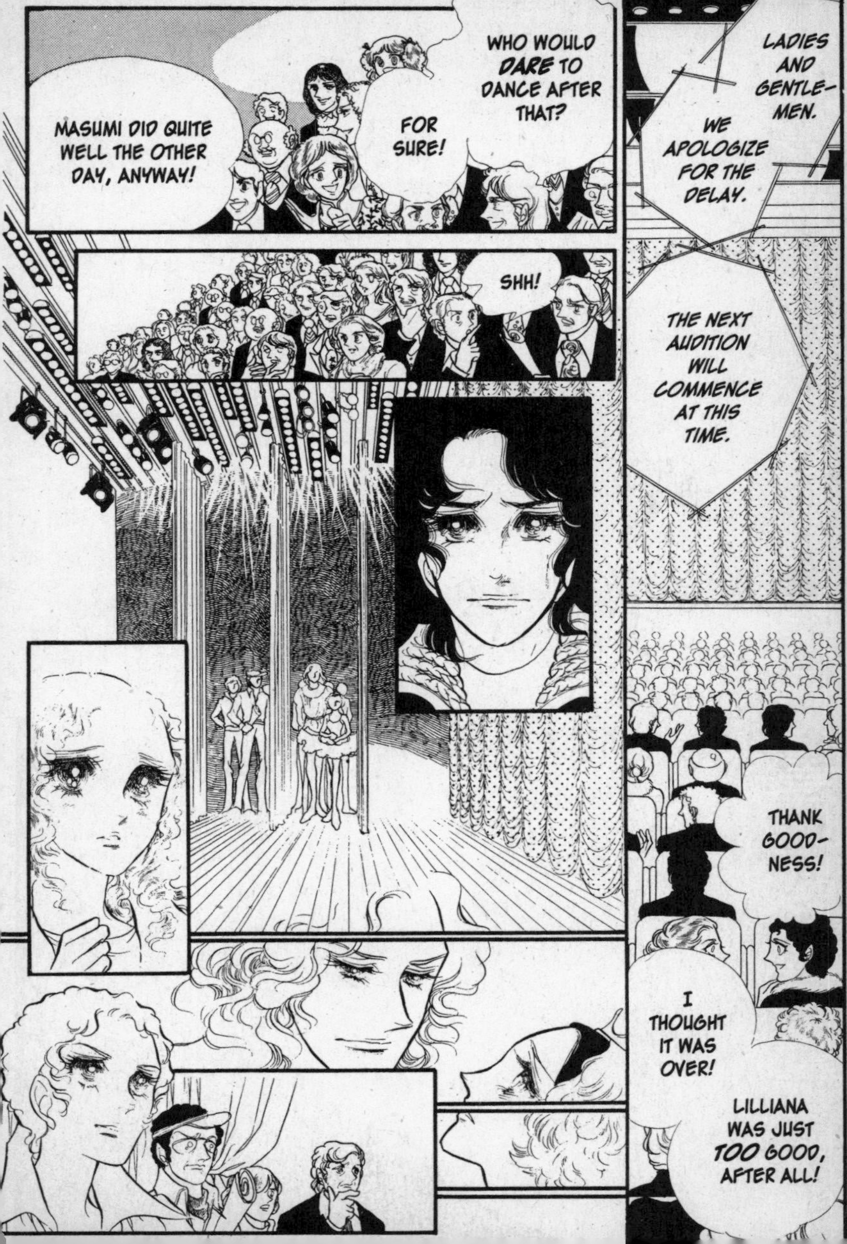
LADIES AND GENTLEMEN.
WE APOLOGIZE FOR THE DELAY.
THE NEXT AUDITION WILL COMMENCE AT THIS TIME.
THANK GOODNESS!
I THOUGHT IT WAS OVER!
LILLIANA WAS JUST TOO GOOD, AFTER ALL!
WHO WOULD DARE TO DANCE AFTER THAT?
FOR SURE!
MASUMI DID QUITE WELL THE OTHER DAY, ANYWAY!
SHH!

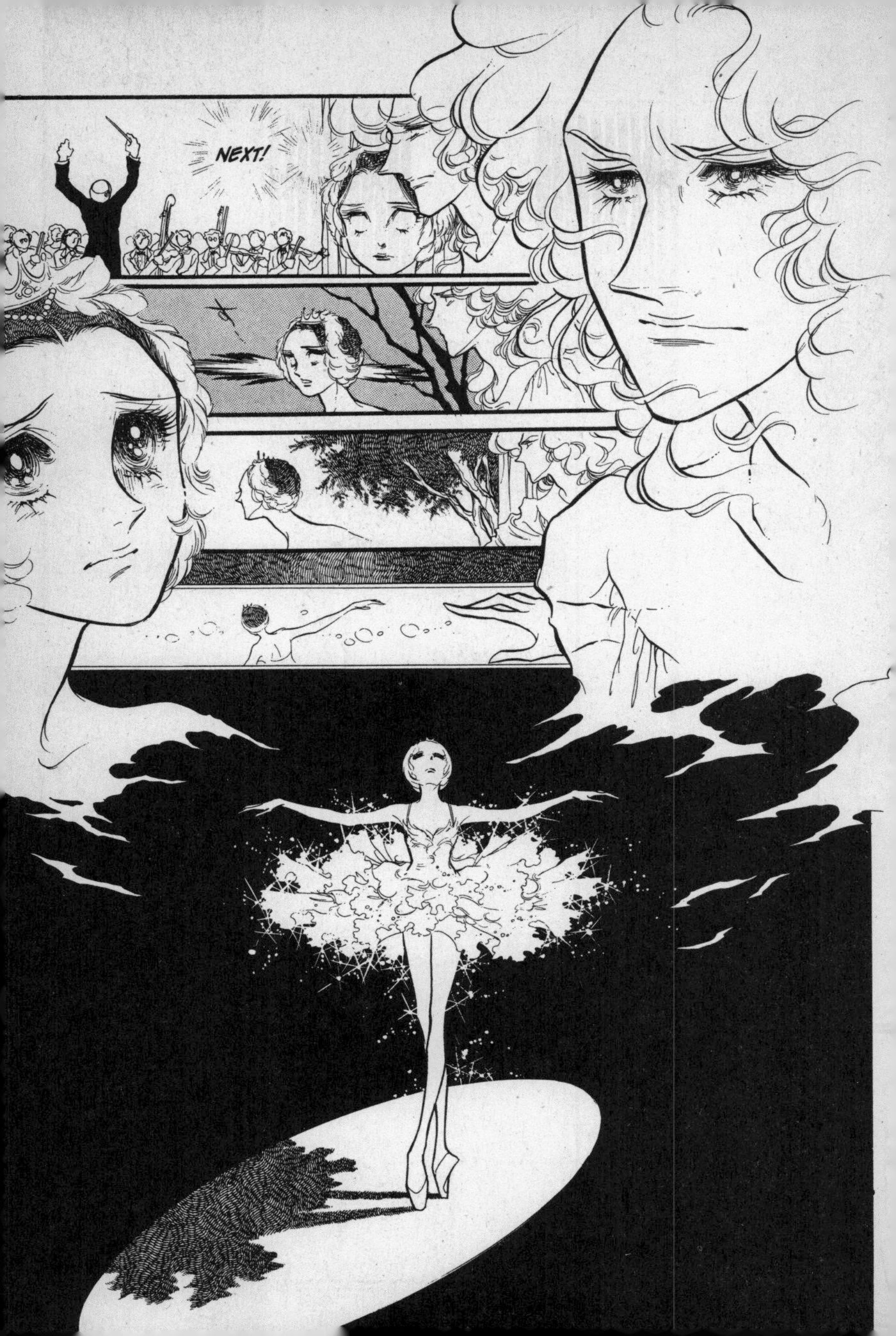
NEXT!

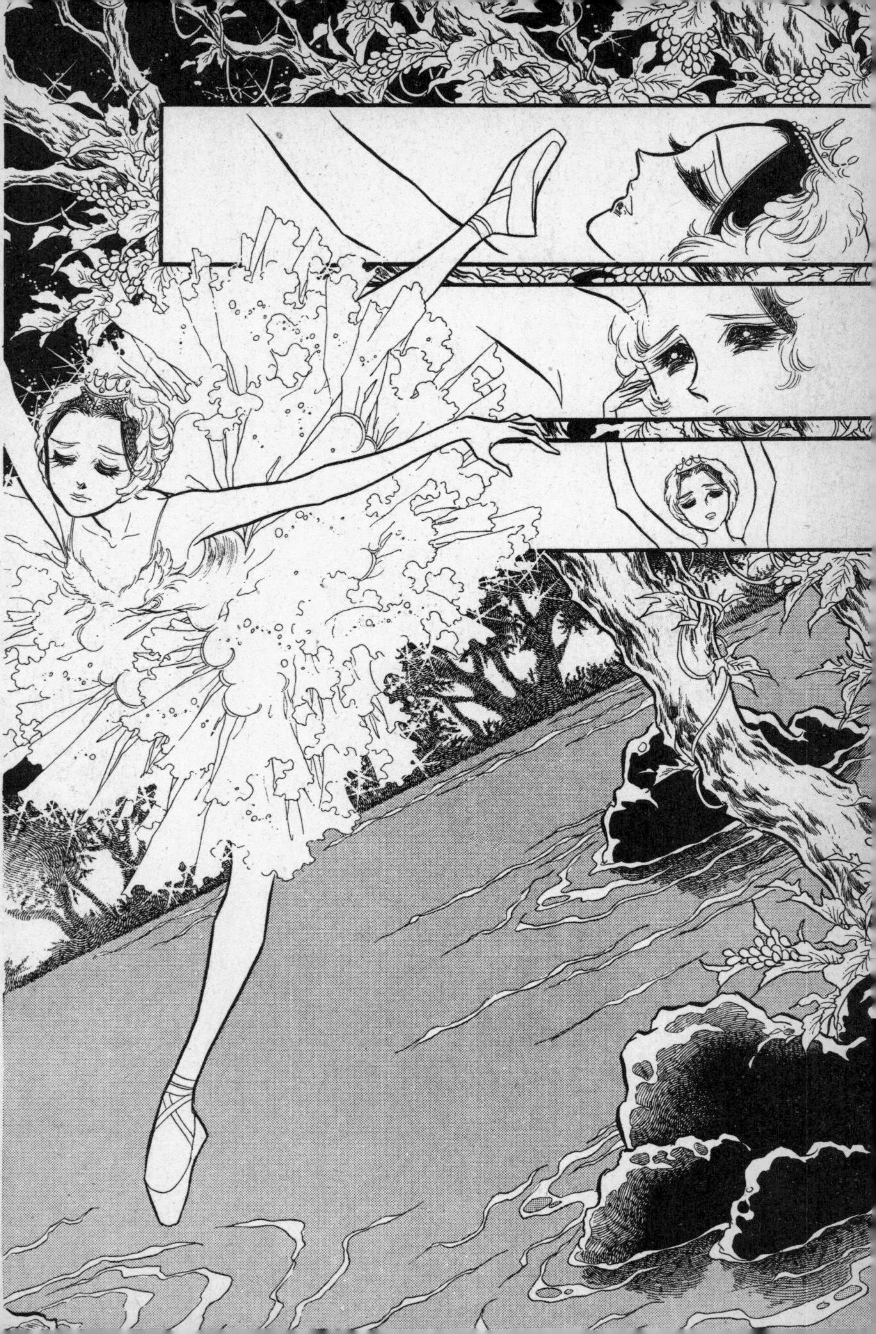

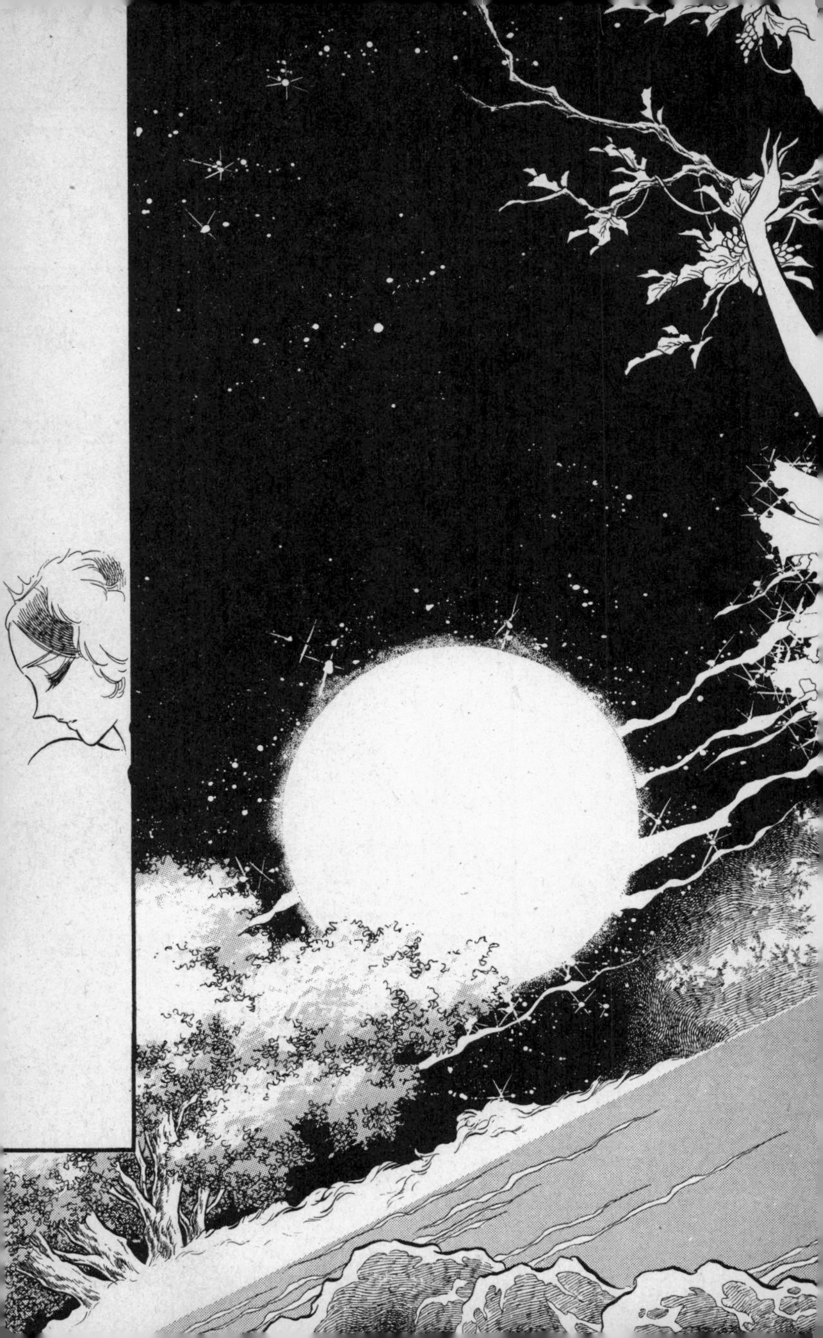

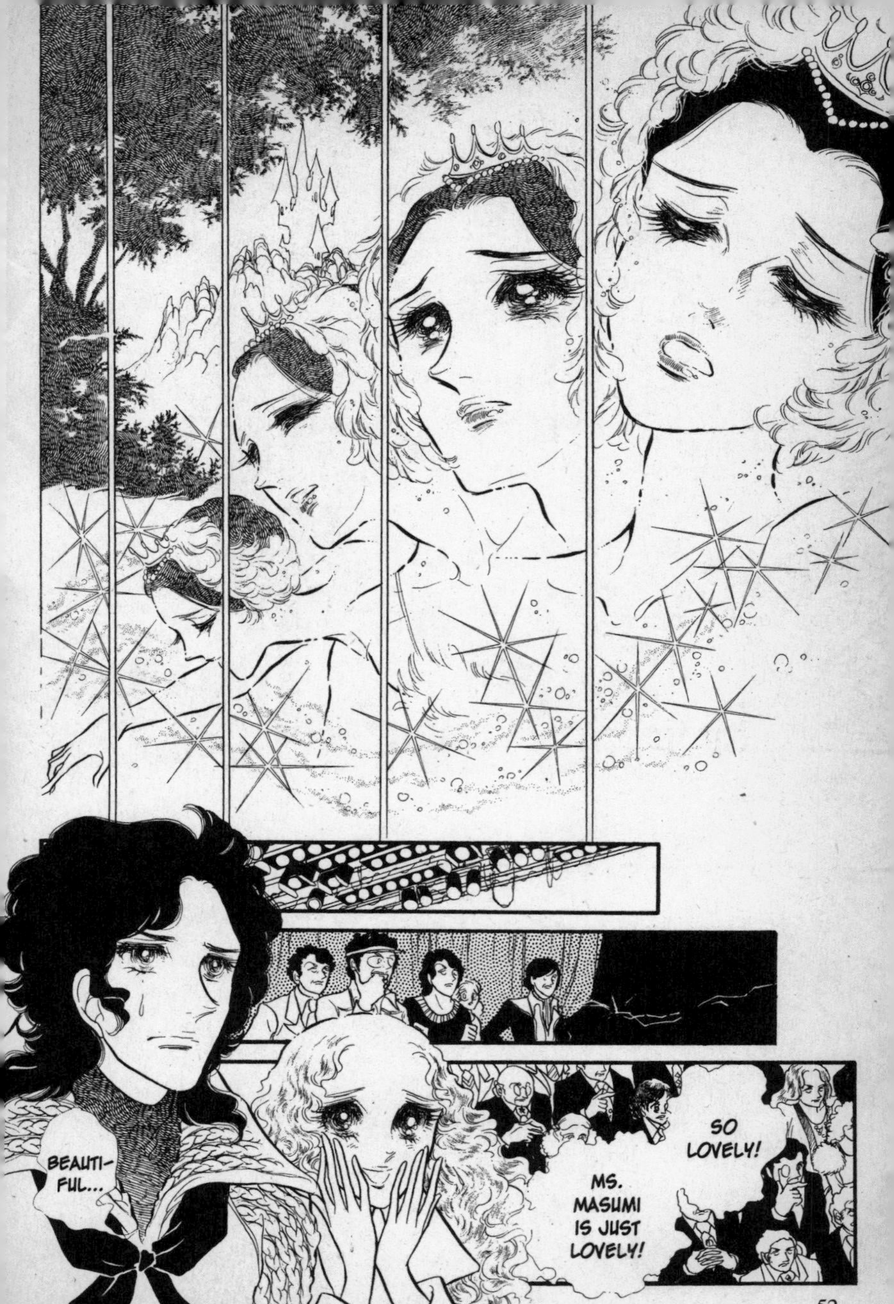
SO LOVELY!
MS. MASUMI IS JUST LOVELY!
BEAUTI-FUL...

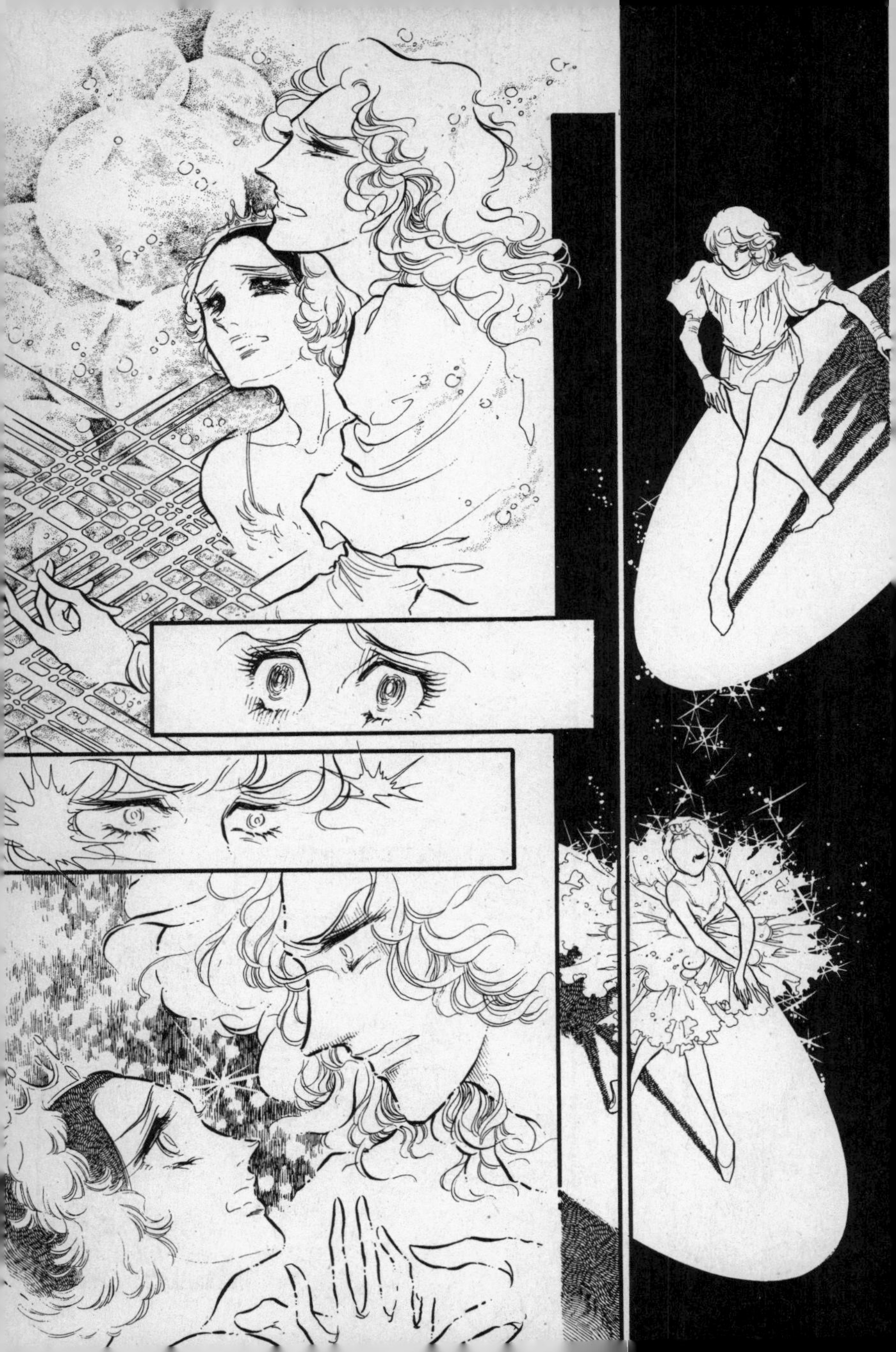

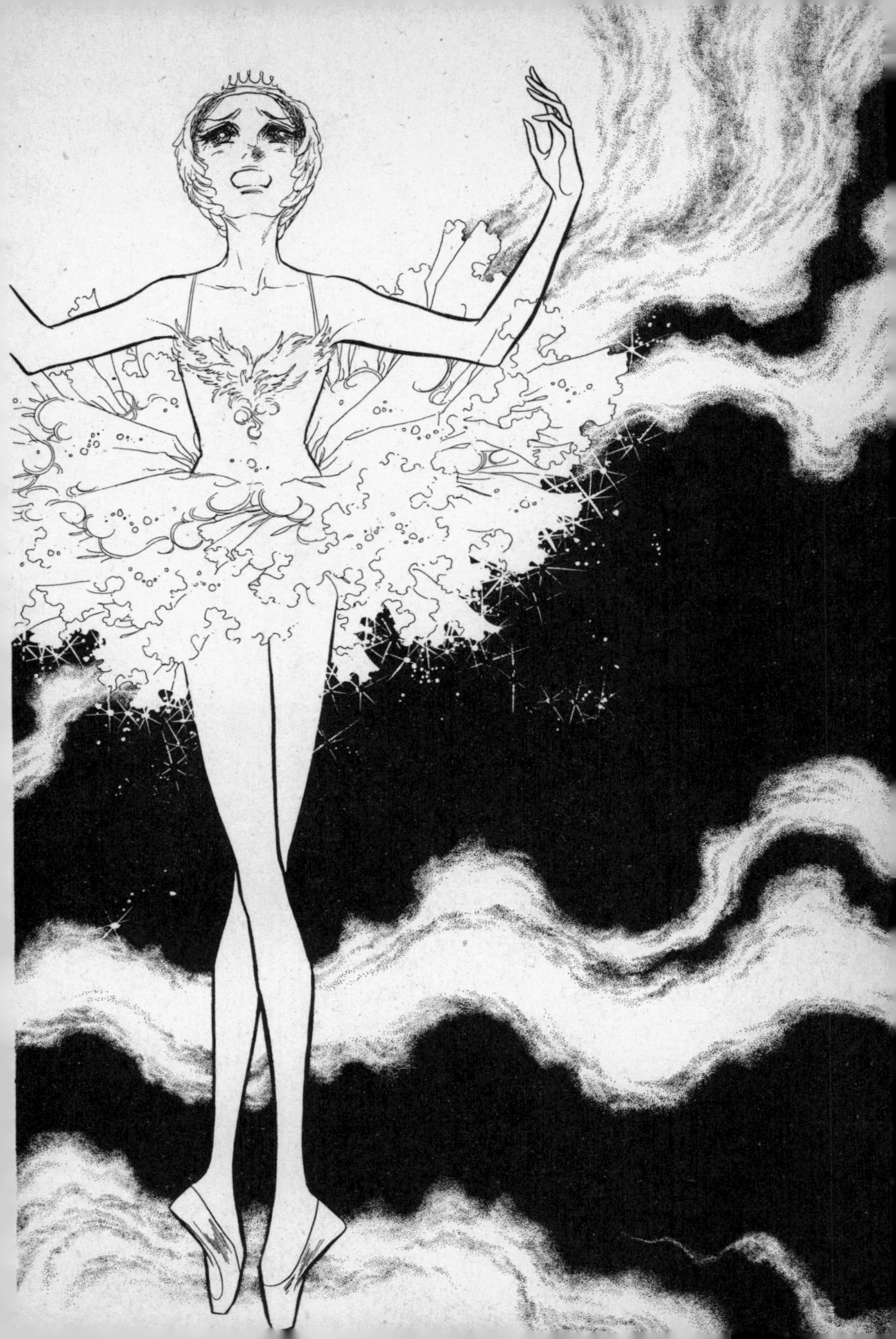

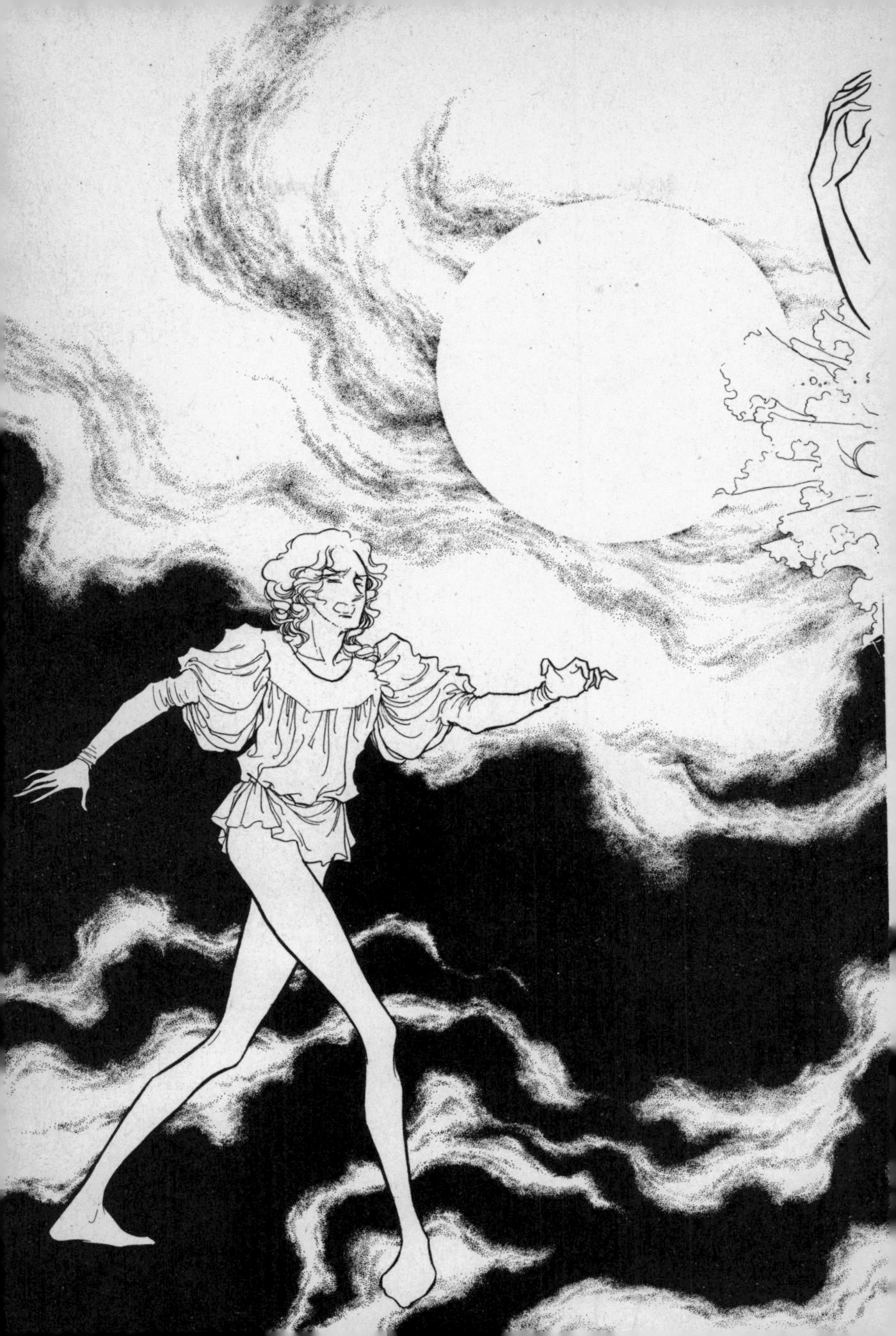

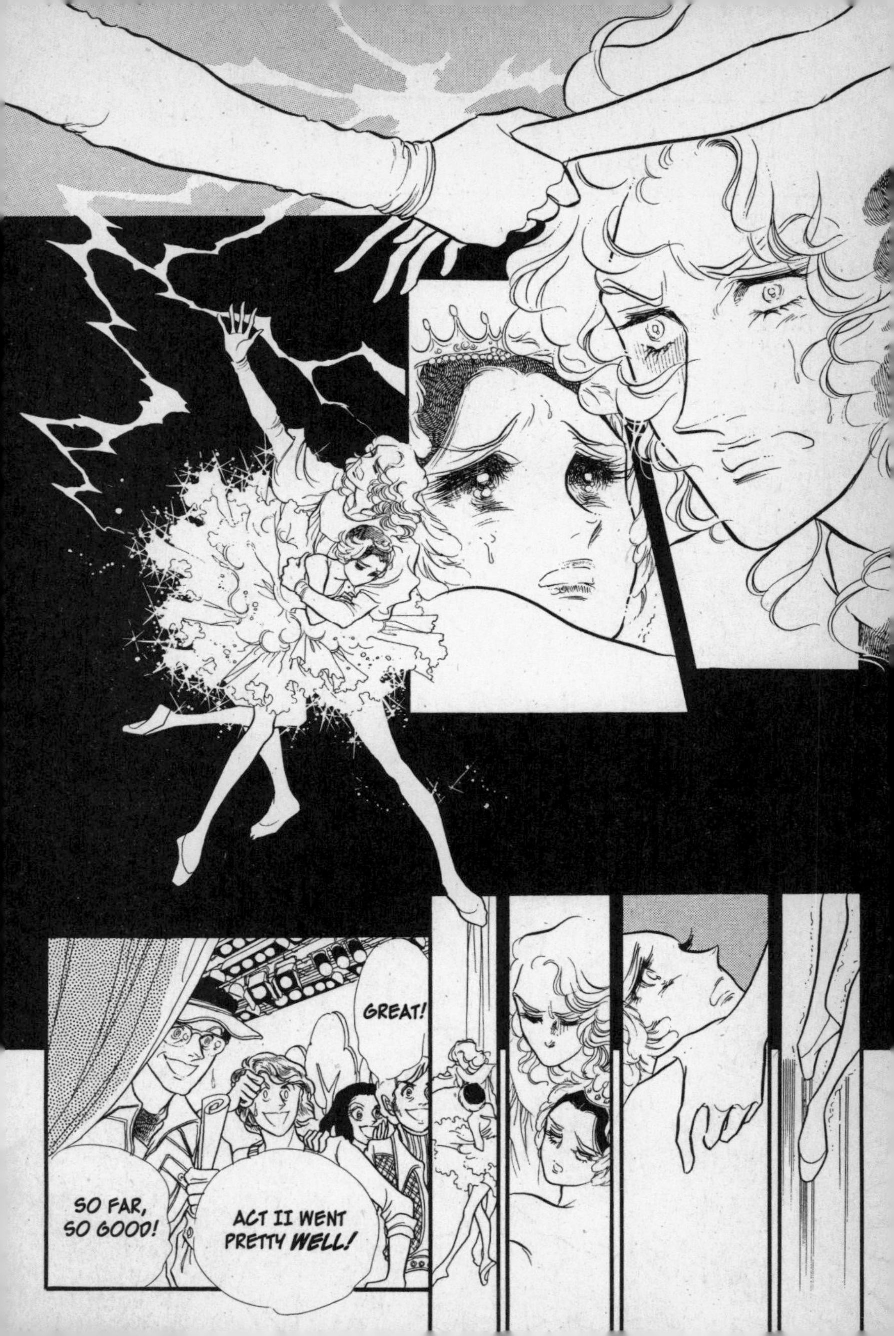
GREAT!
ACT II WENT PRETTY WELL!
SO FAR, SO GOOD!

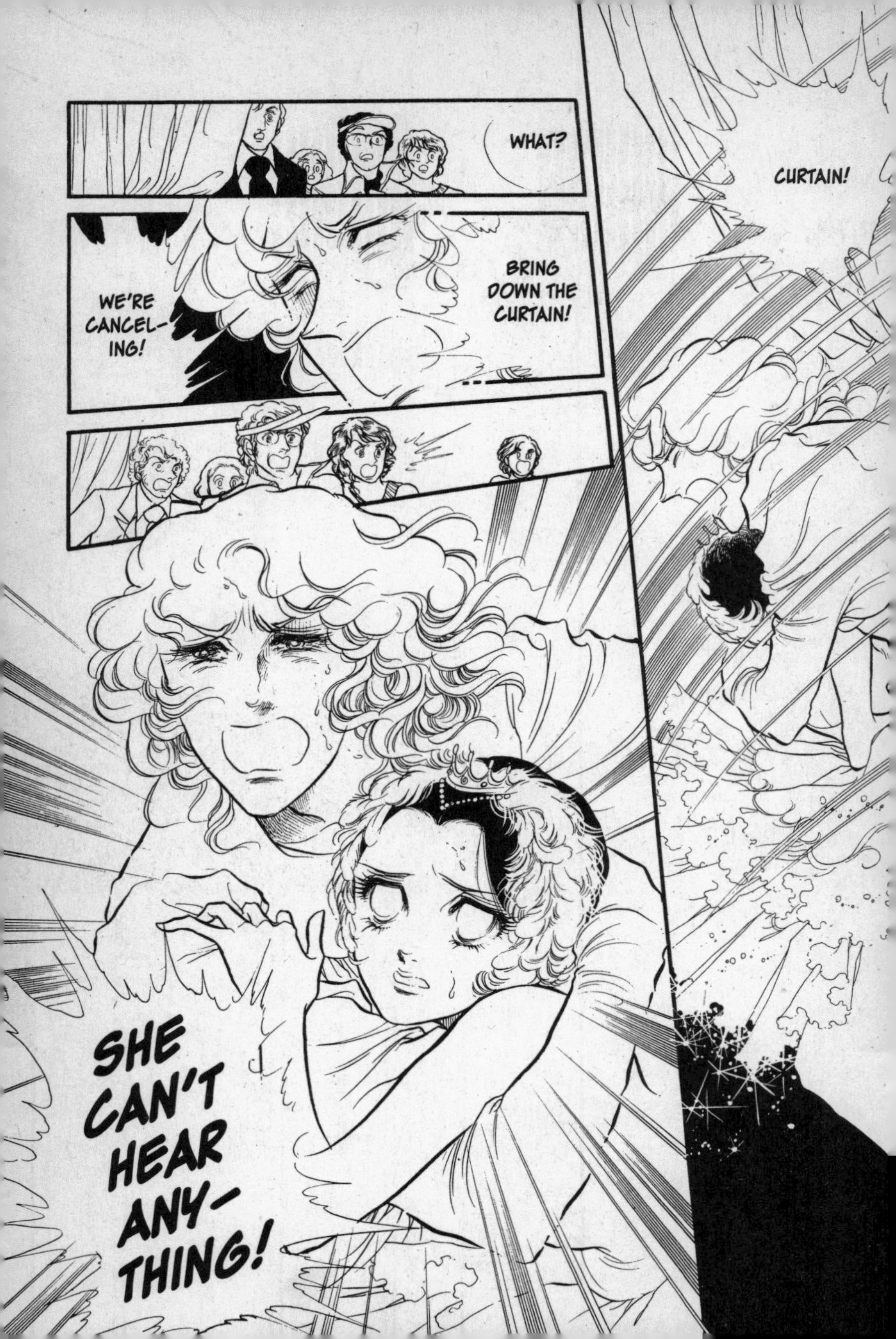
CURTAIN!
WHAT?
BRING DOWN THE CURTAIN!
WE'RE CANCEL-ING!
SHE CAN'T HEAR ANY-THING!

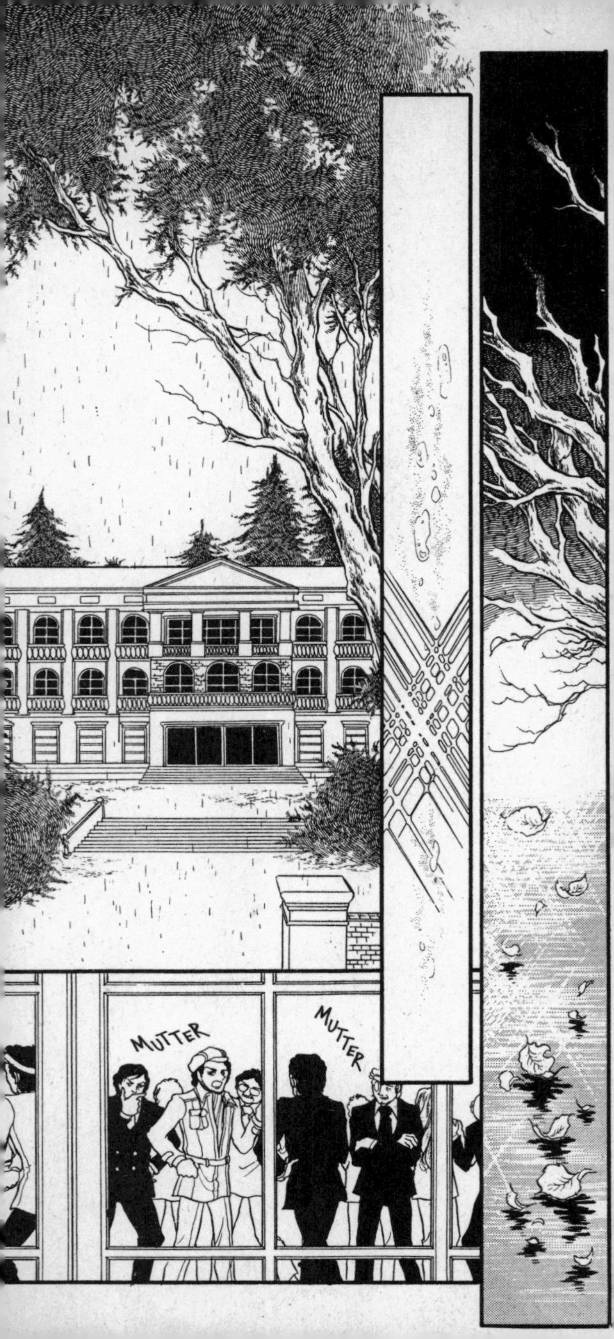
MUTTER
MUTTER

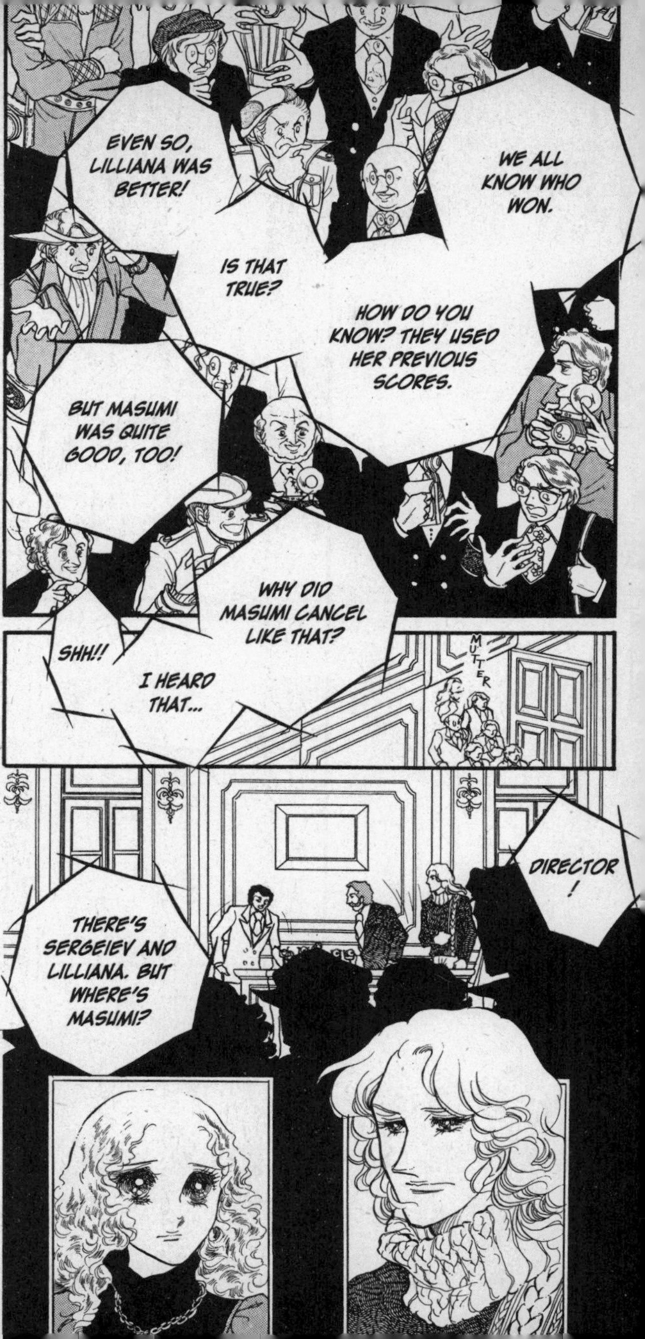
WE ALL KNOW WHO WON.
EVEN SO, LILLIANA WAS BETTER!
HOW DO YOU KNOW? THEY USED HER PREVIOUS SCORES.
IS THAT TRUE?
BUT MASUMI WAS QUITE GOOD, TOO!
WHY DID MASUMI CANCEL LIKE THAT?
MUTTER
I HEARD THAT...
SHH!!
DIRECTOR!
THERE'S SERGEIEV AND LILLIANA. BUT WHERE'S MASUMI?
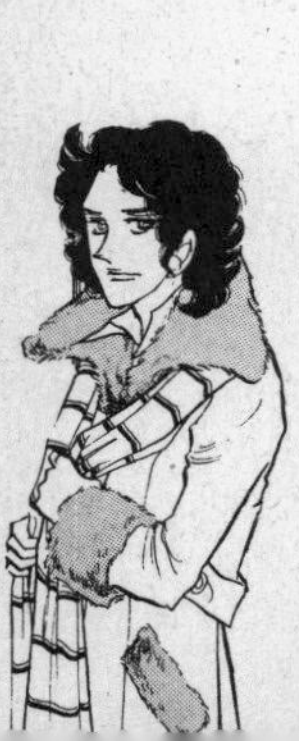

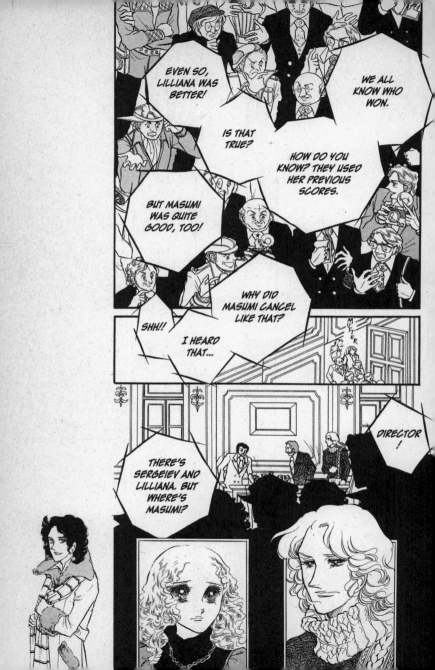

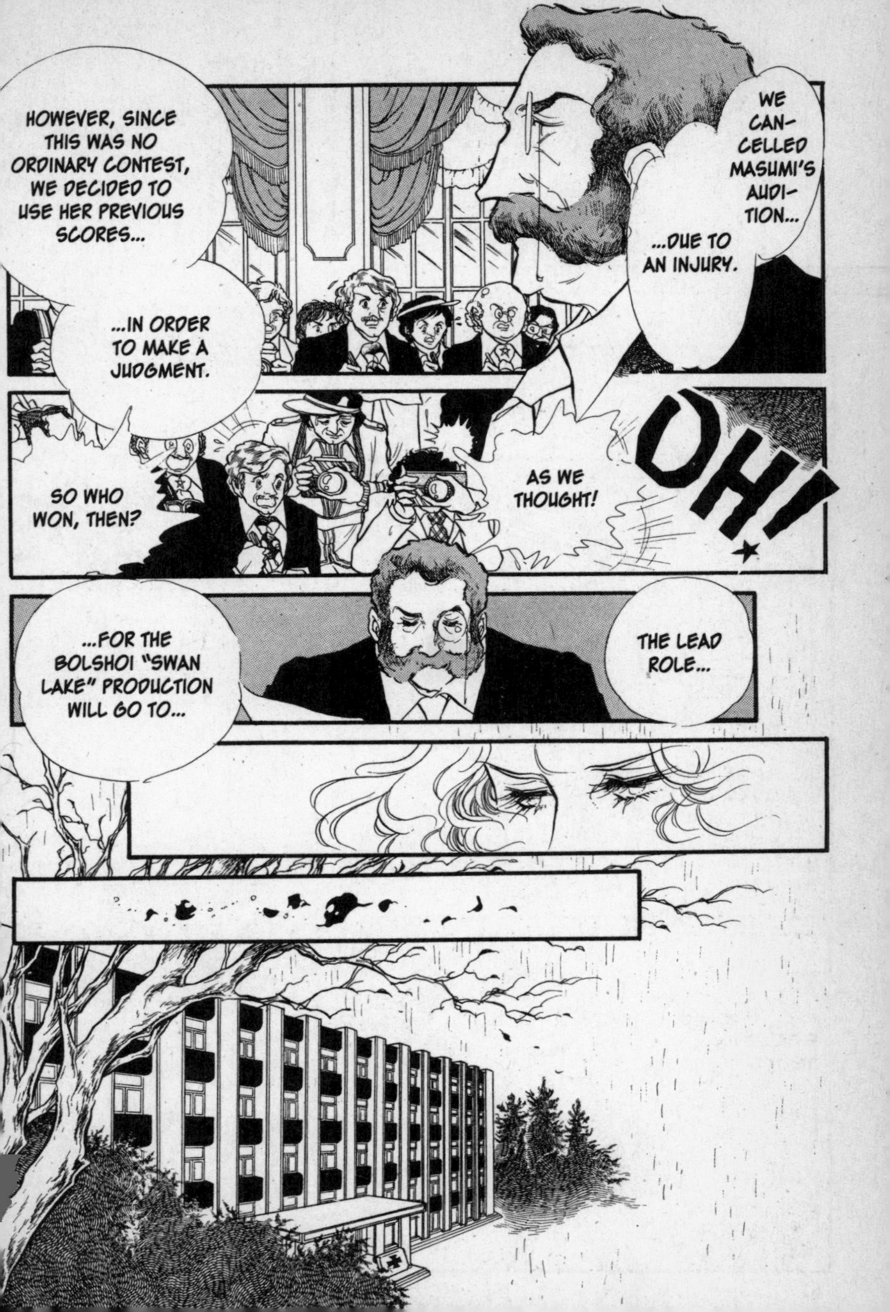
WE CANCELLED MASUMI'S AUDITION...
...DUE TO AN INJURY.
HOWEVER, SINCE THIS WAS NO ORDINARY CONTEST, WE DECIDED TO USE HER PREVIOUS SCORES...
...IN ORDER TO MAKE A JUDGMENT.
OH!
AS WE THOUGHT!
SO WHO WON, THEN?
THE LEAD ROLE...
...FOR THE BOLSHOI "SWAN LAKE" PRODUCTION WILL GO TO...

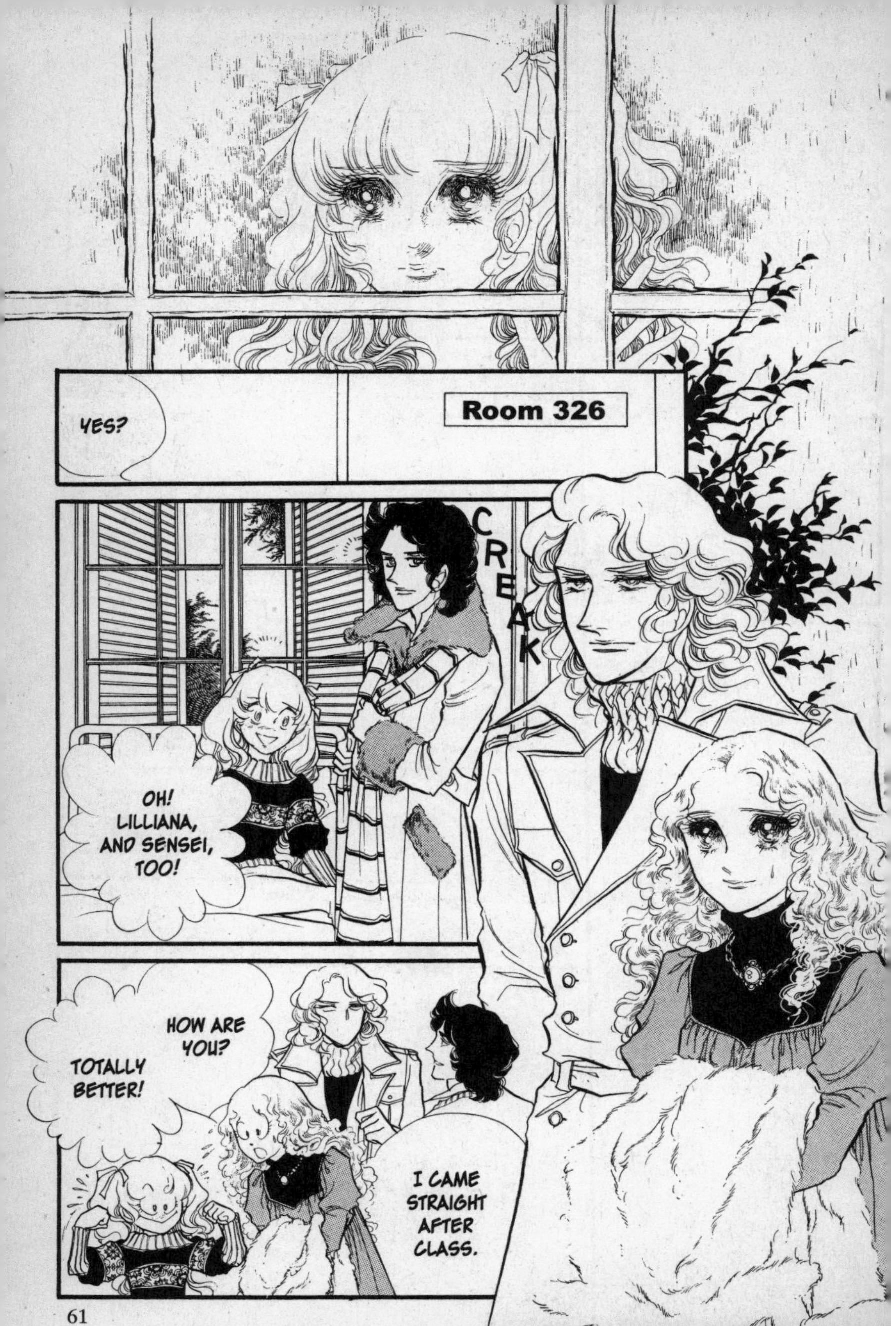
Room 326
YES?
CREAK
OH! LILLIANA, AND SENSEI, TOO!
HOW ARE YOU?
TOTALLY BETTER!
I CAME STRAIGHT AFTER CLASS.

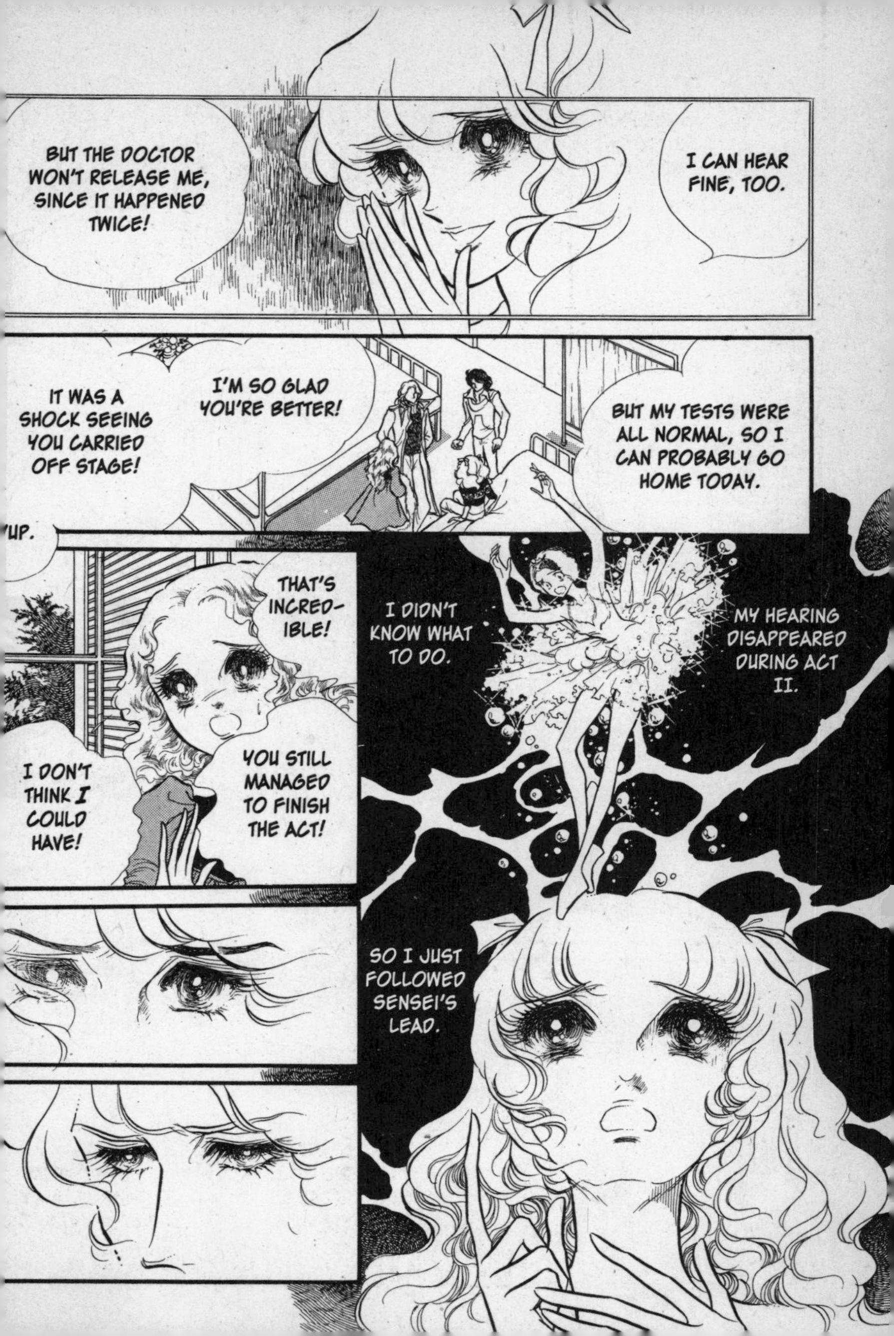
I CAN HEAR FINE, TOO.
BUT THE DOCTOR WON'T RELEASE ME, SINCE IT HAPPENED TWICE!
BUT MY TESTS WERE ALL NORMAL, SO I CAN PROBABLY GO HOME TODAY.
I'M SO GLAD YOU'RE BETTER!
IT WAS A SHOCK SEEING YOU CARRIED OFF STAGE!
YUP.
MY HEARING DISAPPEARED DURING ACT II.
I DIDN'T KNOW WHAT TO DO.
SO I JUST FOLLOWED SENSEI'S LEAD.
THAT'S INCRED-IBLE!
YOU STILL MANAGED TO FINISH THE ACT!
I DON'T THINK I COULD HAVE!

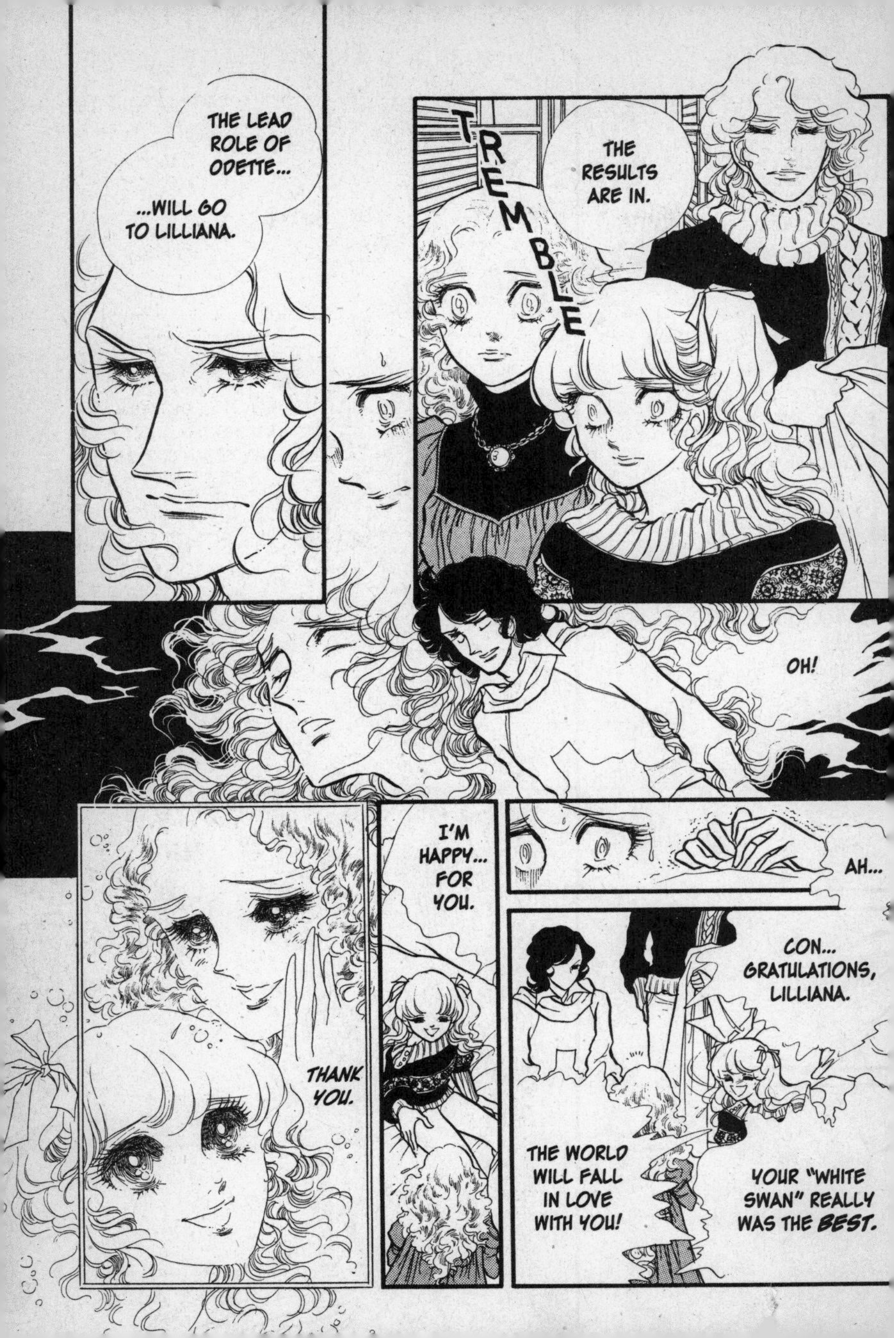
TREMBLE
THE RESULTS ARE IN.
THE LEAD ROLE OF ODETTE...
...WILL GO TO LILLIANA.
OH!
AH...
CON... GRATULATIONS, LILLIANA.
YOUR "WHITE SWAN" REALLY WAS THE *BEST*.
THE WORLD WILL FALL IN LOVE WITH YOU!
I'M HAPPY... FOR YOU.
THANK YOU.

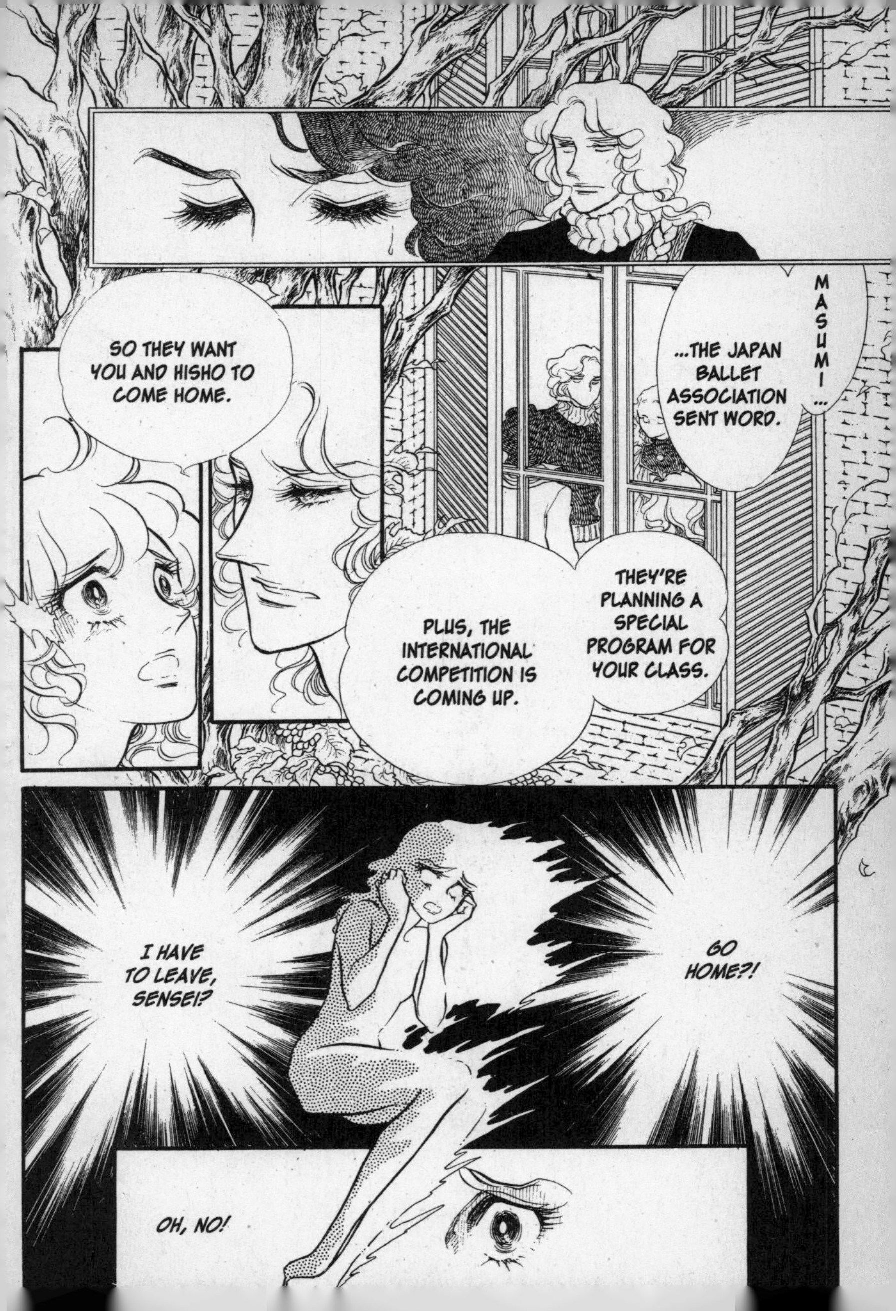
MASUMI...
...THE JAPAN BALLET ASSOCIATION SENT WORD.
THEY'RE PLANNING A SPECIAL PROGRAM FOR YOUR CLASS.
PLUS, THE INTERNATIONAL COMPETITION IS COMING UP.
SO THEY WANT YOU AND HISHO TO COME HOME.
GO HOME?!
I HAVE TO LEAVE, SENSEI?
OH, NO!

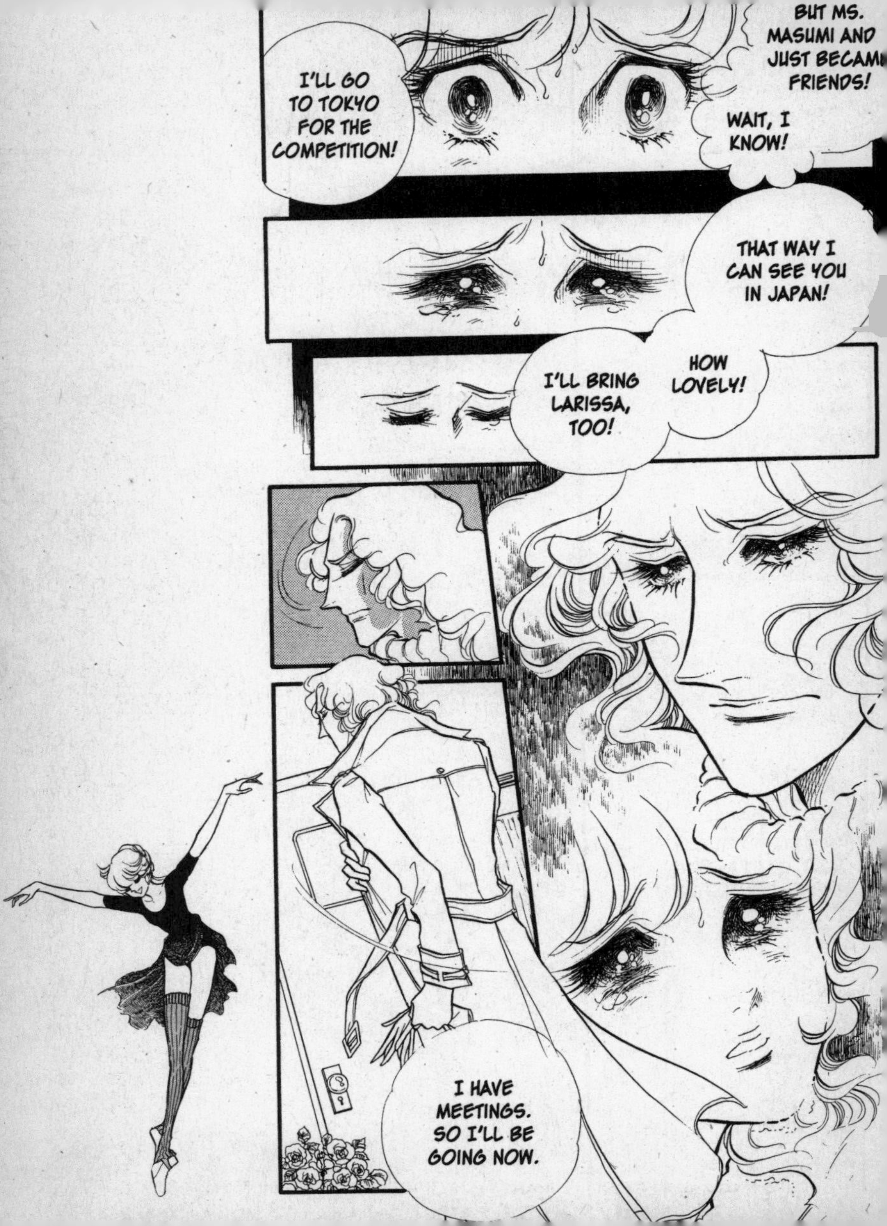
BUT MS. MASUMI AND JUST BECAM FRIENDS!
WAIT, I KNOW!
I'LL GO TO TOKYO FOR THE COMPETITION!
THAT WAY I CAN SEE YOU IN JAPAN!
HOW LOVELY!
I'LL BRING LARISSA, TOO!
I HAVE MEETINGS. SO I'LL BE GOING NOW.

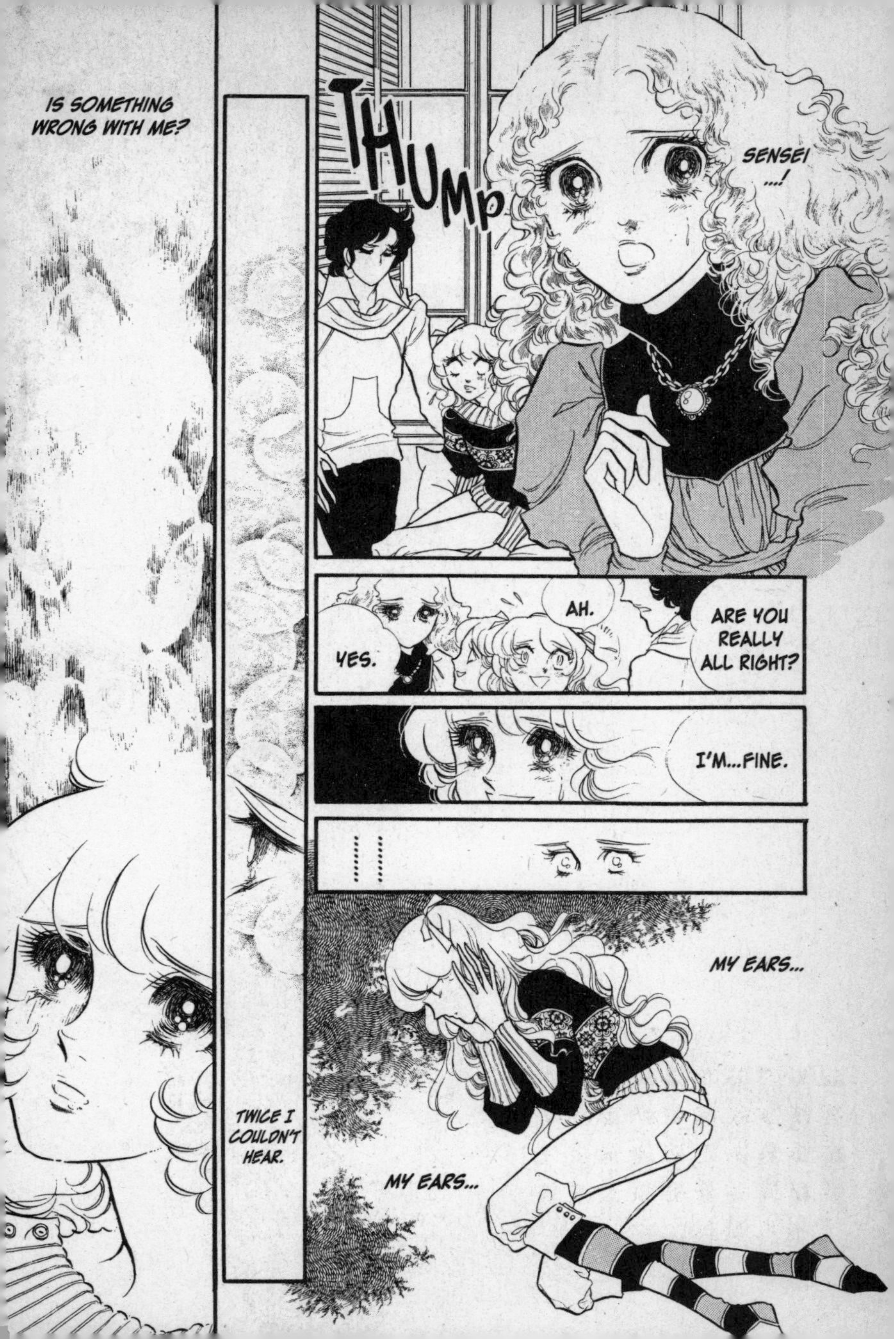
SENSEI ...!
THUMP
ARE YOU REALLY ALL RIGHT?
AH.
YES.
I'M...FINE.
......
MY EARS...
MY EARS...
TWICE I COULDN'T HEAR.
IS SOMETHING WRONG WITH ME?

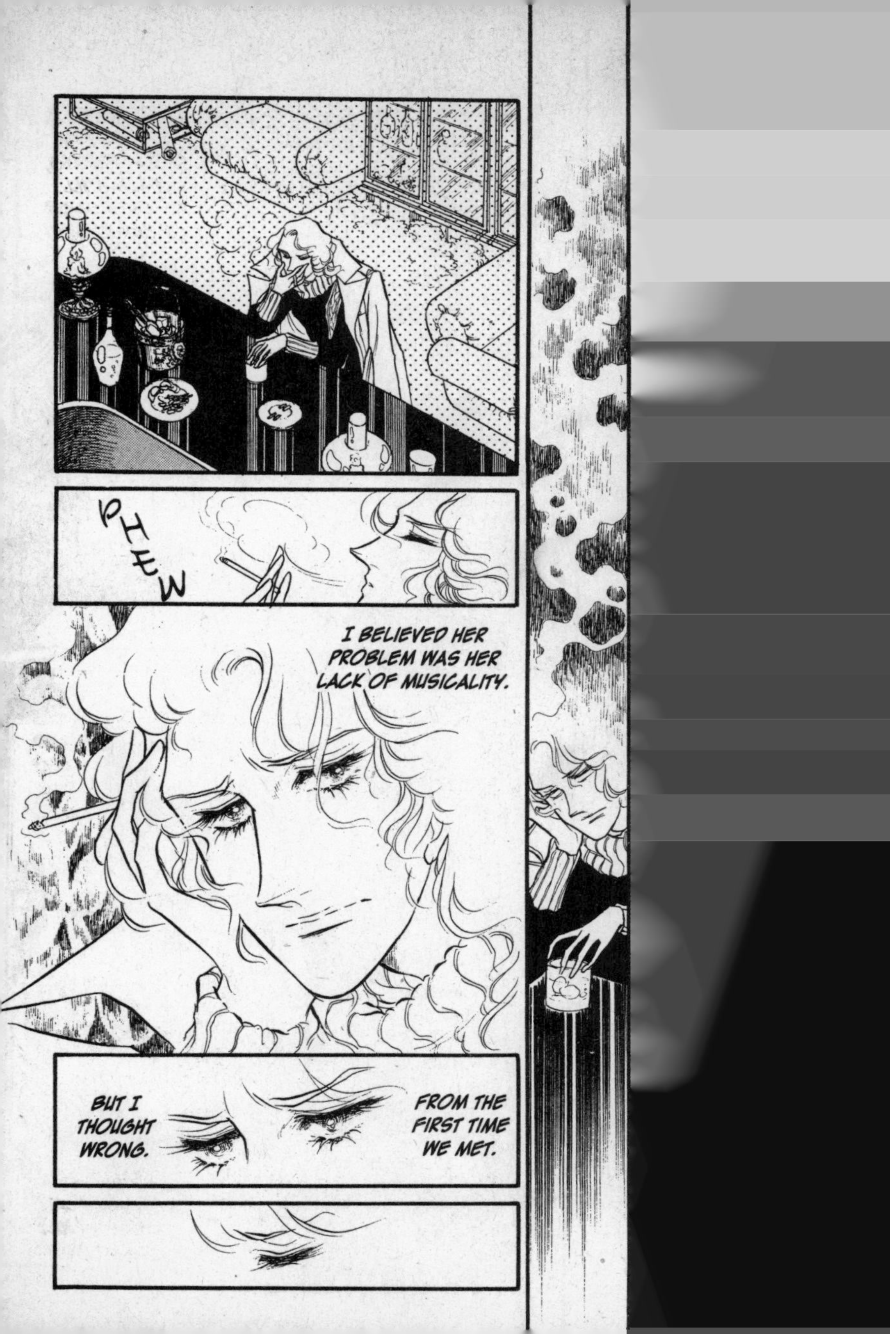
PHEW
I BELIEVED HER PROBLEM WAS HER LACK OF MUSICALITY.
FROM THE FIRST TIME WE MET.
BUT I THOUGHT WRONG.

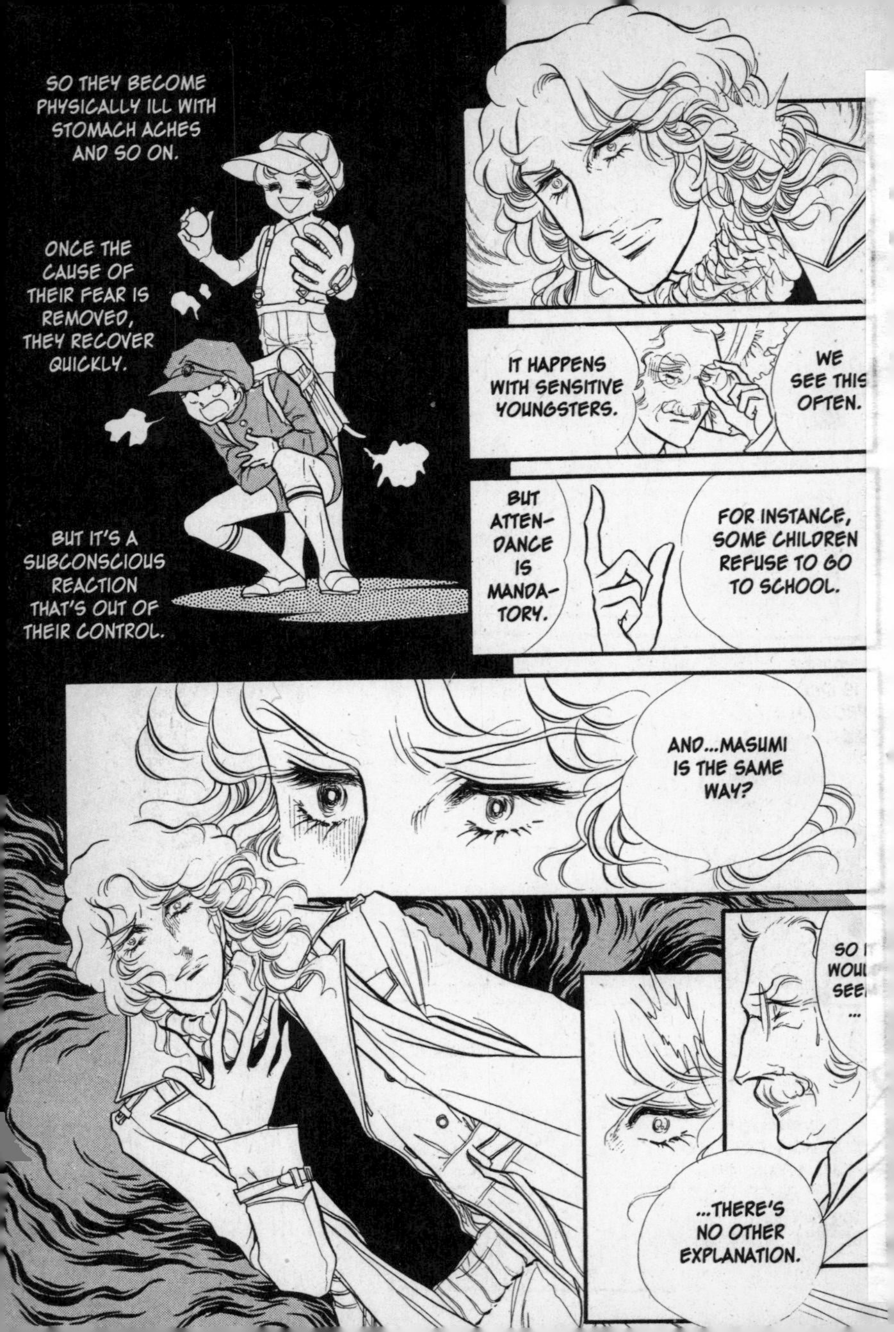
WE SEE THIS OFTEN.
IT HAPPENS WITH SENSITIVE YOUNGSTERS.
FOR INSTANCE, SOME CHILDREN REFUSE TO GO TO SCHOOL.
BUT ATTEN-DANCE IS MANDA-TORY.
SO THEY BECOME PHYSICALLY ILL WITH STOMACH ACHES AND SO ON.
ONCE THE CAUSE OF THEIR FEAR IS REMOVED, THEY RECOVER QUICKLY.
BUT IT'S A SUBCONSCIOUS REACTION THAT'S OUT OF THEIR CONTROL.
AND...MASUMI IS THE SAME WAY?
SO I WOUL SEE ...
...THERE'S NO OTHER EXPLANATION.

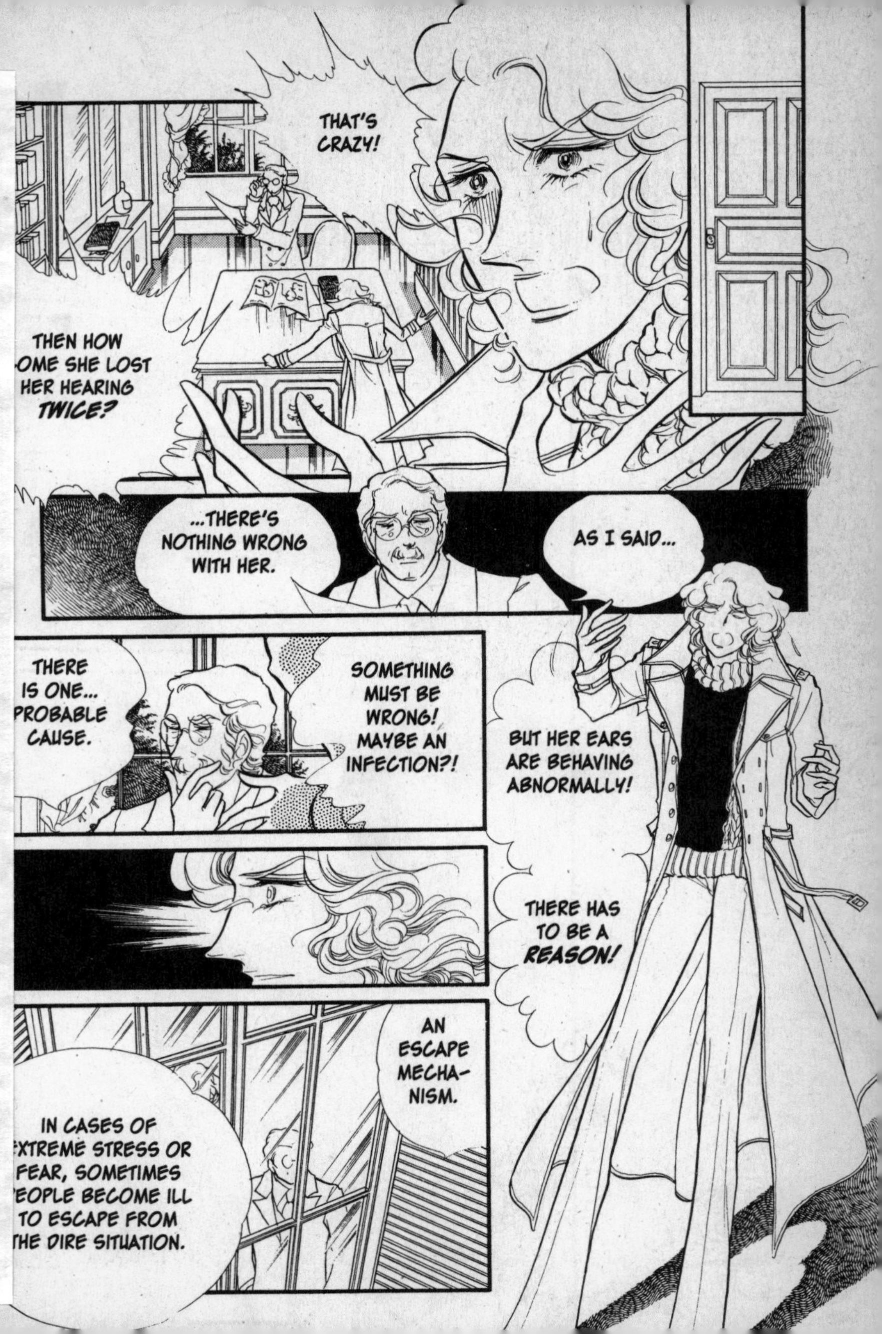
THAT'S CRAZY!
THEN HOW COME SHE LOST HER HEARING *TWICE?*
AS I SAID...
...THERE'S NOTHING WRONG WITH HER.
BUT HER EARS ARE BEHAVING ABNORMALLY!
THERE HAS TO BE A *REASON!*
SOMETHING MUST BE WRONG! MAYBE AN INFECTION?!
THERE IS ONE... PROBABLE CAUSE.
AN ESCAPE MECHA-NISM.
IN CASES OF EXTREME STRESS OR FEAR, SOMETIMES PEOPLE BECOME ILL TO ESCAPE FROM THE DIRE SITUATION.

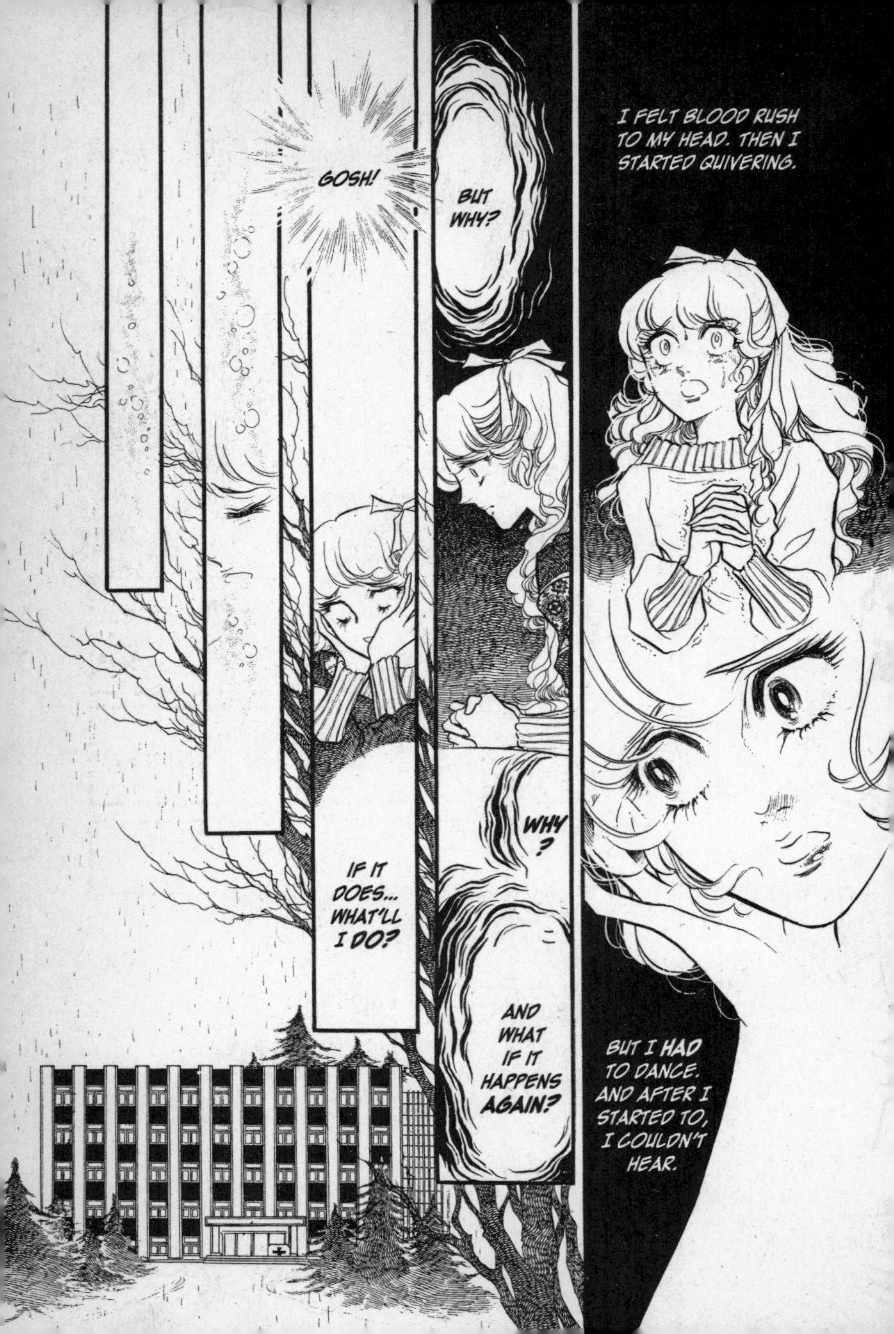
I FELT BLOOD RUSH TO MY HEAD. THEN I STARTED QUIVERING.
BUT I HAD TO DANCE. AND AFTER I STARTED TO, I COULDN'T HEAR.
BUT WHY?
WHY?
AND WHAT IF IT HAPPENS AGAIN?
GOSH!
IF IT DOES... WHAT'LL I DO?

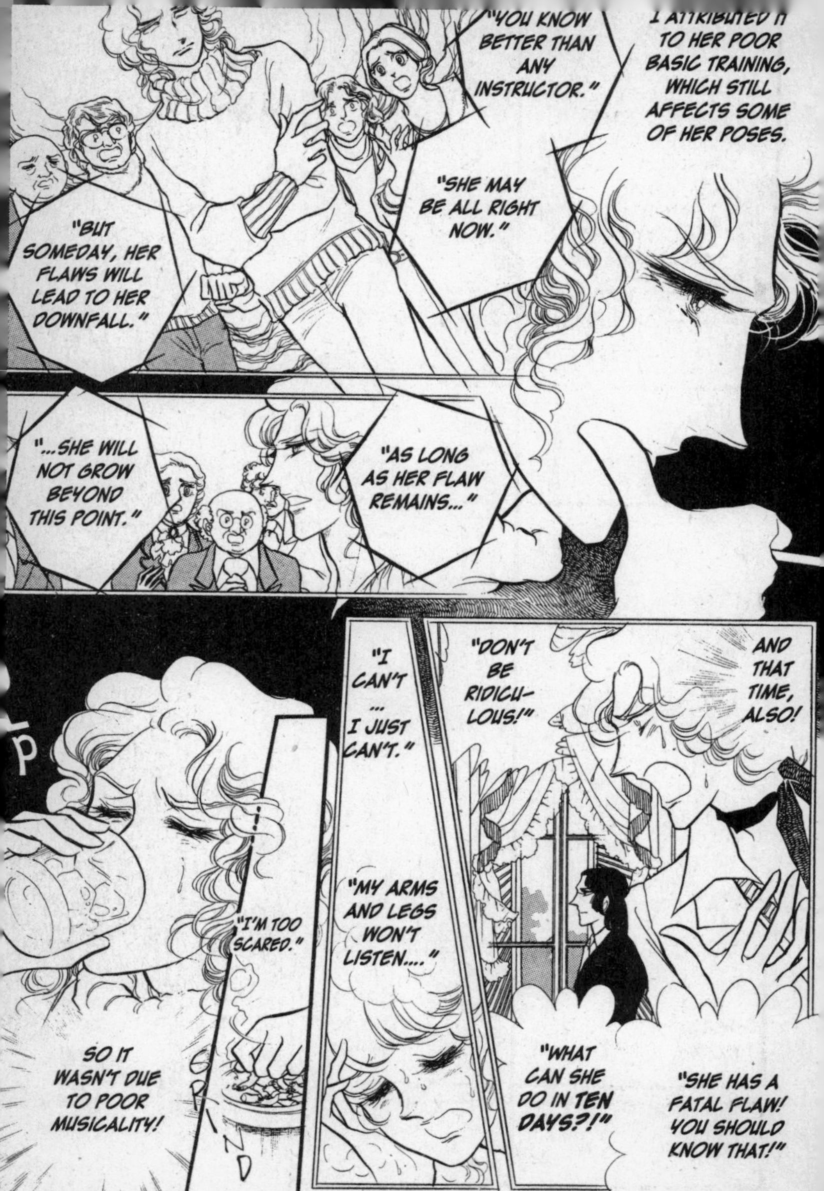
I ATTRIBUTED IT TO HER POOR BASIC TRAINING, WHICH STILL AFFECTS SOME OF HER POSES.
"YOU KNOW BETTER THAN ANY INSTRUCTOR."
"SHE MAY BE ALL RIGHT NOW."
"BUT SOMEDAY, HER FLAWS WILL LEAD TO HER DOWNFALL."
"AS LONG AS HER FLAW REMAINS..."
"...SHE WILL NOT GROW BEYOND THIS POINT."
AND THAT TIME, ALSO!
"DON'T BE RIDICULOUS!"
"SHE HAS A FATAL FLAW! YOU SHOULD KNOW THAT!"
"WHAT CAN SHE DO IN TEN DAYS?!"
"I CAN'T ... I JUST CAN'T."
"MY ARMS AND LEGS WON'T LISTEN...."
"I'M TOO SCARED."
SO IT WASN'T DUE TO POOR MUSICALITY!

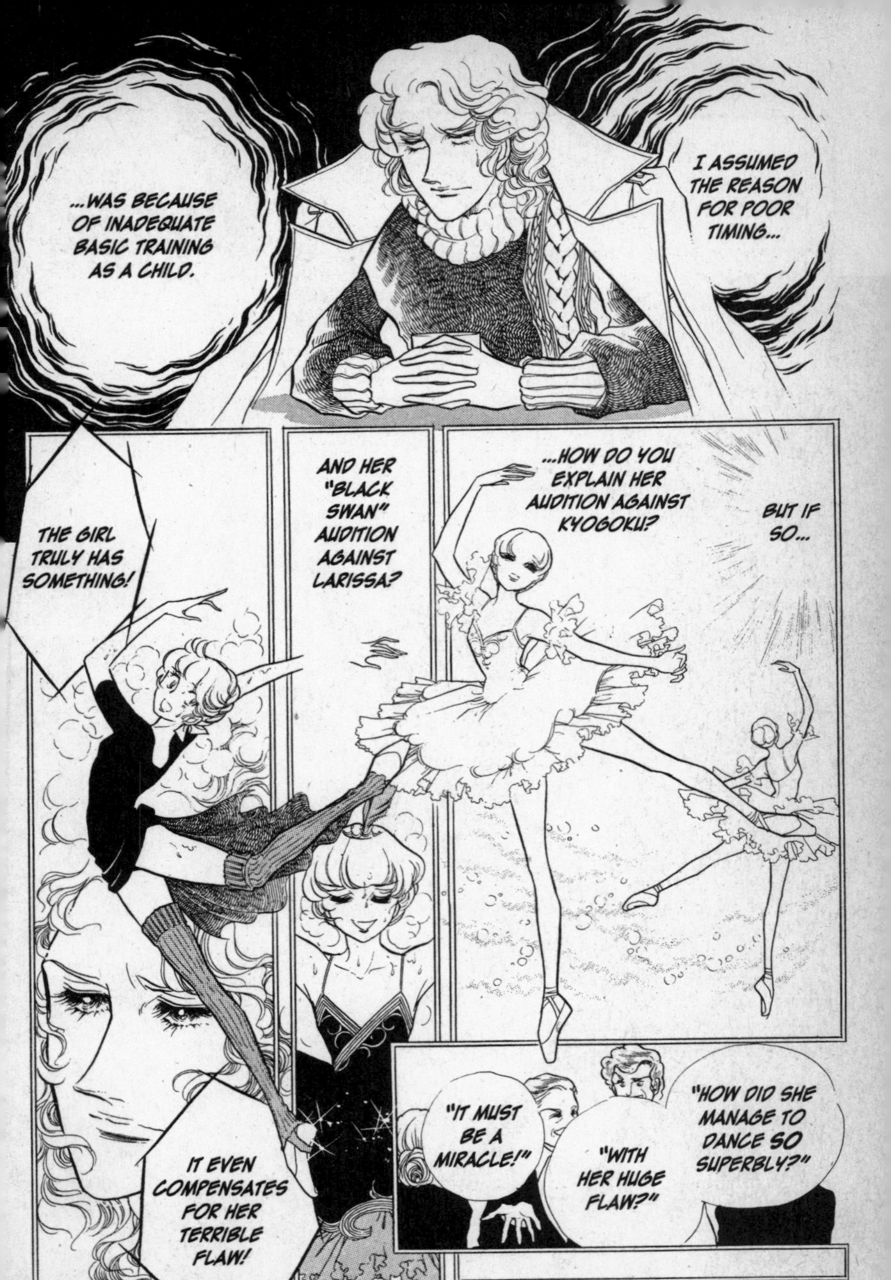
I ASSUMED THE REASON FOR POOR TIMING...
...WAS BECAUSE OF INADEQUATE BASIC TRAINING AS A CHILD.
BUT IF SO...
...HOW DO YOU EXPLAIN HER AUDITION AGAINST KYOGOKU?
"HOW DID SHE MANAGE TO DANCE SO SUPERBLY?"
"WITH HER HUGE FLAW?"
"IT MUST BE A MIRACLE!"
AND HER "BLACK SWAN" AUDITION AGAINST LARISSA?
THE GIRL TRULY HAS SOMETHING!
IT EVEN COMPENSATES FOR HER TERRIBLE FLAW!

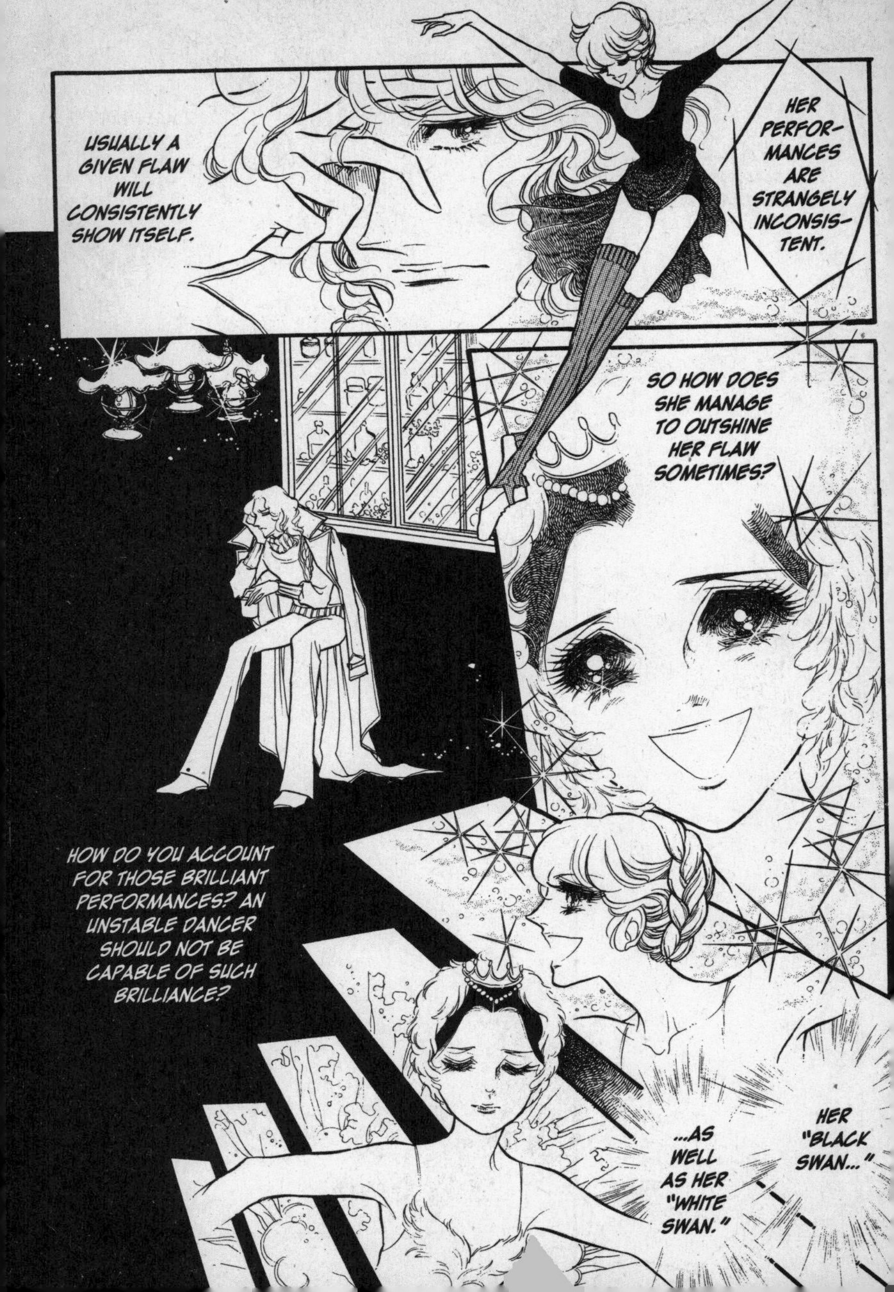
HER PERFORMANCES ARE STRANGELY INCONSISTENT.
USUALLY A GIVEN FLAW WILL CONSISTENTLY SHOW ITSELF.
SO HOW DOES SHE MANAGE TO OUTSHINE HER FLAW SOMETIMES?
HOW DO YOU ACCOUNT FOR THOSE BRILLIANT PERFORMANCES? AN UNSTABLE DANCER SHOULD NOT BE CAPABLE OF SUCH BRILLIANCE?
HER "BLACK SWAN..."
...AS WELL AS HER "WHITE SWAN."

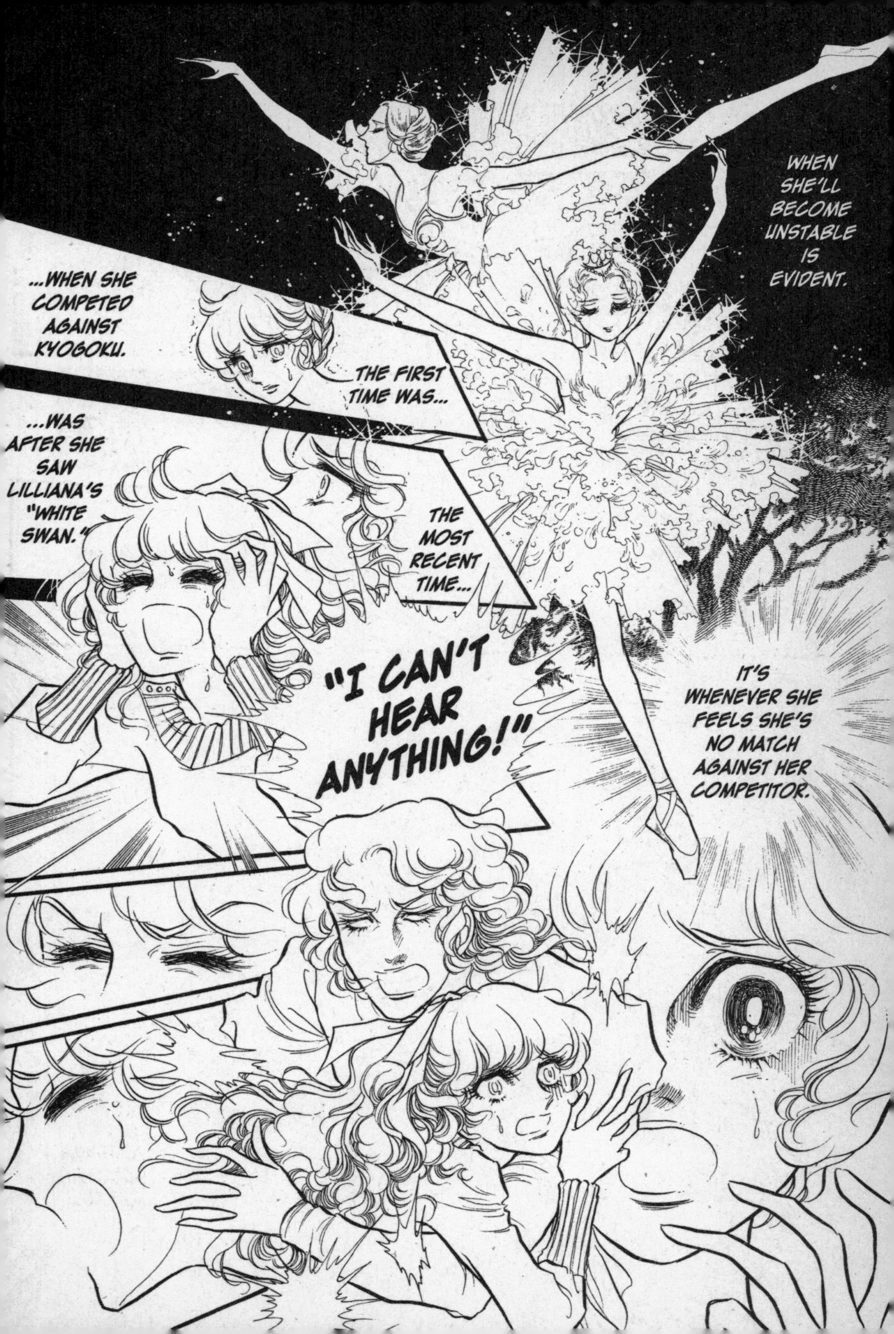
WHEN SHE'LL BECOME UNSTABLE IS EVIDENT.
THE FIRST TIME WAS...
...WHEN SHE COMPETED AGAINST KYOGOKU.
THE MOST RECENT TIME...
...WAS AFTER SHE SAW LILLIANA'S "WHITE SWAN."
"I CAN'T HEAR ANYTHING!"
IT'S WHENEVER SHE FEELS SHE'S NO MATCH AGAINST HER COMPETITOR.

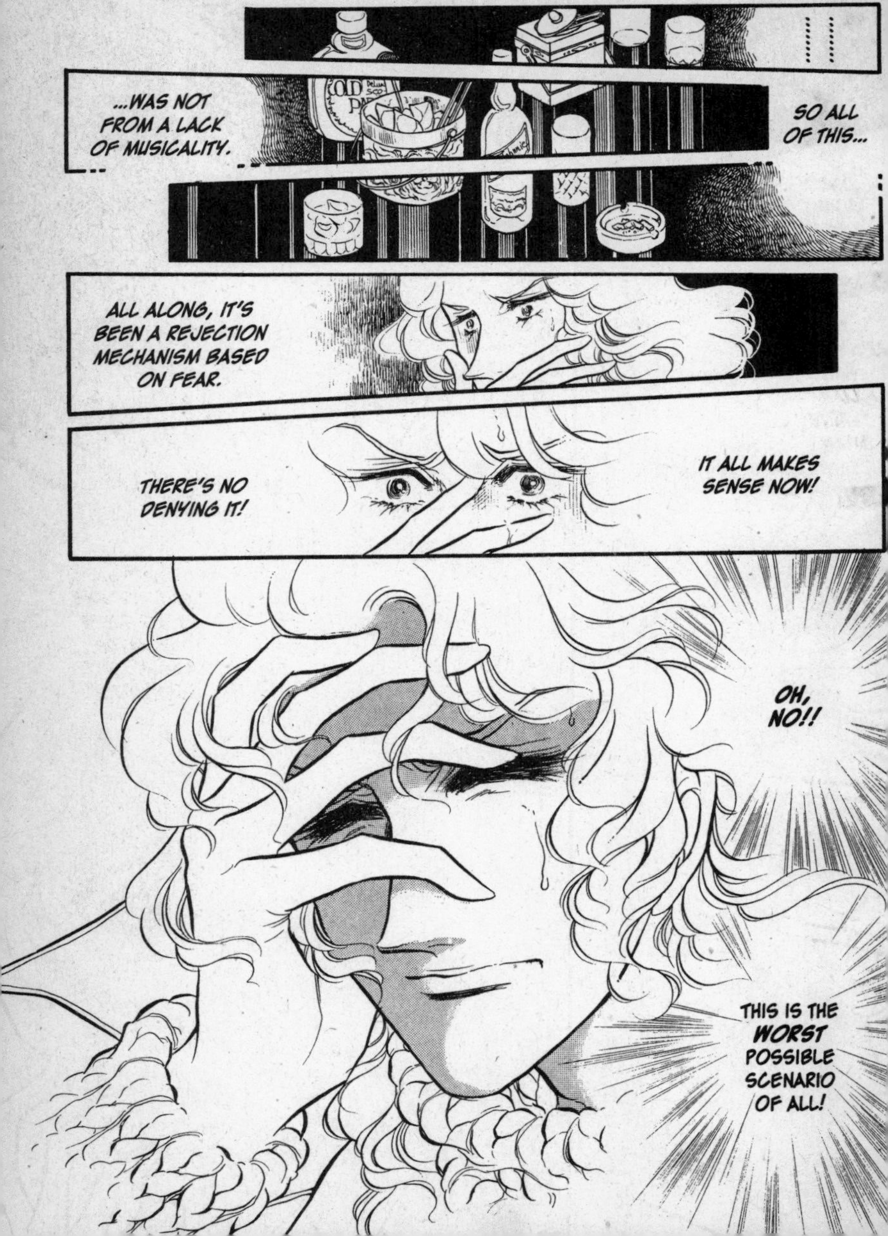
SO ALL OF THIS...
...WAS NOT FROM A LACK OF MUSICALITY.
ALL ALONG, IT'S BEEN A REJECTION MECHANISM BASED ON FEAR.
IT ALL MAKES SENSE NOW!
THERE'S NO DENYING IT!
OH, NO!!
THIS IS THE **WORST** POSSIBLE SCENARIO OF ALL!

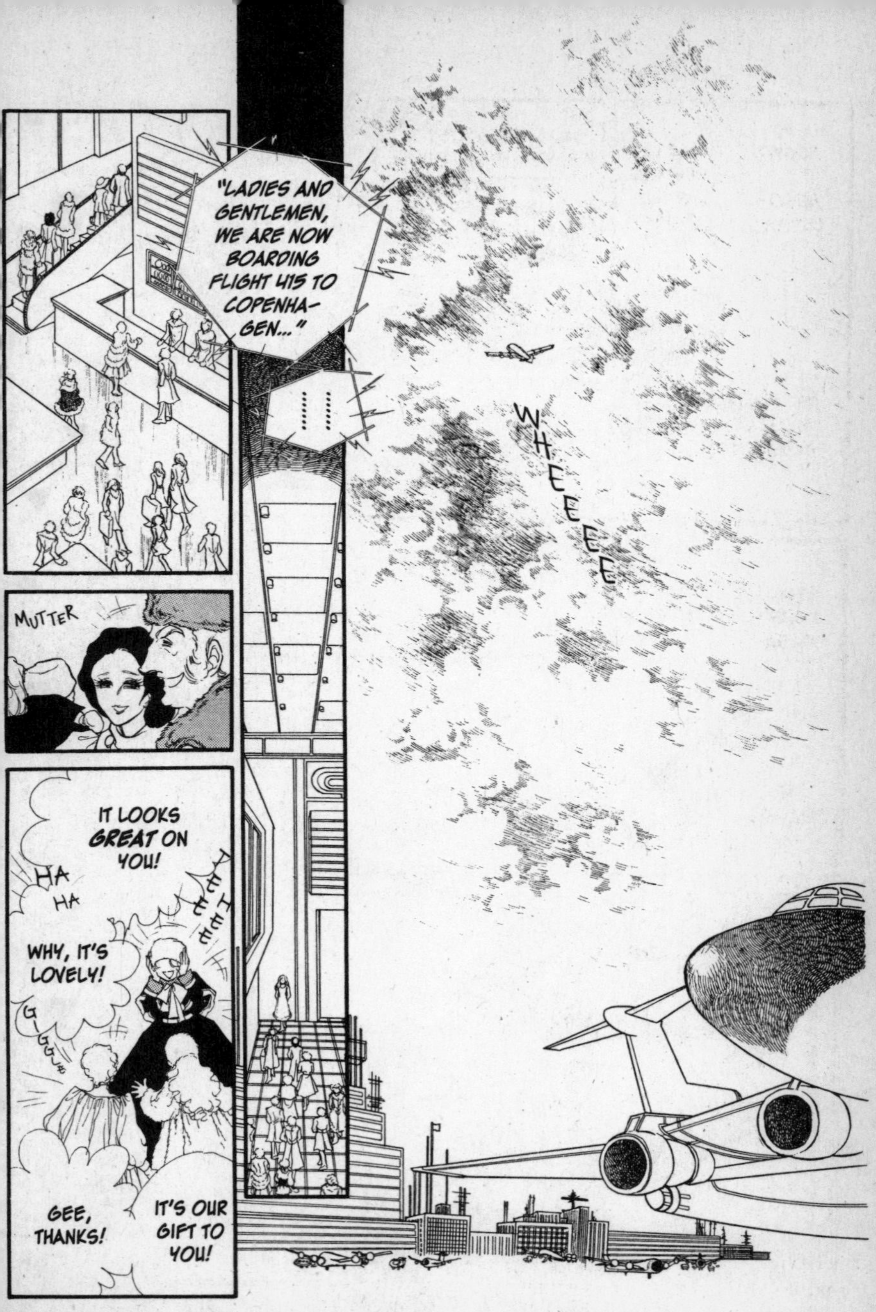
WHEEEEE
"LADIES AND GENTLEMEN, WE ARE NOW BOARDING FLIGHT 415 TO COPENHAGEN..."
...
MUTTER
IT LOOKS GREAT ON YOU!
TEHEEE
HA HA
WHY, IT'S LOVELY!
GIGGLE
IT'S OUR GIFT TO YOU!
GEE, THANKS!

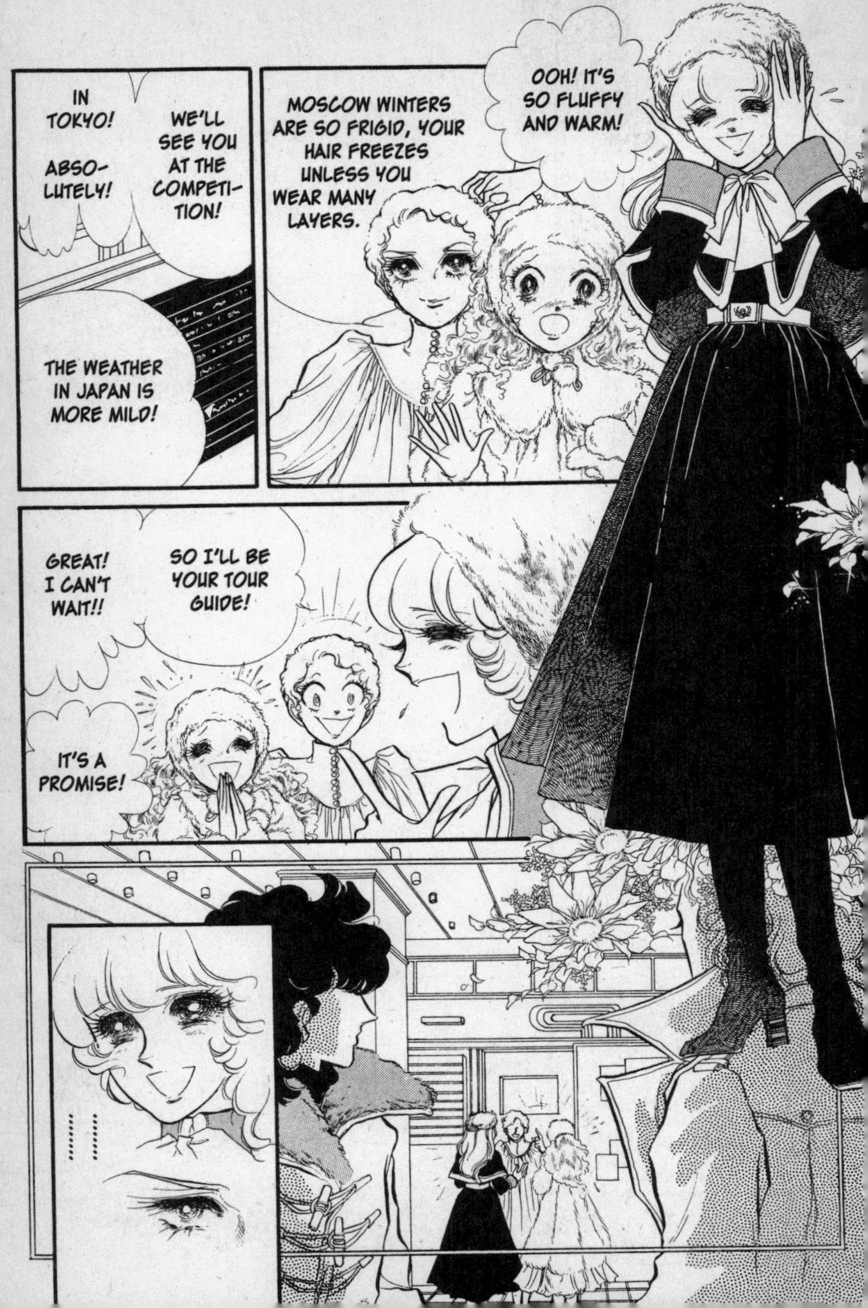
OOH! IT'S SO FLUFFY AND WARM!
MOSCOW WINTERS ARE SO FRIGID, YOUR HAIR FREEZES UNLESS YOU WEAR MANY LAYERS.
WE'LL SEE YOU AT THE COMPETITION!
IN TOKYO!
ABSOLUTELY!
THE WEATHER IN JAPAN IS MORE MILD!
SO I'LL BE YOUR TOUR GUIDE!
GREAT! I CAN'T WAIT!!
IT'S A PROMISE!
....

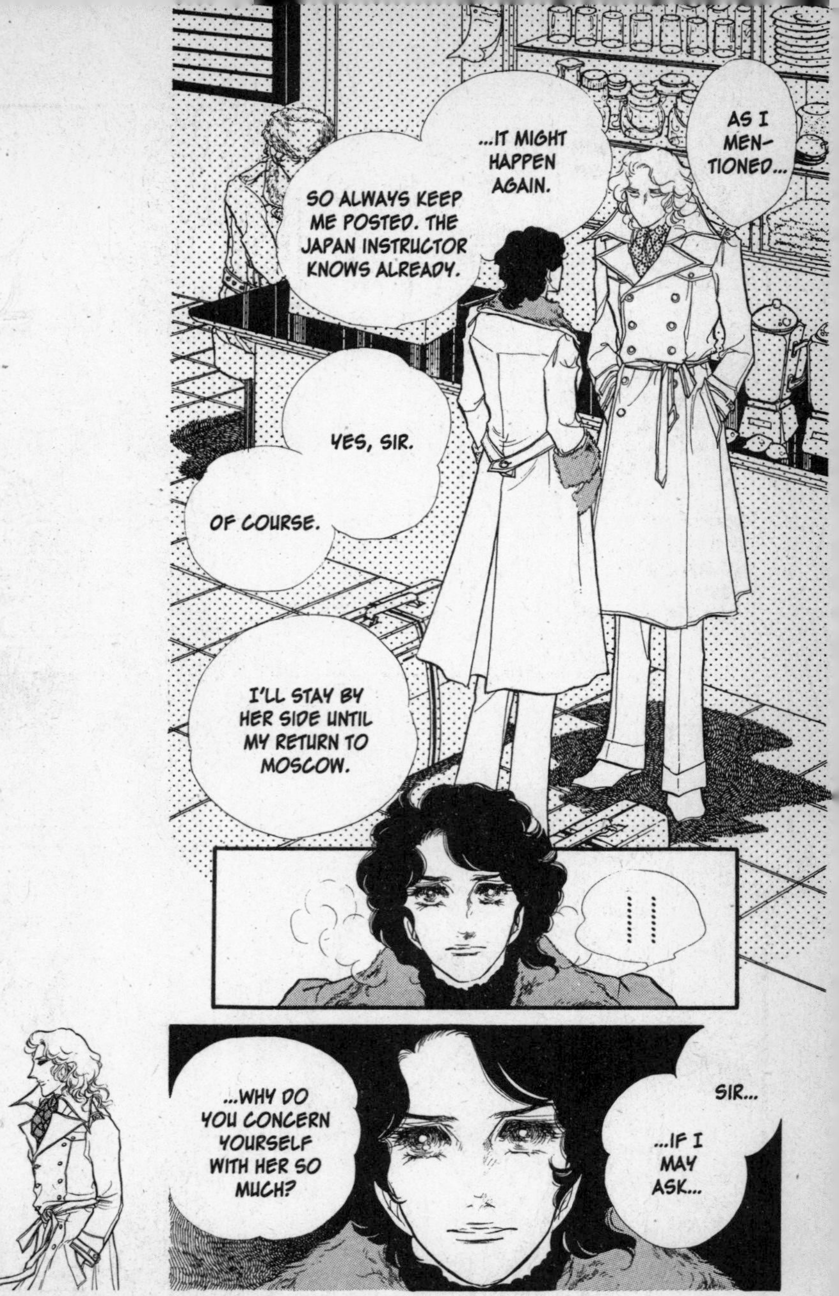
AS I MENTIONED...
...IT MIGHT HAPPEN AGAIN.
SO ALWAYS KEEP ME POSTED. THE JAPAN INSTRUCTOR KNOWS ALREADY.
YES, SIR.
OF COURSE.
I'LL STAY BY HER SIDE UNTIL MY RETURN TO MOSCOW.
SIR...
...IF I MAY ASK...
...WHY DO YOU CONCERN YOURSELF WITH HER SO MUCH?

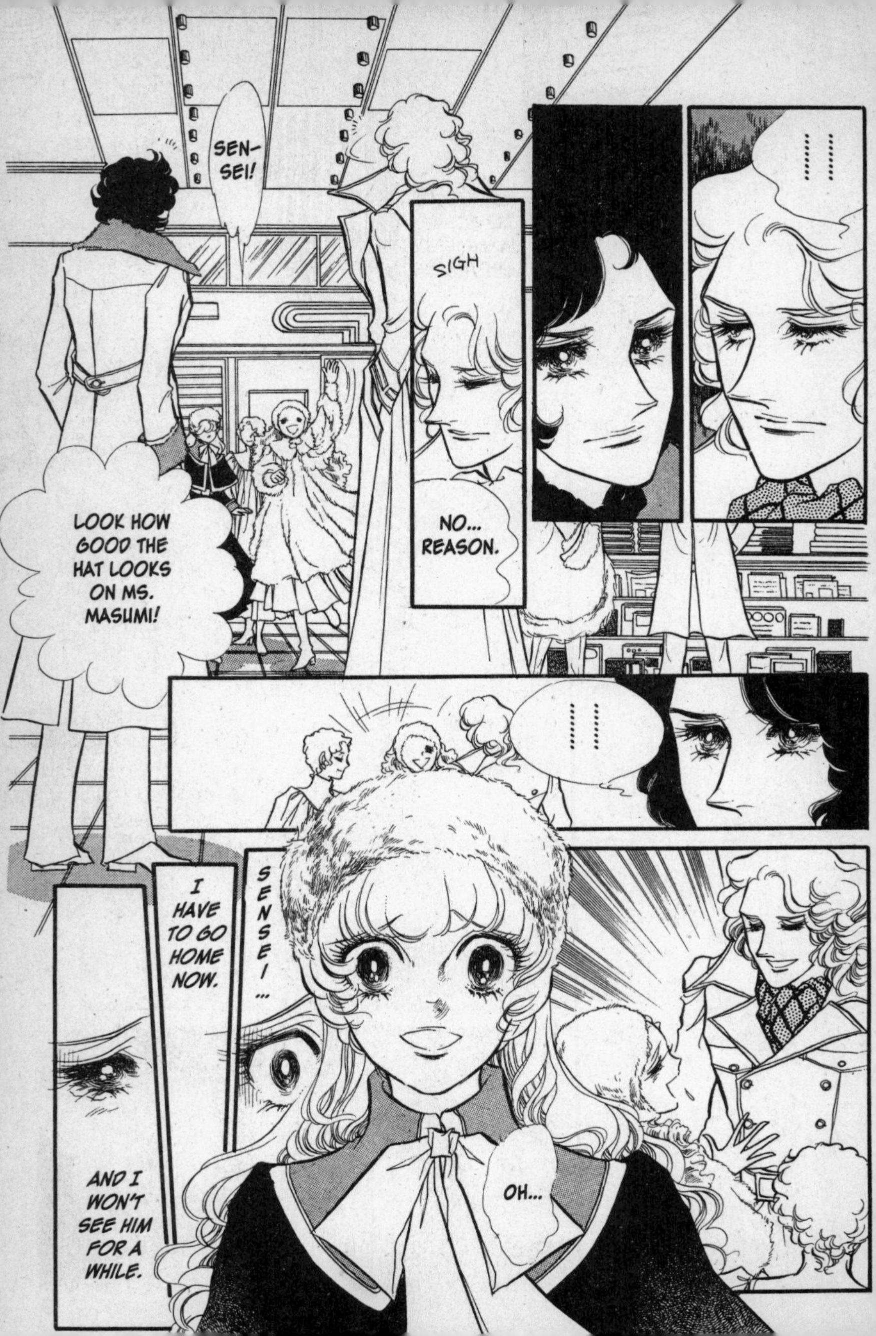
......
SIGH
NO... REASON.
SEN-SEI!
LOOK HOW GOOD THE HAT LOOKS ON MS. MASUMI!
......
SENSEI...
OH...
I HAVE TO GO HOME NOW.
AND I WON'T SEE HIM FOR A WHILE.

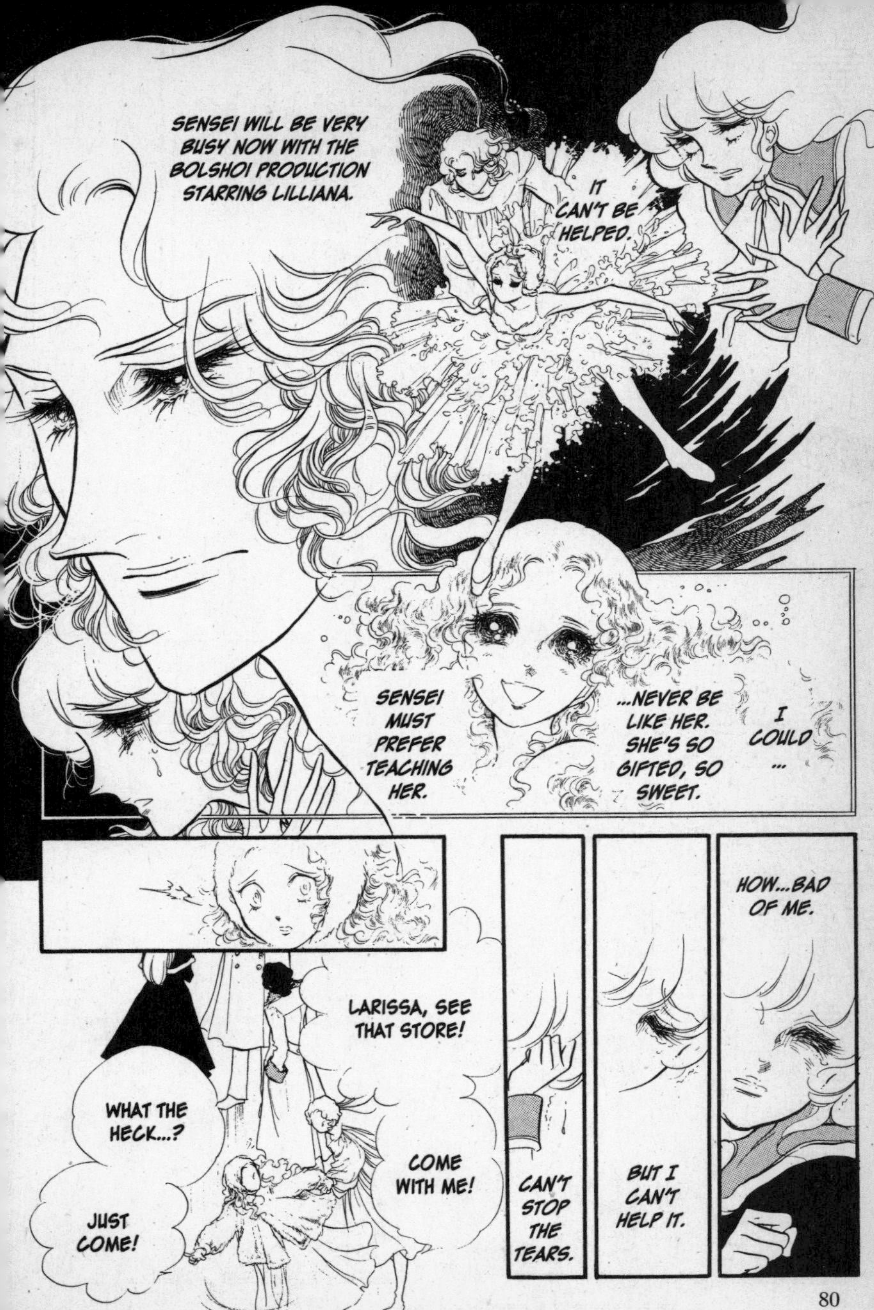

SENSEI WILL BE VERY BUSY NOW WITH THE BOLSHOI PRODUCTION STARRING LILLIANA.
IT CAN'T BE HELPED.
I COULD ...
...NEVER BE LIKE HER. SHE'S SO GIFTED, SO SWEET.
SENSEI MUST PREFER TEACHING HER.
HOW...BAD OF ME.
BUT I CAN'T HELP IT.
CAN'T STOP THE TEARS.
LARISSA, SEE THAT STORE!
COME WITH ME!
WHAT THE HECK...?
JUST COME!

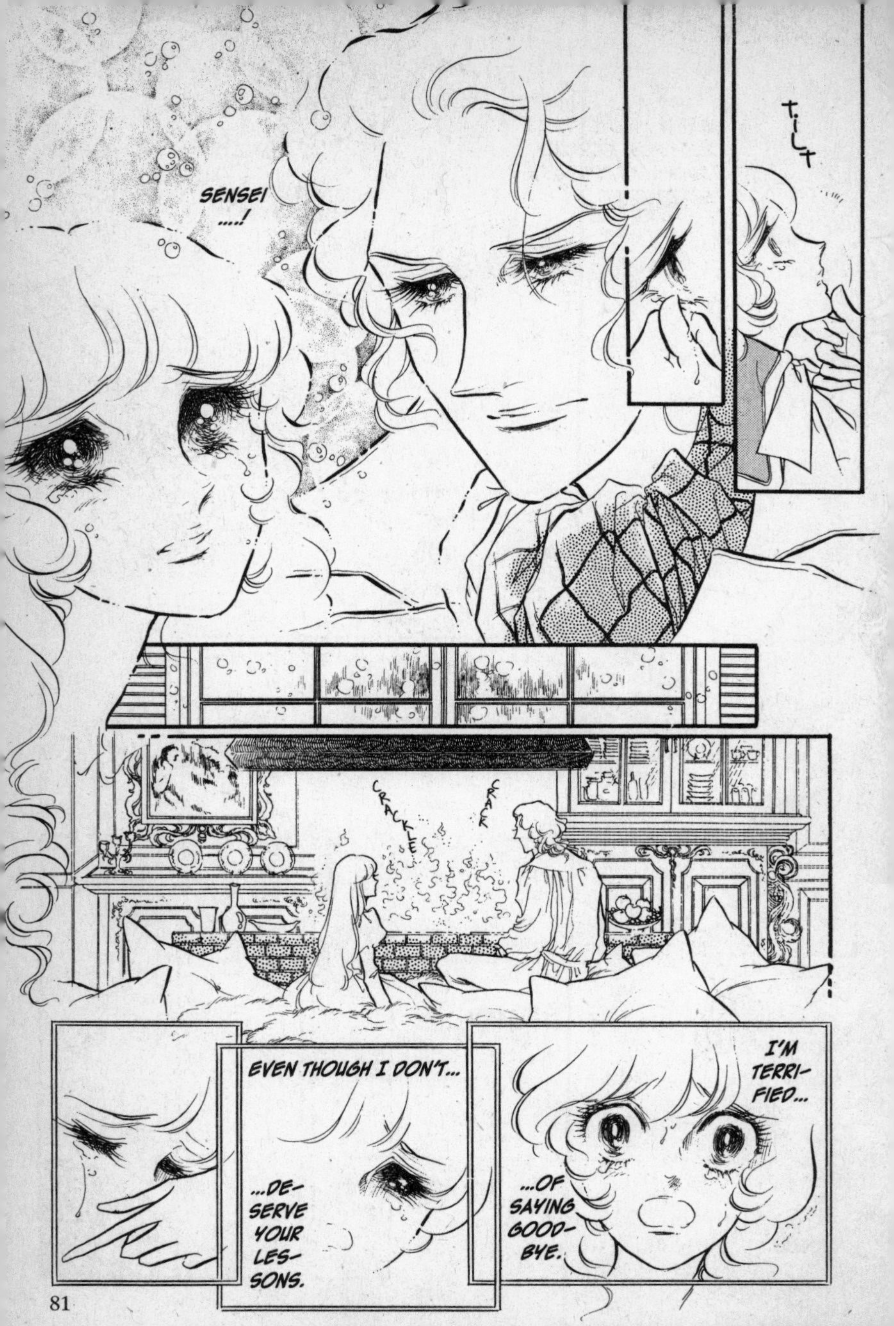
TILT
SENSEI ...!
CRACK
CRACKLE...
I'M TERRI-FIED...
...OF SAYING GOOD-BYE.
EVEN THOUGH I DON'T...
...DE-SERVE YOUR LES-SONS.

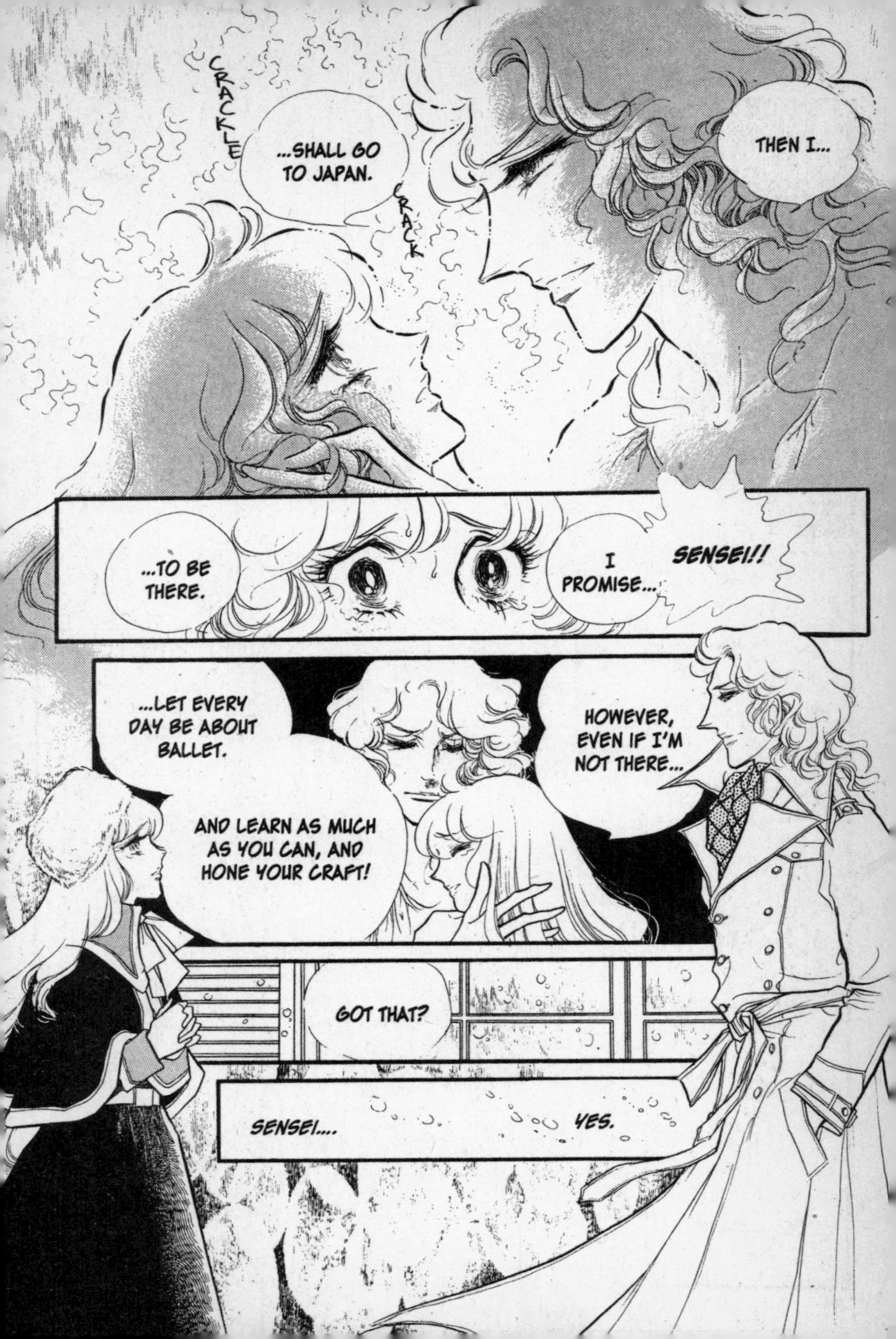
THEN I...
...SHALL GO TO JAPAN.
CRACK
CRACKLE
SENSEI!!
I PROMISE...
...TO BE THERE.
HOWEVER, EVEN IF I'M NOT THERE...
...LET EVERY DAY BE ABOUT BALLET.
AND LEARN AS MUCH AS YOU CAN, AND HONE YOUR CRAFT!
GOT THAT?
YES.
SENSEI....

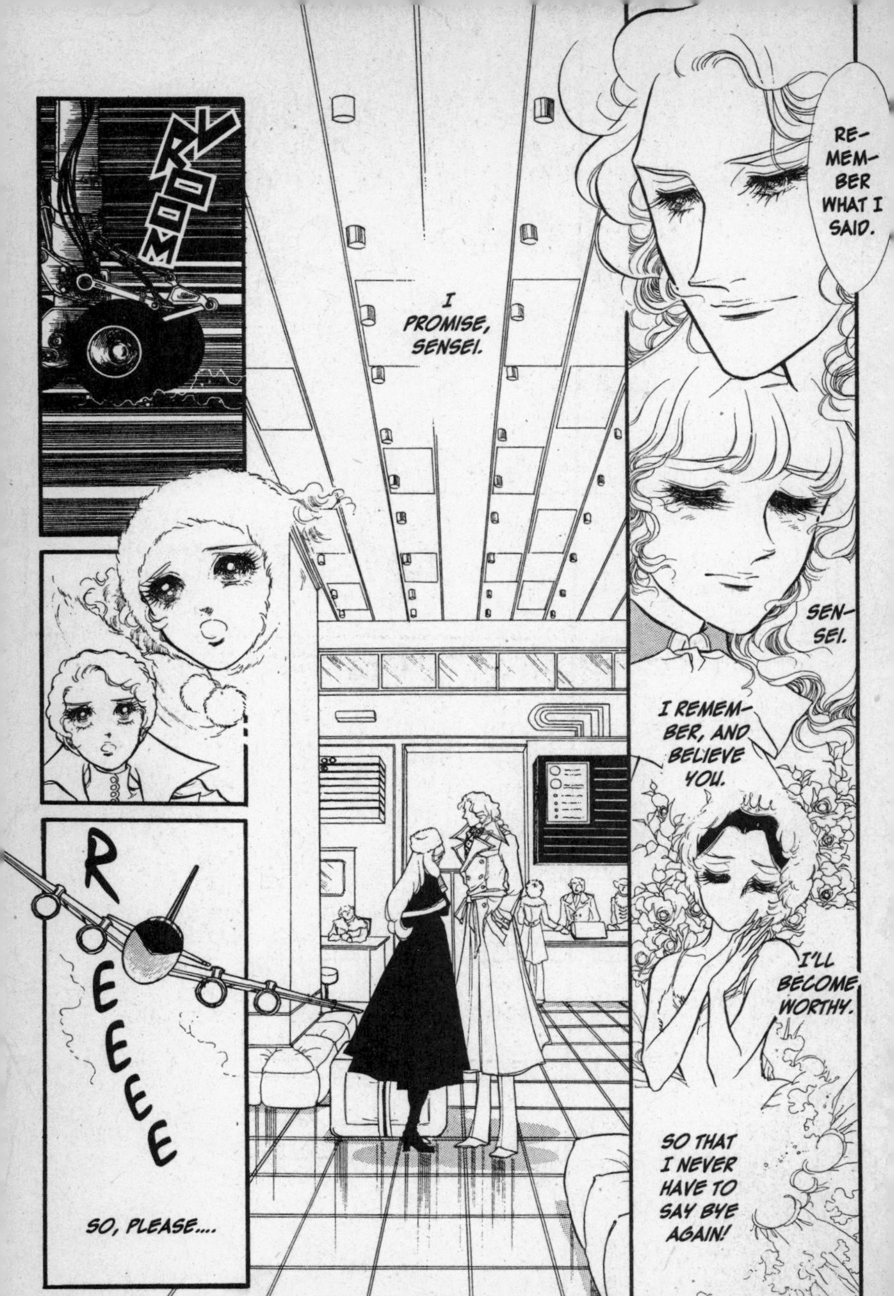
RE-MEM-BER WHAT I SAID.
SEN-SEI.
I REMEMBER, AND BELIEVE YOU.
I'LL BECOME WORTHY.
SO THAT I NEVER HAVE TO SAY BYE AGAIN!
I PROMISE, SENSEI.
VROOM
REEEE
SO, PLEASE....

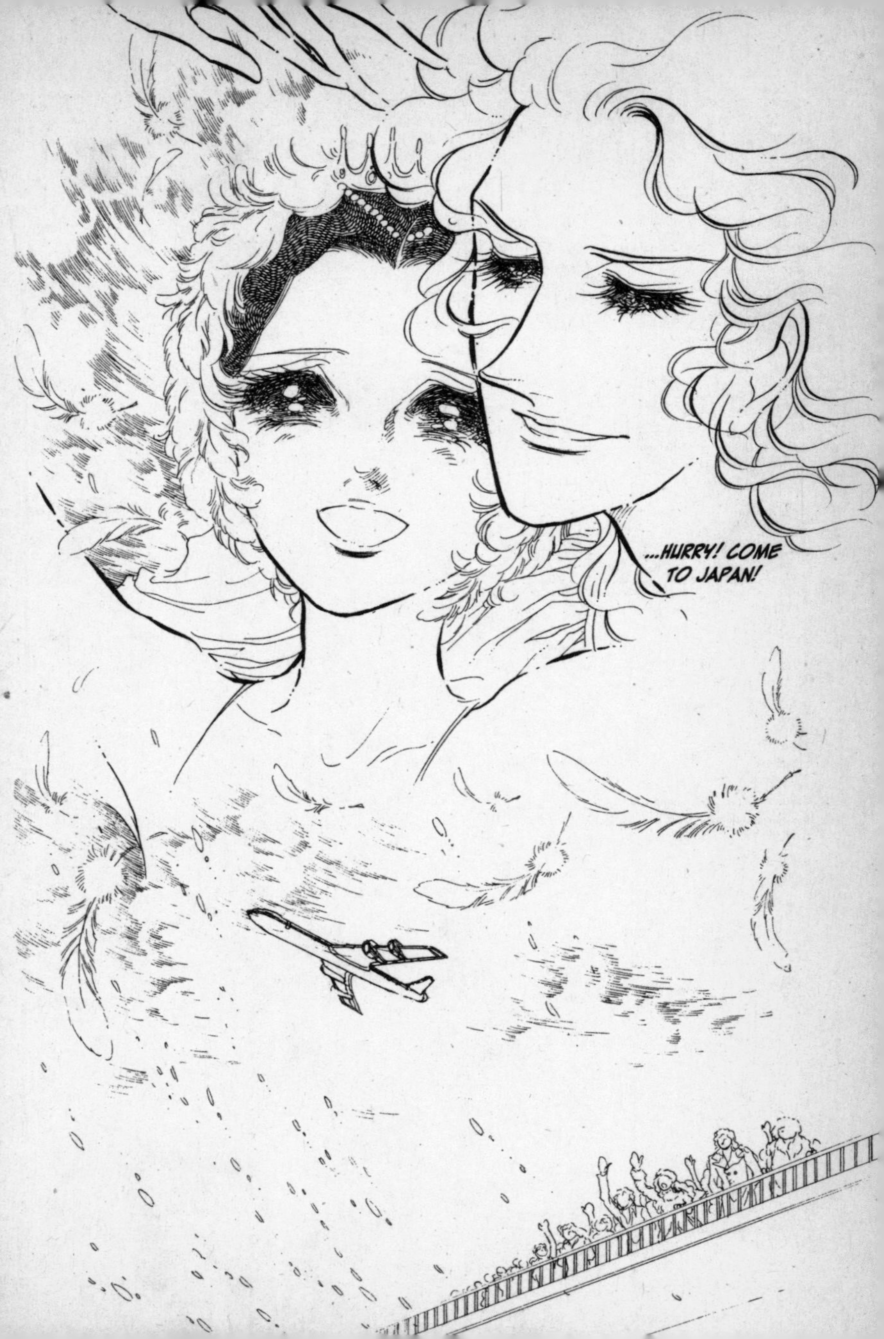
...HURRY! COME TO JAPAN!

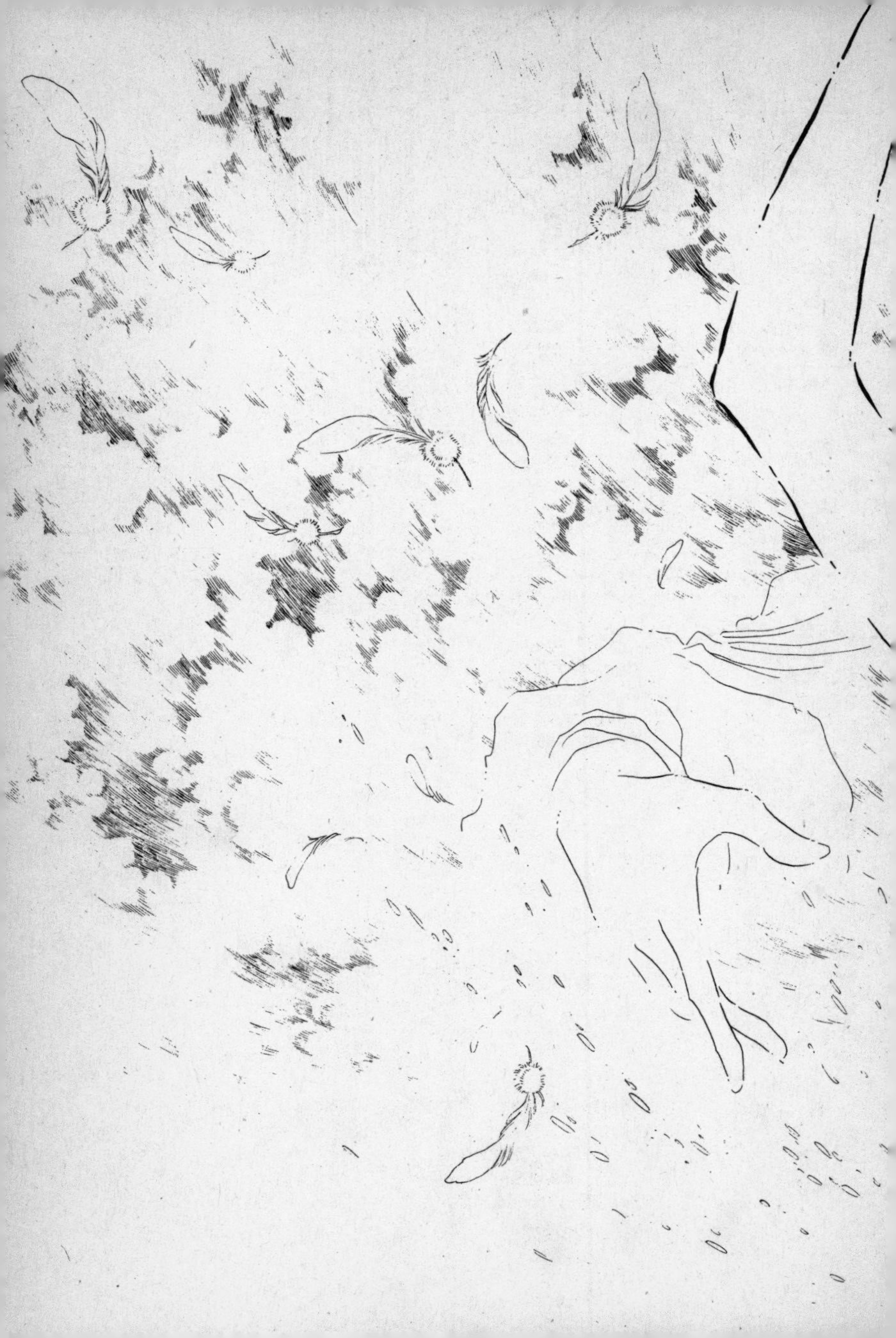

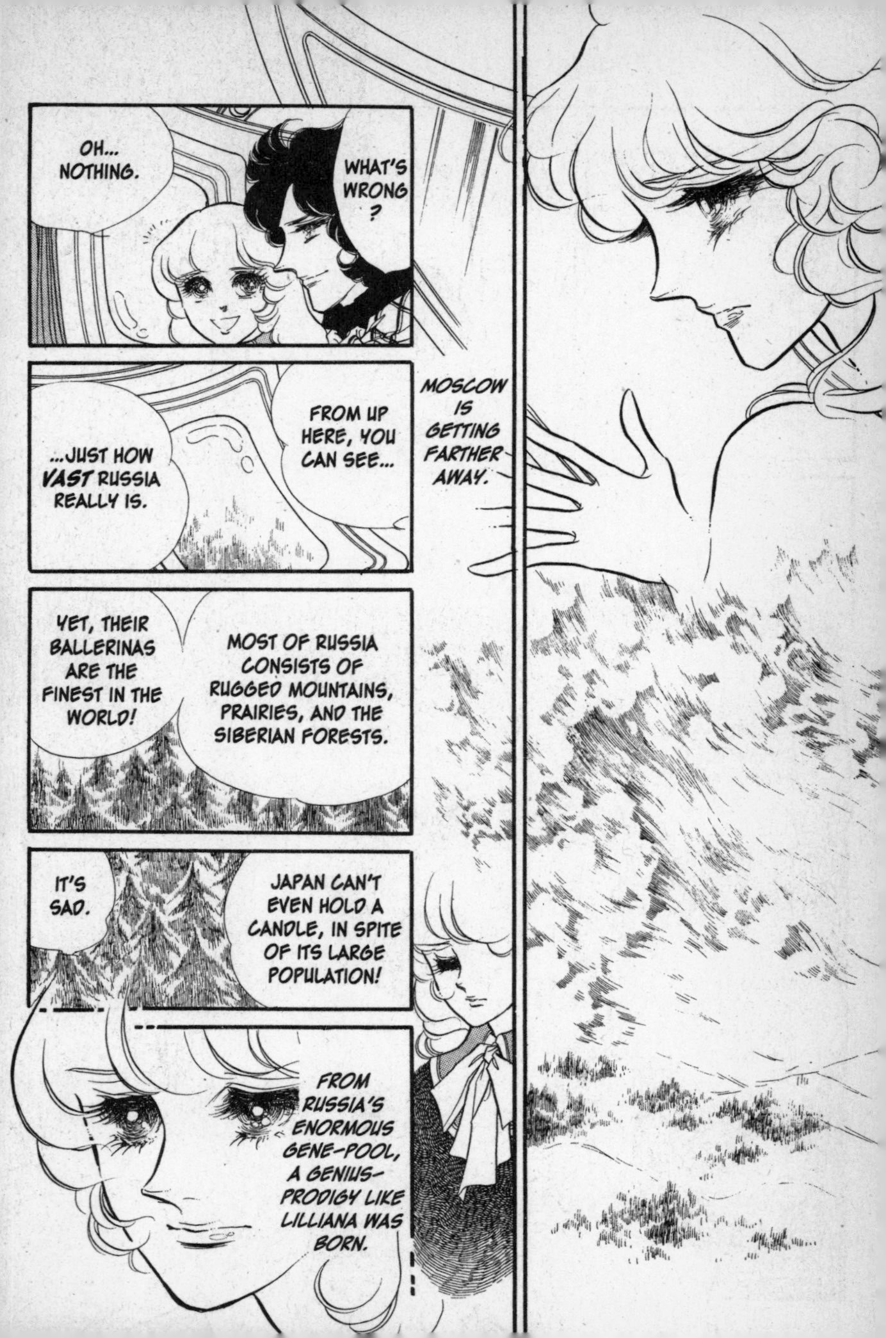
MOSCOW IS GETTING FARTHER AWAY.
WHAT'S WRONG?
OH... NOTHING.
FROM UP HERE, YOU CAN SEE...
...JUST HOW VAST RUSSIA REALLY IS.
MOST OF RUSSIA CONSISTS OF RUGGED MOUNTAINS, PRAIRIES, AND THE SIBERIAN FORESTS.
YET, THEIR BALLERINAS ARE THE FINEST IN THE WORLD!
JAPAN CAN'T EVEN HOLD A CANDLE, IN SPITE OF ITS LARGE POPULATION!
IT'S SAD.
FROM RUSSIA'S ENORMOUS GENE-POOL, A GENIUS-PRODIGY LIKE LILLIANA WAS BORN.

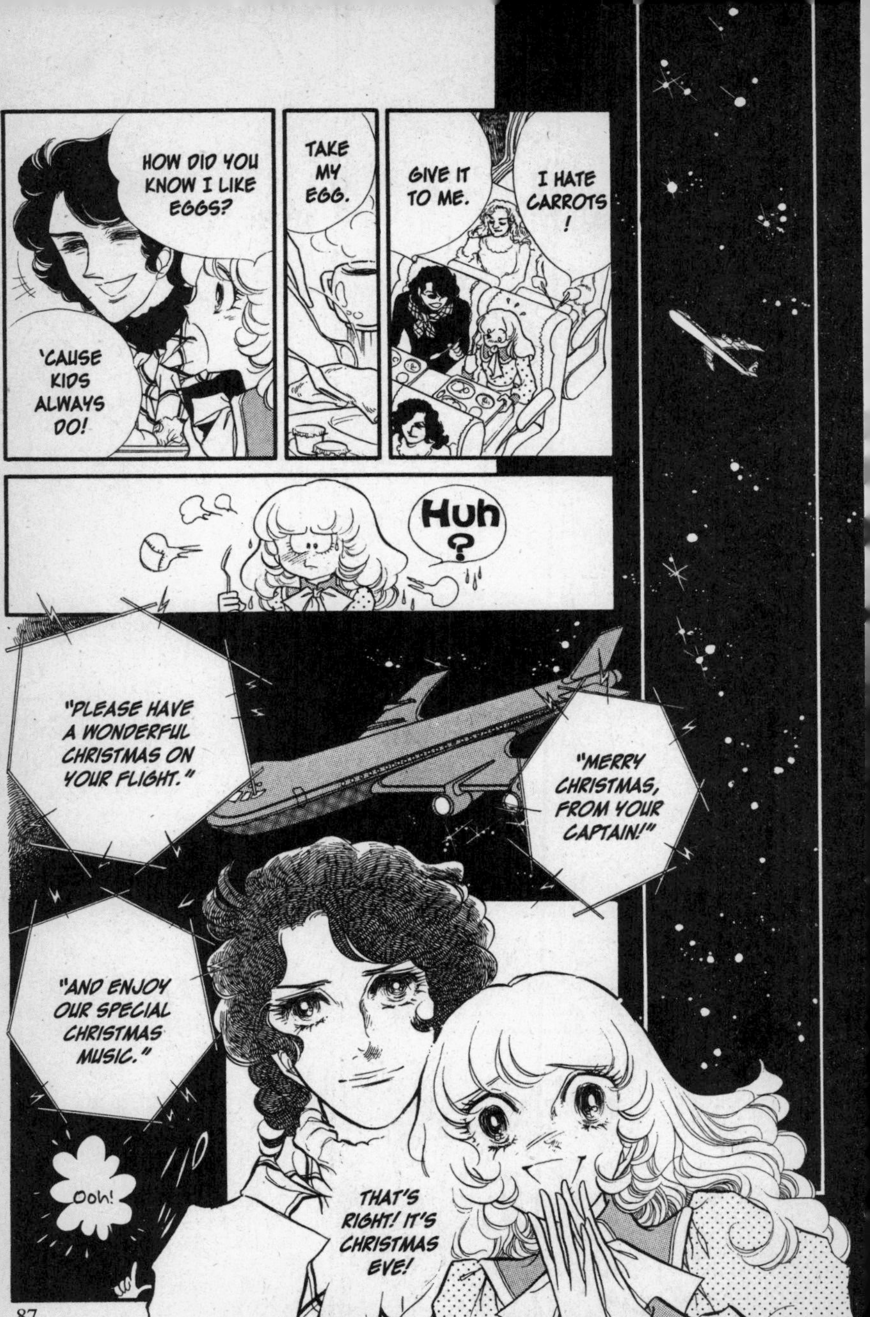
I HATE CARROTS!
GIVE IT TO ME.
TAKE MY EGG.
HOW DID YOU KNOW I LIKE EGGS?
'CAUSE KIDS ALWAYS DO!
Huh?
"MERRY CHRISTMAS, FROM YOUR CAPTAIN!"
"PLEASE HAVE A WONDERFUL CHRISTMAS ON YOUR FLIGHT."
"AND ENJOY OUR SPECIAL CHRISTMAS MUSIC."
Ooh!
THAT'S RIGHT! IT'S CHRISTMAS EVE!

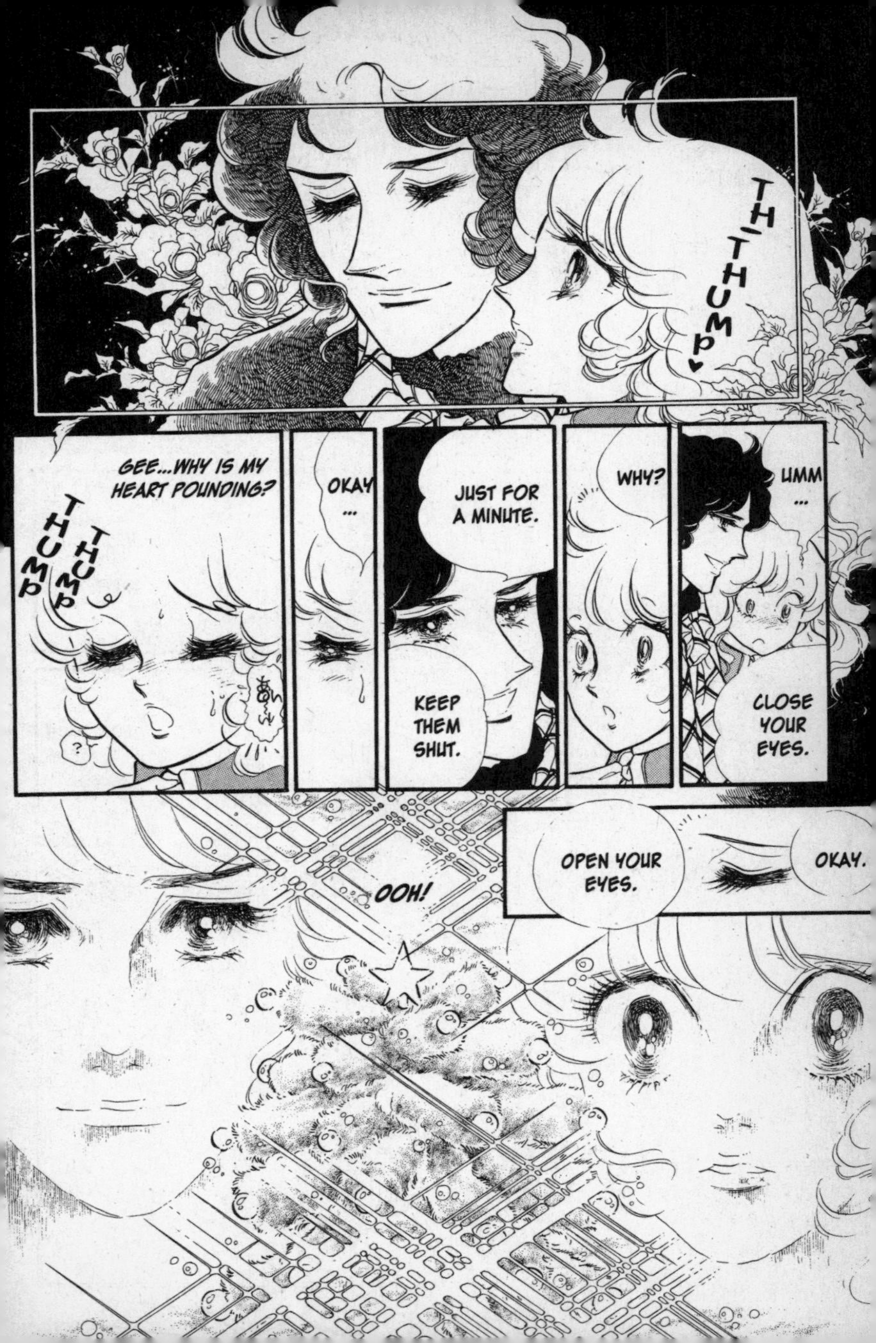
TH-THUMP
UMM ...
CLOSE YOUR EYES.
WHY?
JUST FOR A MINUTE.
KEEP THEM SHUT.
OKAY ...
GEE...WHY IS MY HEART POUNDING?
THUMP THUMP
?
OKAY.
OPEN YOUR EYES.
OOH!

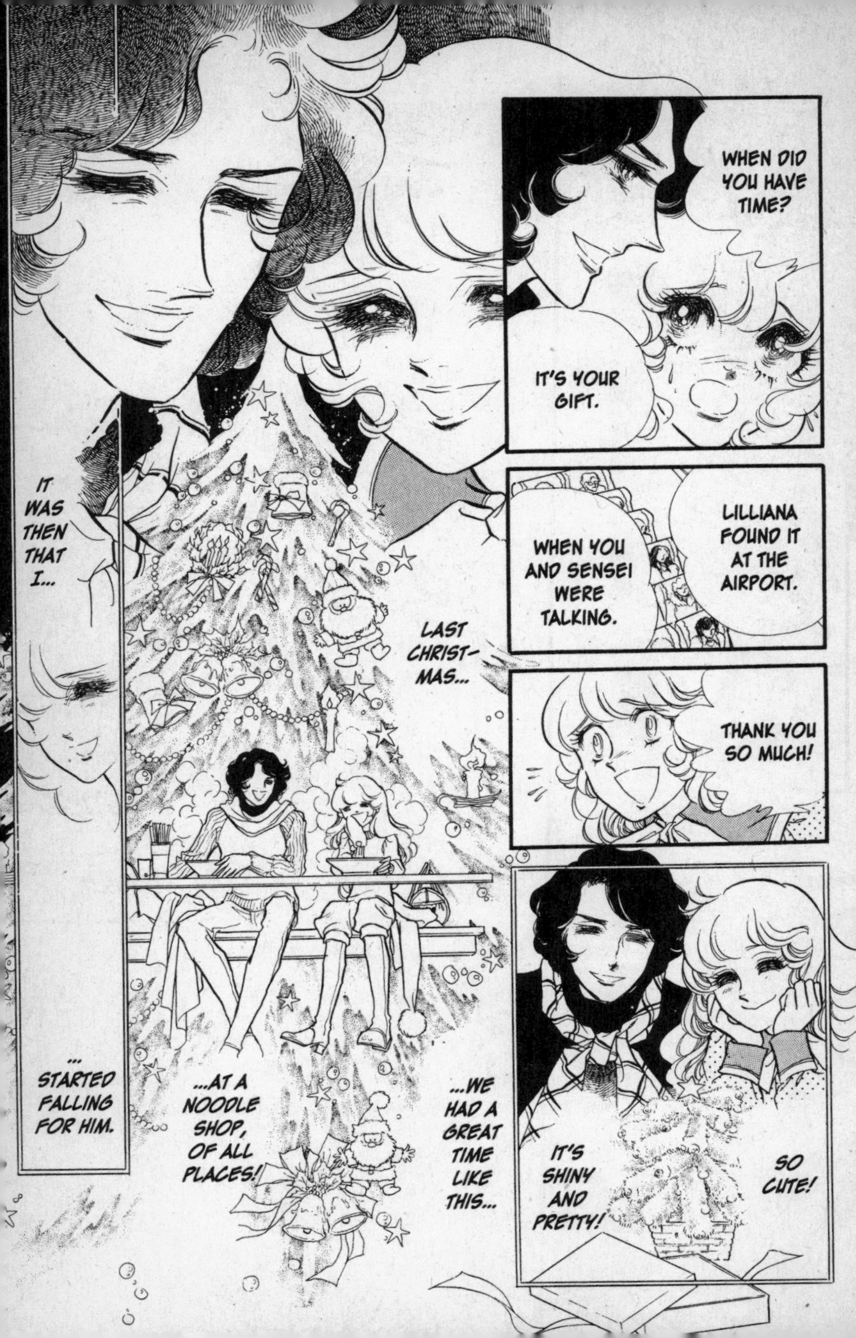
WHEN DID YOU HAVE TIME?
IT'S YOUR GIFT.
LILLIANA FOUND IT AT THE AIRPORT.
WHEN YOU AND SENSEI WERE TALKING.
THANK YOU SO MUCH!
SO CUTE!
IT'S SHINY AND PRETTY!
LAST CHRISTMAS...
...WE HAD A GREAT TIME LIKE THIS...
...AT A NOODLE SHOP, OF ALL PLACES!
IT WAS THEN THAT I...
...STARTED FALLING FOR HIM.

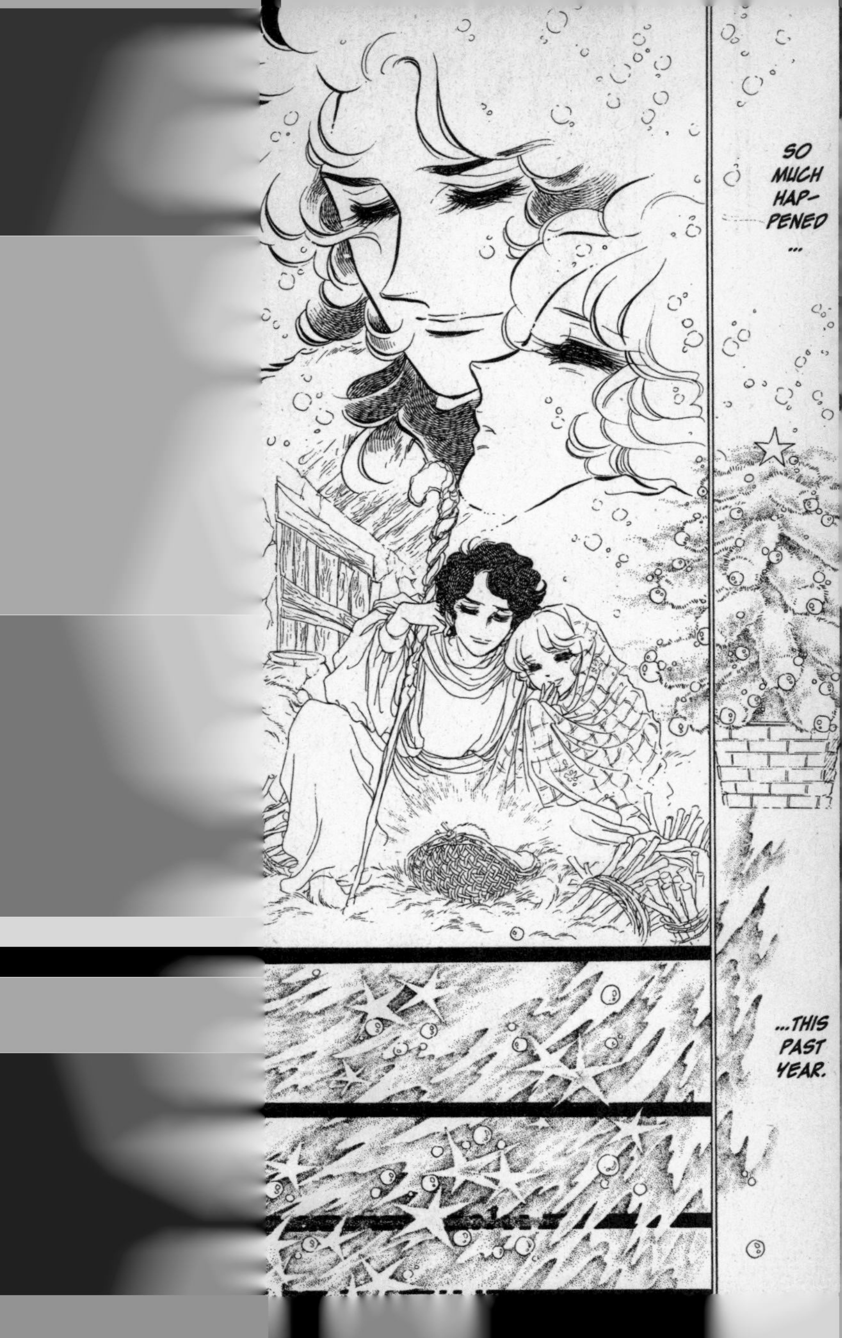
SO MUCH HAPPENED...
...THIS PAST YEAR.

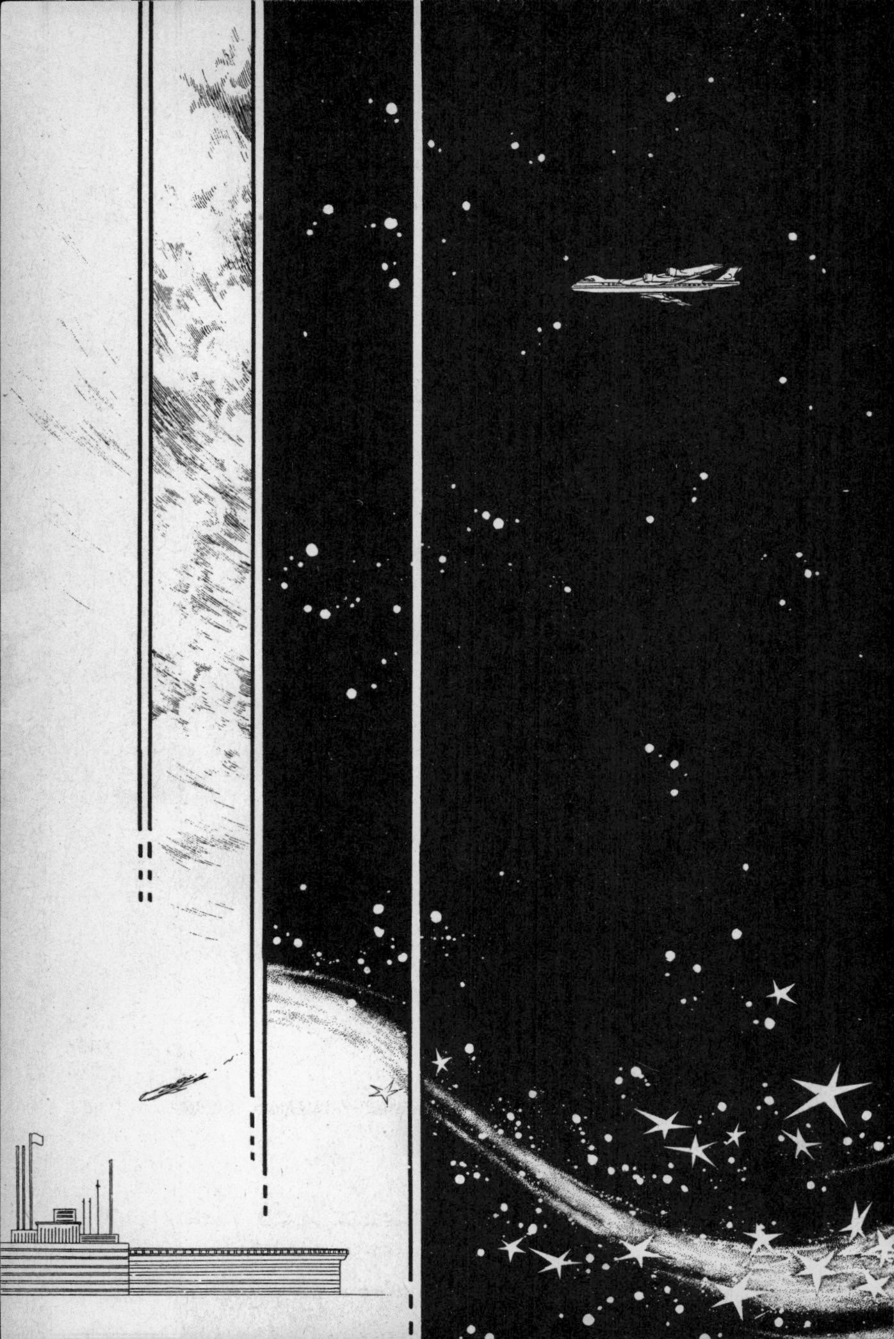

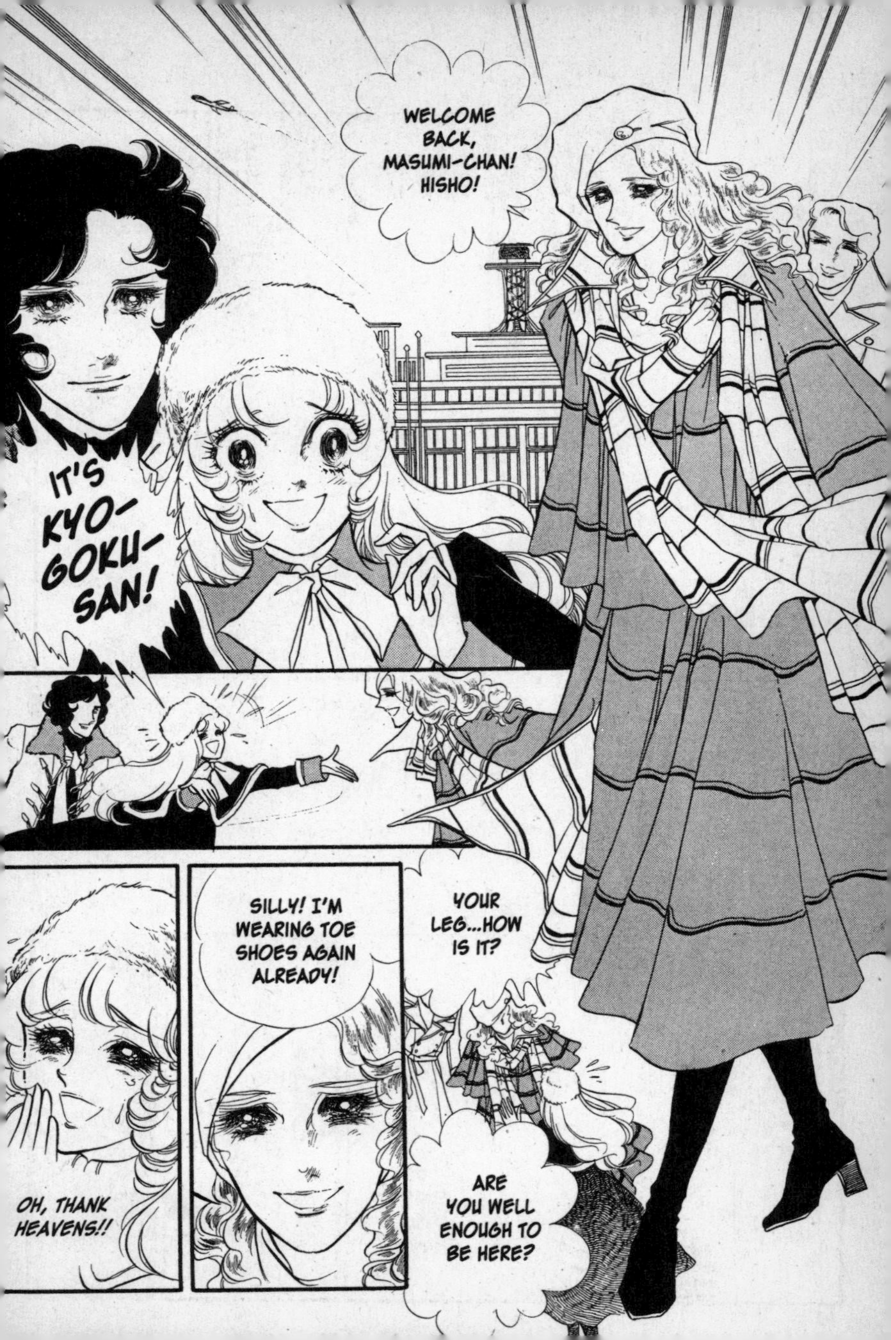
WELCOME BACK, MASUMI-CHAN! HISHO!
IT'S KYO-GOKU-SAN!
YOUR LEG...HOW IS IT?
ARE YOU WELL ENOUGH TO BE HERE?
SILLY! I'M WEARING TOE SHOES AGAIN ALREADY!
OH, THANK HEAVENS!!

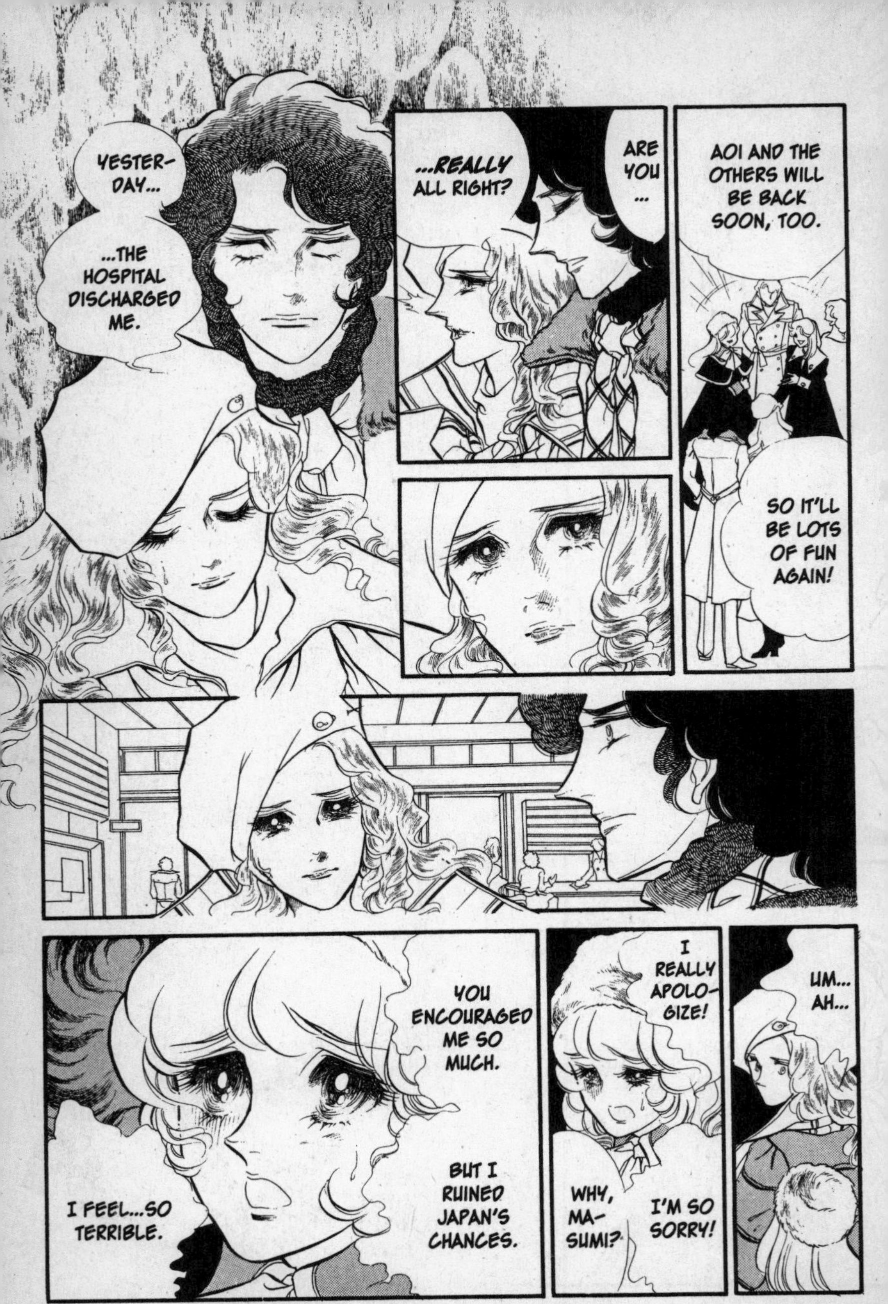
AOI AND THE OTHERS WILL BE BACK SOON, TOO.
SO IT'LL BE LOTS OF FUN AGAIN!
ARE YOU ...
...REALLY ALL RIGHT?
YESTER-DAY...
...THE HOSPITAL DISCHARGED ME.
UM... AH...
I REALLY APOLO-GIZE!
I'M SO SORRY!
WHY, MA-SUMI?
YOU ENCOURAGED ME SO MUCH.
BUT I RUINED JAPAN'S CHANCES.
I FEEL...SO TERRIBLE.

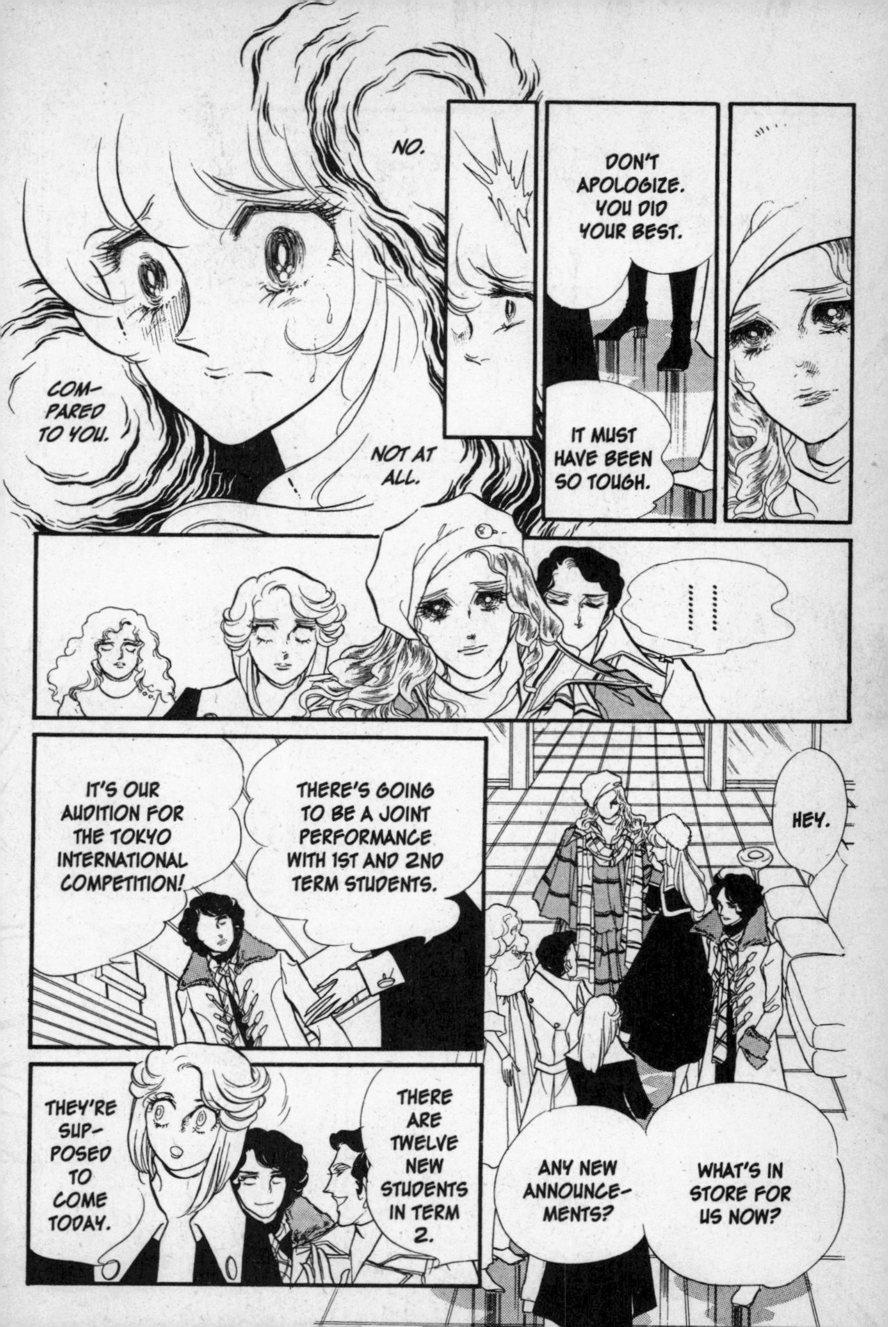
DON'T APOLOGIZE. YOU DID YOUR BEST.
IT MUST HAVE BEEN SO TOUGH.
NO.
NOT AT ALL.
COMPARED TO YOU.
......
HEY.
WHAT'S IN STORE FOR US NOW?
ANY NEW ANNOUNCEMENTS?
THERE'S GOING TO BE A JOINT PERFORMANCE WITH 1ST AND 2ND TERM STUDENTS.
IT'S OUR AUDITION FOR THE TOKYO INTERNATIONAL COMPETITION!
THERE ARE TWELVE NEW STUDENTS IN TERM 2.
THEY'RE SUPPOSED TO COME TODAY.

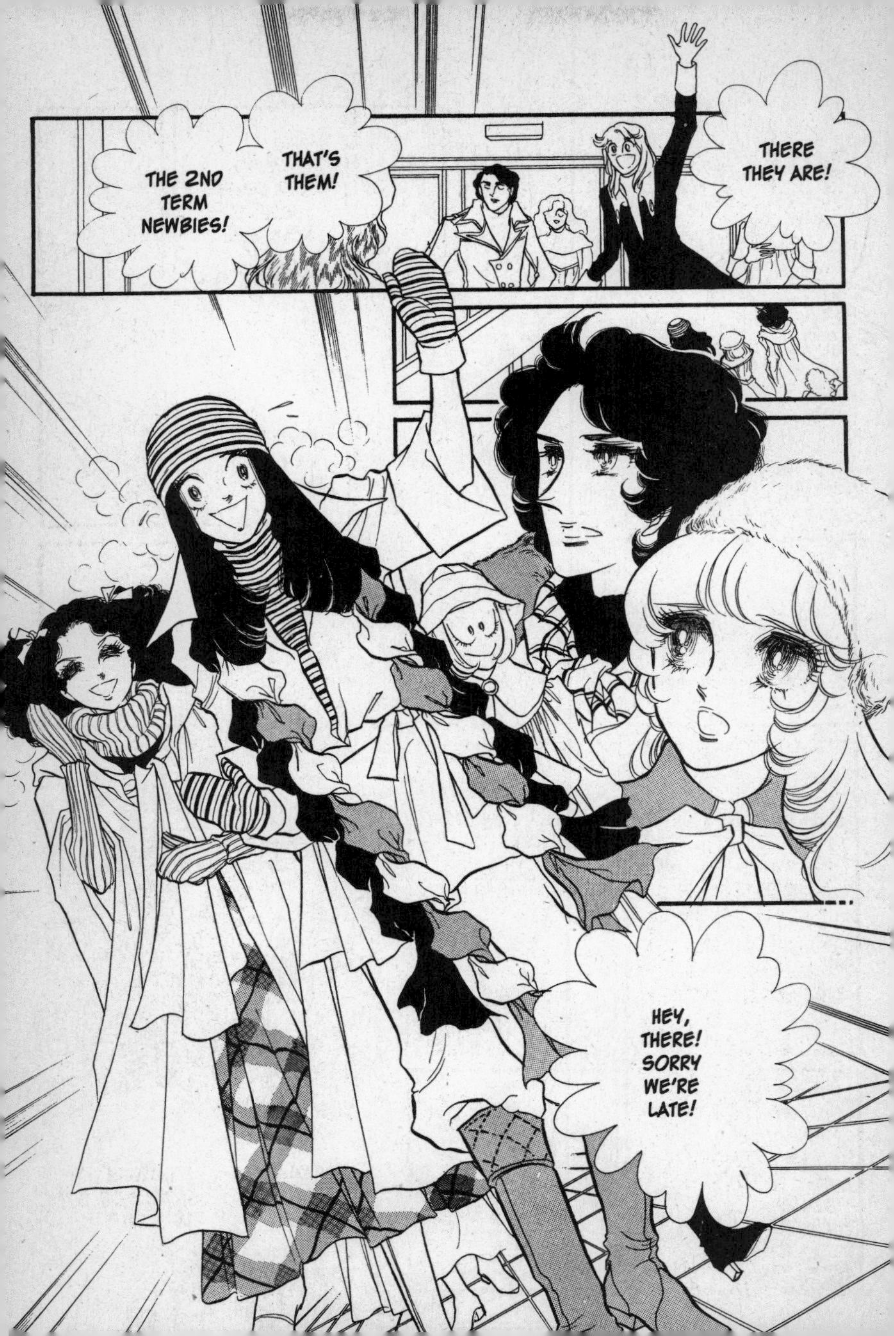
THERE THEY ARE!
THAT'S THEM!
THE 2ND TERM NEWBIES!
HEY, THERE! SORRY WE'RE LATE!

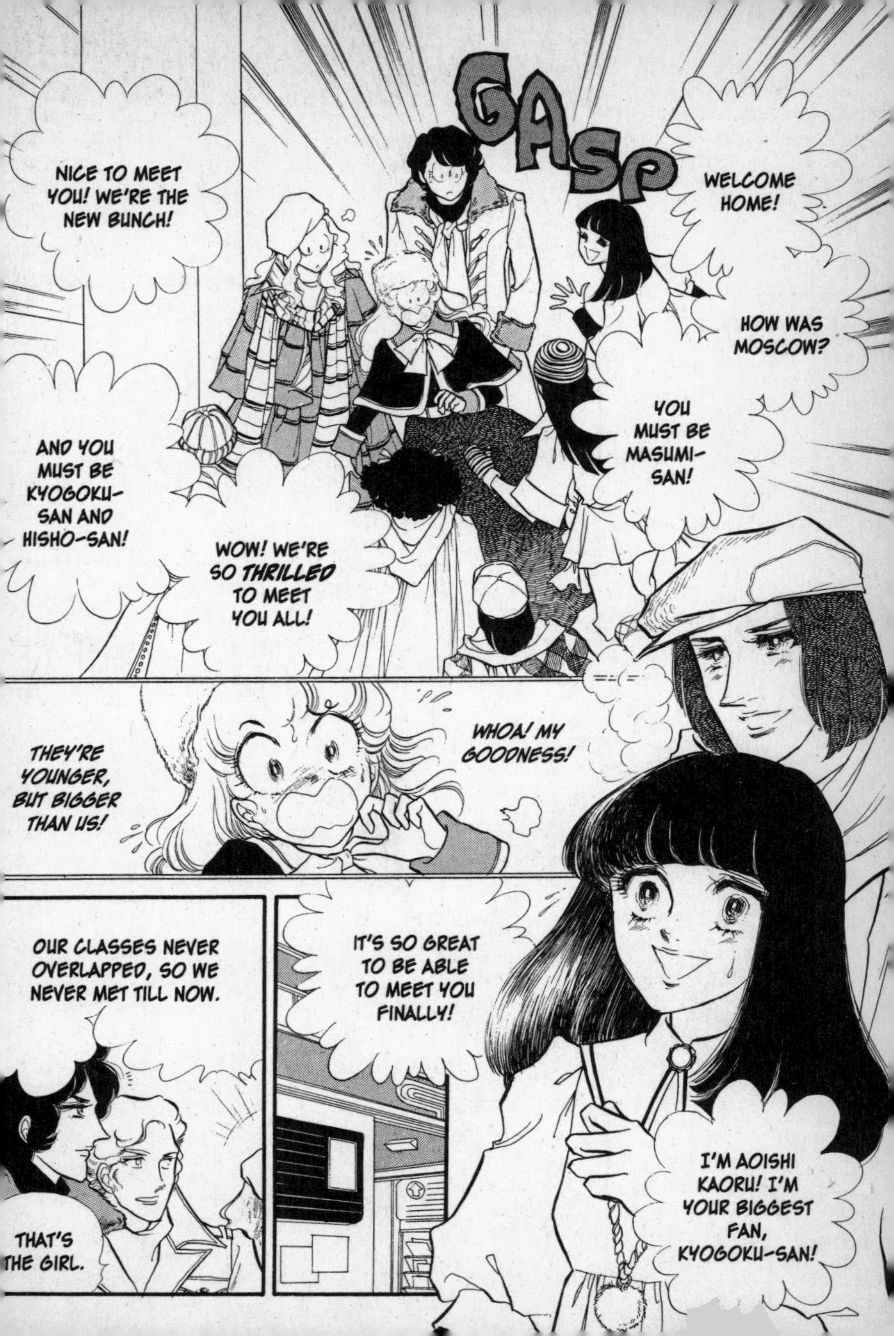
GASP
WELCOME HOME!
HOW WAS MOSCOW?
YOU MUST BE MASUMI-SAN!
NICE TO MEET YOU! WE'RE THE NEW BUNCH!
AND YOU MUST BE KYOGOKU-SAN AND HISHO-SAN!
WOW! WE'RE SO *THRILLED* TO MEET YOU ALL!
I'M AOISHI KAORU! I'M YOUR BIGGEST FAN, KYOGOKU-SAN!
WHOA! MY GOODNESS!
THEY'RE YOUNGER, BUT BIGGER THAN US!
IT'S SO GREAT TO BE ABLE TO MEET YOU FINALLY!
OUR CLASSES NEVER OVERLAPPED, SO WE NEVER MET TILL NOW.
THAT'S THE GIRL.

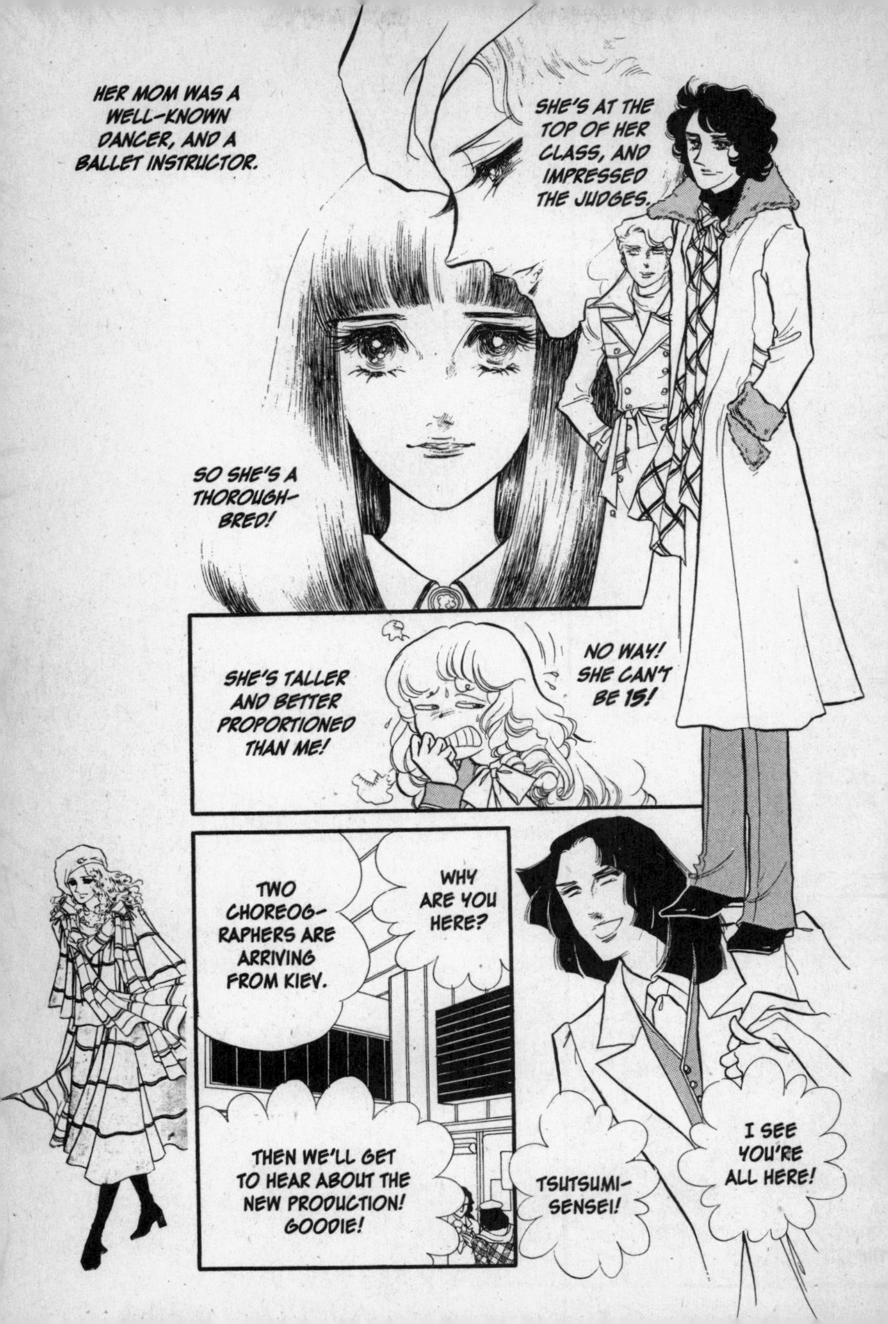
SHE'S AT THE TOP OF HER CLASS, AND IMPRESSED THE JUDGES.
HER MOM WAS A WELL-KNOWN DANCER, AND A BALLET INSTRUCTOR.
SO SHE'S A THOROUGH-BRED!
NO WAY! SHE CAN'T BE 15!
SHE'S TALLER AND BETTER PROPORTIONED THAN ME!
I SEE YOU'RE ALL HERE!
TSUTSUMI-SENSEI!
WHY ARE YOU HERE?
TWO CHOREOG-RAPHERS ARE ARRIVING FROM KIEV.
THEN WE'LL GET TO HEAR ABOUT THE NEW PRODUCTION! GOODIE!

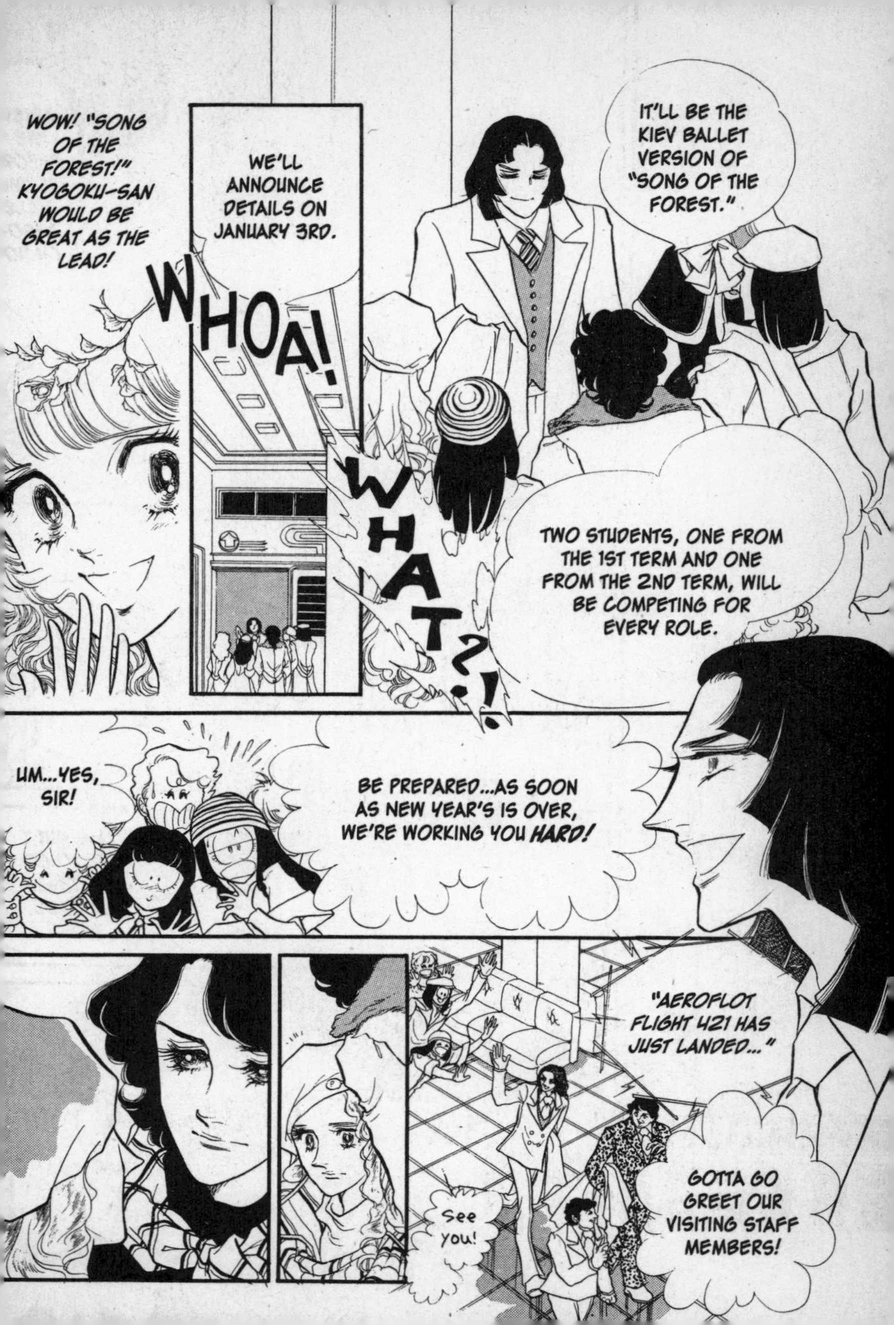
IT'LL BE THE KIEV BALLET VERSION OF "SONG OF THE FOREST."
TWO STUDENTS, ONE FROM THE 1ST TERM AND ONE FROM THE 2ND TERM, WILL BE COMPETING FOR EVERY ROLE.
WE'LL ANNOUNCE DETAILS ON JANUARY 3RD.
WHOA!
WHAT?!
WOW! "SONG OF THE FOREST!" KYOGOKU-SAN WOULD BE GREAT AS THE LEAD!
BE PREPARED...AS SOON AS NEW YEAR'S IS OVER, WE'RE WORKING YOU HARD!
UM...YES, SIR!
"AEROFLOT FLIGHT 421 HAS JUST LANDED..."
GOTTA GO GREET OUR VISITING STAFF MEMBERS!
See you!

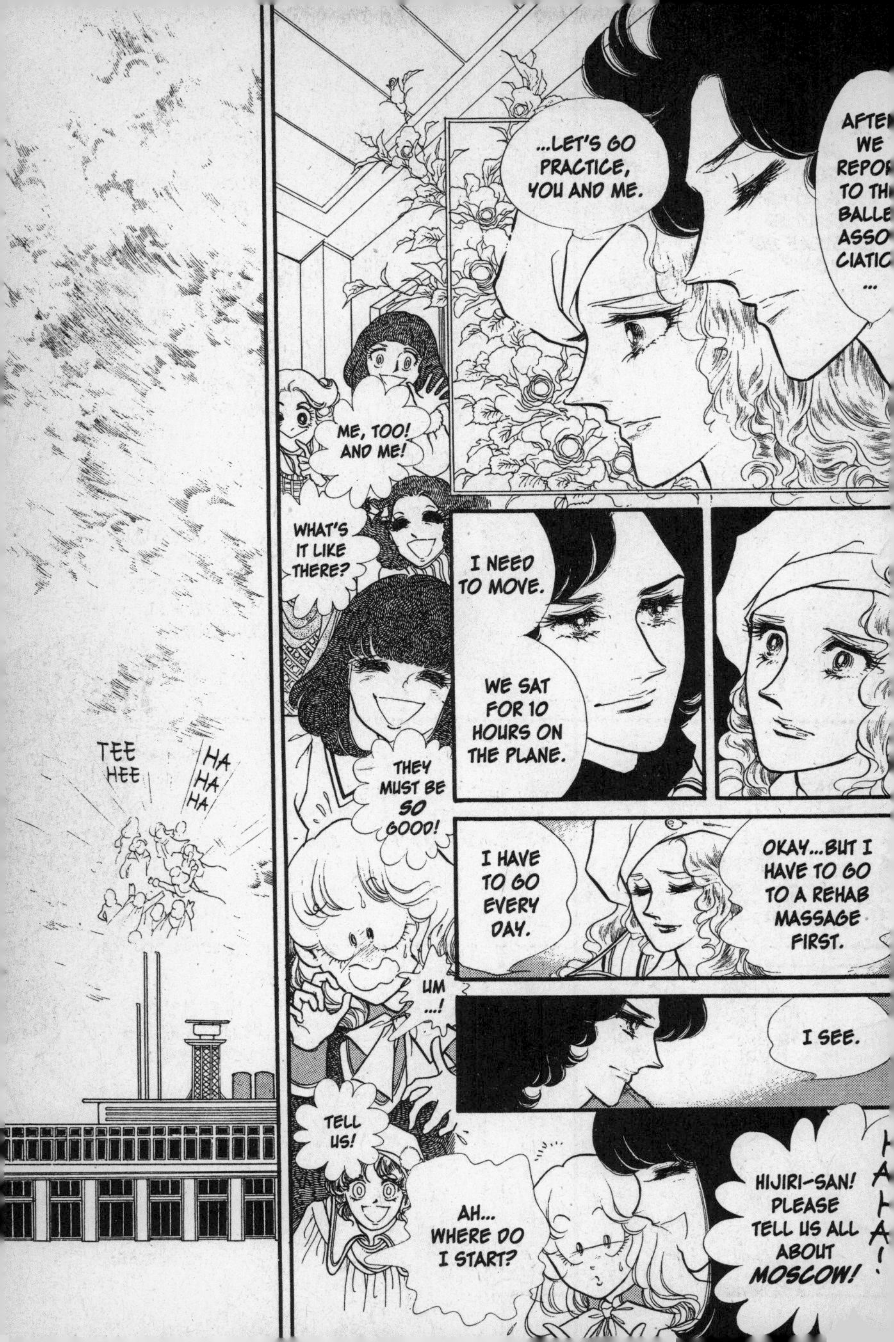
AFTE WE REPO TO TH BALLE ASSO CIATIC ...
...LET'S GO PRACTICE, YOU AND ME.
I NEED TO MOVE.
WE SAT FOR 10 HOURS ON THE PLANE.
OKAY...BUT I HAVE TO GO TO A REHAB MASSAGE FIRST.
I HAVE TO GO EVERY DAY.
I SEE.
HA HA!
HIJIRI-SAN! PLEASE TELL US ALL ABOUT MOSCOW!
AH... WHERE DO I START?
ME, TOO! AND ME!
WHAT'S IT LIKE THERE?
THEY MUST BE SO GOOD!
UM ...!
TELL US!
TEE HEE
HA HA HA

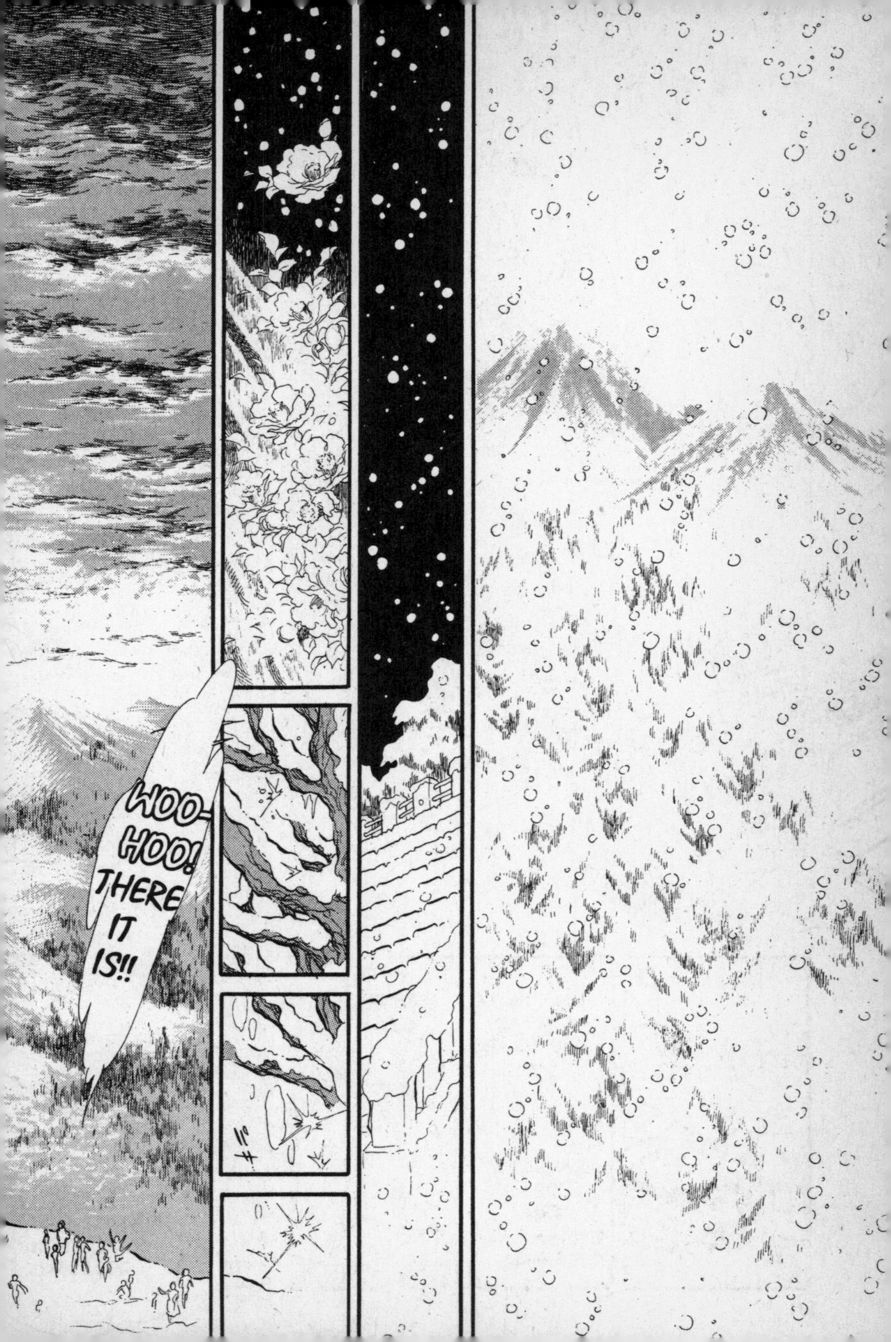
WOO-HOO! THERE IT IS!!

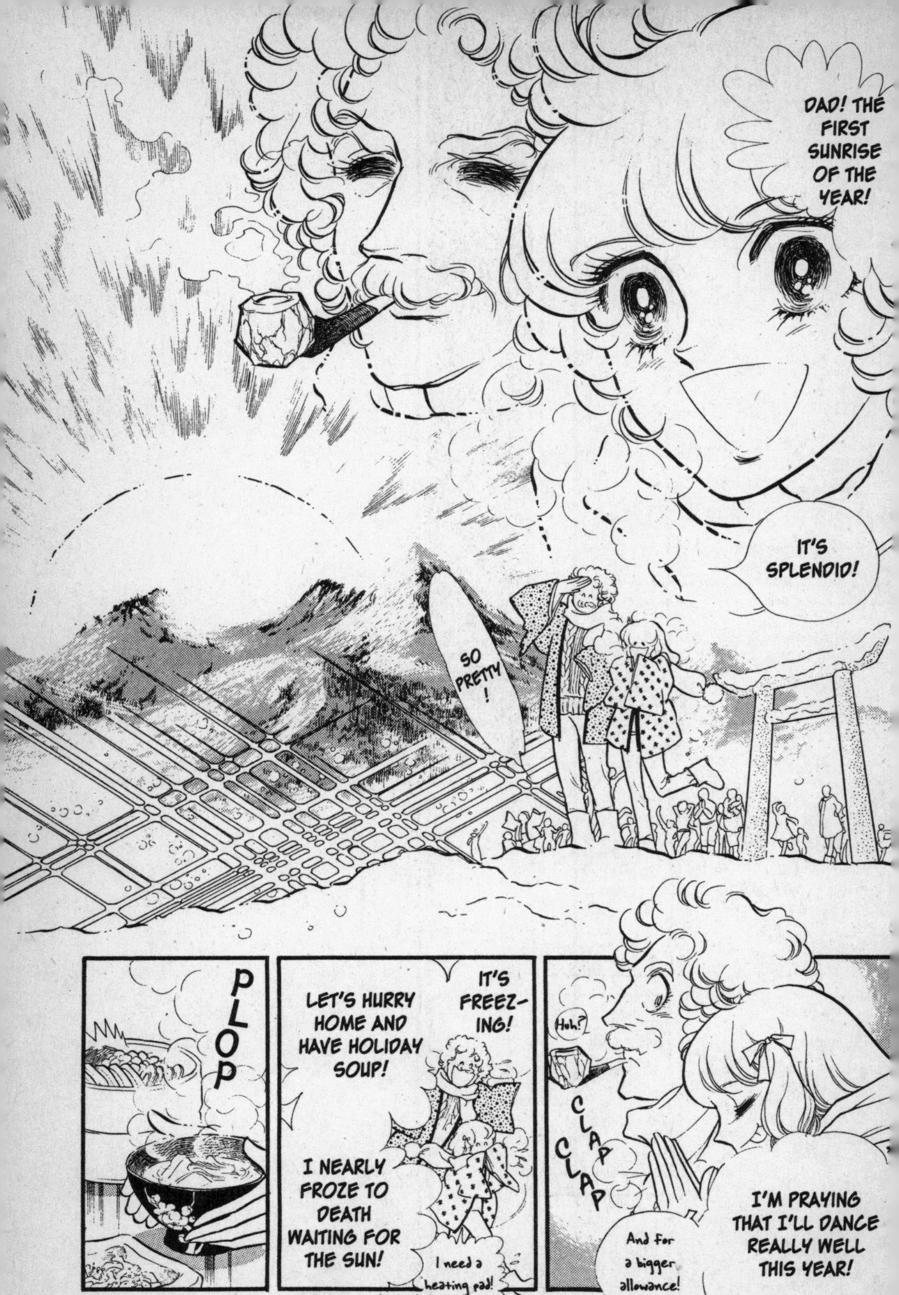
DAD! THE FIRST SUNRISE OF THE YEAR!
IT'S SPLENDID!
SO PRETTY!
I'M PRAYING THAT I'LL DANCE REALLY WELL THIS YEAR!
And for a bigger allowance!
Huh?
CLAP CLAP
IT'S FREEZ-ING!
LET'S HURRY HOME AND HAVE HOLIDAY SOUP!
I NEARLY FROZE TO DEATH WAITING FOR THE SUN!
I need a heating pad!
PLOP

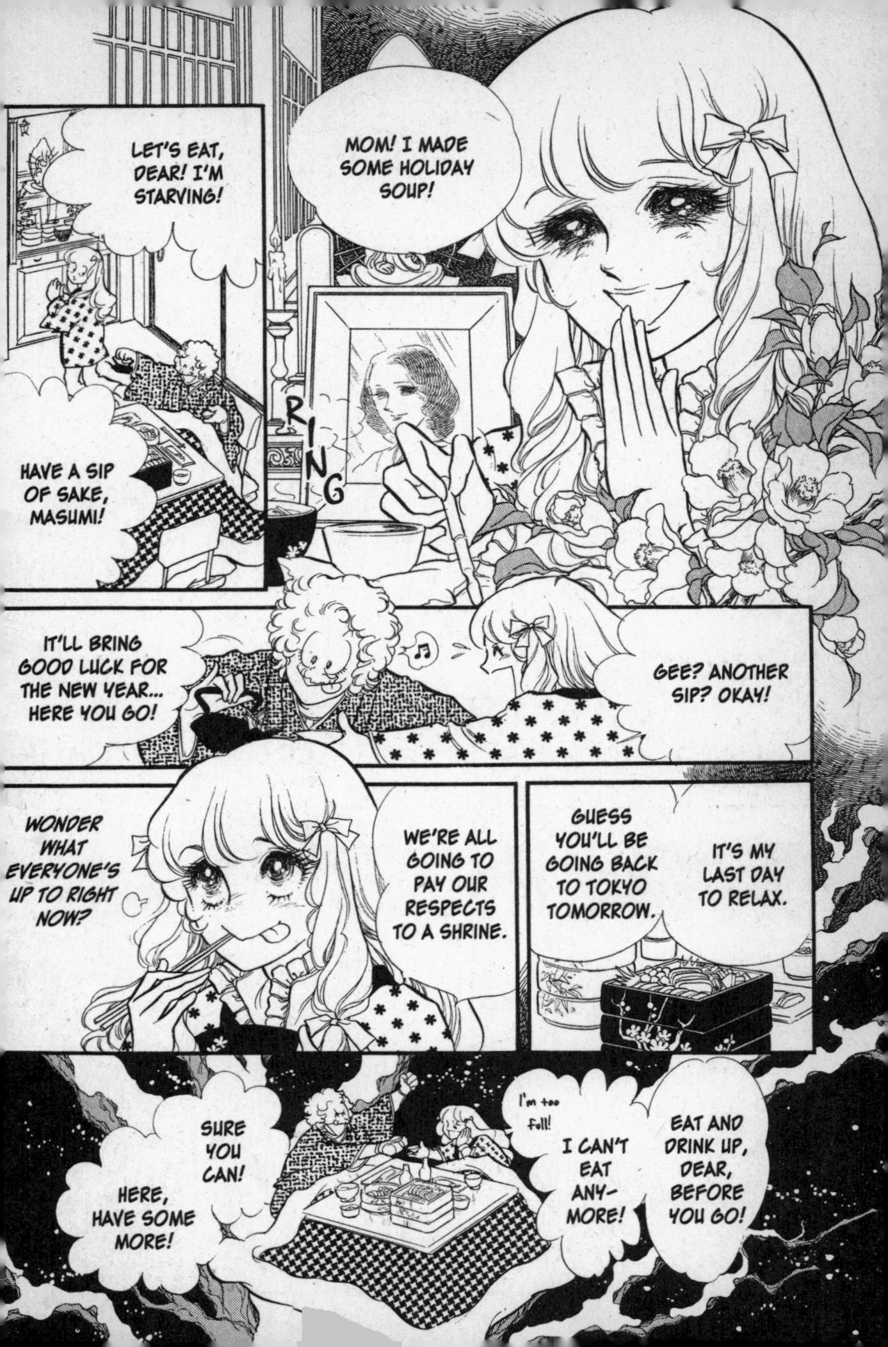

MOM! I MADE SOME HOLIDAY SOUP!
RING
LET'S EAT, DEAR! I'M STARVING!
HAVE A SIP OF SAKE, MASUMI!
GEE? ANOTHER SIP? OKAY!
IT'LL BRING GOOD LUCK FOR THE NEW YEAR... HERE YOU GO!
IT'S MY LAST DAY TO RELAX.
GUESS YOU'LL BE GOING BACK TO TOKYO TOMORROW.
WE'RE ALL GOING TO PAY OUR RESPECTS TO A SHRINE.
WONDER WHAT EVERYONE'S UP TO RIGHT NOW?
EAT AND DRINK UP, DEAR, BEFORE YOU GO!
I CAN'T EAT ANY-MORE!
I'm too full!
SURE YOU CAN!
HERE, HAVE SOME MORE!

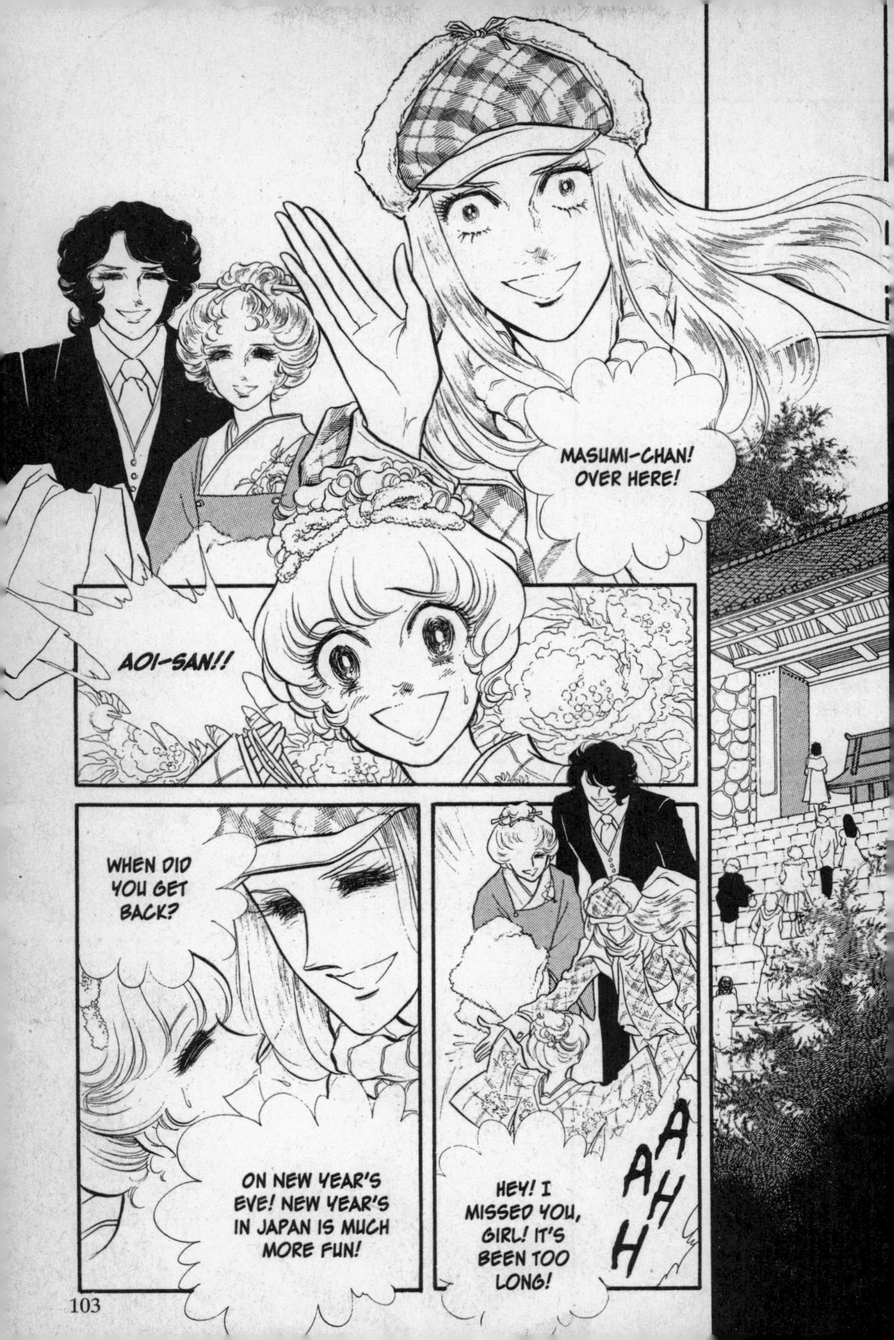

MASUMI-CHAN! OVER HERE!
AOI-SAN!!
HEY! I MISSED YOU, GIRL! IT'S BEEN TOO LONG!
AAHH
WHEN DID YOU GET BACK?
ON NEW YEAR'S EVE! NEW YEAR'S IN JAPAN IS MUCH MORE FUN!

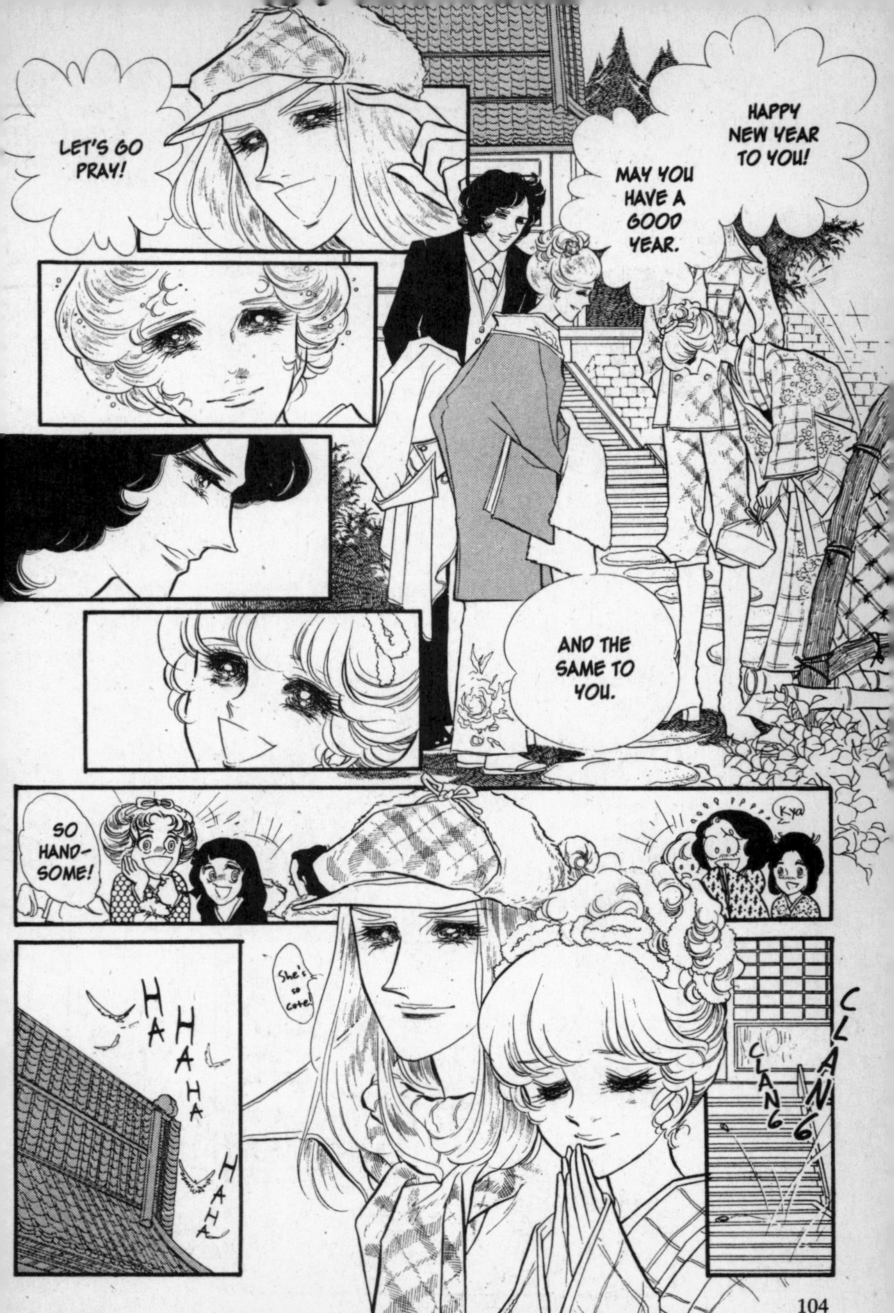
HAPPY NEW YEAR TO YOU!
MAY YOU HAVE A GOOD YEAR.
AND THE SAME TO YOU.
LET'S GO PRAY!
Kya
SO HAND-SOME!
CLANG CLANG
She's so cute!
HA HA HA HA HA HA

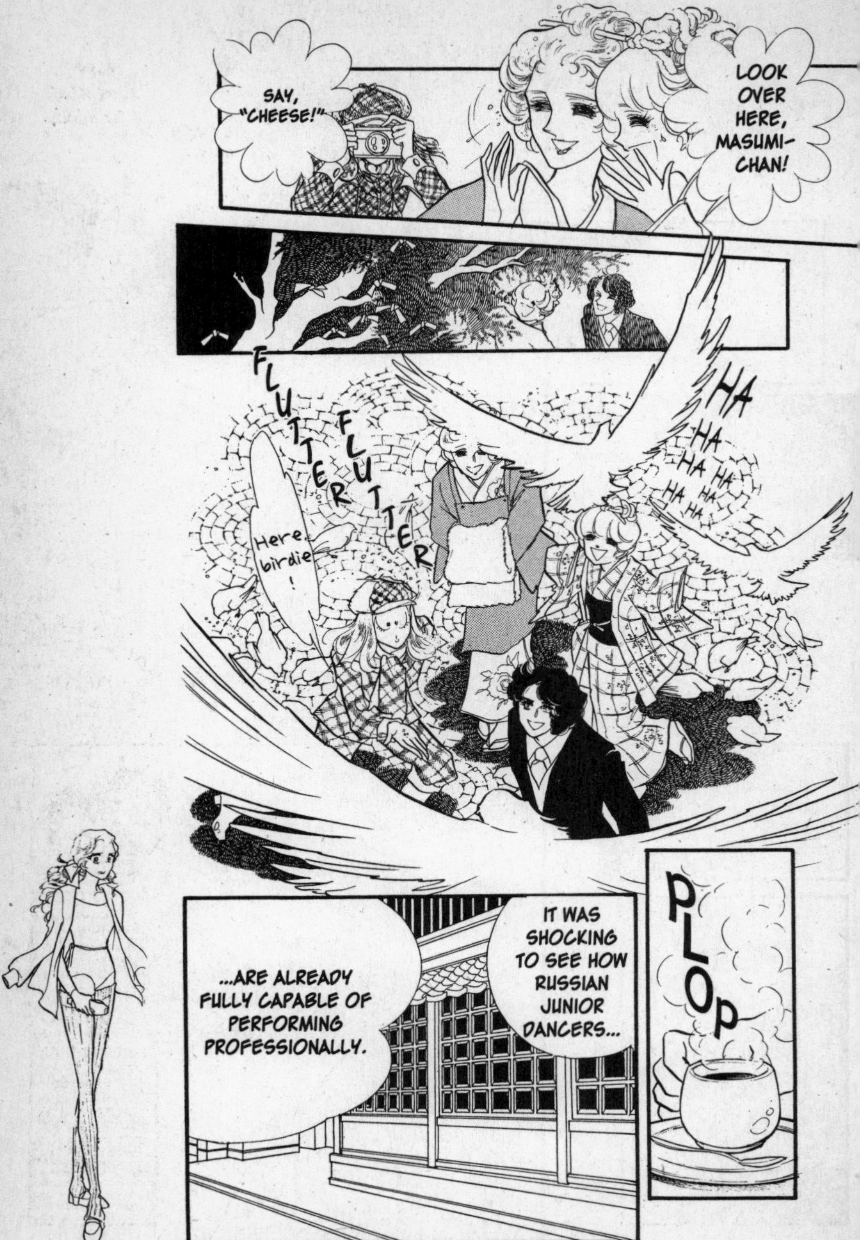
LOOK OVER HERE, MASUMI-CHAN!
SAY, "CHEESE!"
HA HA HA HA HA HA HA HA
FLUTTER FLUTTER
Here birdie!
PLOP
IT WAS SHOCKING TO SEE HOW RUSSIAN JUNIOR DANCERS...
...ARE ALREADY FULLY CAPABLE OF PERFORMING PROFESSIONALLY.

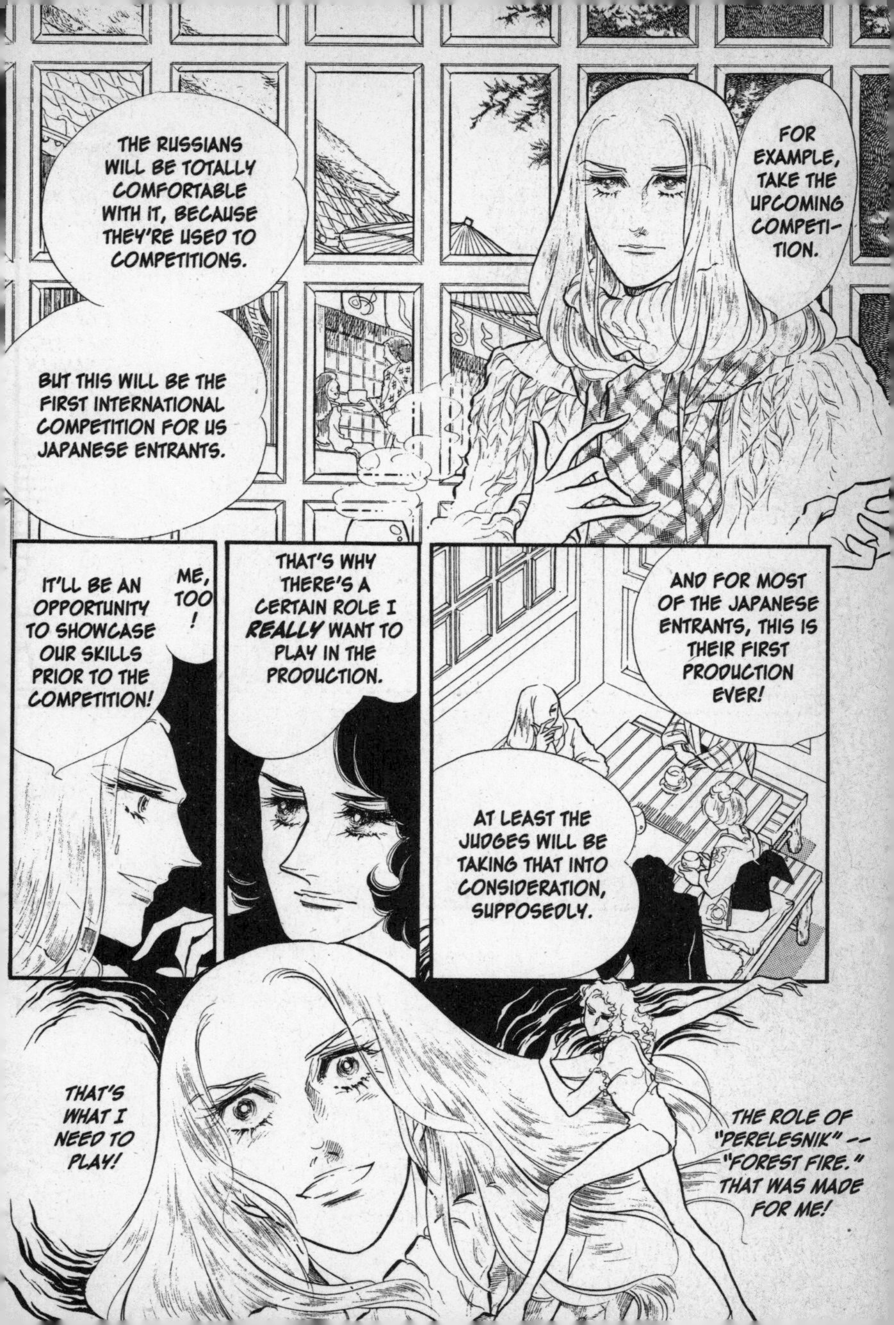
FOR EXAMPLE, TAKE THE UPCOMING COMPETI-TION.
THE RUSSIANS WILL BE TOTALLY COMFORTABLE WITH IT, BECAUSE THEY'RE USED TO COMPETITIONS.
BUT THIS WILL BE THE FIRST INTERNATIONAL COMPETITION FOR US JAPANESE ENTRANTS.
AND FOR MOST OF THE JAPANESE ENTRANTS, THIS IS THEIR FIRST PRODUCTION EVER!
AT LEAST THE JUDGES WILL BE TAKING THAT INTO CONSIDERATION, SUPPOSEDLY.
THAT'S WHY THERE'S A CERTAIN ROLE I *REALLY* WANT TO PLAY IN THE PRODUCTION.
ME, TOO!
IT'LL BE AN OPPORTUNITY TO SHOWCASE OUR SKILLS PRIOR TO THE COMPETITION!
THE ROLE OF "PERELESNIK" -- "FOREST FIRE." THAT WAS MADE FOR ME!
THAT'S WHAT I NEED TO PLAY!

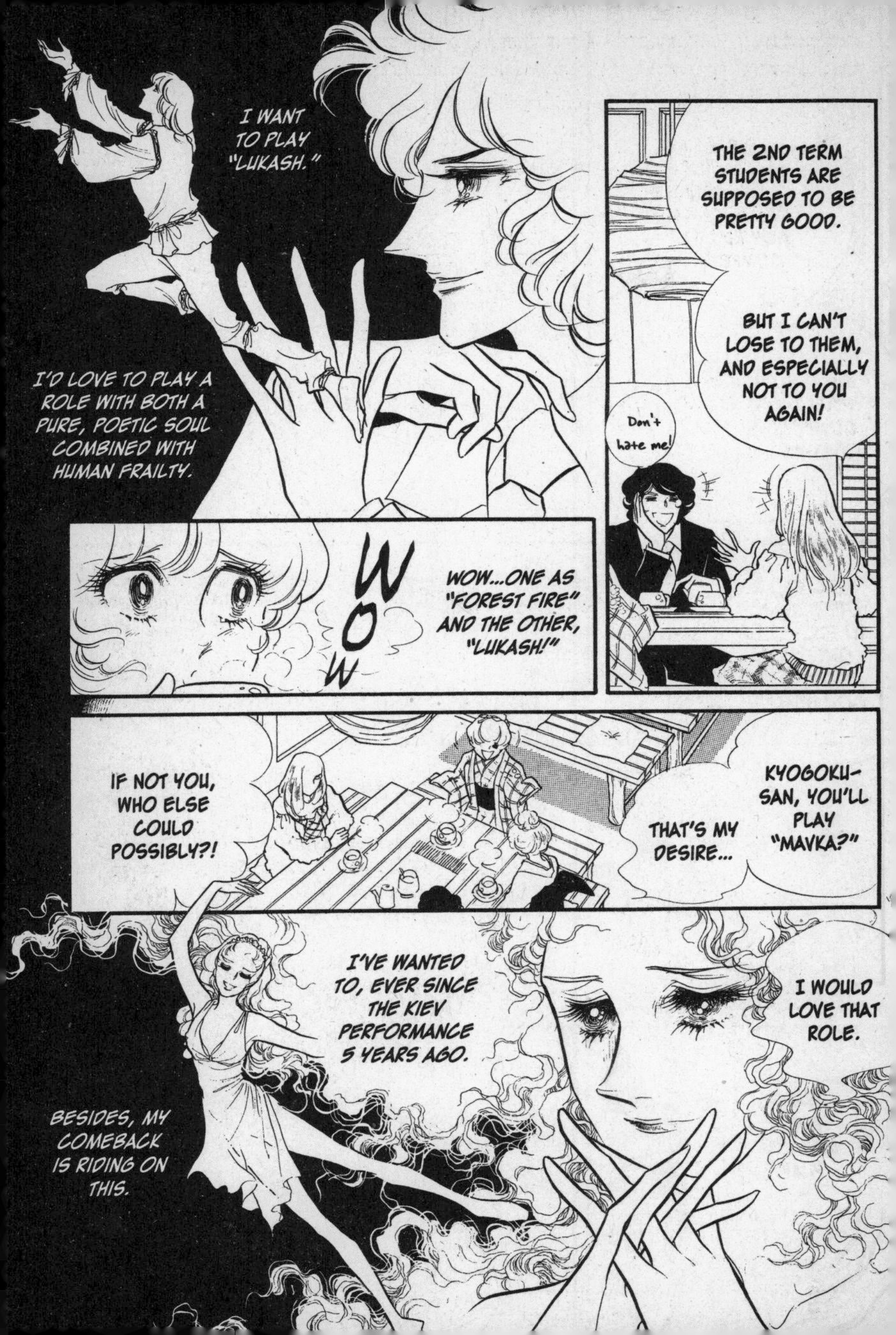
THE 2ND TERM STUDENTS ARE SUPPOSED TO BE PRETTY GOOD.
BUT I CAN'T LOSE TO THEM, AND ESPECIALLY NOT TO YOU AGAIN!
Don't hate me!
I WANT TO PLAY "LUKASH."
I'D LOVE TO PLAY A ROLE WITH BOTH A PURE, POETIC SOUL COMBINED WITH HUMAN FRAILTY.
WOW...ONE AS "FOREST FIRE" AND THE OTHER, "LUKASH!"
WOW
KYOGOKU-SAN, YOU'LL PLAY "MAVKA?"
THAT'S MY DESIRE...
IF NOT YOU, WHO ELSE COULD POSSIBLY?!
I WOULD LOVE THAT ROLE.
I'VE WANTED TO, EVER SINCE THE KIEV PERFORMANCE 5 YEARS AGO.
BESIDES, MY COMEBACK IS RIDING ON THIS.

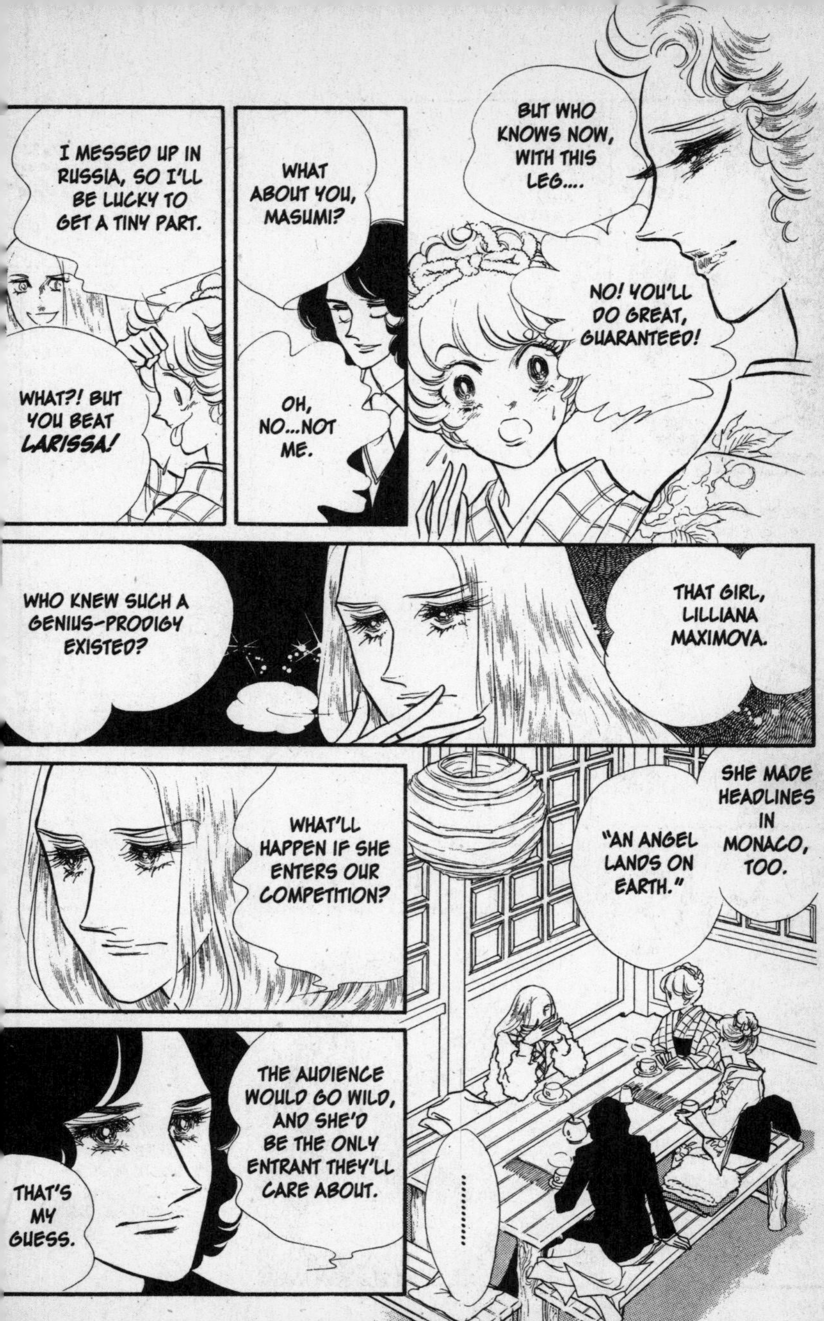
BUT WHO KNOWS NOW, WITH THIS LEG....
NO! YOU'LL DO GREAT, GUARANTEED!
WHAT ABOUT YOU, MASUMI?
OH, NO...NOT ME.
I MESSED UP IN RUSSIA, SO I'LL BE LUCKY TO GET A TINY PART.
WHAT?! BUT YOU BEAT ***LARISSA!***
THAT GIRL, LILLIANA MAXIMOVA.
WHO KNEW SUCH A GENIUS-PRODIGY EXISTED?
SHE MADE HEADLINES IN MONACO, TOO.
"AN ANGEL LANDS ON EARTH."
......
WHAT'LL HAPPEN IF SHE ENTERS OUR COMPETITION?
THE AUDIENCE WOULD GO WILD, AND SHE'D BE THE ONLY ENTRANT THEY'LL CARE ABOUT.
THAT'S MY GUESS.

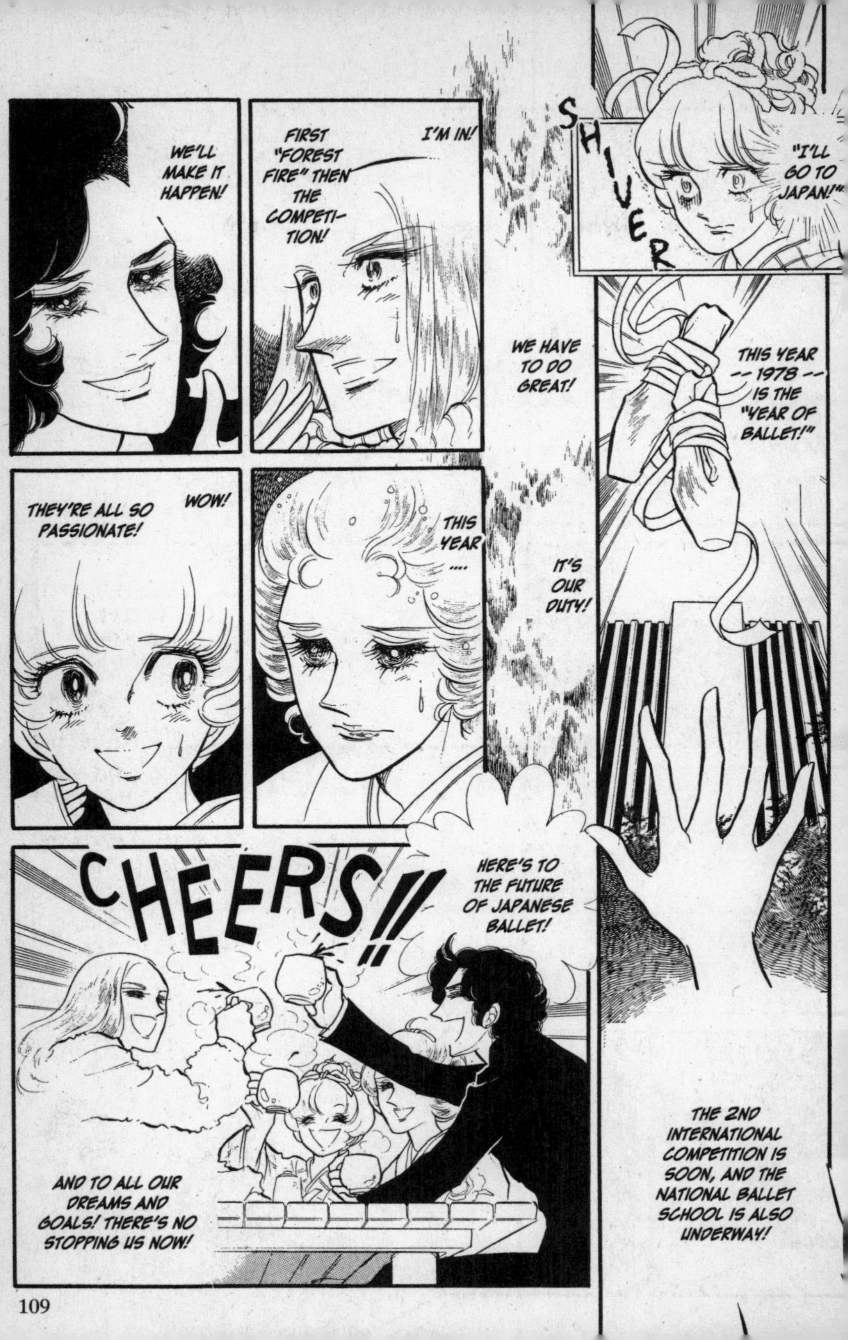

"I'LL GO TO JAPAN!"
SHIVER
THIS YEAR -- 1978 -- IS THE "YEAR OF BALLET!"
THE 2ND INTERNATIONAL COMPETITION IS SOON, AND THE NATIONAL BALLET SCHOOL IS ALSO UNDERWAY!
WE HAVE TO DO GREAT!
I'M IN!
FIRST "FOREST FIRE" THEN THE COMPETITION!
WE'LL MAKE IT HAPPEN!
IT'S OUR DUTY!
THIS YEAR ....
WOW!
THEY'RE ALL SO PASSIONATE!
HERE'S TO THE FUTURE OF JAPANESE BALLET!
CHEERS!!
AND TO ALL OUR DREAMS AND GOALS! THERE'S NO STOPPING US NOW!

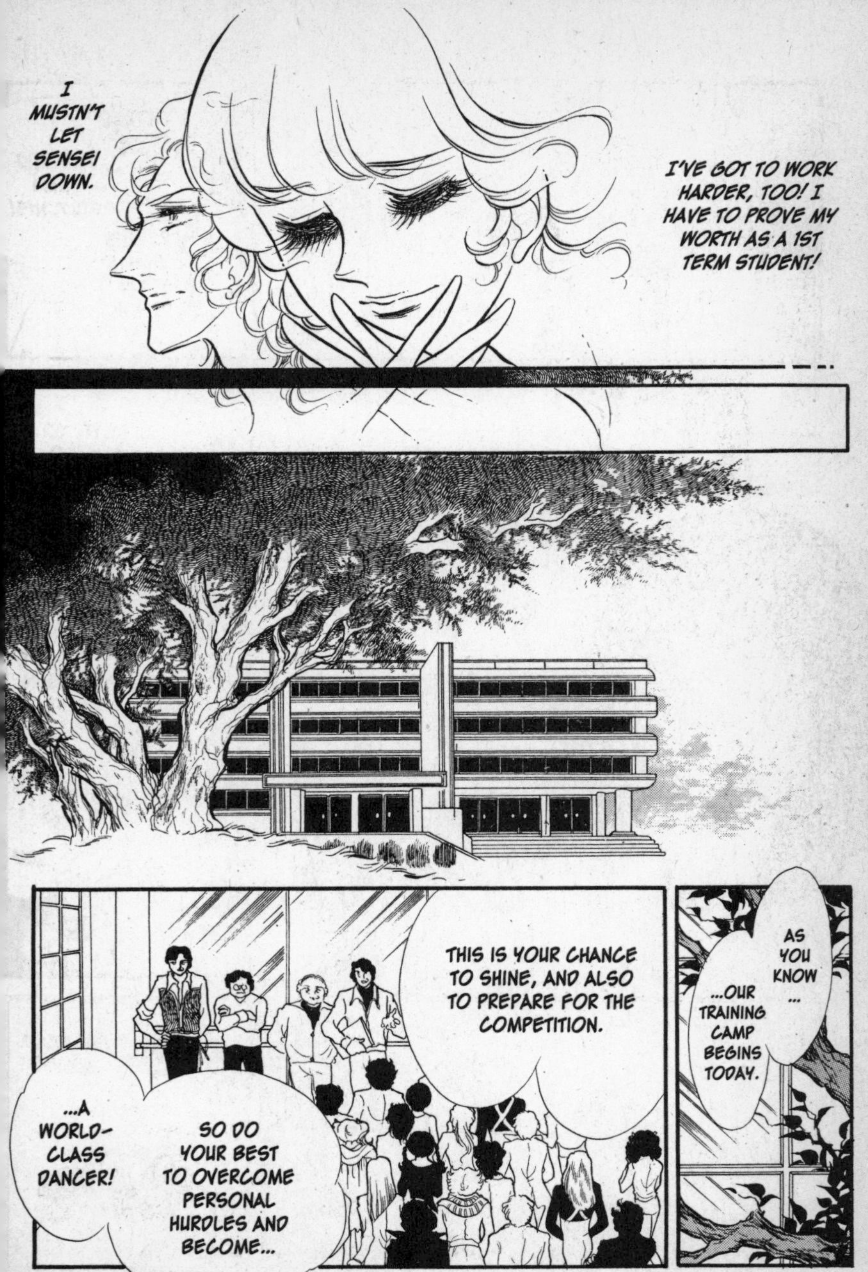
I'VE GOT TO WORK HARDER, TOO! I HAVE TO PROVE MY WORTH AS A 1ST TERM STUDENT!
I MUSTN'T LET SENSEI DOWN.
AS YOU KNOW...
...OUR TRAINING CAMP BEGINS TODAY.
THIS IS YOUR CHANCE TO SHINE, AND ALSO TO PREPARE FOR THE COMPETITION.
SO DO YOUR BEST TO OVERCOME PERSONAL HURDLES AND BECOME...
...A WORLD-CLASS DANCER!

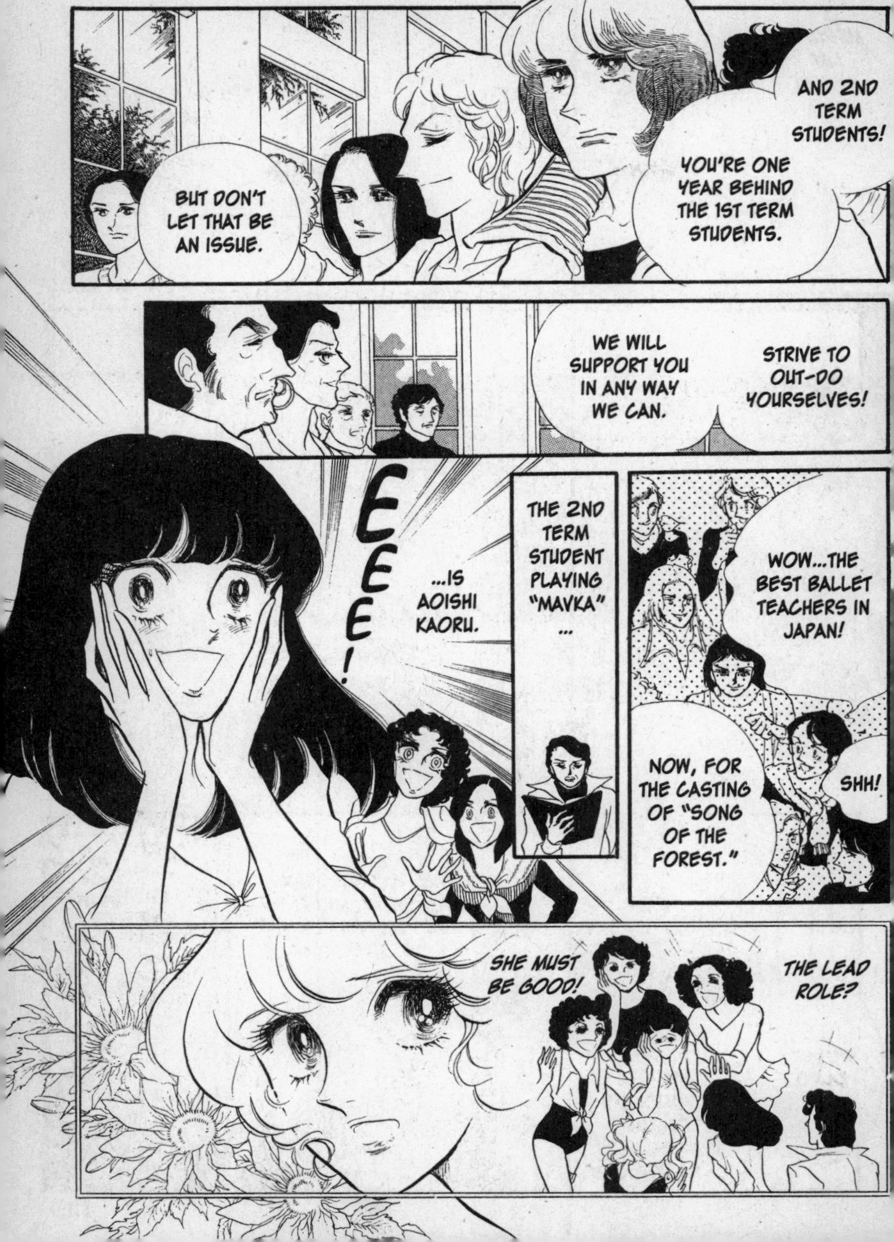
AND 2ND TERM STUDENTS!
YOU'RE ONE YEAR BEHIND THE 1ST TERM STUDENTS.
BUT DON'T LET THAT BE AN ISSUE.
STRIVE TO OUT-DO YOURSELVES!
WE WILL SUPPORT YOU IN ANY WAY WE CAN.
WOW...THE BEST BALLET TEACHERS IN JAPAN!
SHH!
NOW, FOR THE CASTING OF "SONG OF THE FOREST."
THE 2ND TERM STUDENT PLAYING "MAVKA" ...
...IS AOISHI KAORU.
EEEE!
THE LEAD ROLE?
SHE MUST BE GOOD!

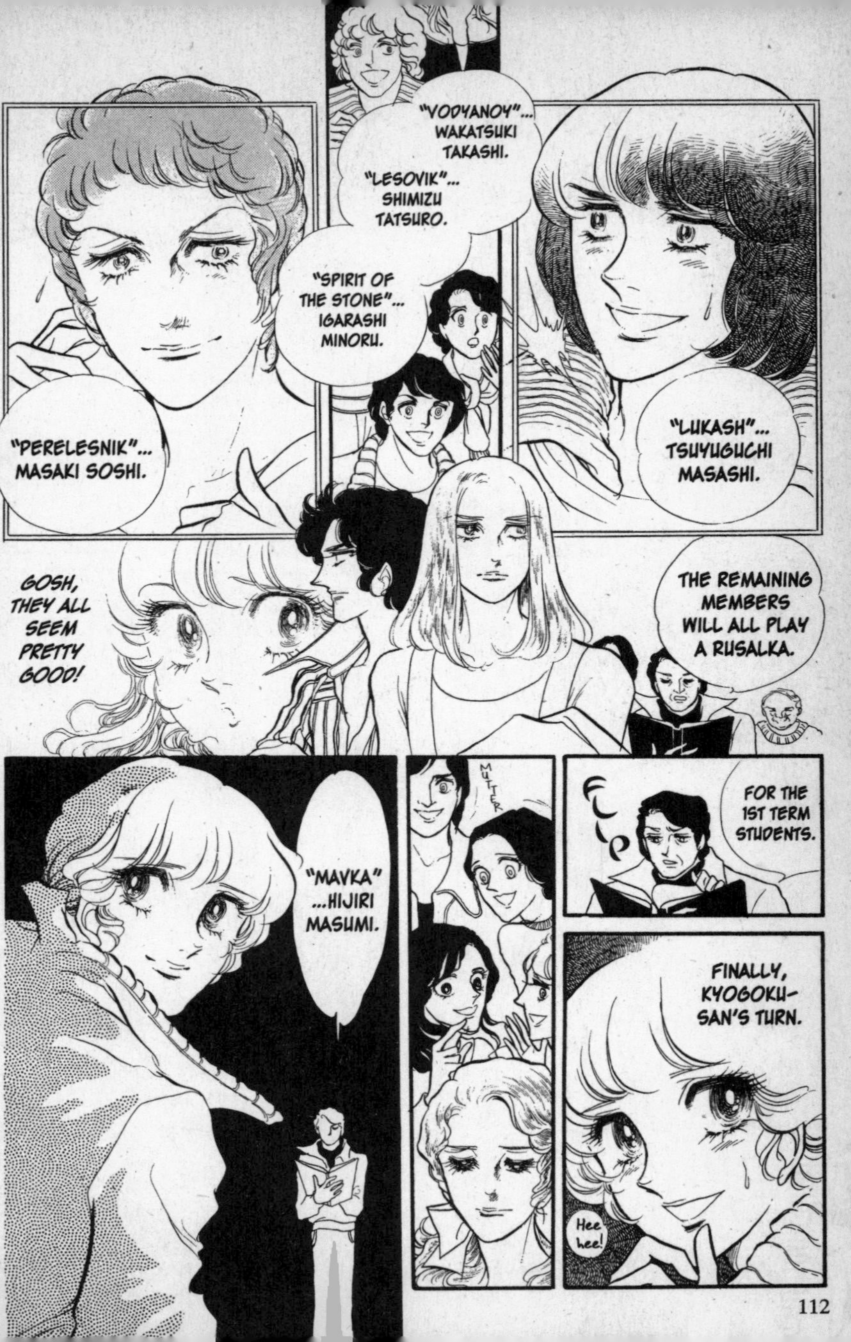
"LUKASH"... TSUYUGUCHI MASASHI.
"VODYANOY"... WAKATSUKI TAKASHI.
"LESOVIK"... SHIMIZU TATSURO.
"SPIRIT OF THE STONE"... IGARASHI MINORU.
"PERELESNIK"... MASAKI SOSHI.
THE REMAINING MEMBERS WILL ALL PLAY A RUSALKA.
GOSH, THEY ALL SEEM PRETTY GOOD!
FLIP
FOR THE 1ST TERM STUDENTS.
FINALLY, KYOGOKU-SAN'S TURN.
Hee hee!
MUTTER
"MAVKA" ...HIJIRI MASUMI.

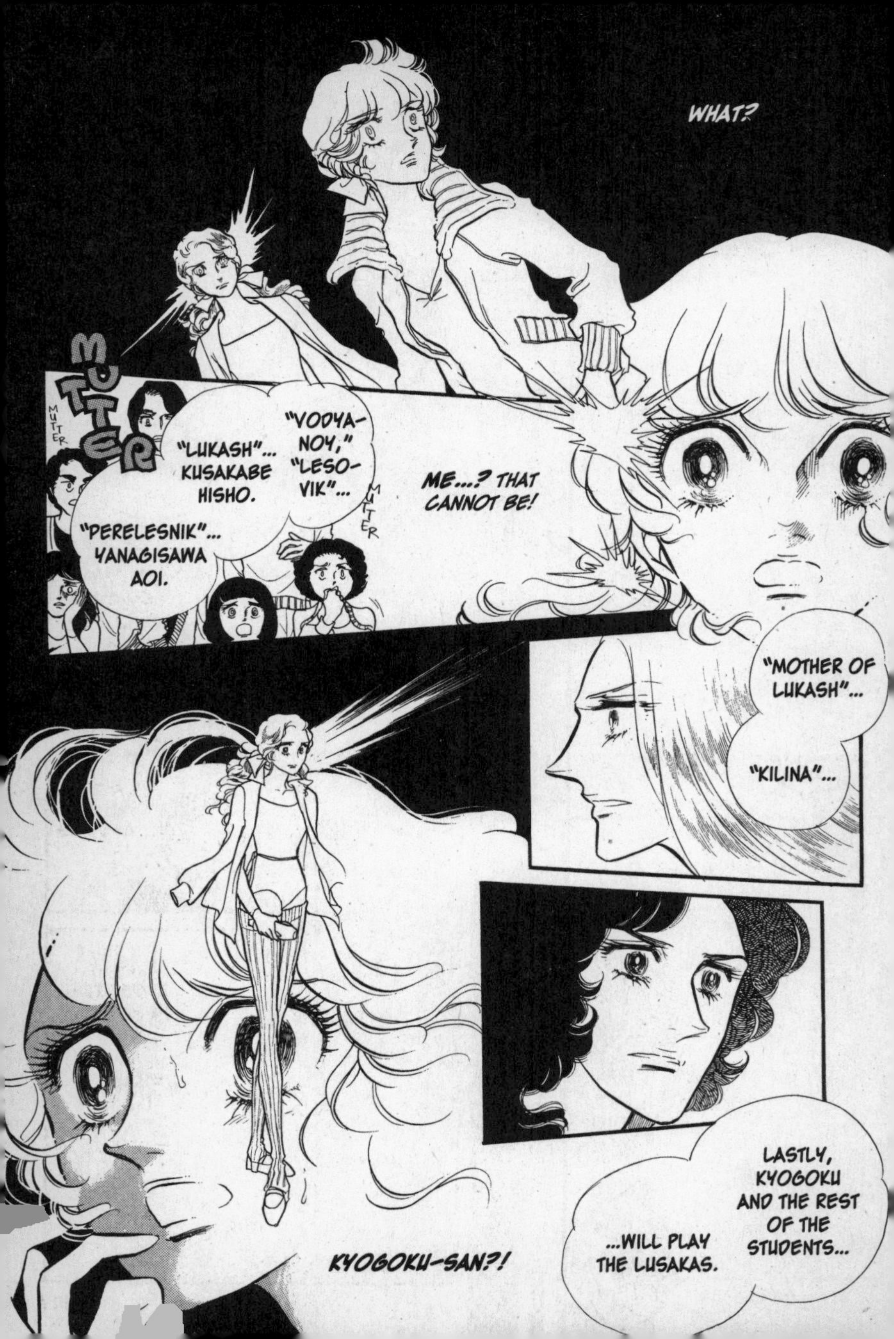
WHAT?
"LUKASH"... KUSAKABE HISHO.
"VODYA-NOY," "LESO-VIK"...
"PERELESNIK"... YANAGISAWA AOI.
ME...? THAT CANNOT BE!
MUTTER
MUTTER
MUTTER
"MOTHER OF LUKASH"...
"KILINA"...
LASTLY, KYOGOKU AND THE REST OF THE STUDENTS...
...WILL PLAY THE LUSAKAS.
KYOGOKU-SAN?!

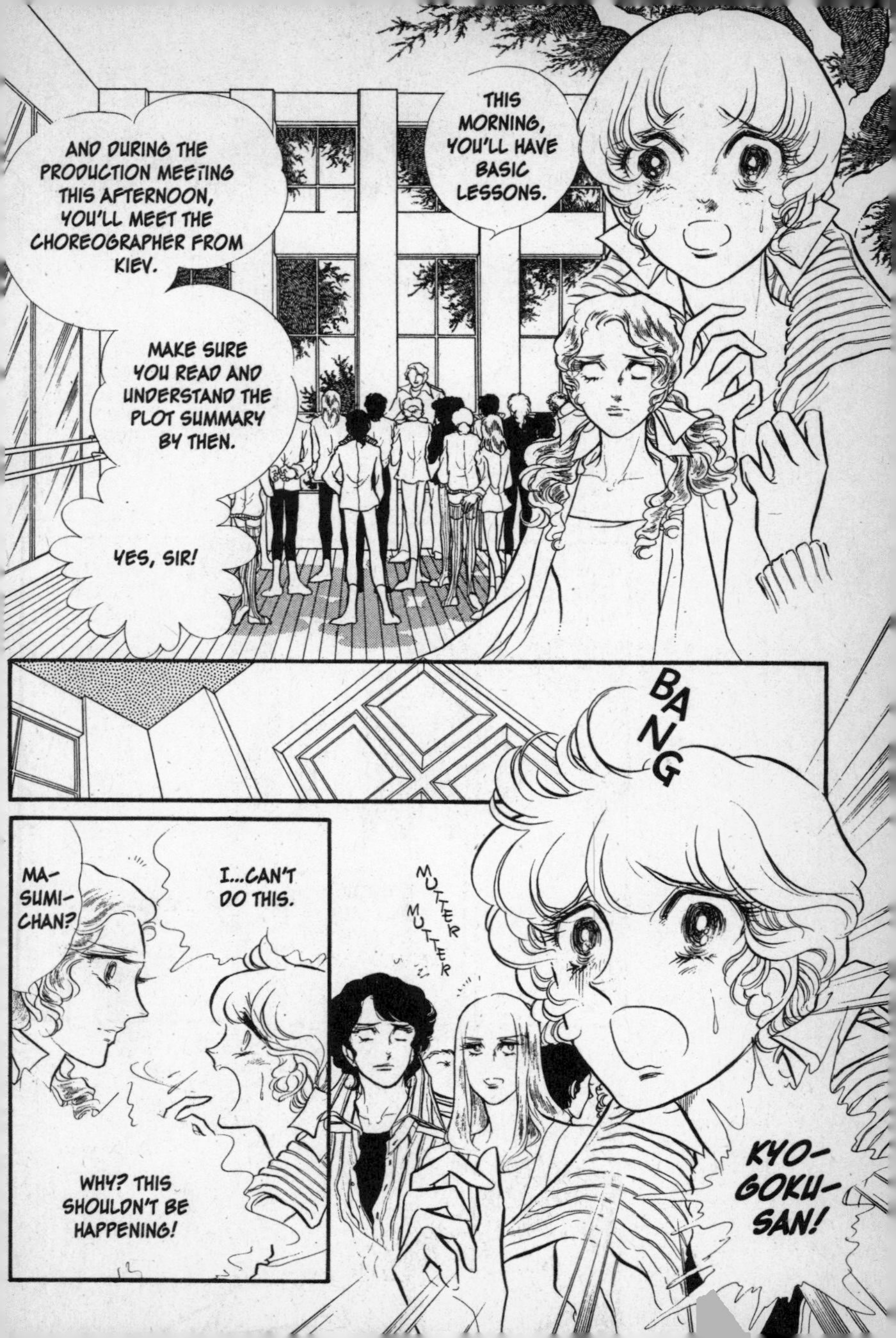
THIS MORNING, YOU'LL HAVE BASIC LESSONS.
AND DURING THE PRODUCTION MEETING THIS AFTERNOON, YOU'LL MEET THE CHOREOGRAPHER FROM KIEV.
MAKE SURE YOU READ AND UNDERSTAND THE PLOT SUMMARY BY THEN.
YES, SIR!
BANG
KYO-GOKU-SAN!
MUTTER MUTTER
I...CAN'T DO THIS.
MA-SUMI-CHAN?
WHY? THIS SHOULDN'T BE HAPPENING!

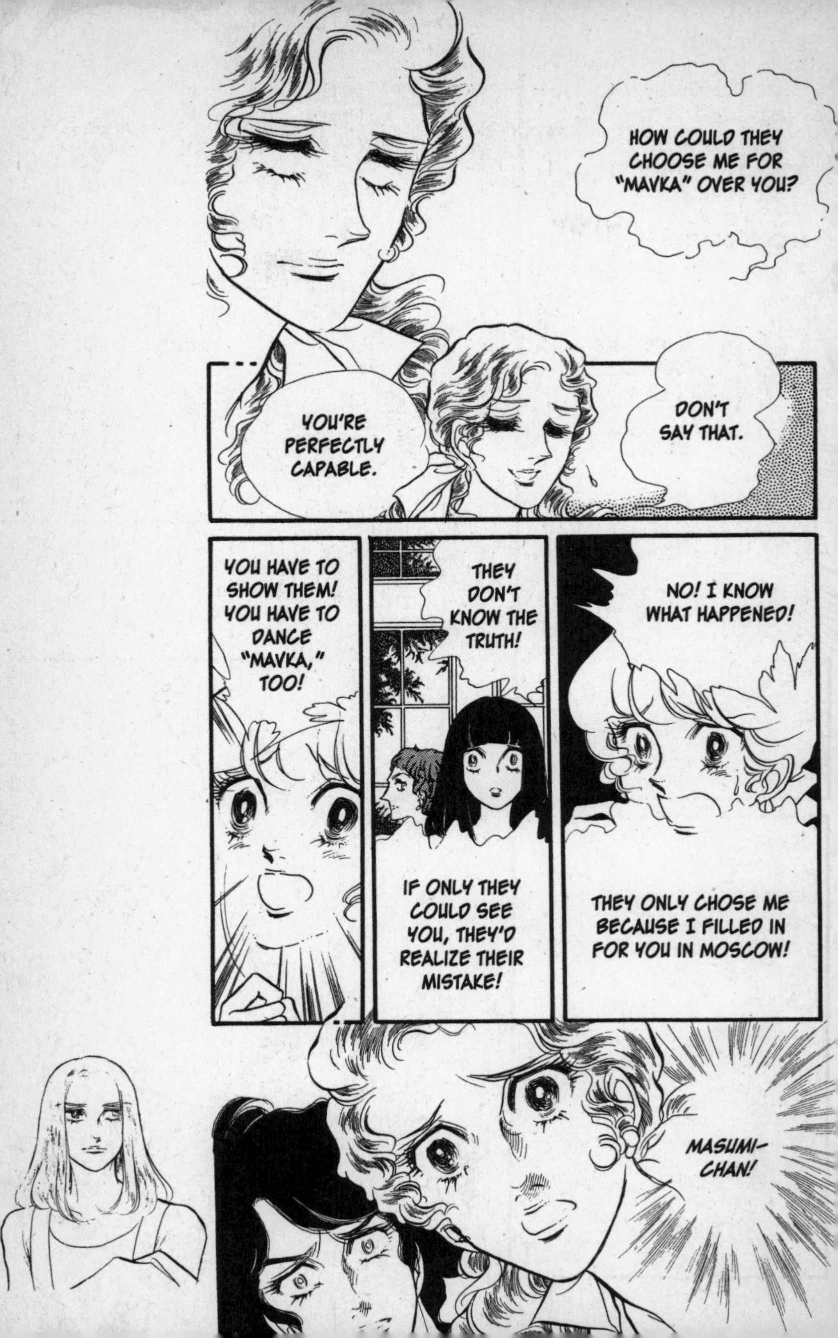
HOW COULD THEY CHOOSE ME FOR "MAVKA" OVER YOU?
DON'T SAY THAT.
YOU'RE PERFECTLY CAPABLE.
NO! I KNOW WHAT HAPPENED!
THEY ONLY CHOSE ME BECAUSE I FILLED IN FOR YOU IN MOSCOW!
THEY DON'T KNOW THE TRUTH!
IF ONLY THEY COULD SEE YOU, THEY'D REALIZE THEIR MISTAKE!
YOU HAVE TO SHOW THEM! YOU HAVE TO DANCE "MAVKA," TOO!
MASUMI-CHAN!

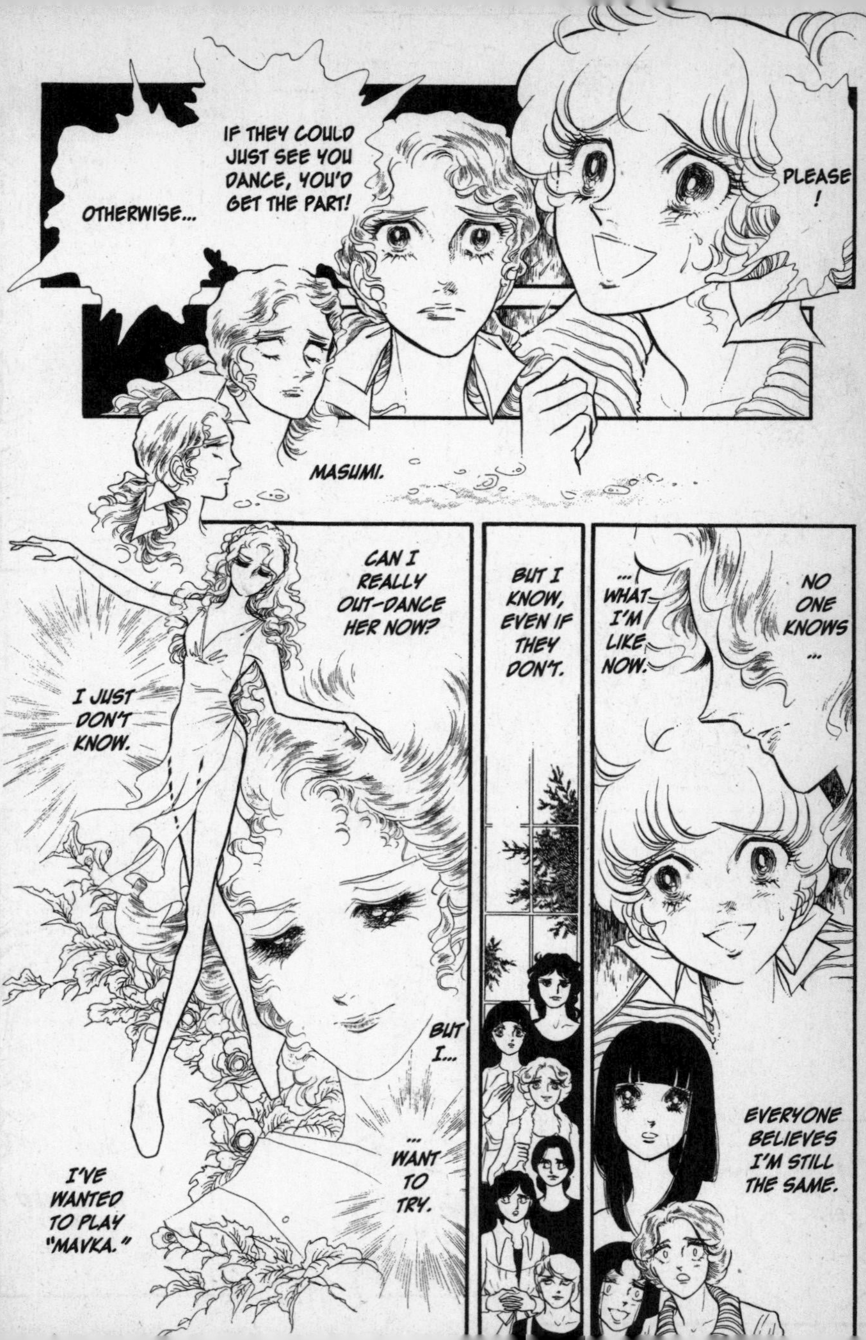
PLEASE !
IF THEY COULD JUST SEE YOU DANCE, YOU'D GET THE PART!
OTHERWISE...
MASUMI.
NO ONE KNOWS ...
...WHAT I'M LIKE NOW.
EVERYONE BELIEVES I'M STILL THE SAME.
BUT I KNOW, EVEN IF THEY DON'T.
CAN I REALLY OUT-DANCE HER NOW?
I JUST DON'T KNOW.
BUT I...
...WANT TO TRY.
I'VE WANTED TO PLAY "MAVKA."

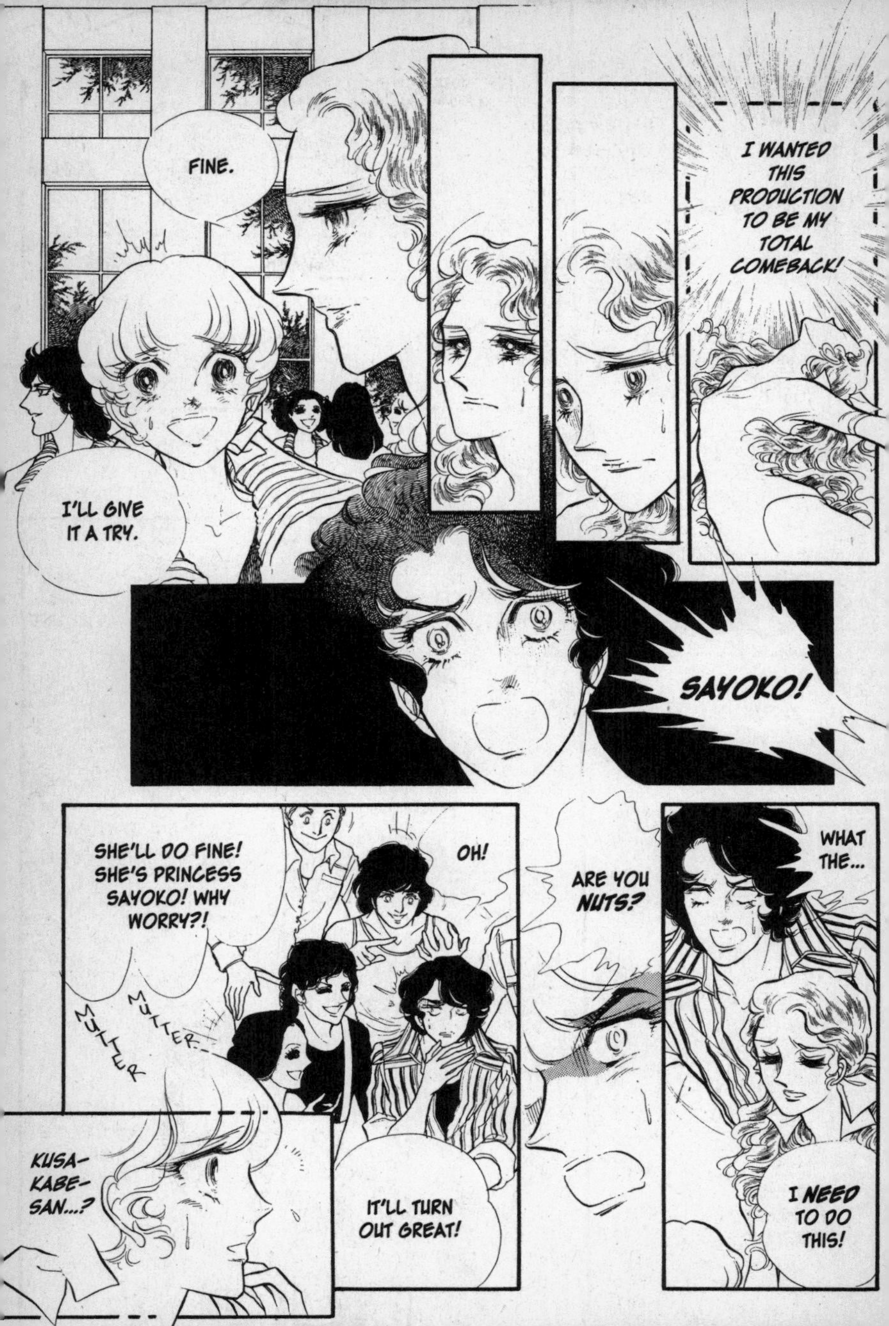
I WANTED THIS PRODUCTION TO BE MY TOTAL COMEBACK!
FINE.
I'LL GIVE IT A TRY.
SAYOKO!
WHAT THE...
I NEED TO DO THIS!
ARE YOU NUTS?
OH!
SHE'LL DO FINE! SHE'S PRINCESS SAYOKO! WHY WORRY?!
MUTTER
MUTTER
IT'LL TURN OUT GREAT!
KUSA-KABE-SAN...?

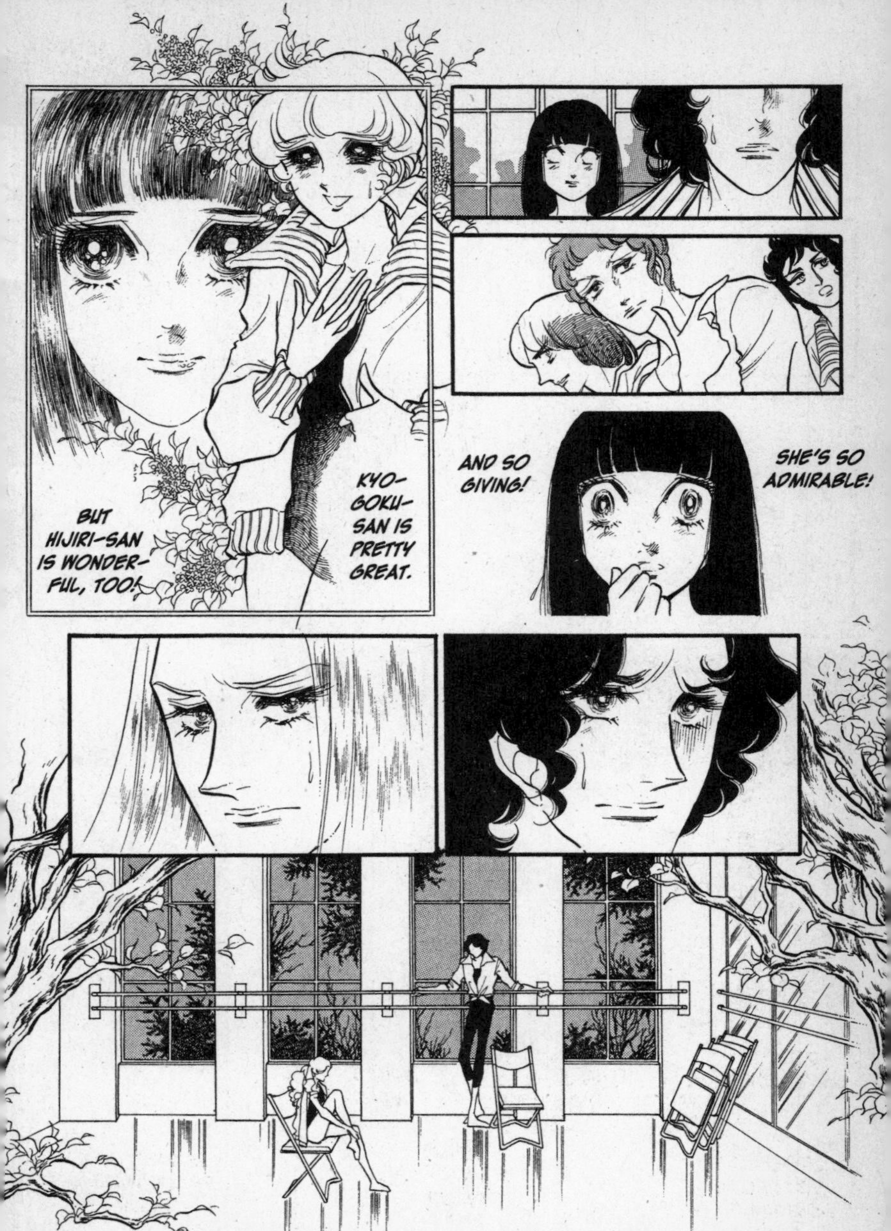
SHE'S SO ADMIRABLE!
AND SO GIVING!
KYO-GOKU-SAN IS PRETTY GREAT.
BUT HIJIRI-SAN IS WONDER-FUL, TOO!

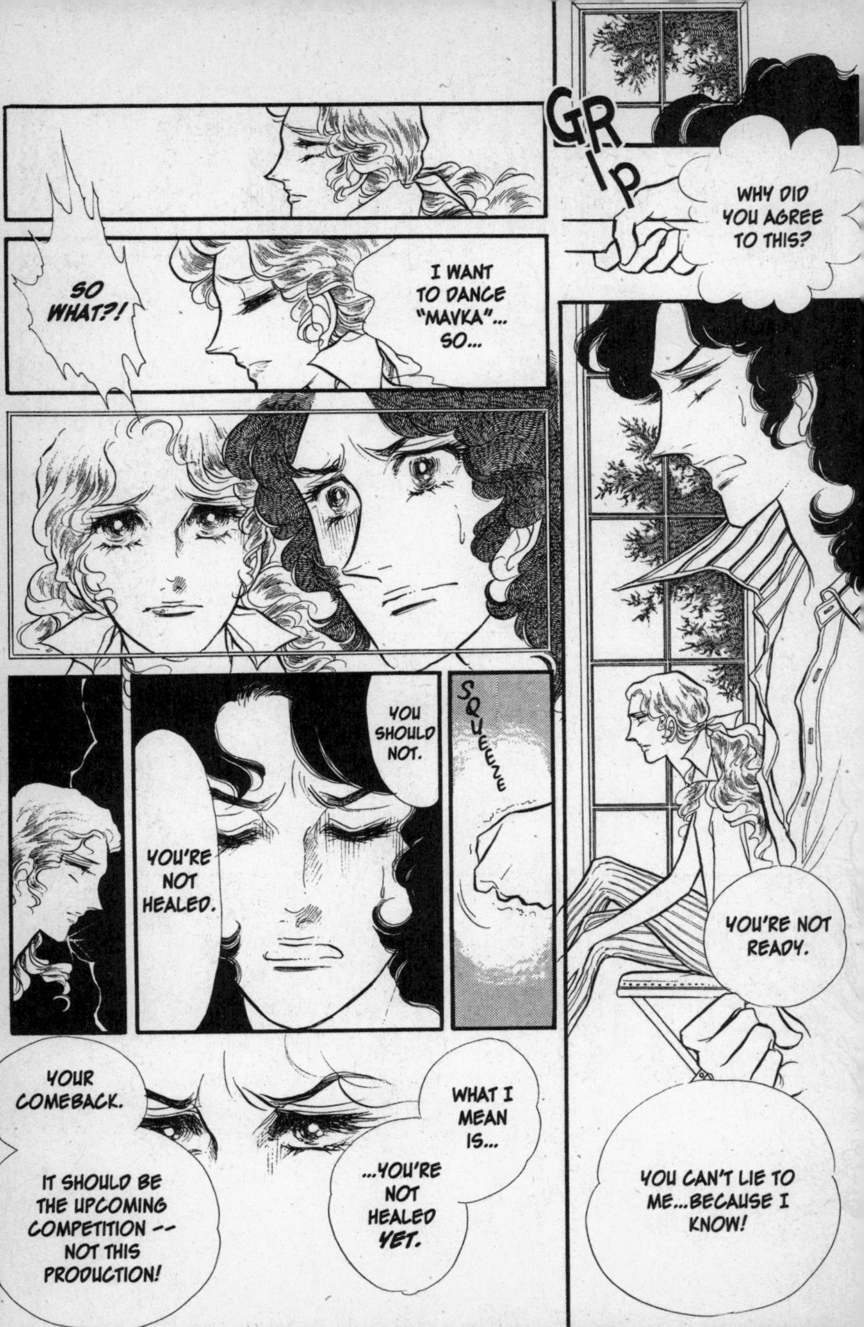
GRIP
WHY DID YOU AGREE TO THIS?
YOU'RE NOT READY.
YOU CAN'T LIE TO ME...BECAUSE I KNOW!
I WANT TO DANCE "MAVKA"... SO...
SO WHAT?!
SQUEEZE
YOU SHOULD NOT.
YOU'RE NOT HEALED.
WHAT I MEAN IS...
...YOU'RE NOT HEALED YET.
YOUR COMEBACK.
IT SHOULD BE THE UPCOMING COMPETITION -- NOT THIS PRODUCTION!

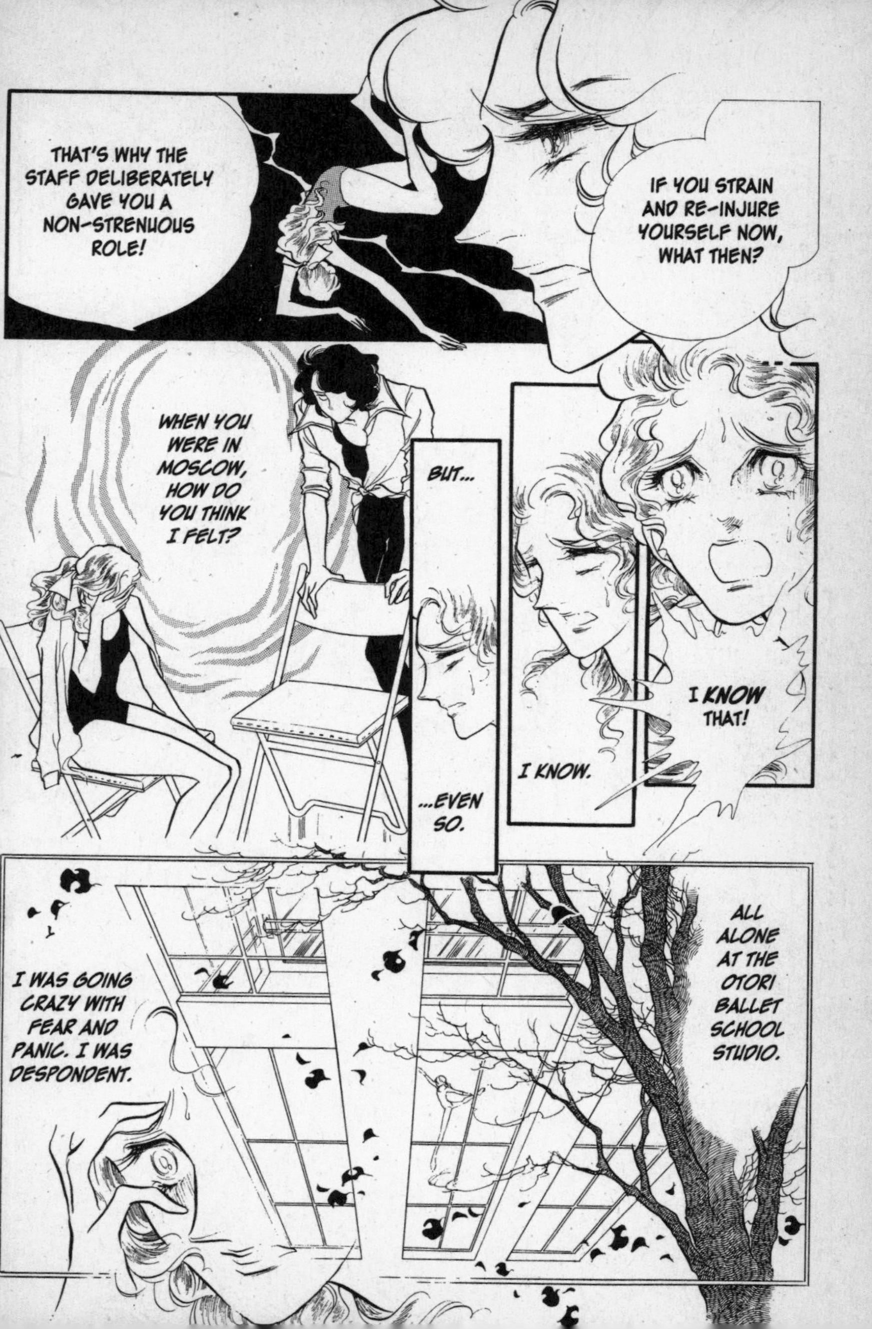
IF YOU STRAIN AND RE-INJURE YOURSELF NOW, WHAT THEN?
THAT'S WHY THE STAFF DELIBERATELY GAVE YOU A NON-STRENUOUS ROLE!
I KNOW THAT!
I KNOW.
BUT...
...EVEN SO.
WHEN YOU WERE IN MOSCOW, HOW DO YOU THINK I FELT?
ALL ALONE AT THE OTORI BALLET SCHOOL STUDIO.
I WAS GOING CRAZY WITH FEAR AND PANIC. I WAS DESPONDENT.

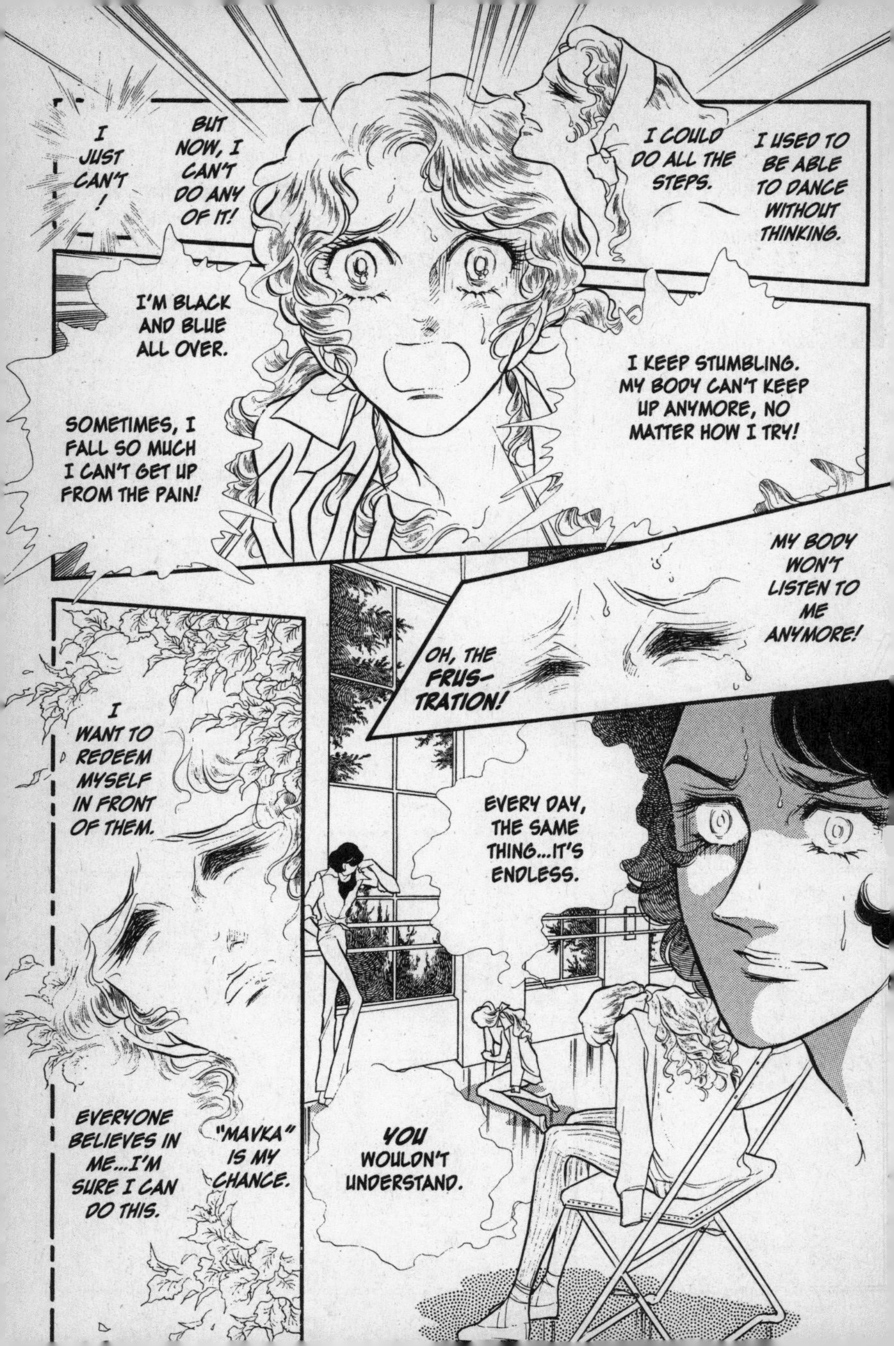
I USED TO BE ABLE TO DANCE WITHOUT THINKING.
I COULD DO ALL THE STEPS.
BUT NOW, I CAN'T DO ANY OF IT!
I JUST CAN'T!
I KEEP STUMBLING. MY BODY CAN'T KEEP UP ANYMORE, NO MATTER HOW I TRY!
I'M BLACK AND BLUE ALL OVER.
SOMETIMES, I FALL SO MUCH I CAN'T GET UP FROM THE PAIN!
MY BODY WON'T LISTEN TO ME ANYMORE!
OH, THE FRUS-TRATION!
EVERY DAY, THE SAME THING...IT'S ENDLESS.
YOU WOULDN'T UNDERSTAND.
I WANT TO REDEEM MYSELF IN FRONT OF THEM.
"MAVKA" IS MY CHANCE.
EVERYONE BELIEVES IN ME...I'M SURE I CAN DO THIS.

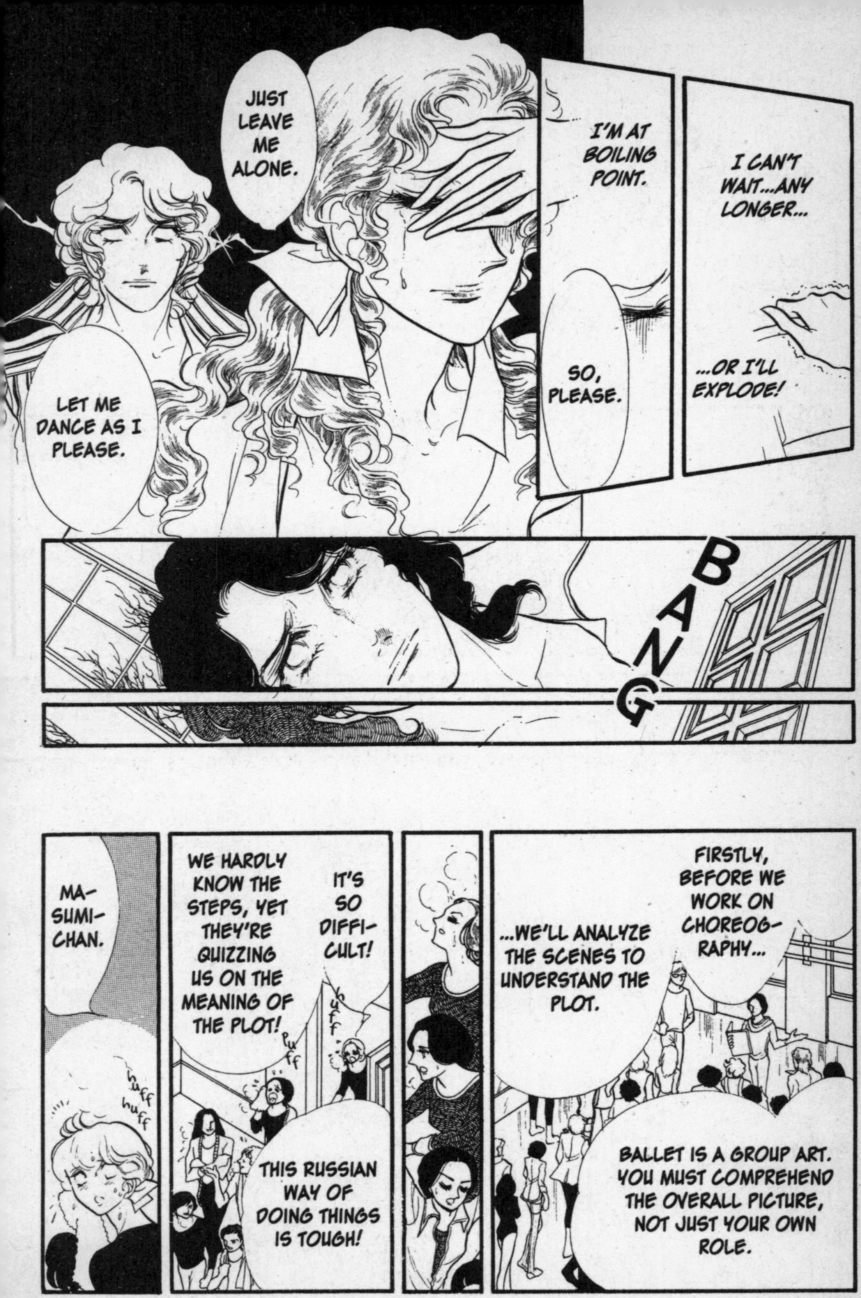

I CAN'T WAIT...ANY LONGER...
...OR I'LL EXPLODE!
I'M AT BOILING POINT.
SO, PLEASE.
JUST LEAVE ME ALONE.
LET ME DANCE AS I PLEASE.
BANG
FIRSTLY, BEFORE WE WORK ON CHOREOG-RAPHY...
...WE'LL ANALYZE THE SCENES TO UNDERSTAND THE PLOT.
BALLET IS A GROUP ART. YOU MUST COMPREHEND THE OVERALL PICTURE, NOT JUST YOUR OWN ROLE.
IT'S SO DIFFI-CULT!
huff
puff
WE HARDLY KNOW THE STEPS, YET THEY'RE QUIZZING US ON THE MEANING OF THE PLOT!
THIS RUSSIAN WAY OF DOING THINGS IS TOUGH!
huff huff
MA-SUMI-CHAN.

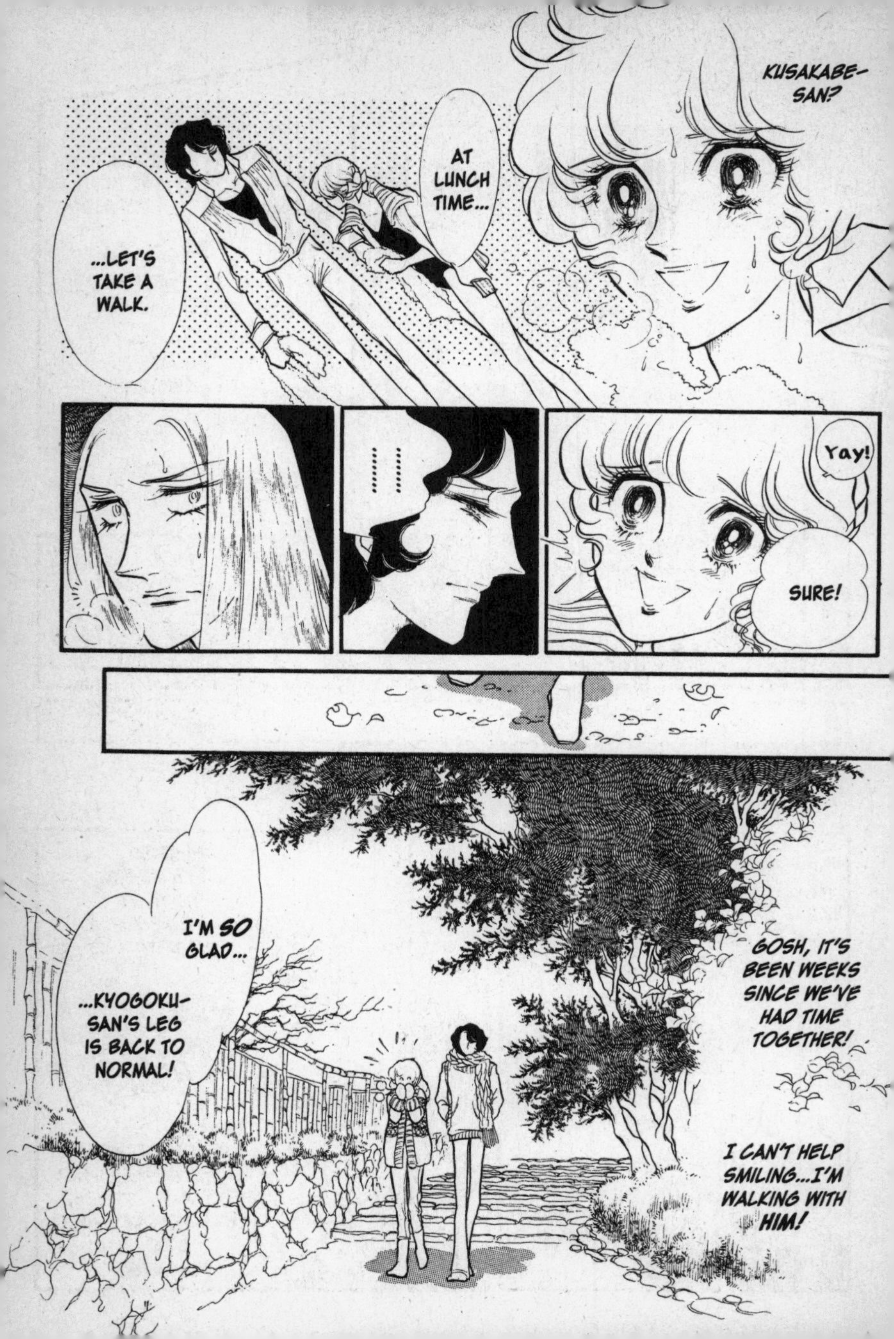
KUSAKABE-SAN?
AT LUNCH TIME...
...LET'S TAKE A WALK.
Yay!
SURE!
......
GOSH, IT'S BEEN WEEKS SINCE WE'VE HAD TIME TOGETHER!
I CAN'T HELP SMILING...I'M WALKING WITH HIM!
I'M SO GLAD...
...KYOGOKU-SAN'S LEG IS BACK TO NORMAL!

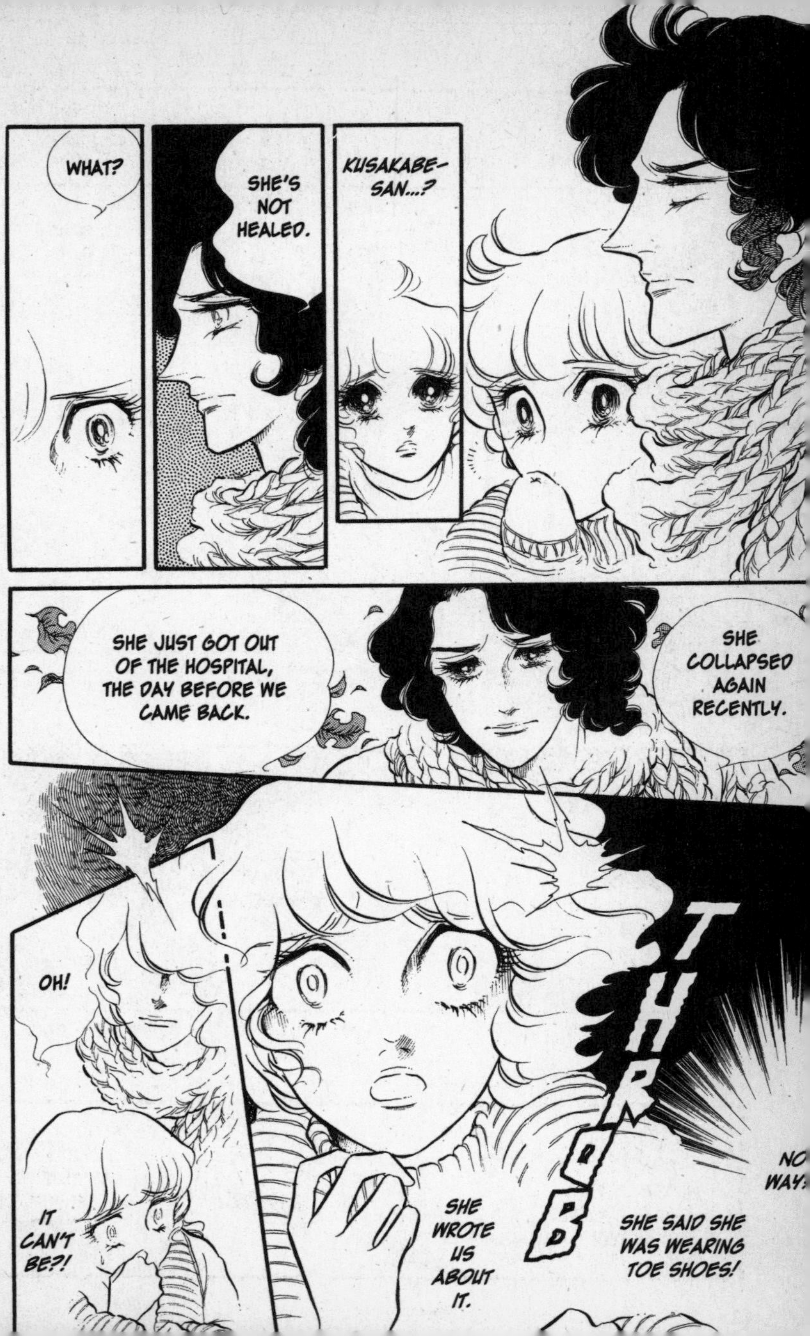
KUSAKABE-SAN...?
SHE'S NOT HEALED.
WHAT?
SHE COLLAPSED AGAIN RECENTLY.
SHE JUST GOT OUT OF THE HOSPITAL, THE DAY BEFORE WE CAME BACK.
NO WAY
THROB
SHE SAID SHE WAS WEARING TOE SHOES!
SHE WROTE US ABOUT IT.
OH!
IT CAN'T BE?!

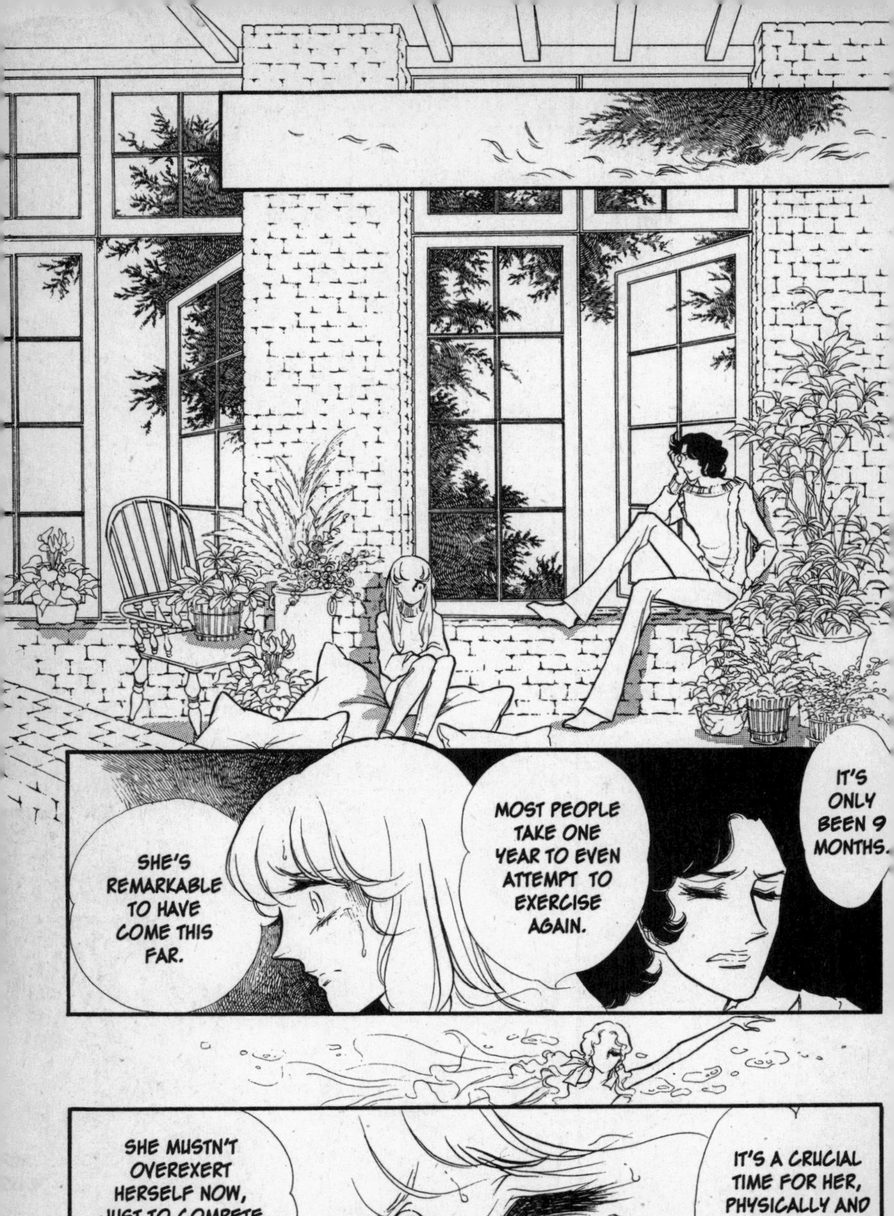
IT'S ONLY BEEN 9 MONTHS.
MOST PEOPLE TAKE ONE YEAR TO EVEN ATTEMPT TO EXERCISE AGAIN.
SHE'S REMARKABLE TO HAVE COME THIS FAR.
IT'S A CRUCIAL TIME FOR HER, PHYSICALLY AND EMOTIONALLY.
SHE MUSTN'T OVEREXERT HERSELF NOW, JUST TO COMPETE WITH YOU.

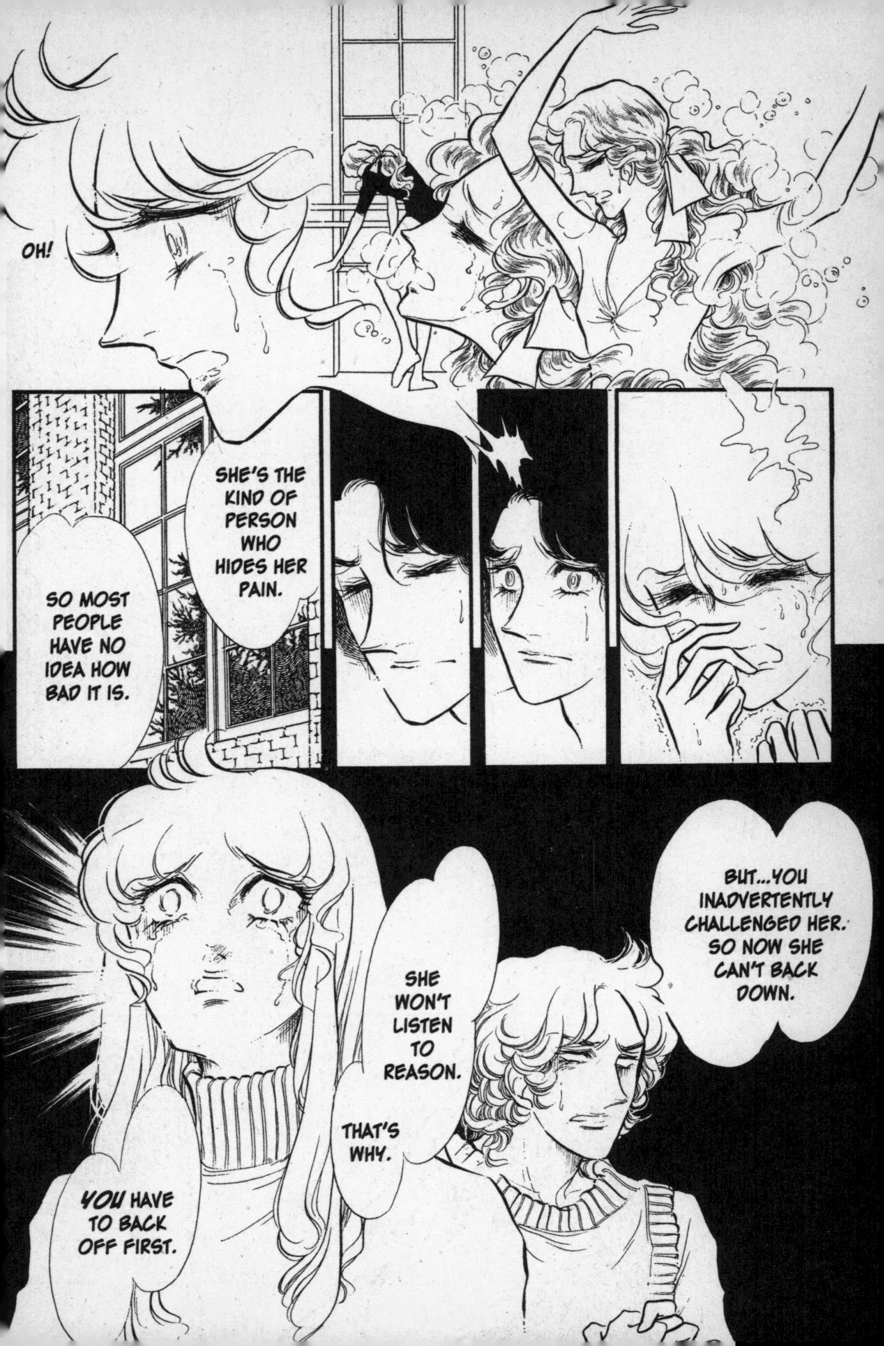
OH!
SHE'S THE KIND OF PERSON WHO HIDES HER PAIN.
SO MOST PEOPLE HAVE NO IDEA HOW BAD IT IS.
BUT...YOU INADVERTENTLY CHALLENGED HER. SO NOW SHE CAN'T BACK DOWN.
SHE WON'T LISTEN TO REASON.
THAT'S WHY.
YOU HAVE TO BACK OFF FIRST.

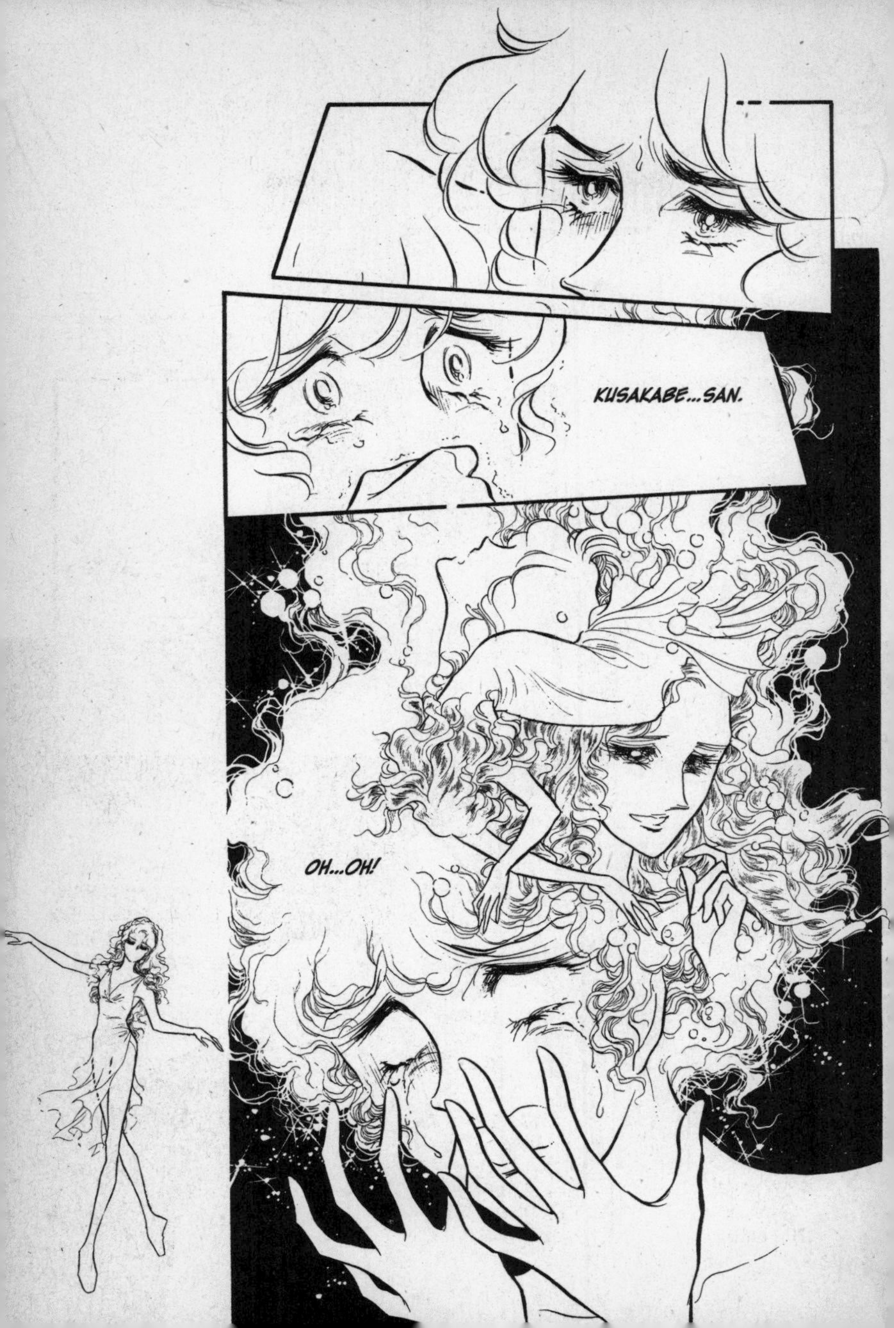
KUSAKABE...SAN.
OH...OH!

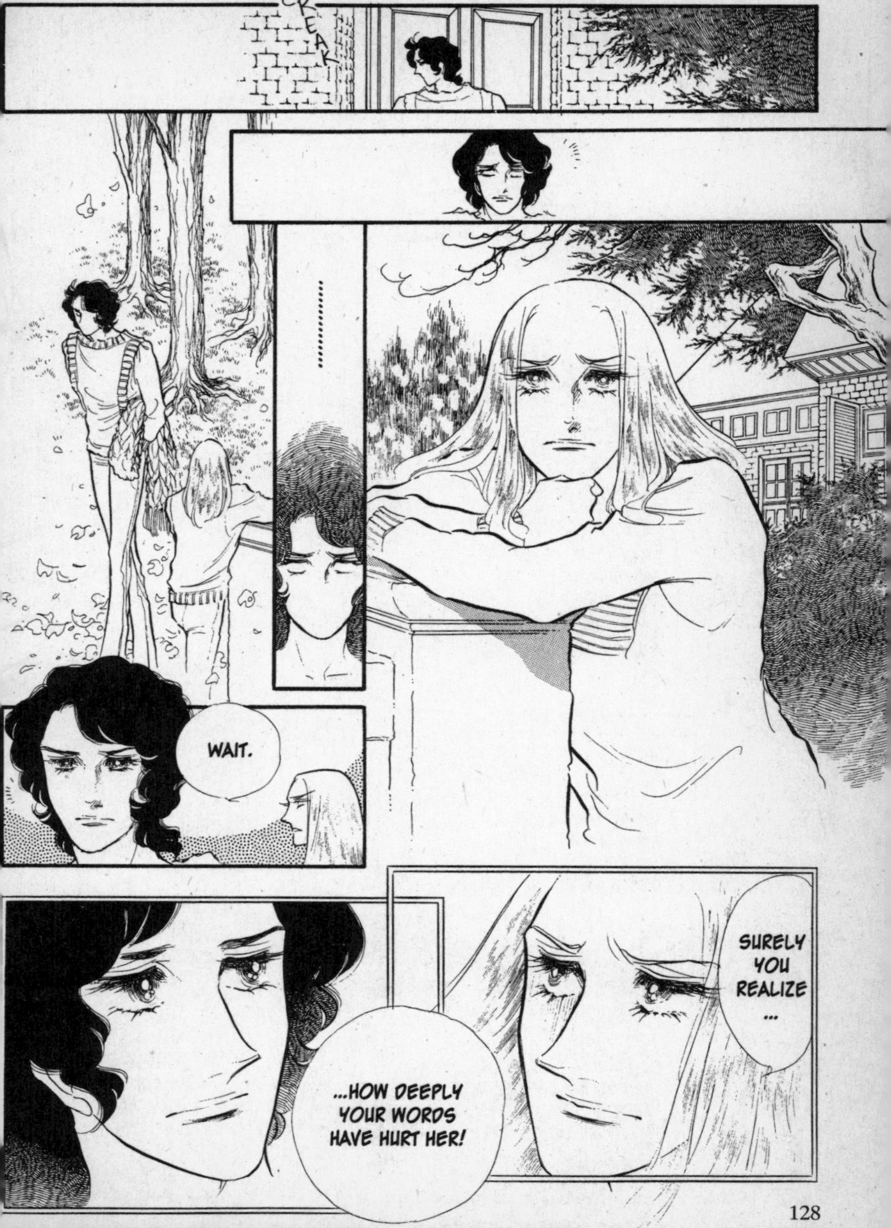
CREAK
......
WAIT.
SURELY YOU REALIZE ...
...HOW DEEPLY YOUR WORDS HAVE HURT HER!

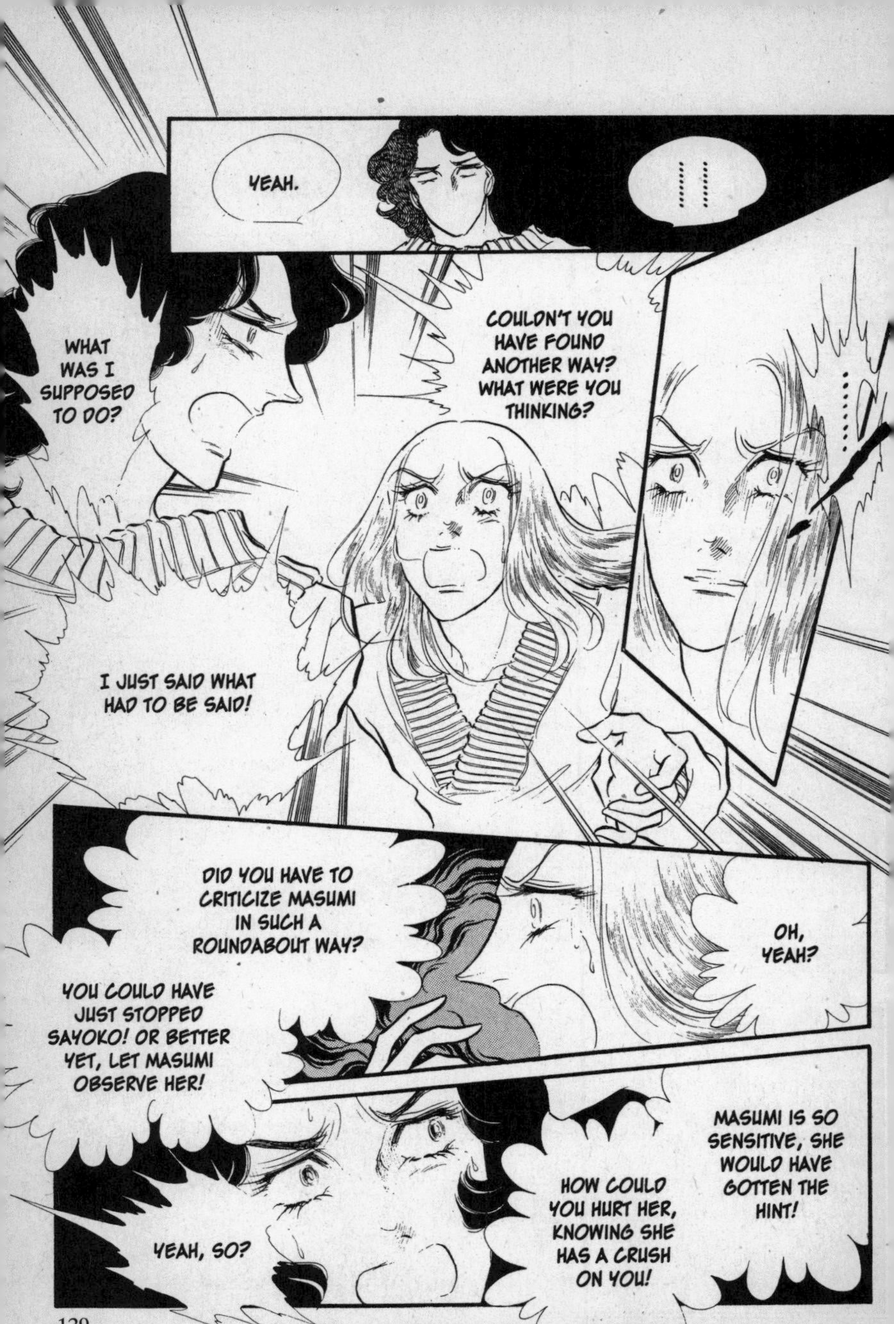

......
YEAH.
......
COULDN'T YOU HAVE FOUND ANOTHER WAY? WHAT WERE YOU THINKING?
WHAT WAS I SUPPOSED TO DO?
I JUST SAID WHAT HAD TO BE SAID!
OH, YEAH?
DID YOU HAVE TO CRITICIZE MASUMI IN SUCH A ROUNDABOUT WAY?
YOU COULD HAVE JUST STOPPED SAYOKO! OR BETTER YET, LET MASUMI OBSERVE HER!
MASUMI IS SO SENSITIVE, SHE WOULD HAVE GOTTEN THE HINT!
HOW COULD YOU HURT HER, KNOWING SHE HAS A CRUSH ON YOU!
YEAH, SO?

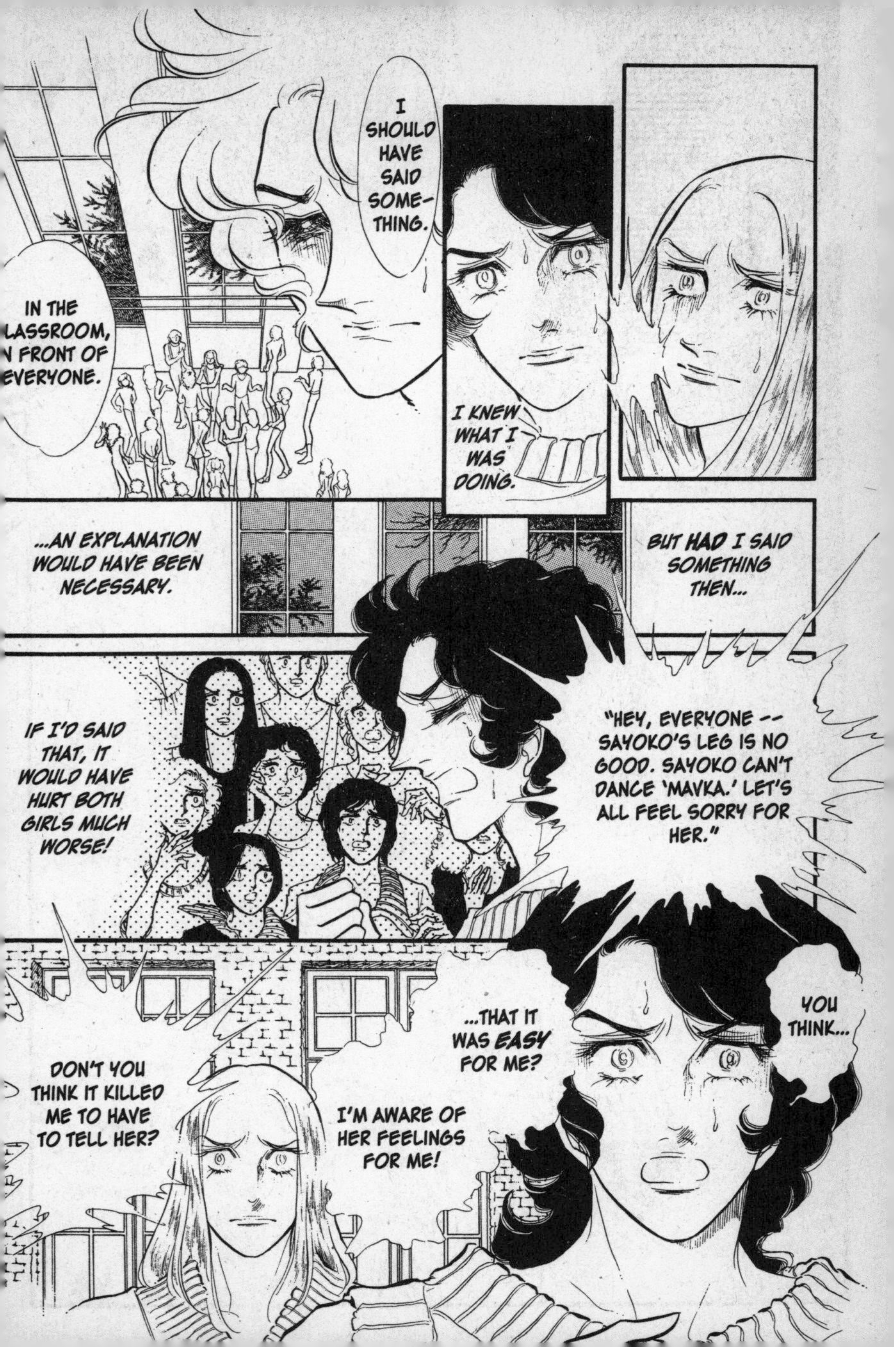
I KNEW WHAT I WAS DOING.
I SHOULD HAVE SAID SOME-THING.
IN THE LASSROOM, N FRONT OF EVERYONE.
BUT HAD I SAID SOMETHING THEN...
...AN EXPLANATION WOULD HAVE BEEN NECESSARY.
"HEY, EVERYONE -- SAYOKO'S LEG IS NO GOOD. SAYOKO CAN'T DANCE 'MAVKA.' LET'S ALL FEEL SORRY FOR HER."
IF I'D SAID THAT, IT WOULD HAVE HURT BOTH GIRLS MUCH WORSE!
YOU THINK...
...THAT IT WAS *EASY* FOR ME?
I'M AWARE OF HER FEELINGS FOR ME!
DON'T YOU THINK IT KILLED ME TO HAVE TO TELL HER?

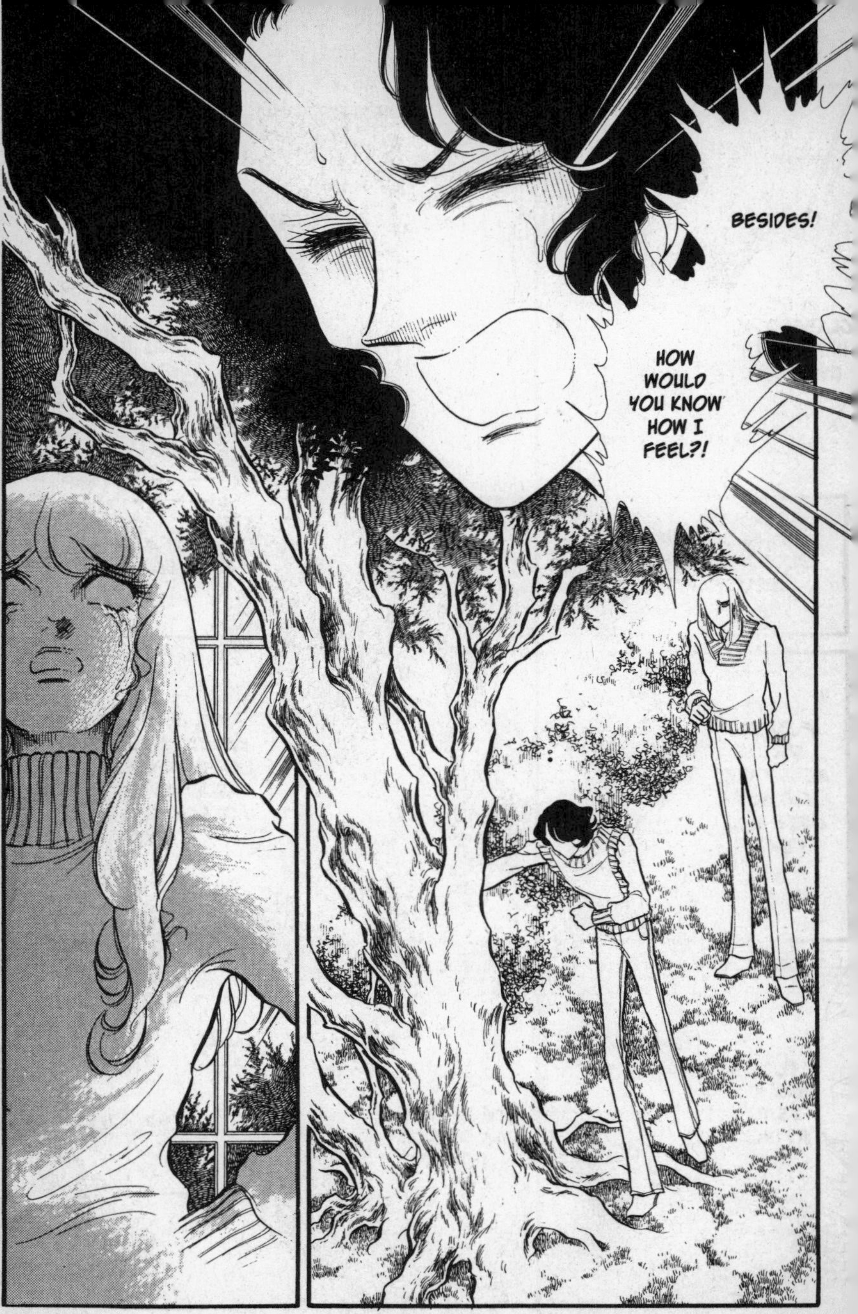
BESIDES!
HOW WOULD YOU KNOW HOW I FEEL?!

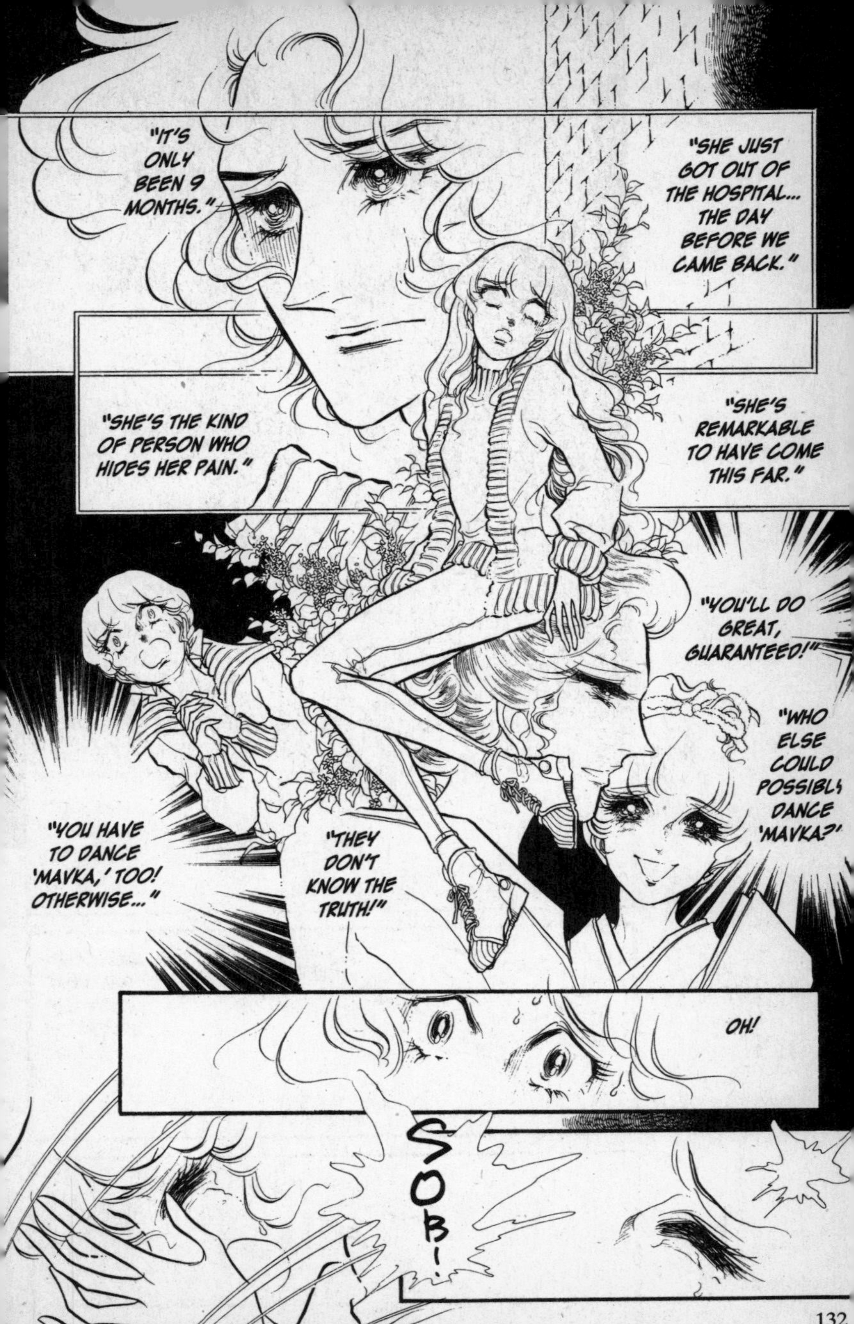
"SHE JUST GOT OUT OF THE HOSPITAL... THE DAY BEFORE WE CAME BACK."
"IT'S ONLY BEEN 9 MONTHS."
"SHE'S REMARKABLE TO HAVE COME THIS FAR."
"SHE'S THE KIND OF PERSON WHO HIDES HER PAIN."
"YOU'LL DO GREAT, GUARANTEED!"
"WHO ELSE COULD POSSIBLY DANCE 'MAVKA?'"
"THEY DON'T KNOW THE TRUTH!"
"YOU HAVE TO DANCE 'MAVKA,' TOO! OTHERWISE..."
OH!
SOB!

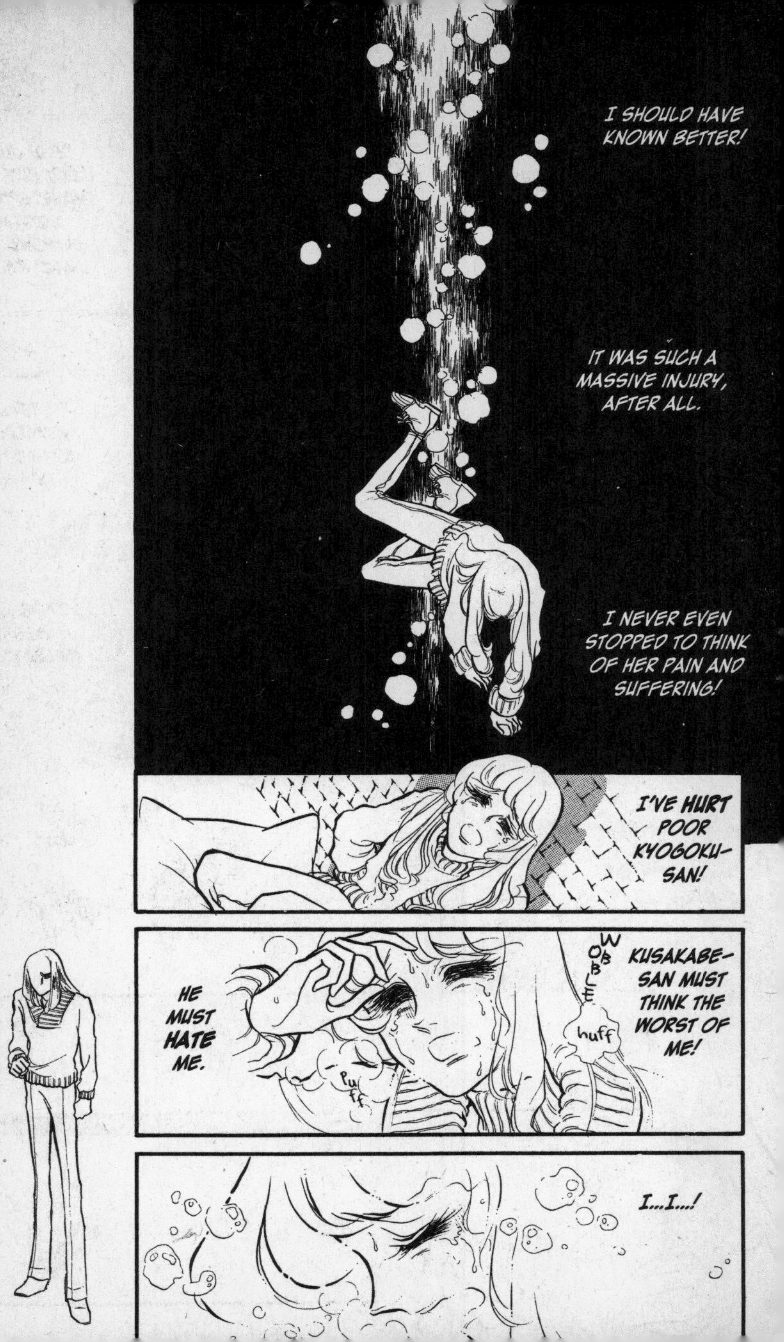
I SHOULD HAVE KNOWN BETTER!
IT WAS SUCH A MASSIVE INJURY, AFTER ALL.
I NEVER EVEN STOPPED TO THINK OF HER PAIN AND SUFFERING!
I'VE HURT POOR KYOGOKU-SAN!
KUSAKABE-SAN MUST THINK THE WORST OF ME!
WOBBLE
huff
HE MUST HATE ME.
Puff
I...I...!

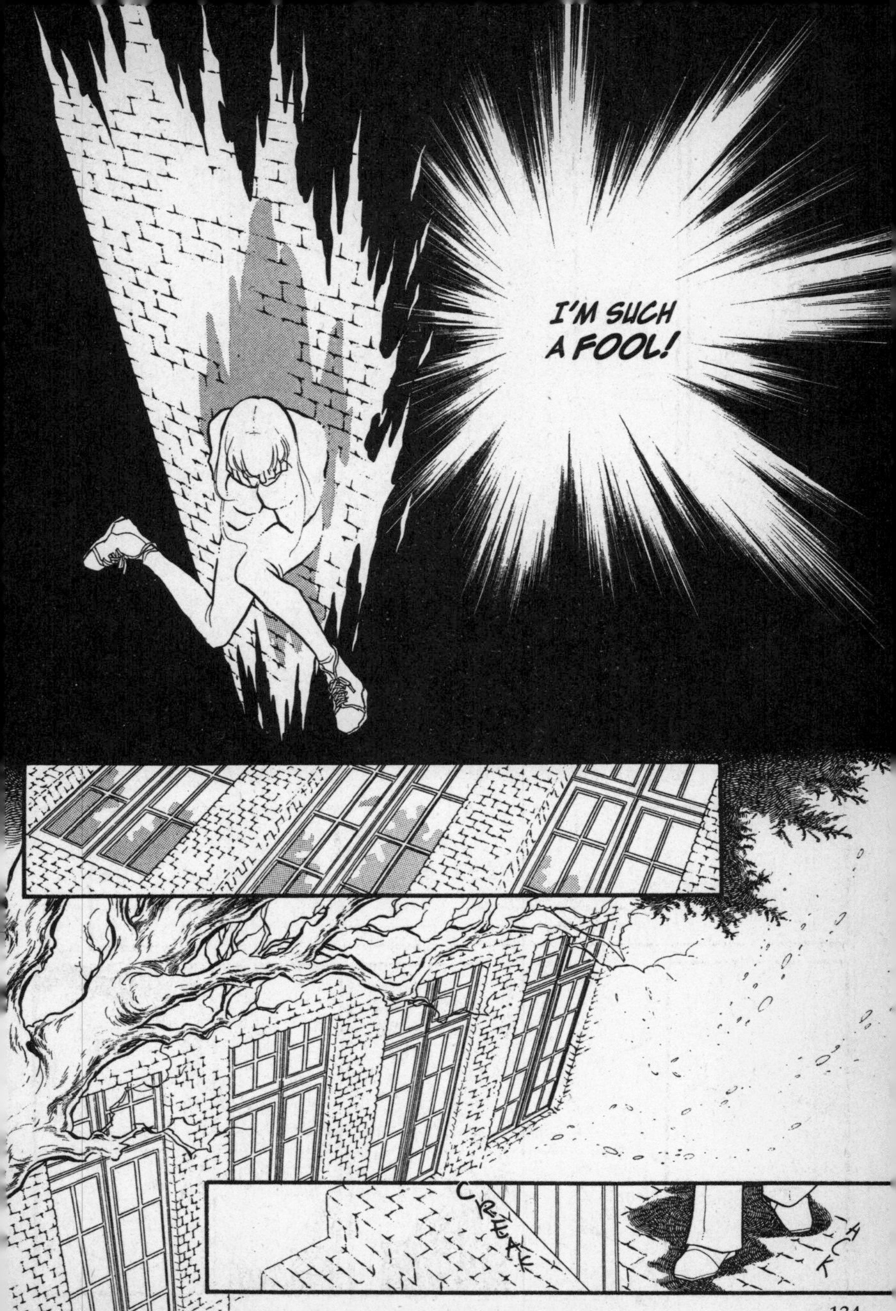
I'M SUCH A FOOL!
CREAK
HUCK

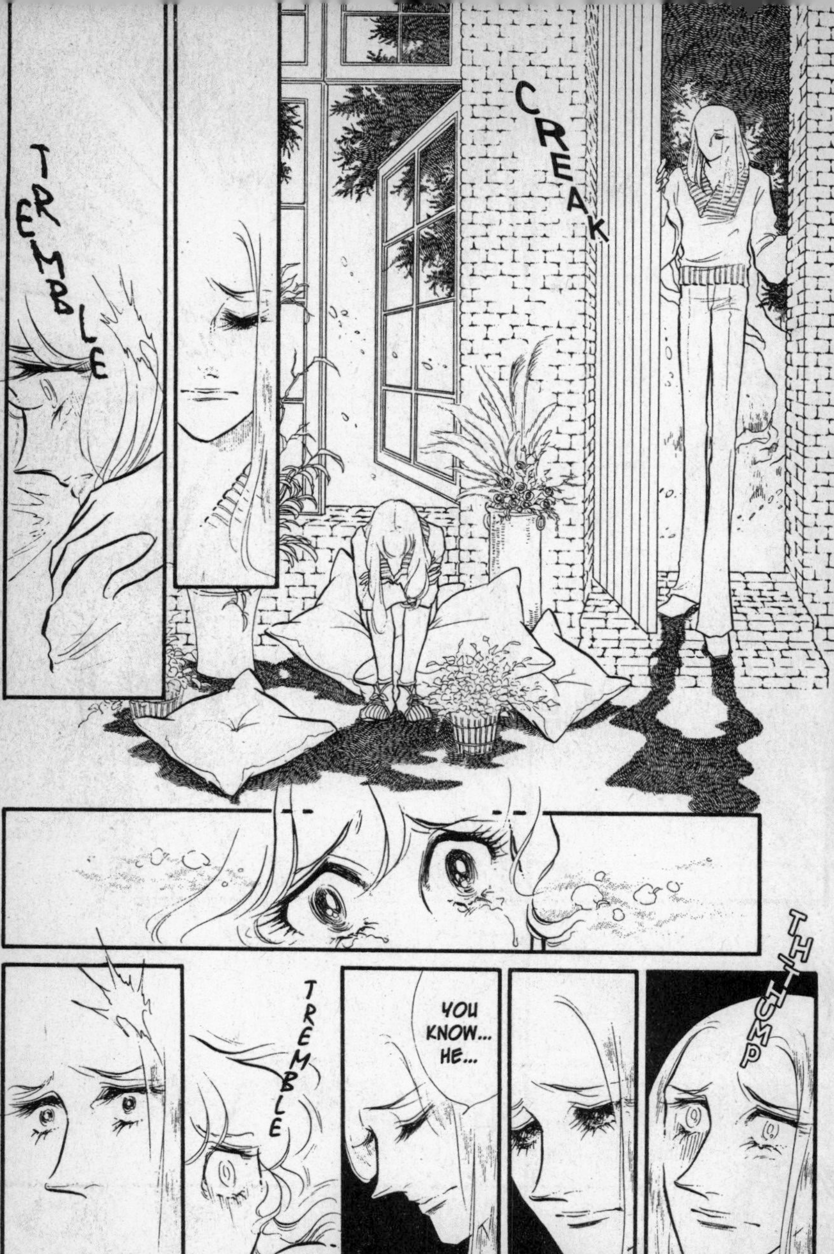
CREAK
TREMBLE
THTHUMP
YOU KNOW... HE...
TREMBLE

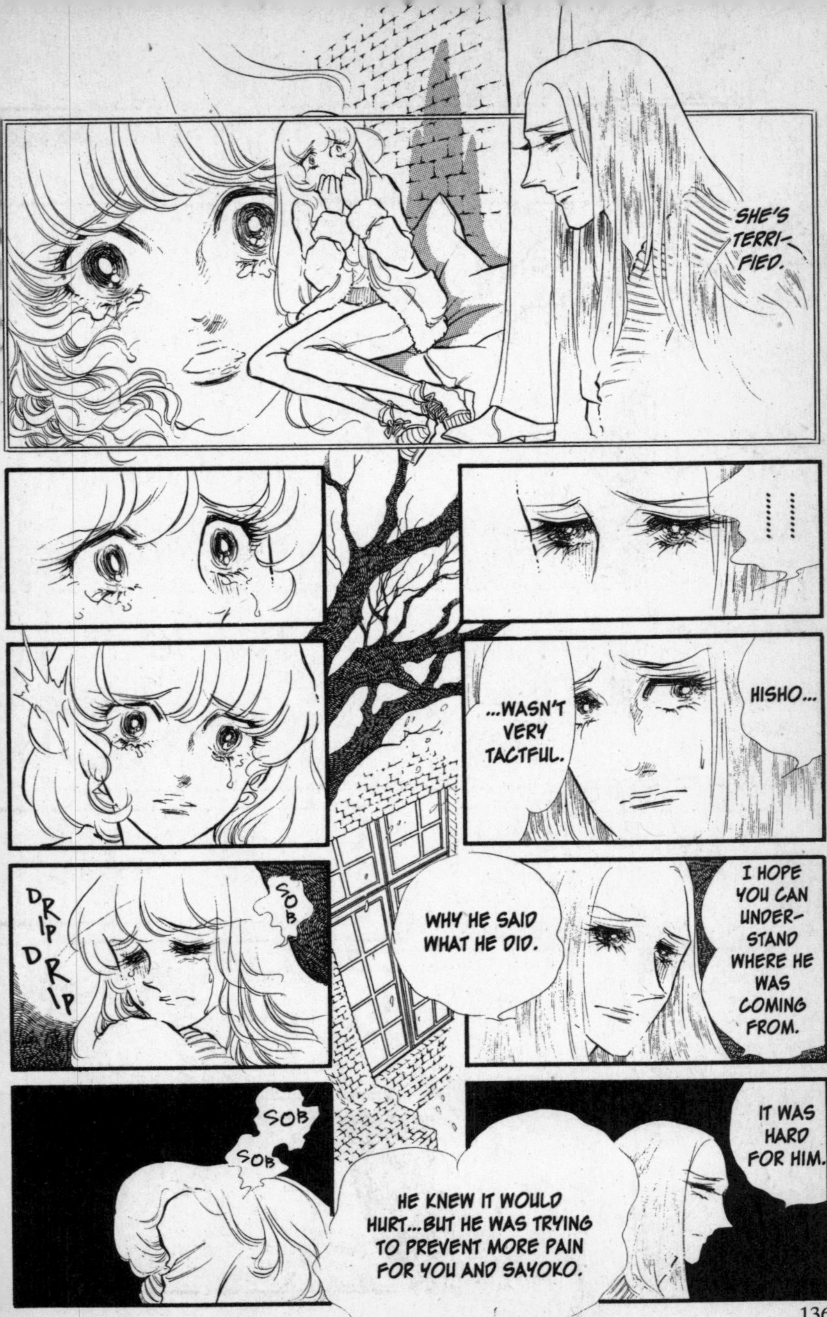
SHE'S TERRI-FIED.
......
HISHO...
...WASN'T VERY TACTFUL.
I HOPE YOU CAN UNDER-STAND WHERE HE WAS COMING FROM.
WHY HE SAID WHAT HE DID.
SOB
DRIP DRIP
IT WAS HARD FOR HIM.
HE KNEW IT WOULD HURT...BUT HE WAS TRYING TO PREVENT MORE PAIN FOR YOU AND SAYOKO.
SOB
SOB

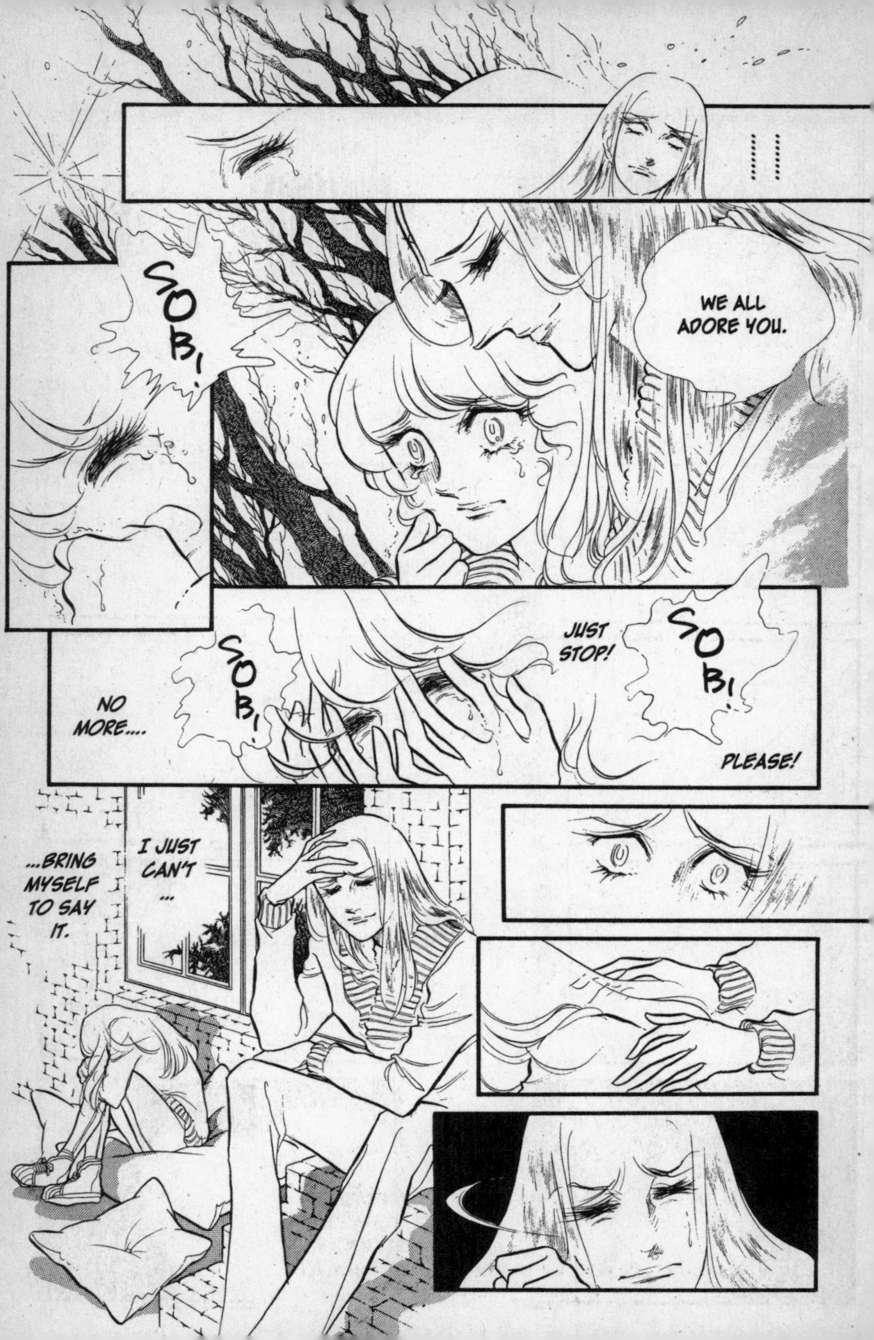

WE ALL ADORE YOU.
SOB!
SOB!
JUST STOP!
PLEASE!
SOB!
NO MORE....
I JUST CAN'T ...
...BRING MYSELF TO SAY IT.

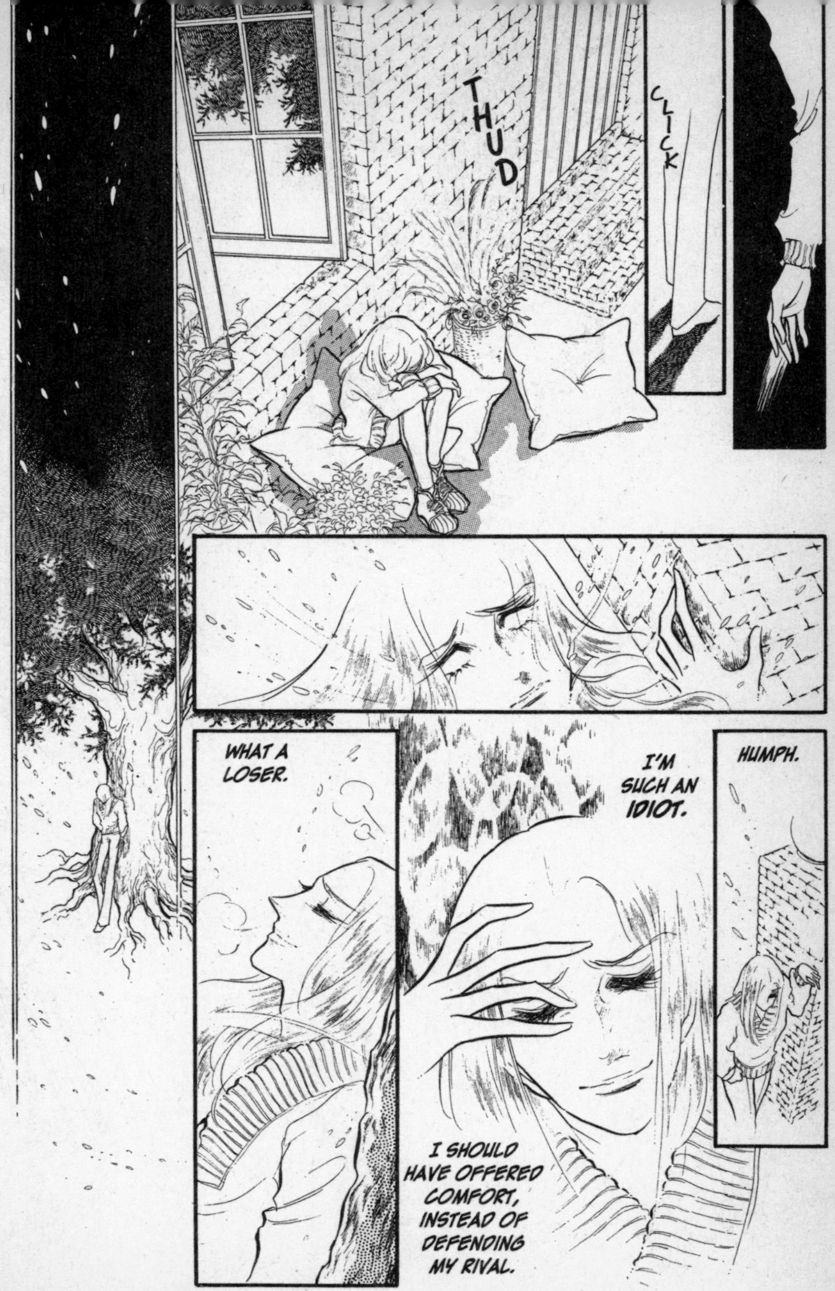
CLICK
THUD
HUMPH.
I'M SUCH AN IDIOT.
I SHOULD HAVE OFFERED COMFORT, INSTEAD OF DEFENDING MY RIVAL.
WHAT A LOSER.

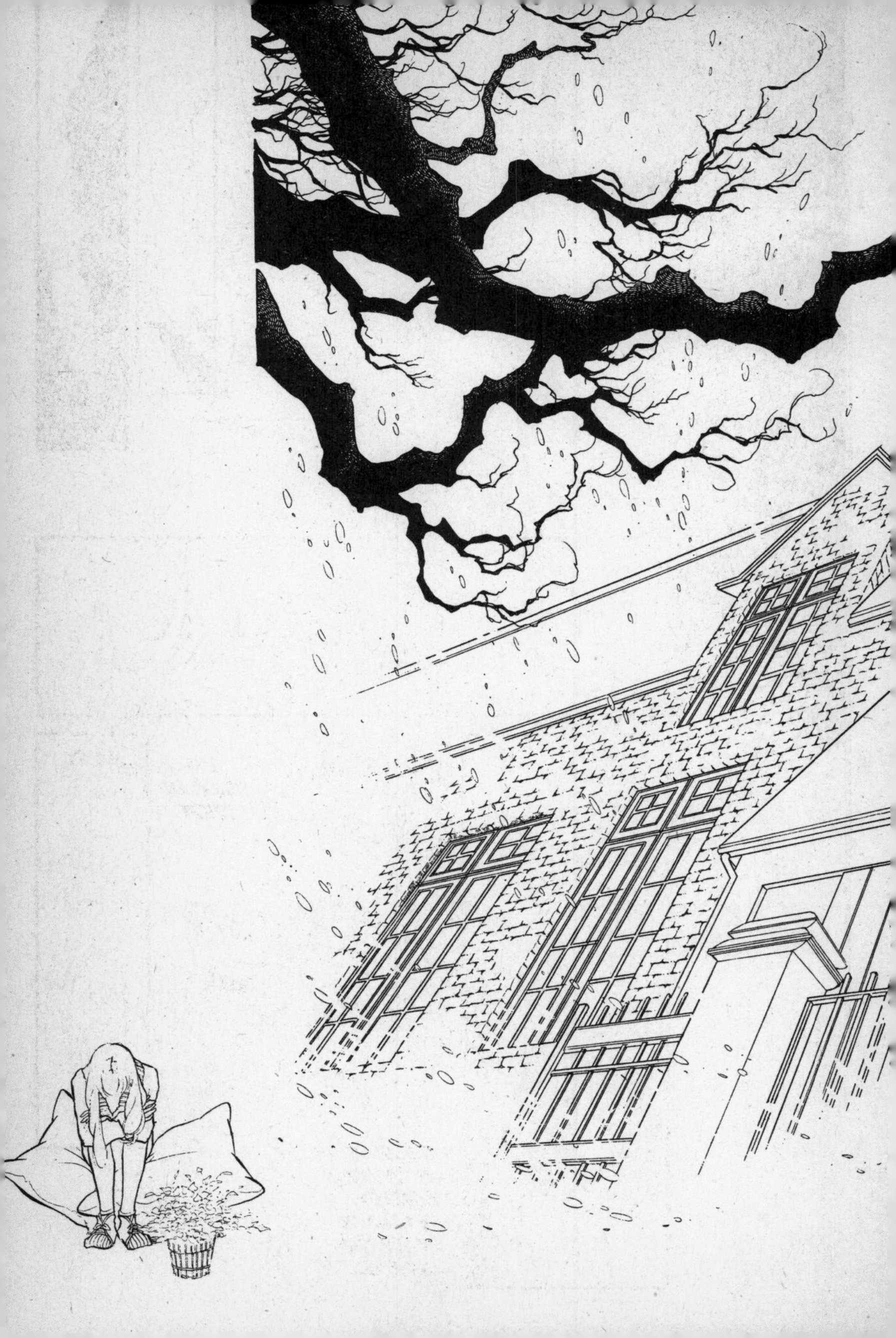

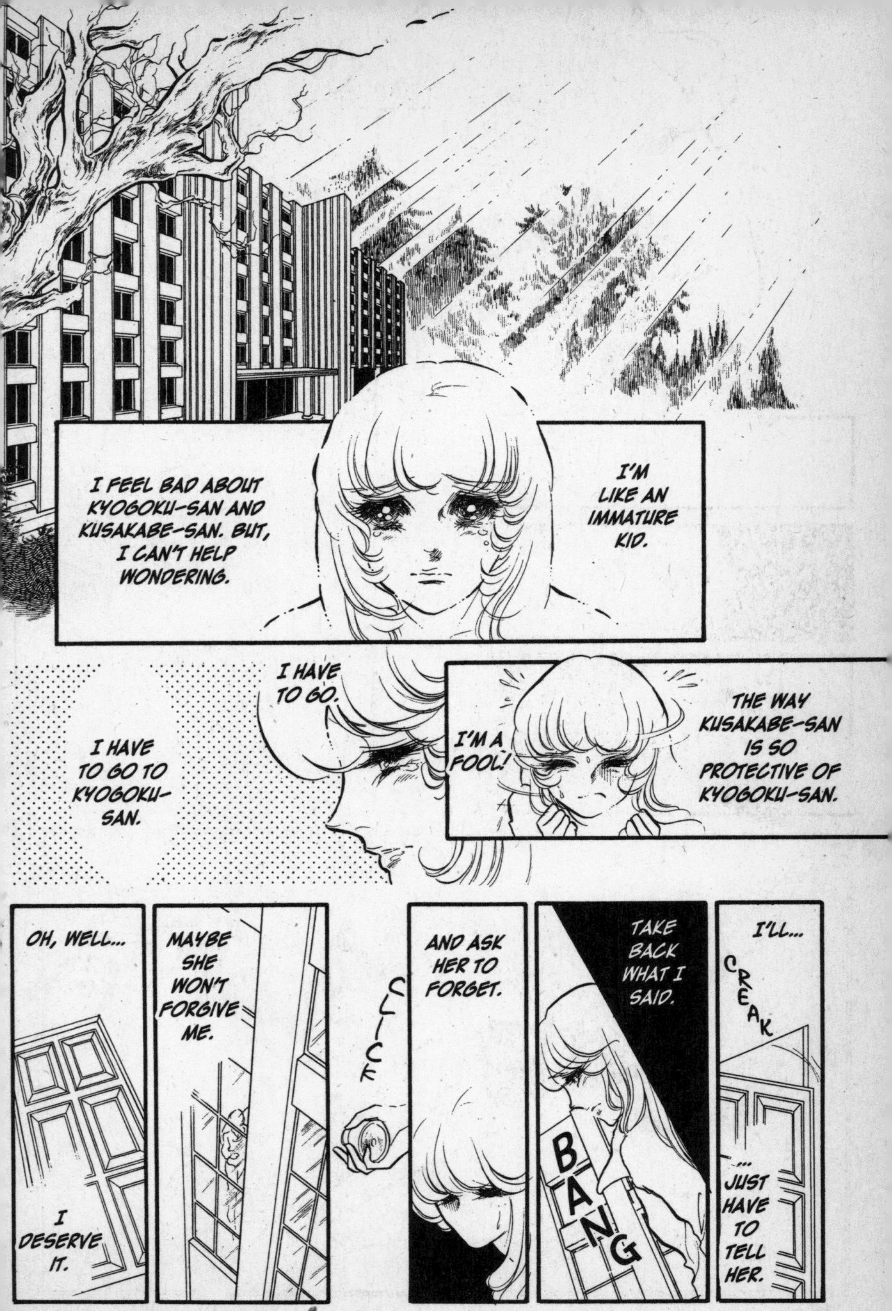
I'M LIKE AN IMMATURE KID.
I FEEL BAD ABOUT KYOGOKU-SAN AND KUSAKABE-SAN. BUT, I CAN'T HELP WONDERING.
THE WAY KUSAKABE-SAN IS SO PROTECTIVE OF KYOGOKU-SAN.
I'M A FOOL!
I HAVE TO GO.
I HAVE TO GO TO KYOGOKU-SAN.
I'LL...
CREAK
...JUST HAVE TO TELL HER.
TAKE BACK WHAT I SAID.
BANG
AND ASK HER TO FORGET.
CLICK
MAYBE SHE WON'T FORGIVE ME.
OH, WELL...
I DESERVE IT.

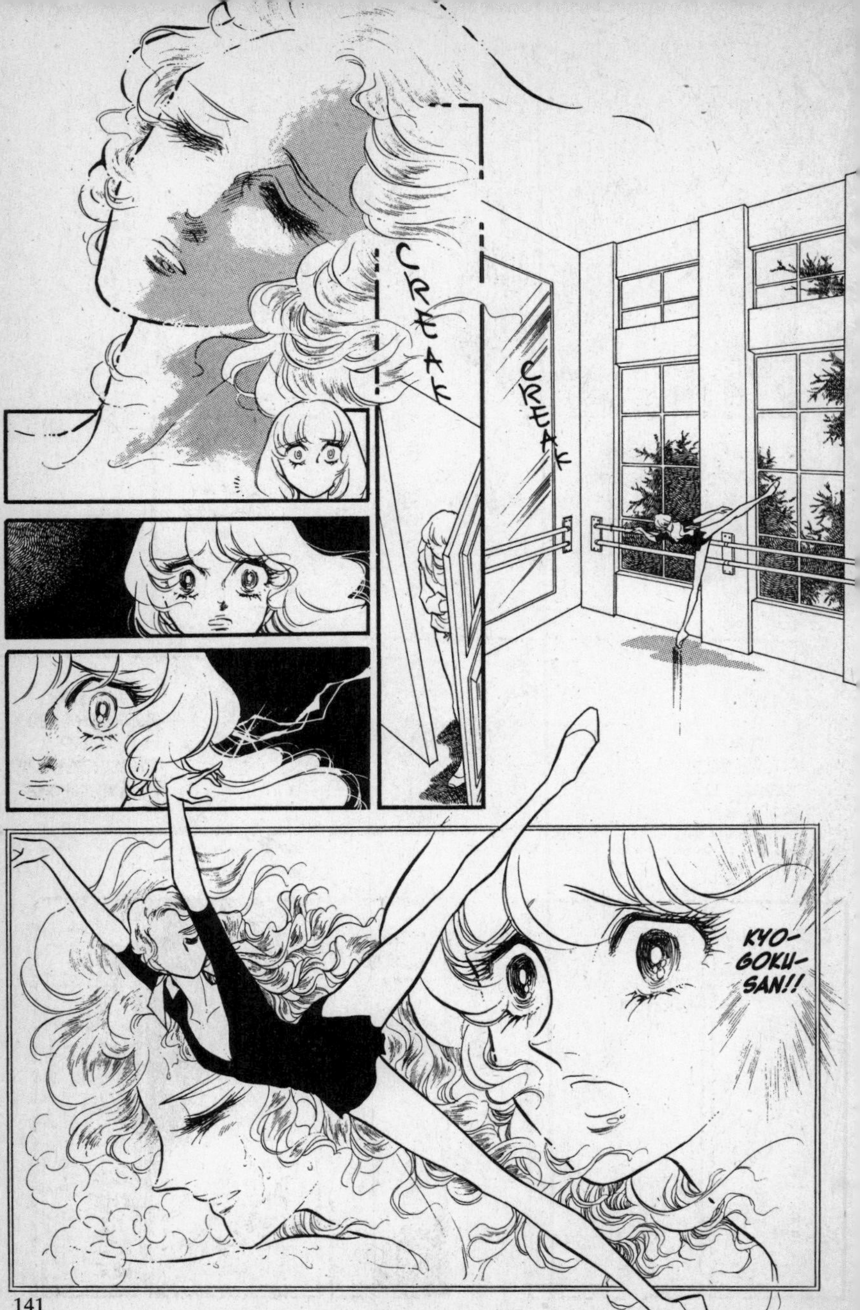
CREAK
CREAK
KYO-GOKU-SAN!!

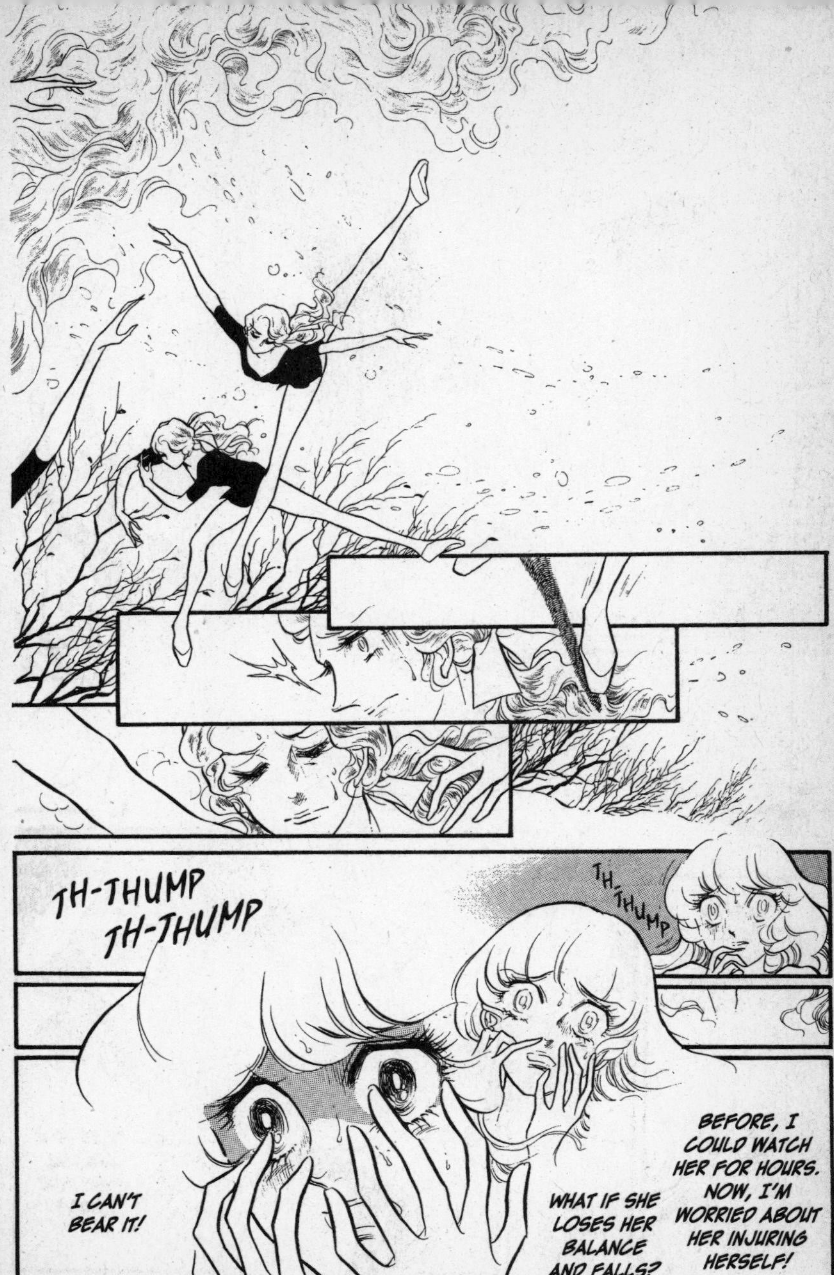
TH-THUMP
TH-THUMP
TH-THUMP
BEFORE, I COULD WATCH HER FOR HOURS. NOW, I'M WORRIED ABOUT HER INJURING HERSELF!
WHAT IF SHE LOSES HER BALANCE AND FALLS?
I CAN'T BEAR IT!

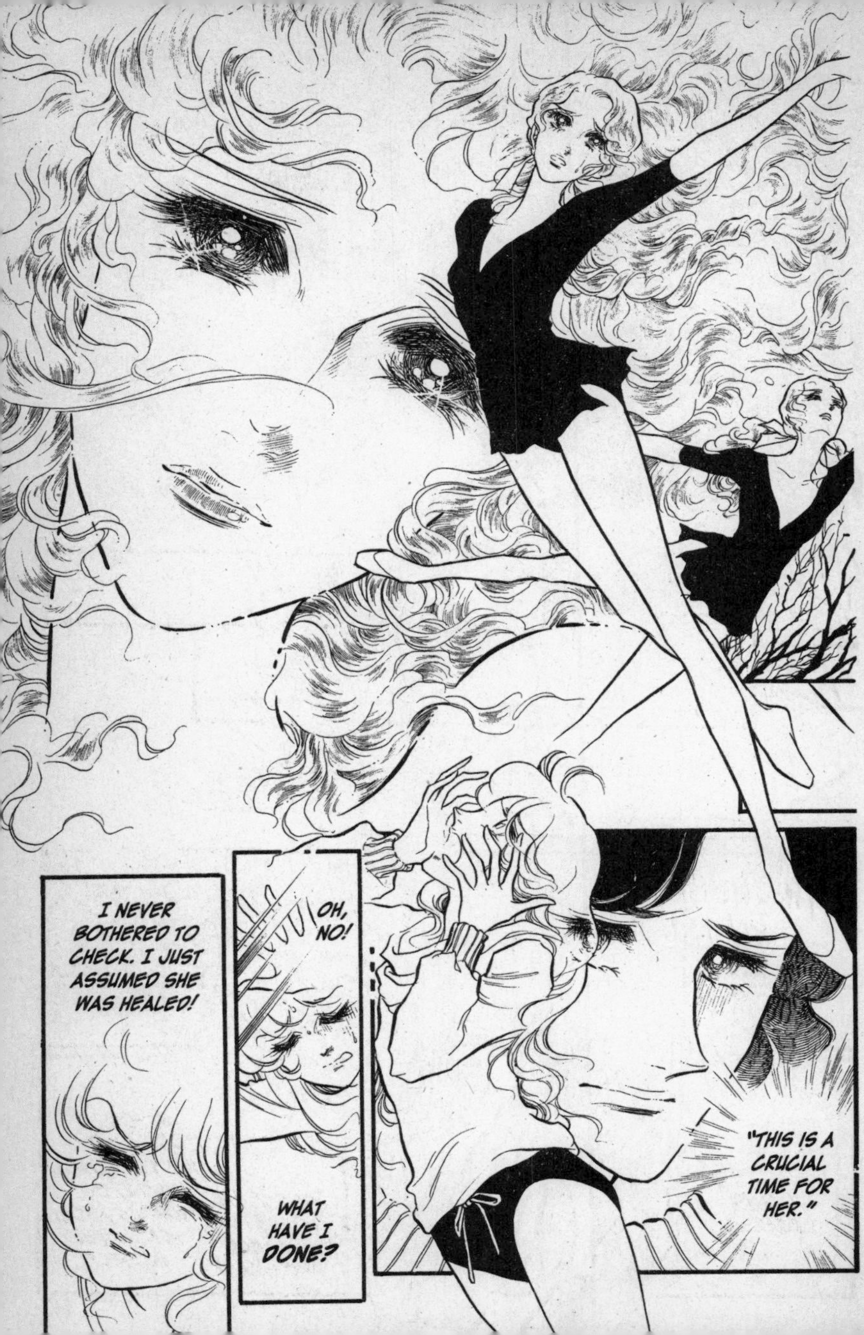
"THIS IS A CRUCIAL TIME FOR HER."
OH, NO!
WHAT HAVE I DONE?
I NEVER BOTHERED TO CHECK. I JUST ASSUMED SHE WAS HEALED!

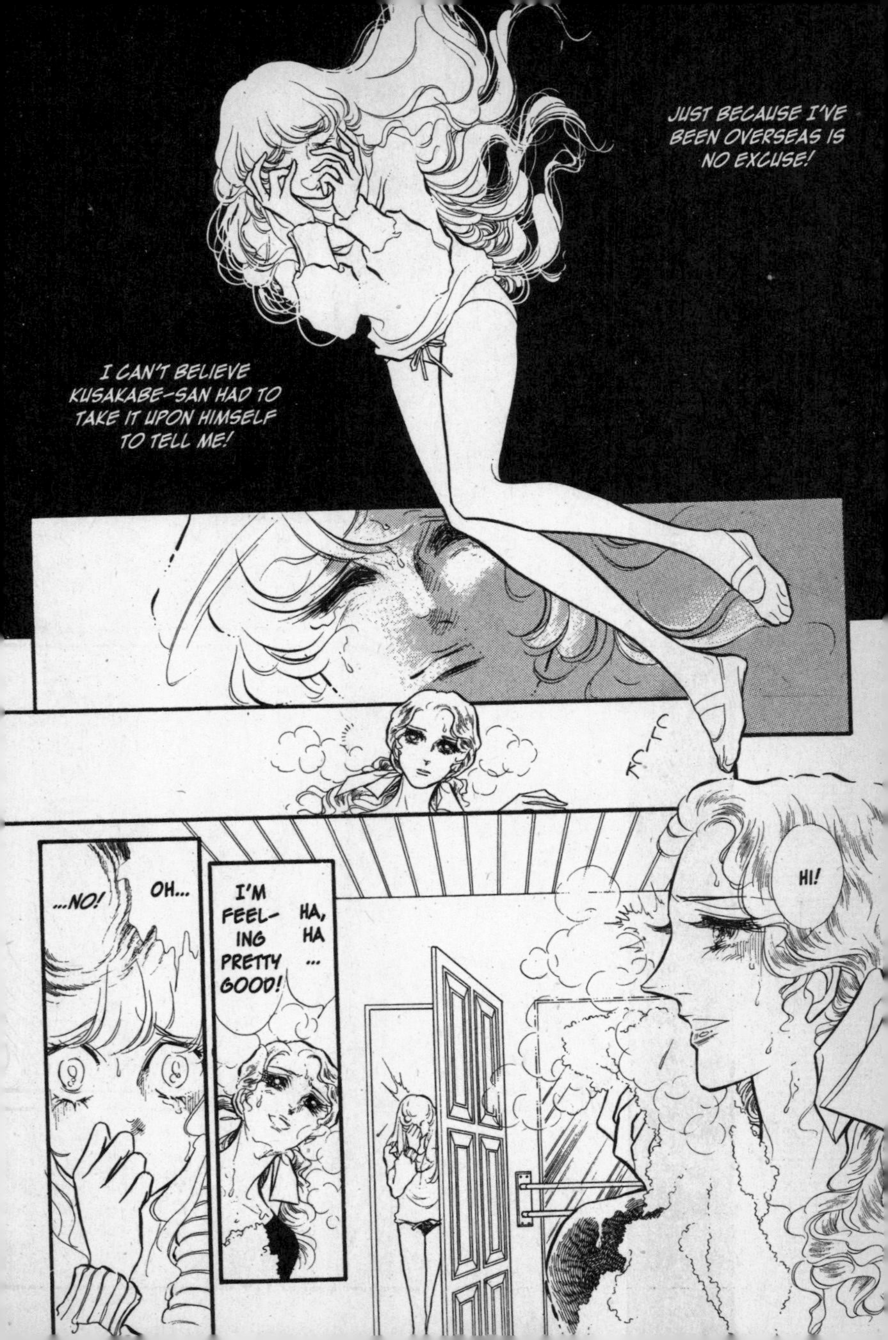
JUST BECAUSE I'VE BEEN OVERSEAS IS NO EXCUSE!
I CAN'T BELIEVE KUSAKABE-SAN HAD TO TAKE IT UPON HIMSELF TO TELL ME!
HI!
HA, HA ...
I'M FEELING PRETTY GOOD!
OH...
...NO!

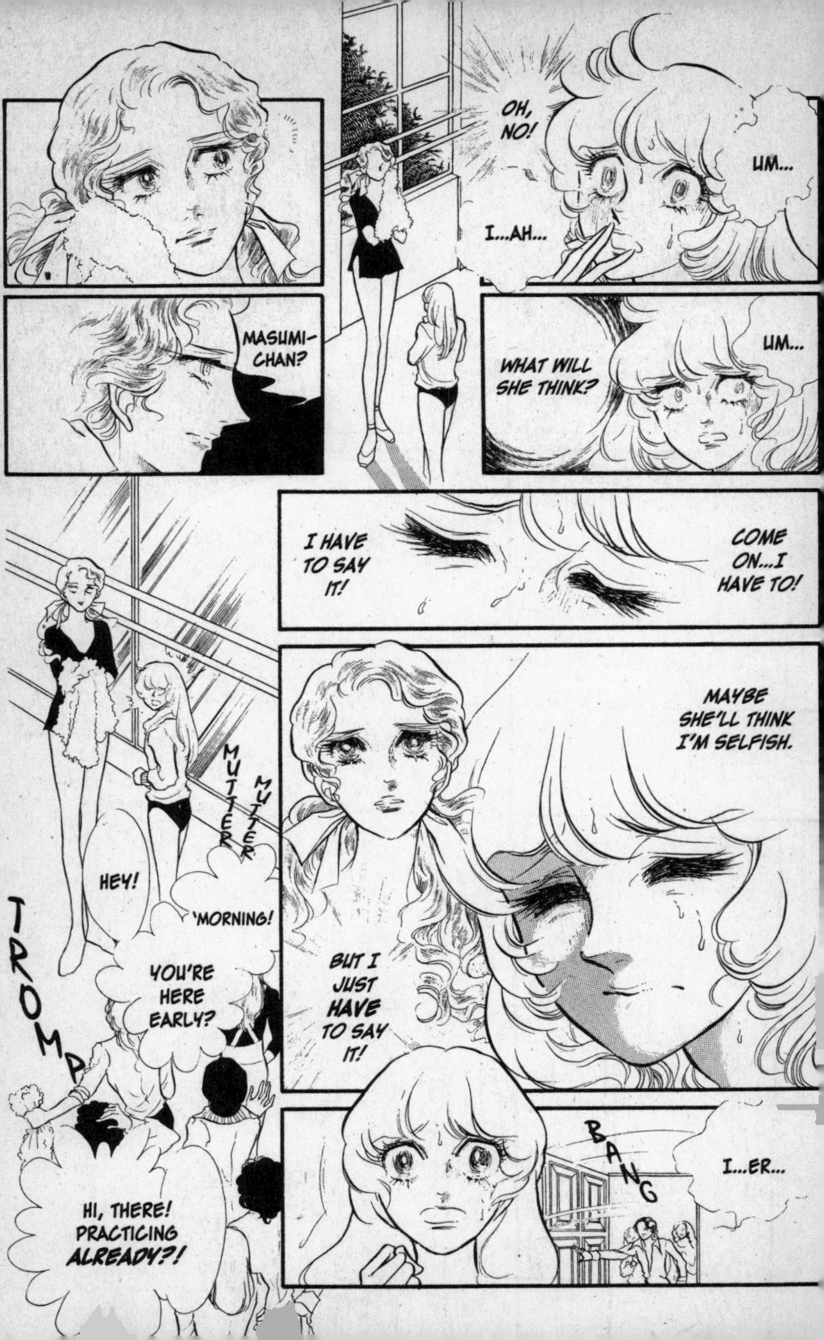

OH, NO!
UM...
I...AH...
UM...
WHAT WILL SHE THINK?
MASUMI-CHAN?
COME ON...I HAVE TO!
I HAVE TO SAY IT!
MAYBE SHE'LL THINK I'M SELFISH.
BUT I JUST HAVE TO SAY IT!
I...ER...
BANG
MUTTER MUTTER
'MORNING!
HEY!
YOU'RE HERE EARLY?
TROMP
HI, THERE! PRACTICING ALREADY?!

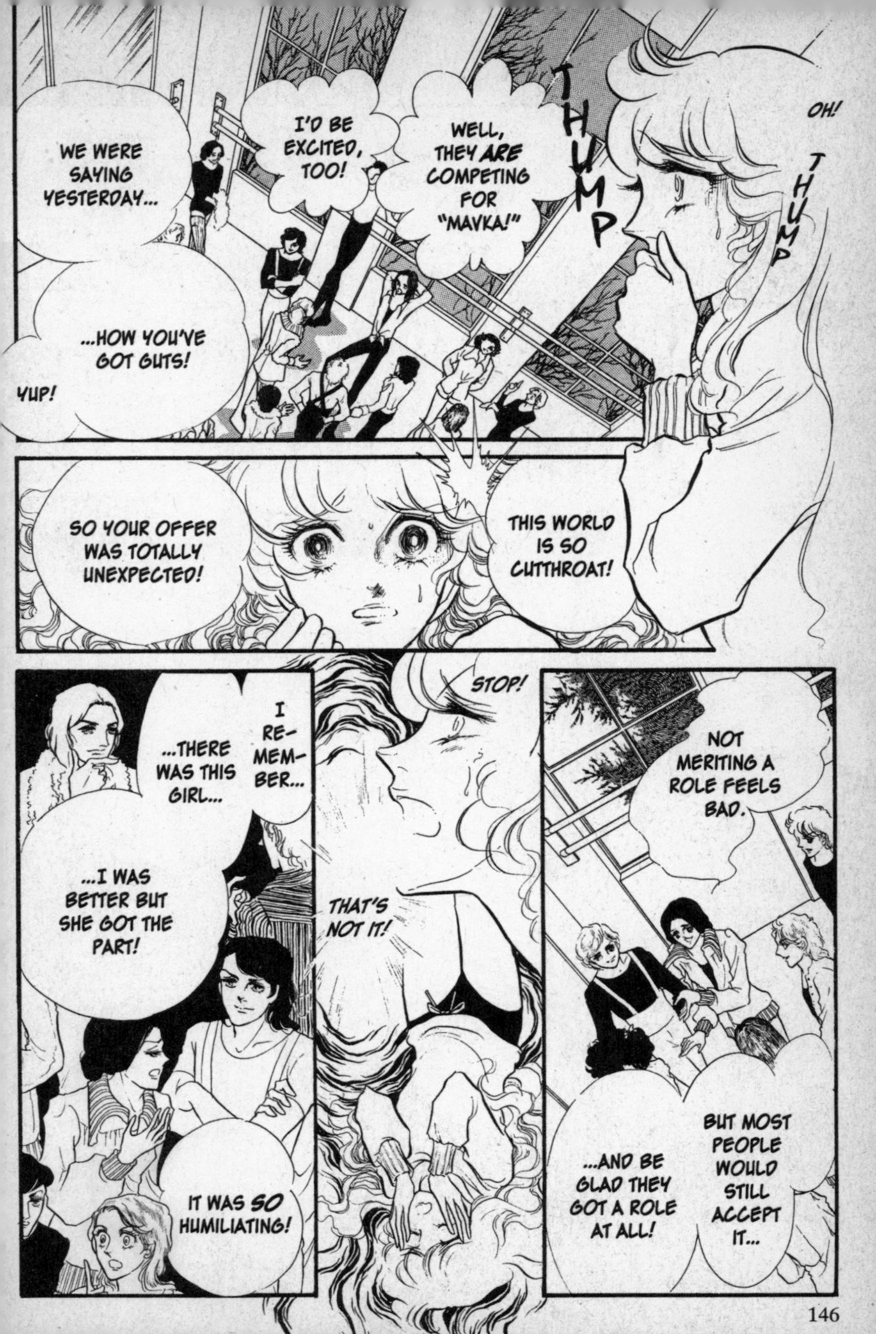
OH!
THUMP
THUMP
WELL, THEY ARE COMPETING FOR "MAVKA!"
I'D BE EXCITED, TOO!
WE WERE SAYING YESTERDAY...
...HOW YOU'VE GOT GUTS!
YUP!
THIS WORLD IS SO CUTTHROAT!
SO YOUR OFFER WAS TOTALLY UNEXPECTED!
NOT MERITING A ROLE FEELS BAD.
BUT MOST PEOPLE WOULD STILL ACCEPT IT...
...AND BE GLAD THEY GOT A ROLE AT ALL!
STOP!
THAT'S NOT IT!
I RE-MEM-BER...
...THERE WAS THIS GIRL...
...I WAS BETTER BUT SHE GOT THE PART!
IT WAS SO HUMILIATING!

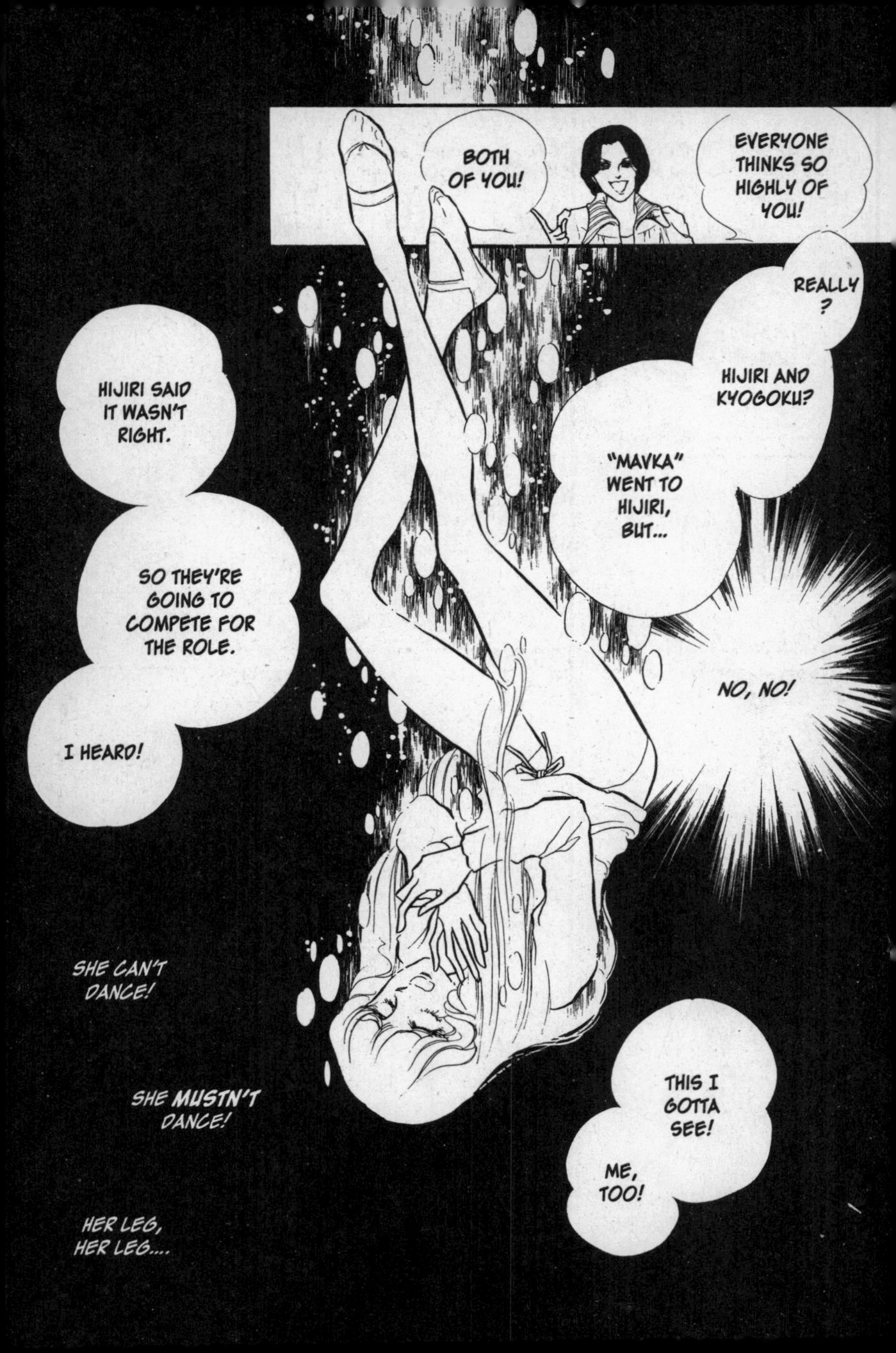
EVERYONE THINKS SO HIGHLY OF YOU!
BOTH OF YOU!
REALLY?
HIJIRI AND KYOGOKU?
"MAVKA" WENT TO HIJIRI, BUT...
HIJIRI SAID IT WASN'T RIGHT.
SO THEY'RE GOING TO COMPETE FOR THE ROLE.
I HEARD!
NO, NO!
THIS I GOTTA SEE!
ME, TOO!
SHE CAN'T DANCE!
SHE MUSTN'T DANCE!
HER LEG, HER LEG....

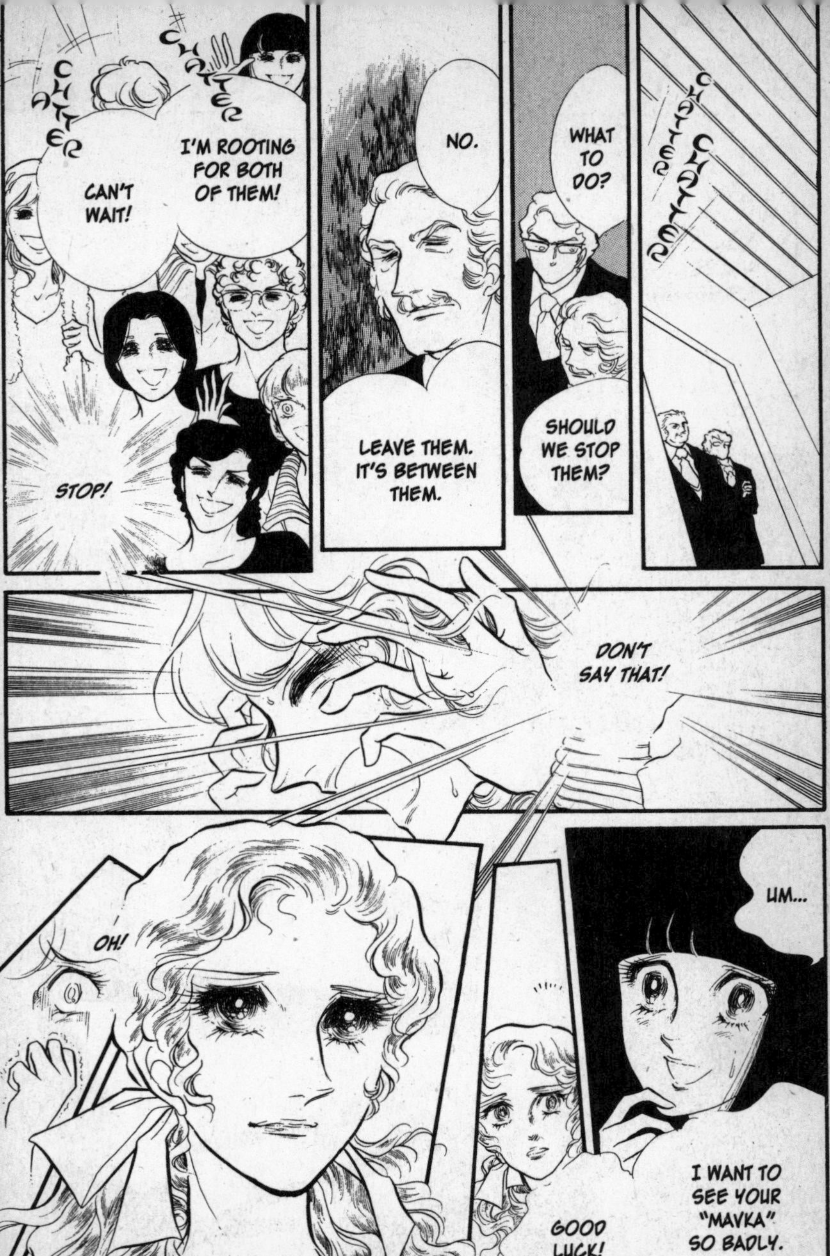
CHATTER
CHATTER
WHAT TO DO?
SHOULD WE STOP THEM?
NO.
LEAVE THEM. IT'S BETWEEN THEM.
CHATTER
I'M ROOTING FOR BOTH OF THEM!
CHATTER
CAN'T WAIT!
STOP!
DON'T SAY THAT!
UM...
I WANT TO SEE YOUR "MAVKA" SO BADLY.
GOOD LUCK!
OH!

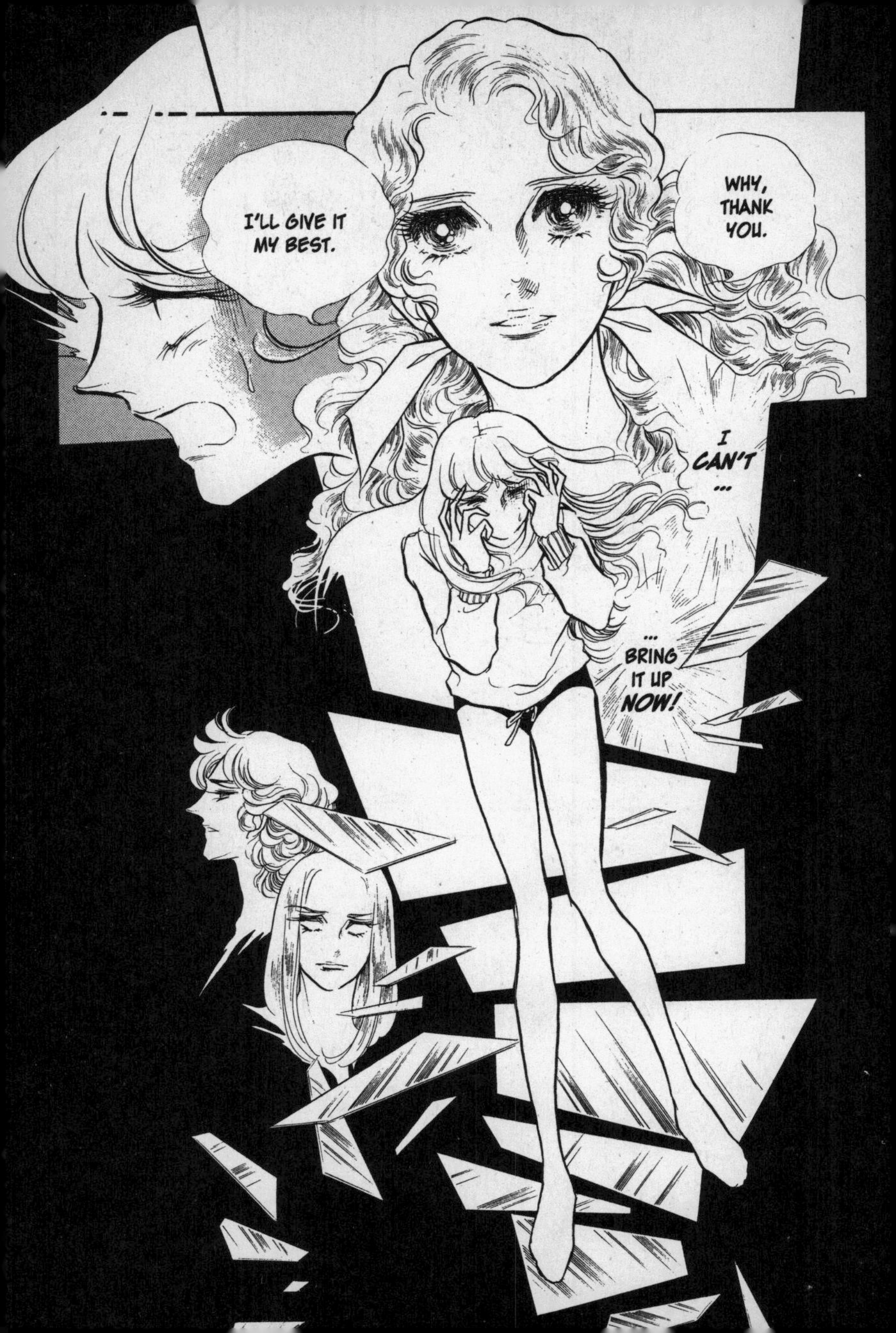
WHY, THANK YOU.
I'LL GIVE IT MY BEST.
I CAN'T ...
... BRING IT UP NOW!

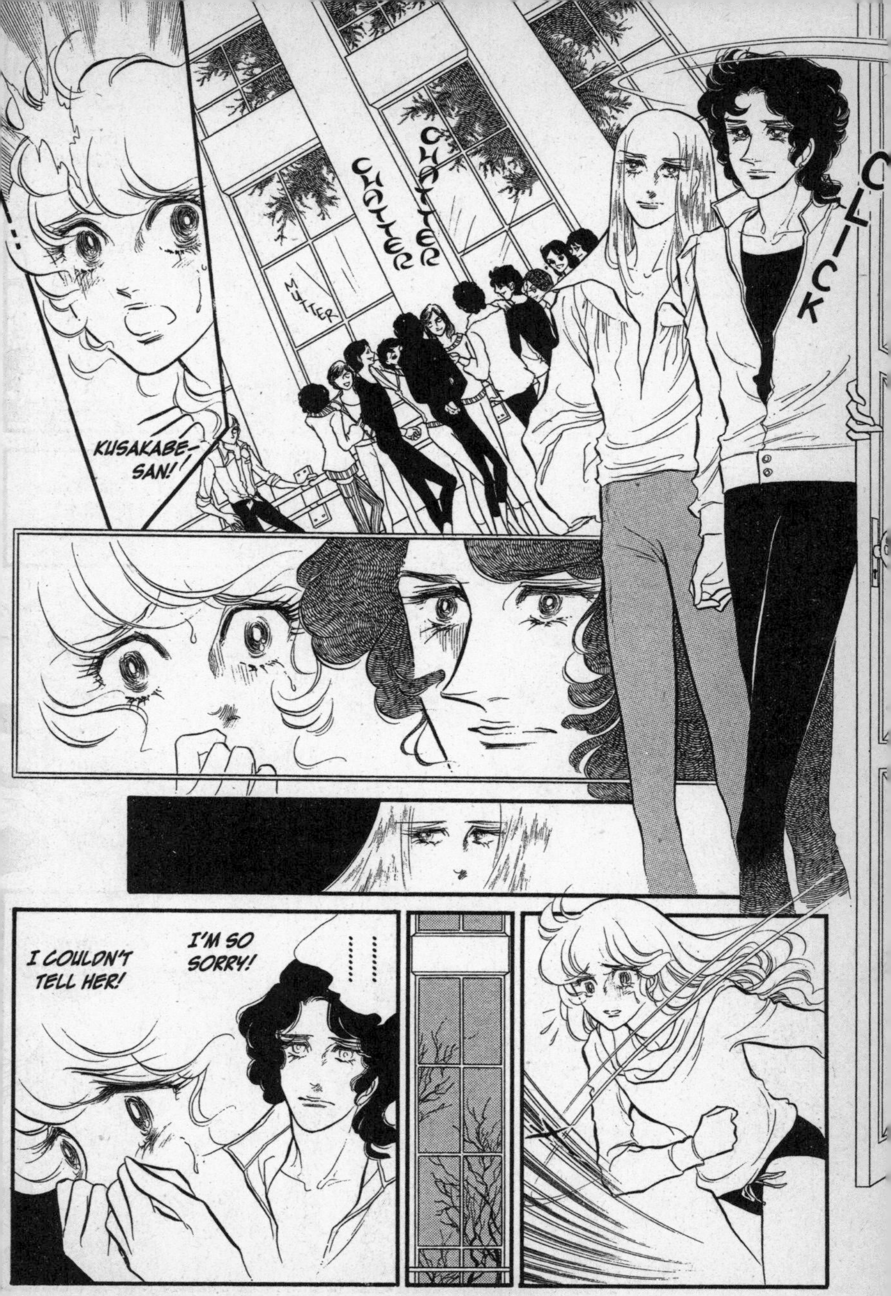
CLICK
CHATTER
CHATTER
MUTTER
KUSAKABE-SAN!
......
I'M SO SORRY!
I COULDN'T TELL HER!

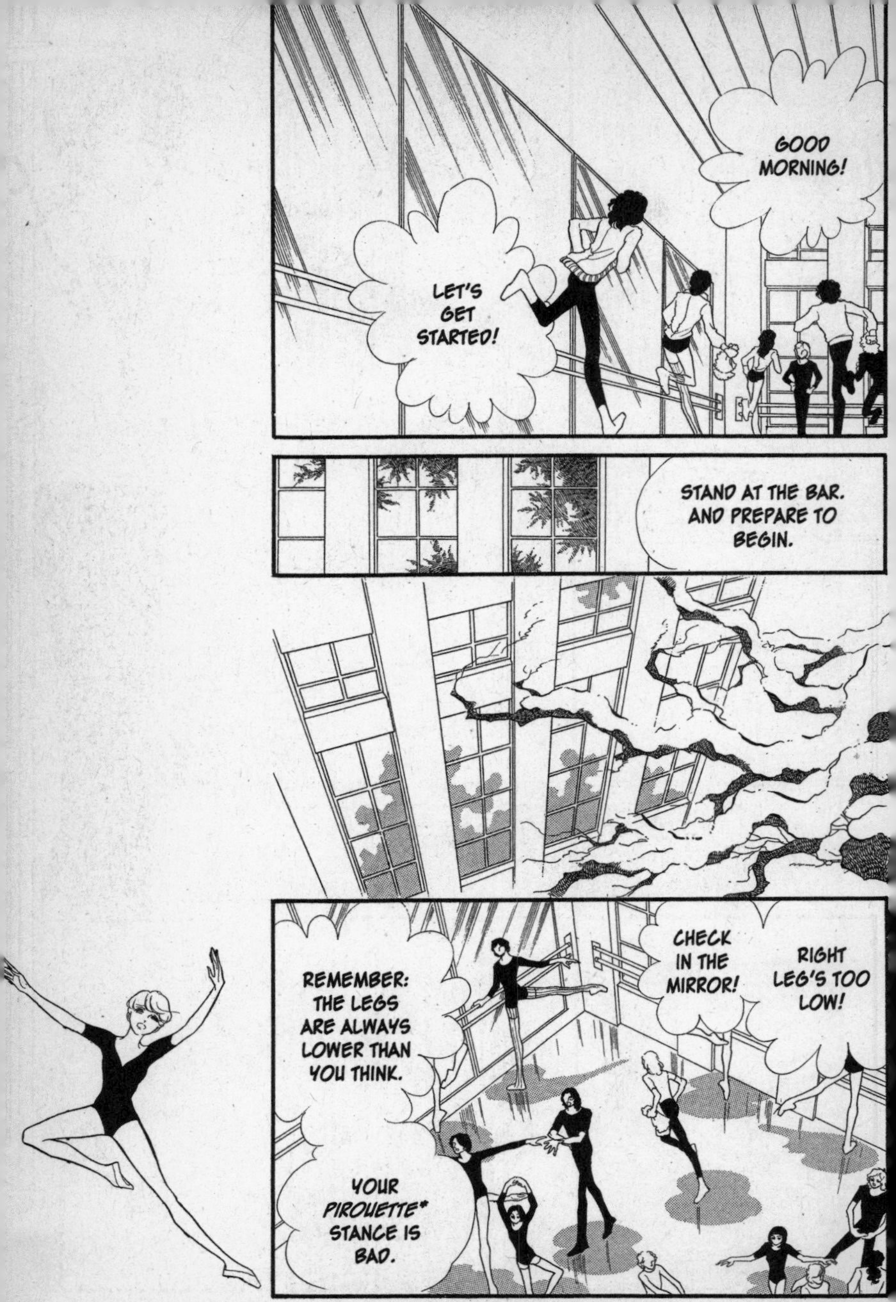
GOOD MORNING!
LET'S GET STARTED!
STAND AT THE BAR. AND PREPARE TO BEGIN.
RIGHT LEG'S TOO LOW!
CHECK IN THE MIRROR!
REMEMBER: THE LEGS ARE ALWAYS LOWER THAN YOU THINK.
YOUR PIROUETTE* STANCE IS BAD.

**pirouette:* Complete turn of the body on one foot.

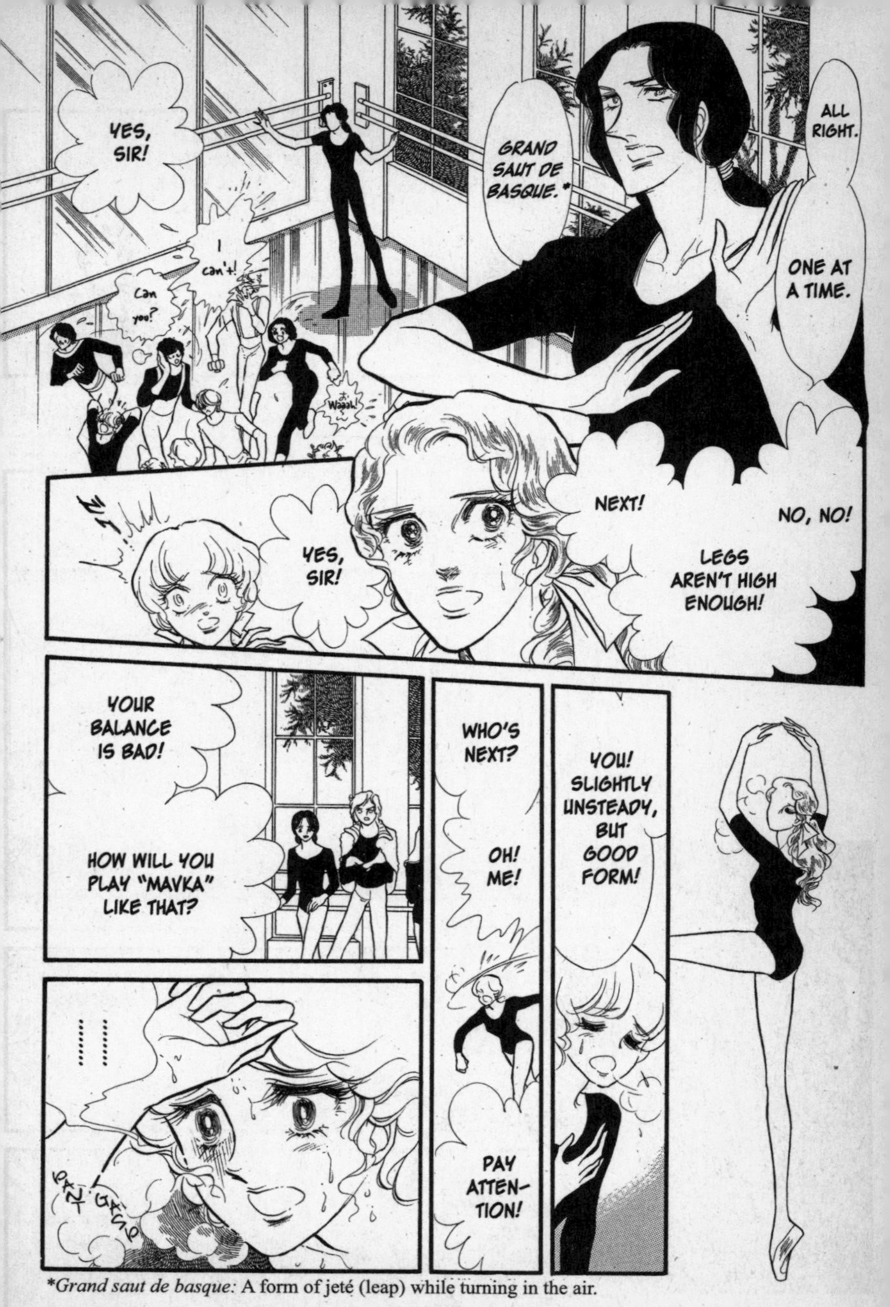
ALL RIGHT.
ONE AT A TIME.
GRAND SAUT DE BASQUE.*
YES, SIR!
I can't!
Can you?
Waaah!
NO, NO!
LEGS AREN'T HIGH ENOUGH!
NEXT!
YES, SIR!
YOU! SLIGHTLY UNSTEADY, BUT GOOD FORM!
WHO'S NEXT?
OH! ME!
PAY ATTEN-TION!
YOUR BALANCE IS BAD!
HOW WILL YOU PLAY "MAVKA" LIKE THAT?
......
PANT
GASP

Grand saut de basque: A form of jeté (leap) while turning in the air.

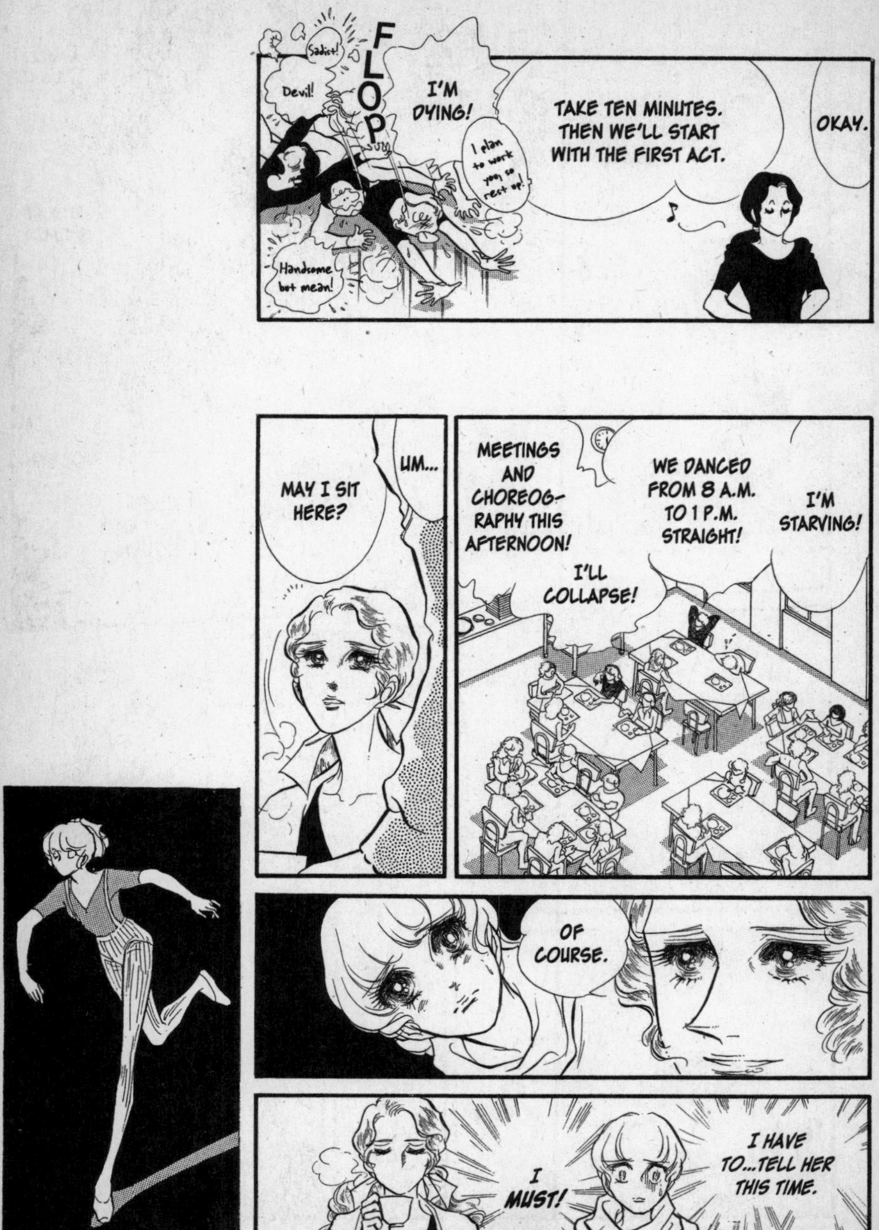
OKAY.
TAKE TEN MINUTES. THEN WE'LL START WITH THE FIRST ACT.
I plan to work you so rest up!
I'M DYING!
FLOP
Sadist!
Devil!
Handsome but mean!
I'M STARVING!
WE DANCED FROM 8 A.M. TO 1 P.M. STRAIGHT!
MEETINGS AND CHOREOG-RAPHY THIS AFTERNOON!
I'LL COLLAPSE!
UM...
MAY I SIT HERE?
OF COURSE.
I HAVE TO...TELL HER THIS TIME.
I MUST!

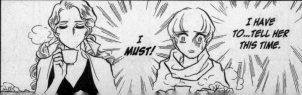

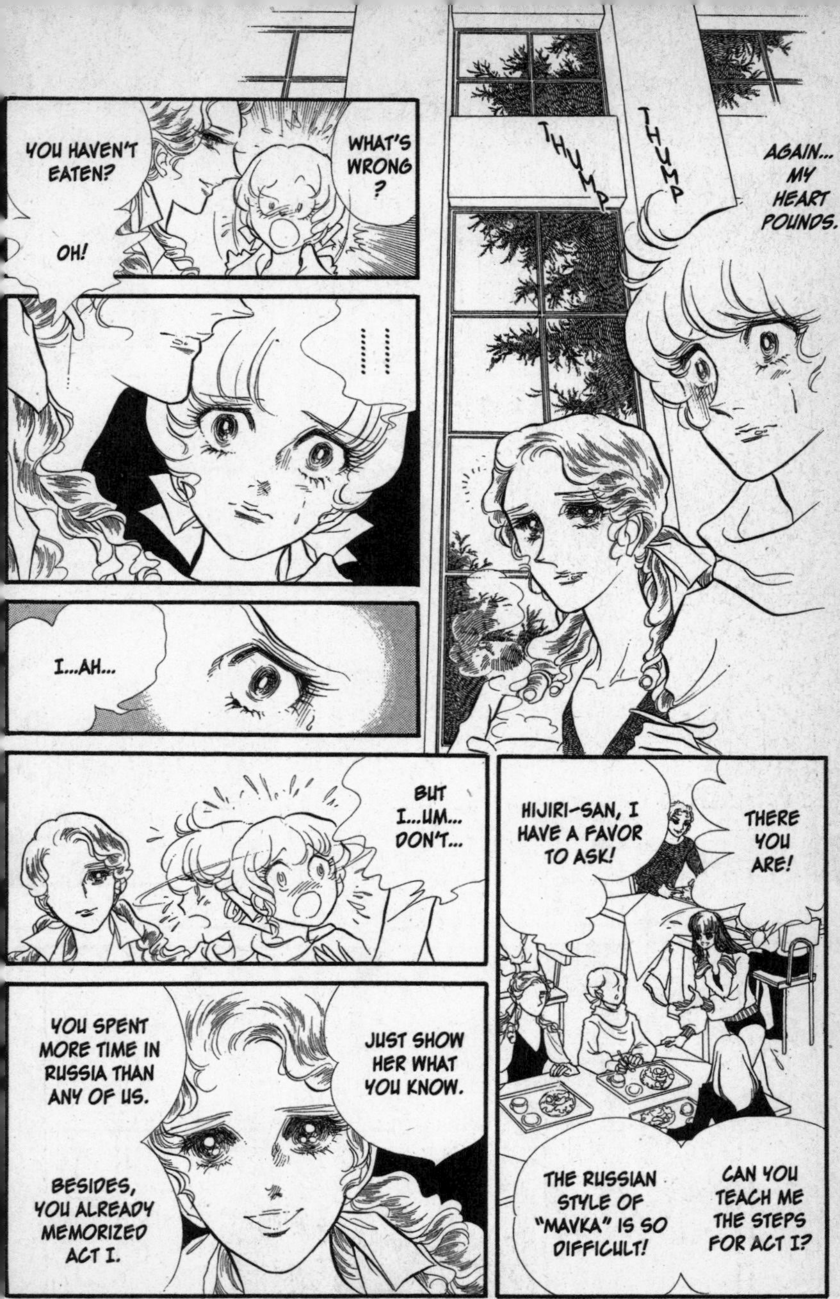
THUMP
THUMP
AGAIN... MY HEART POUNDS.
WHAT'S WRONG?
YOU HAVEN'T EATEN?
OH!
I...AH...
THERE YOU ARE!
HIJIRI-SAN, I HAVE A FAVOR TO ASK!
CAN YOU TEACH ME THE STEPS FOR ACT I?
THE RUSSIAN STYLE OF "MAVKA" IS SO DIFFICULT!
BUT I...UM... DON'T...
JUST SHOW HER WHAT YOU KNOW.
YOU SPENT MORE TIME IN RUSSIA THAN ANY OF US.
BESIDES, YOU ALREADY MEMORIZED ACT I.

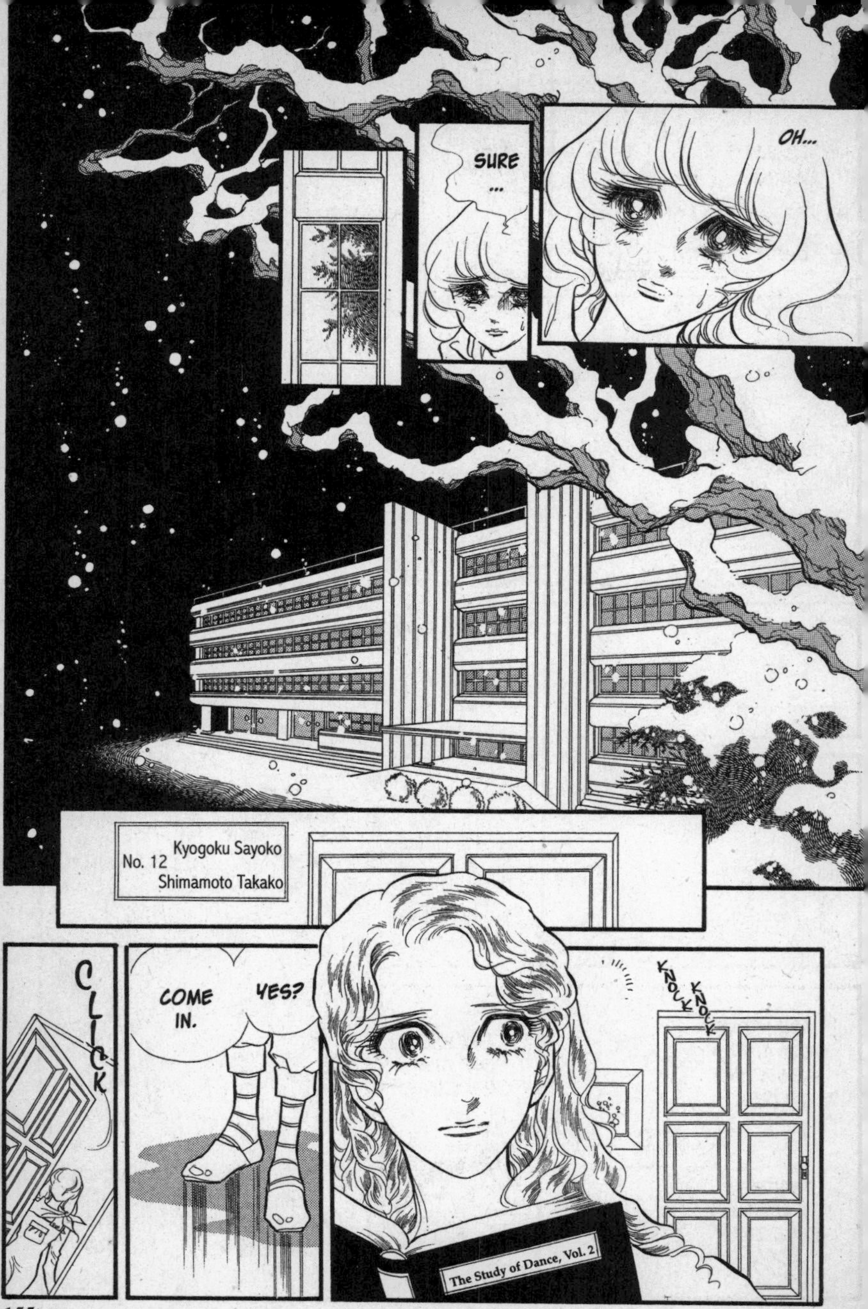
OH...
SURE ...
No. 12 Kyogoku Sayoko
Shimamoto Takako
KNOCK KNOCK
The Study of Dance, Vol. 2
YES?
COME IN.
CLICK

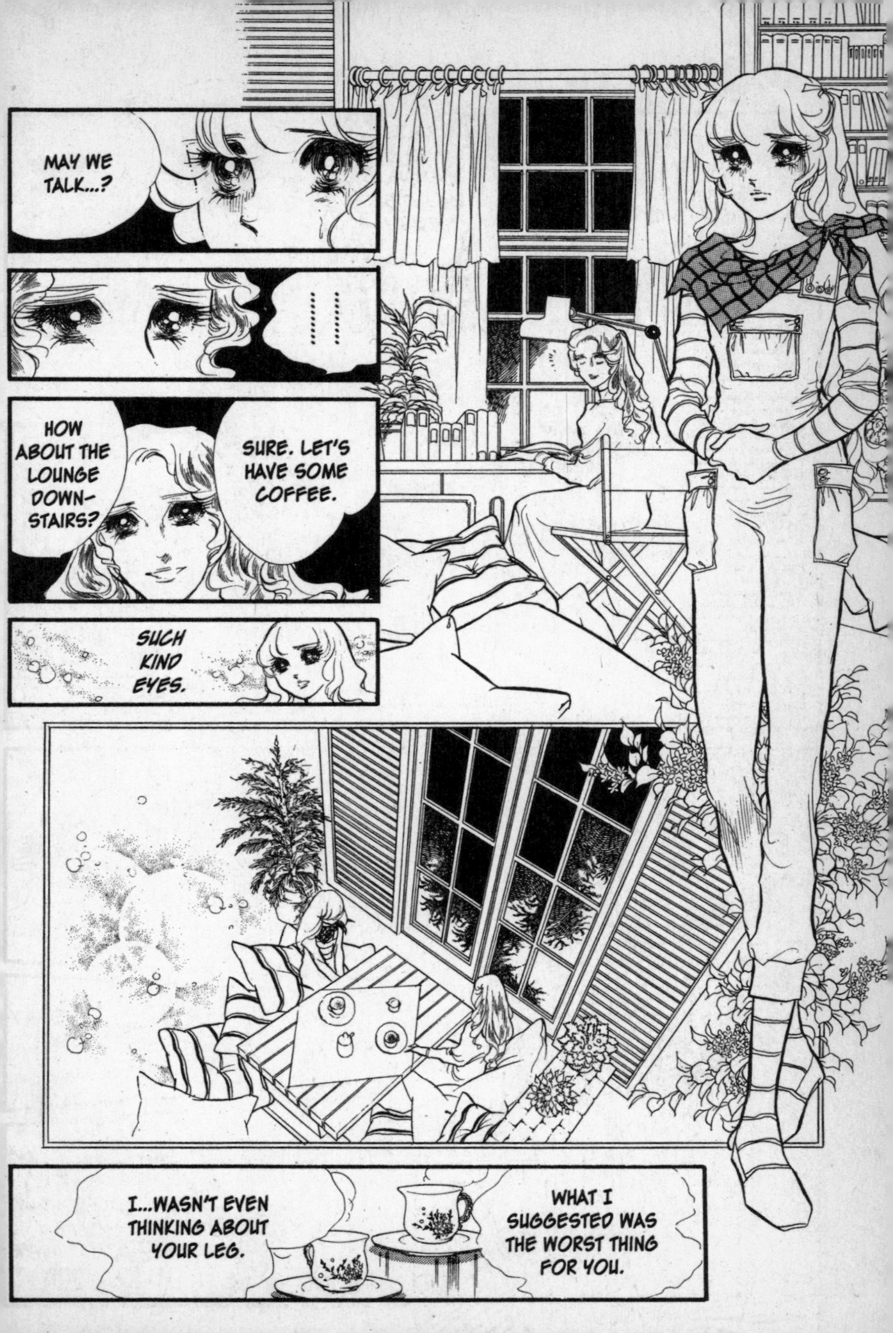
MAY WE TALK...?
......
HOW ABOUT THE LOUNGE DOWN-STAIRS?
SURE. LET'S HAVE SOME COFFEE.
SUCH KIND EYES.
I...WASN'T EVEN THINKING ABOUT YOUR LEG.
WHAT I SUGGESTED WAS THE WORST THING FOR YOU.

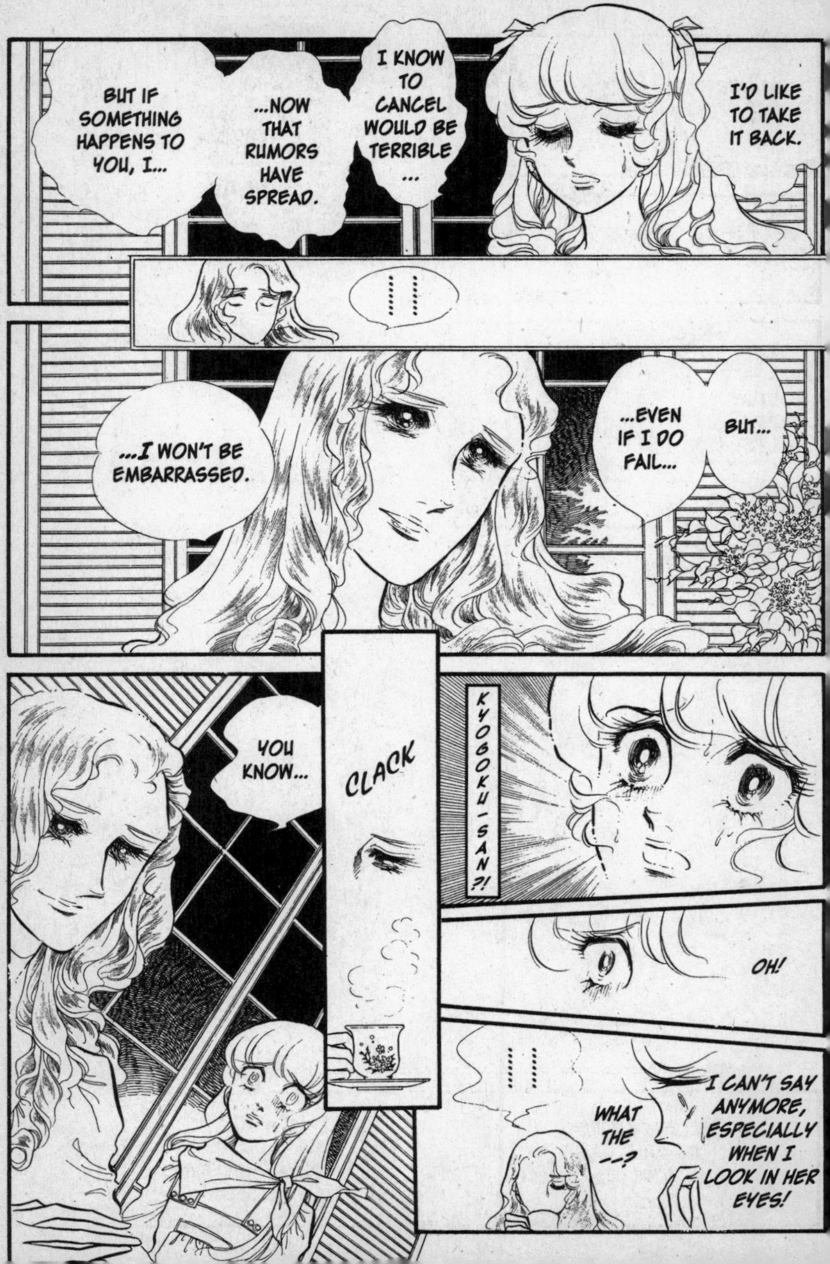
I'D LIKE TO TAKE IT BACK.
I KNOW TO CANCEL WOULD BE TERRIBLE...
...NOW THAT RUMORS HAVE SPREAD.
BUT IF SOMETHING HAPPENS TO YOU, I...
......
BUT...
...EVEN IF I DO FAIL...
...I WON'T BE EMBARRASSED.
KYOGOKU-SAN?!
OH!
I CAN'T SAY ANYMORE, ESPECIALLY WHEN I LOOK IN HER EYES!
WHAT THE--?
......
CLACK
YOU KNOW...

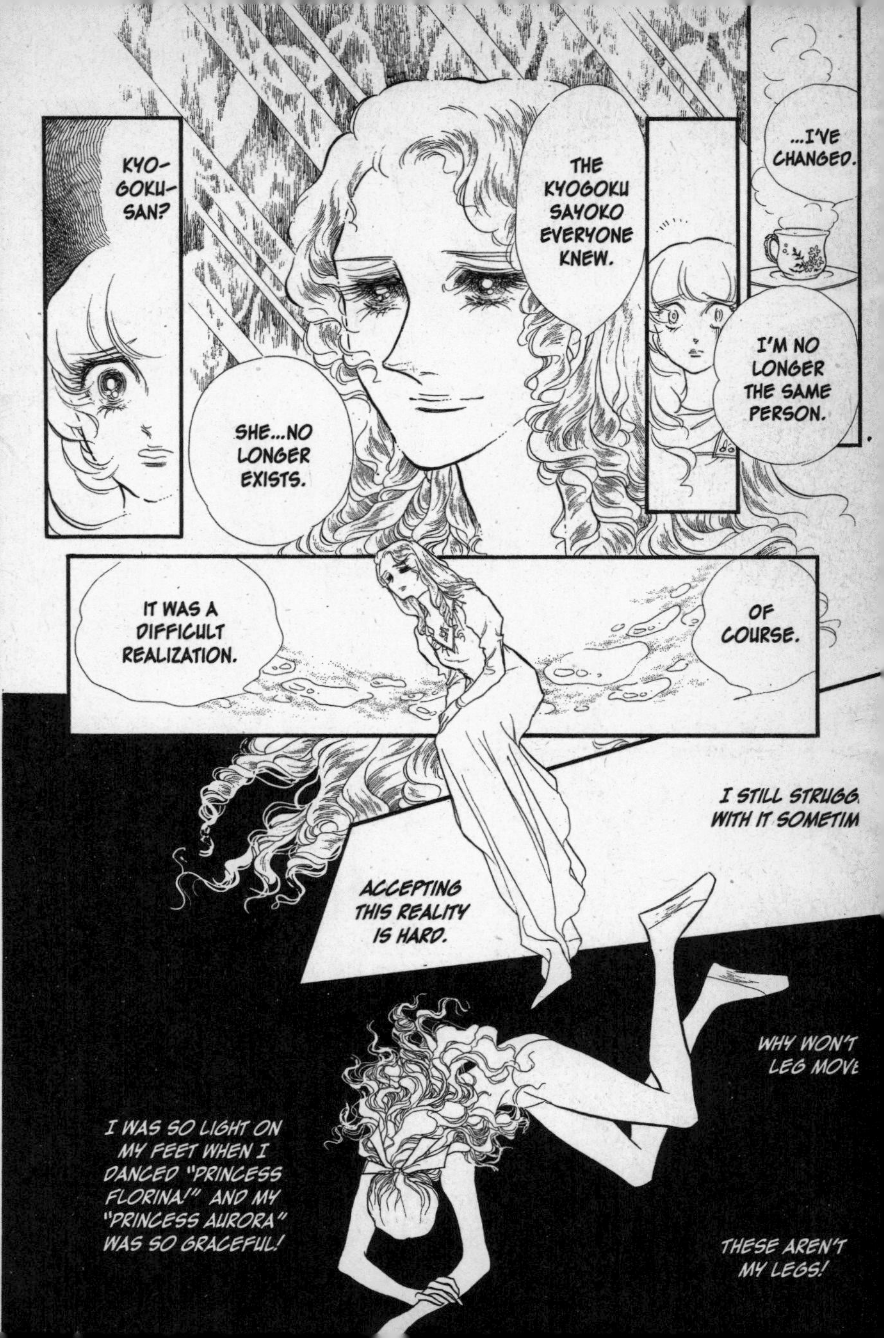
...I'VE CHANGED.
I'M NO LONGER THE SAME PERSON.
THE KYOGOKU SAYOKO EVERYONE KNEW.
SHE...NO LONGER EXISTS.
KYO-GOKU-SAN?
OF COURSE.
IT WAS A DIFFICULT REALIZATION.
I STILL STRUGG WITH IT SOMETIM
ACCEPTING THIS REALITY IS HARD.
WHY WON'T LEG MOVE
THESE AREN'T MY LEGS!
I WAS SO LIGHT ON MY FEET WHEN I DANCED "PRINCESS FLORINA!" AND MY "PRINCESS AURORA" WAS SO GRACEFUL!

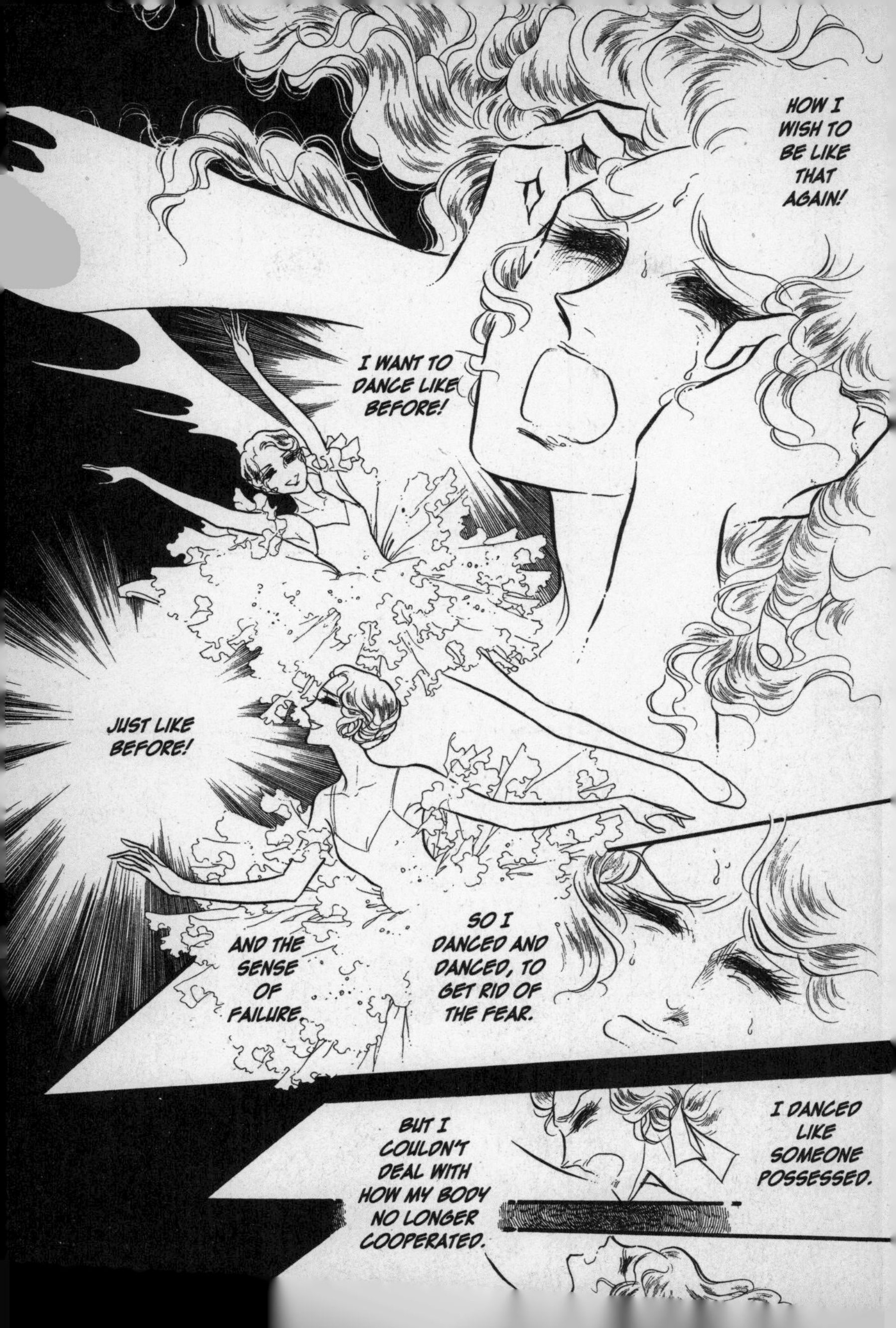
HOW I WISH TO BE LIKE THAT AGAIN!
I WANT TO DANCE LIKE BEFORE!
JUST LIKE BEFORE!
SO I DANCED AND DANCED, TO GET RID OF THE FEAR.
AND THE SENSE OF FAILURE.
I DANCED LIKE SOMEONE POSSESSED.
BUT I COULDN'T DEAL WITH HOW MY BODY NO LONGER COOPERATED.

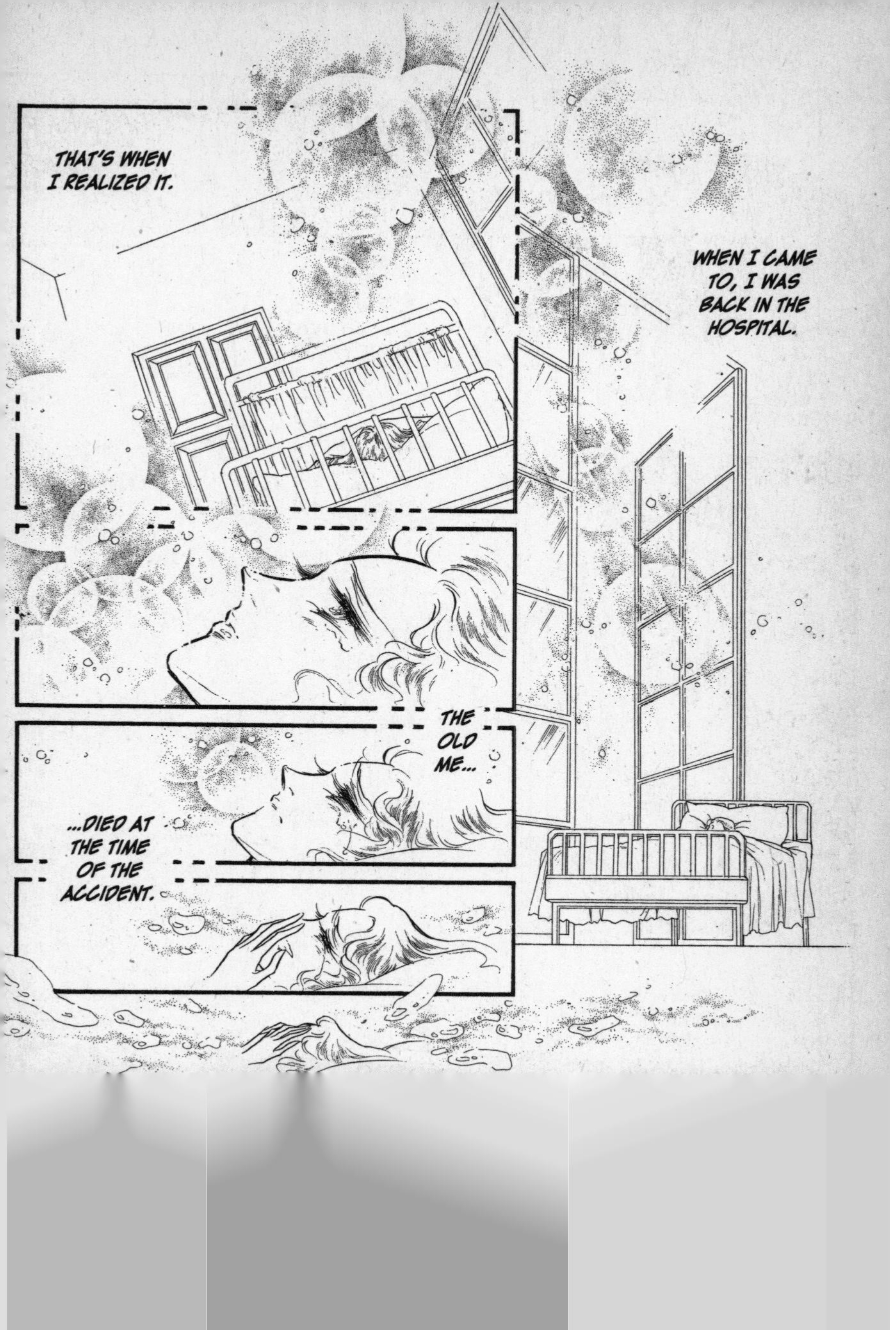
WHEN I CAME TO, I WAS BACK IN THE HOSPITAL.
THAT'S WHEN I REALIZED IT.
THE OLD ME...
...DIED AT THE TIME OF THE ACCIDENT.

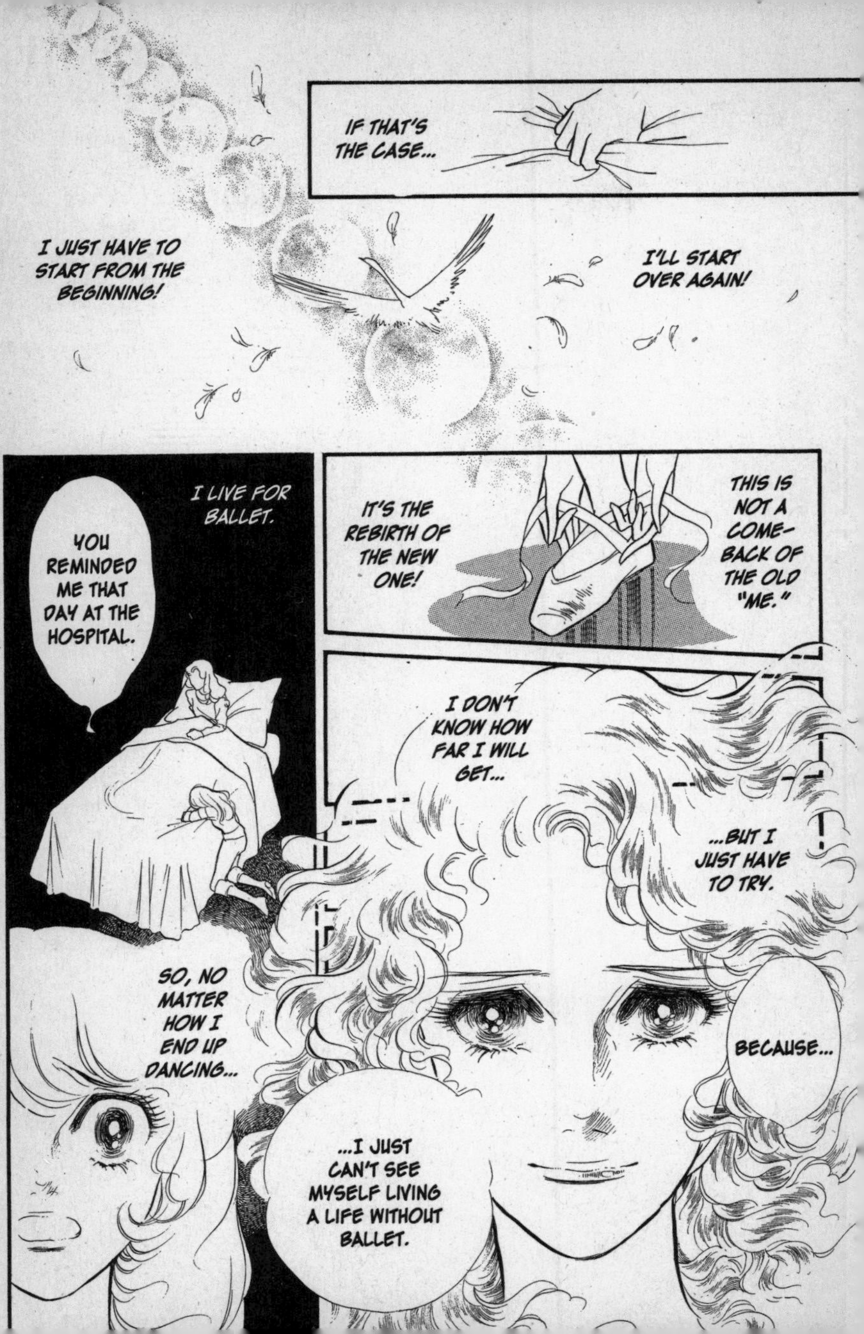
IF THAT'S THE CASE...
I'LL START OVER AGAIN!
I JUST HAVE TO START FROM THE BEGINNING!
THIS IS NOT A COME-BACK OF THE OLD "ME."
IT'S THE REBIRTH OF THE NEW ONE!
I DON'T KNOW HOW FAR I WILL GET...
...BUT I JUST HAVE TO TRY.
BECAUSE...
I LIVE FOR BALLET.
YOU REMINDED ME THAT DAY AT THE HOSPITAL.
SO, NO MATTER HOW I END UP DANCING...
...I JUST CAN'T SEE MYSELF LIVING A LIFE WITHOUT BALLET.

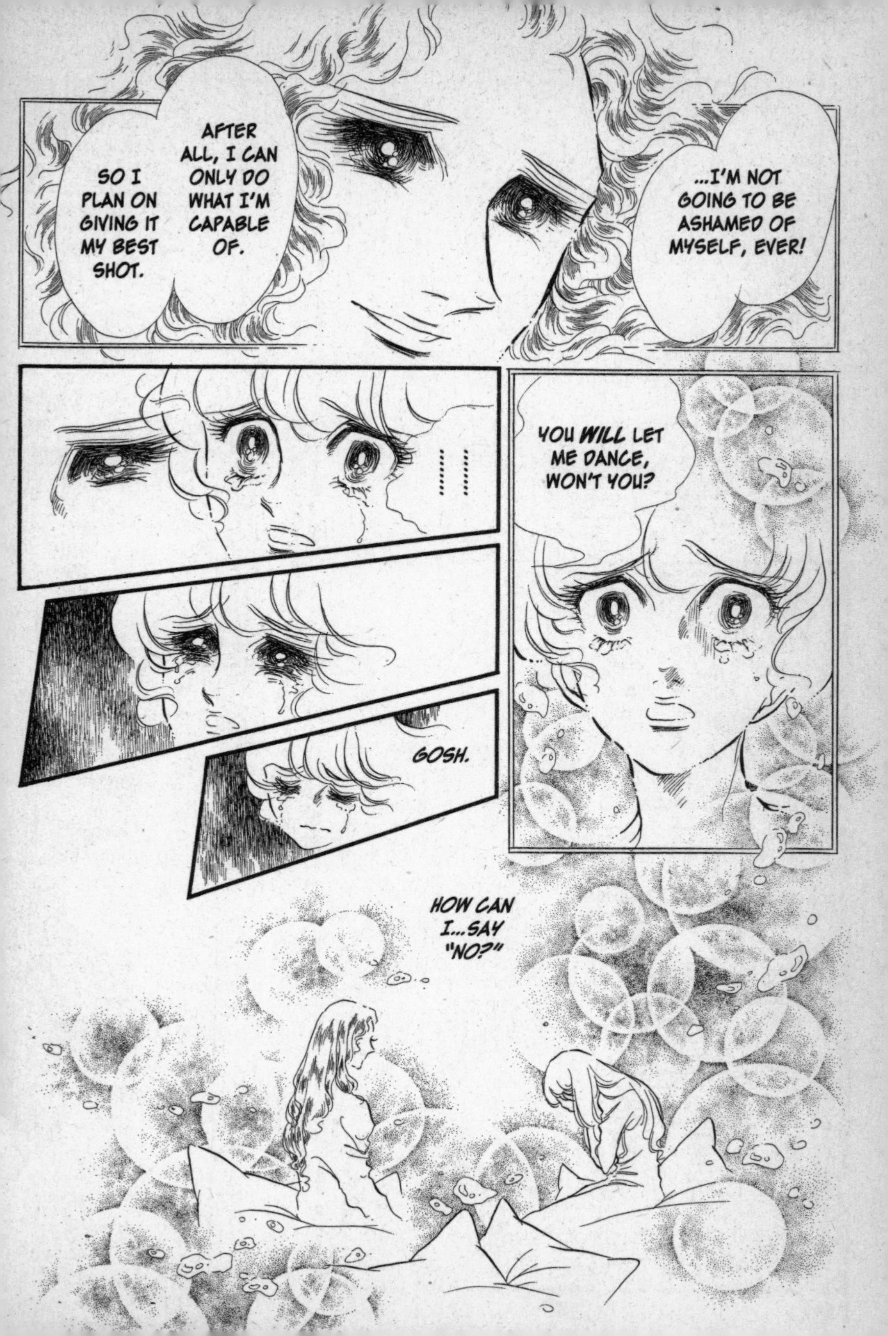
...I'M NOT GOING TO BE ASHAMED OF MYSELF, EVER!
AFTER ALL, I CAN ONLY DO WHAT I'M CAPABLE OF.
SO I PLAN ON GIVING IT MY BEST SHOT.
YOU *WILL* LET ME DANCE, WON'T YOU?
......
GOSH.
HOW CAN I...SAY "NO?"

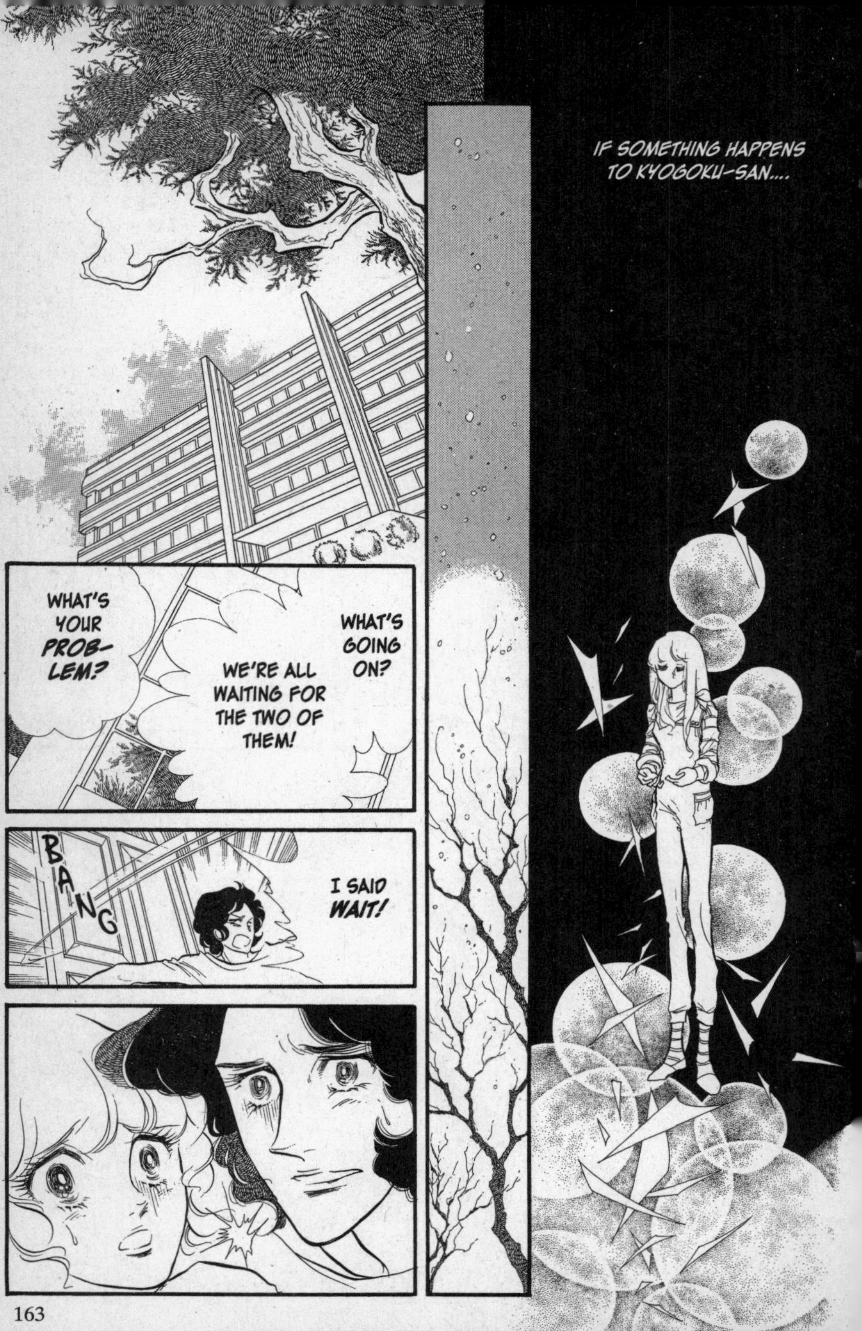
IF SOMETHING HAPPENS TO KYOGOKU-SAN....
WHAT'S GOING ON?
WE'RE ALL WAITING FOR THE TWO OF THEM!
WHAT'S YOUR PROB-LEM?
I SAID WAIT!
BANG

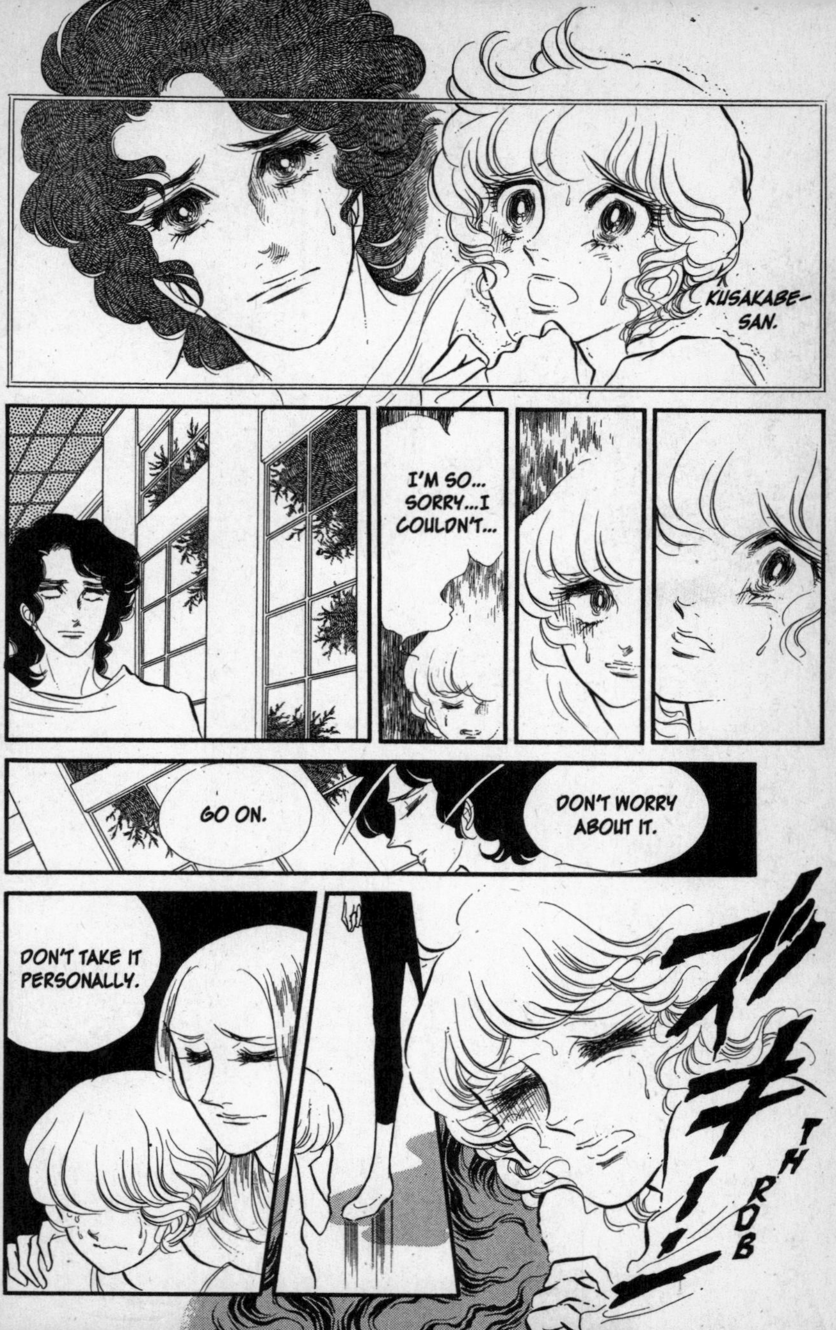
KUSAKABE-SAN.
I'M SO... SORRY...I COULDN'T...
DON'T WORRY ABOUT IT.
GO ON.
THROB
DON'T TAKE IT PERSONALLY.

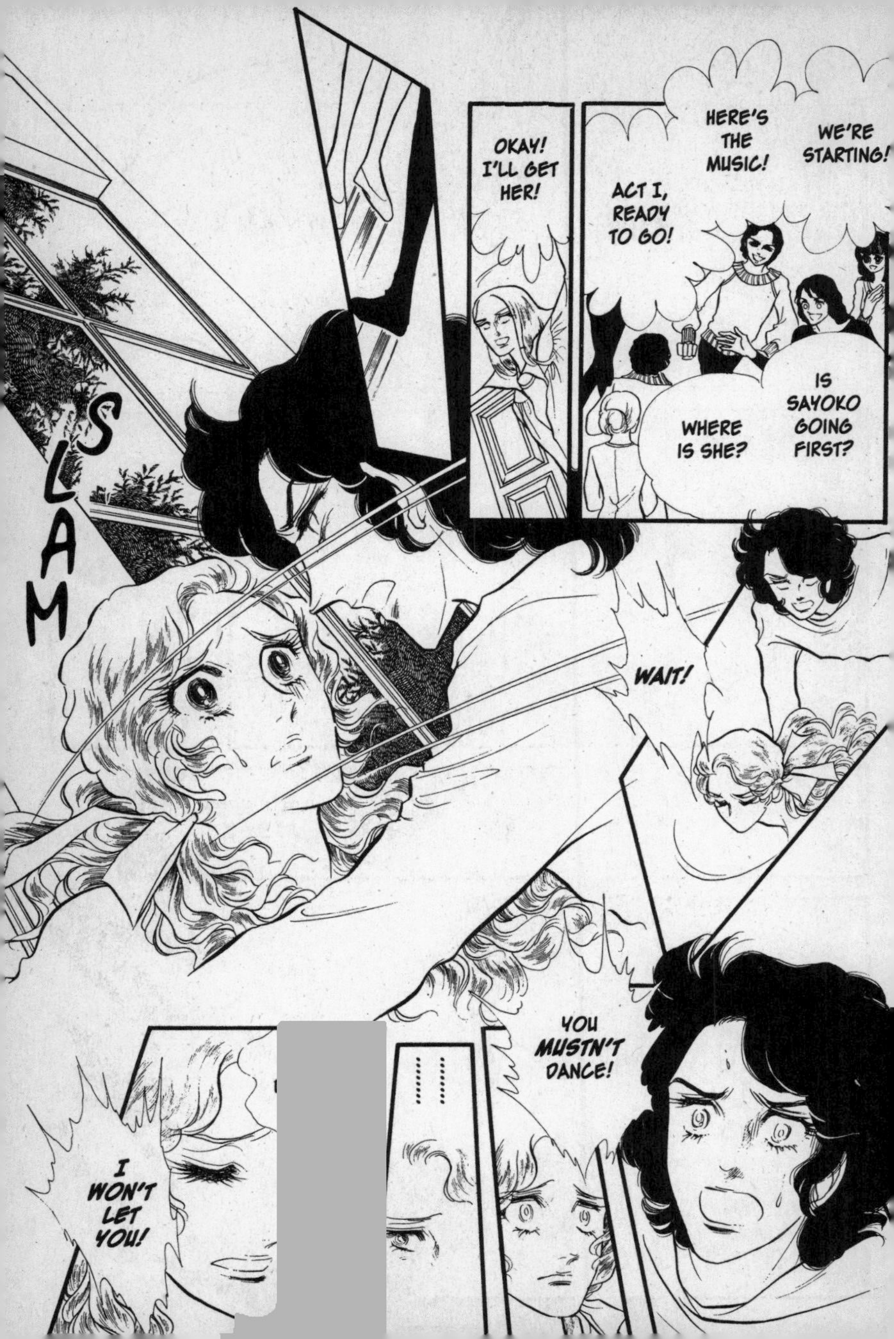
WE'RE STARTING!
HERE'S THE MUSIC!
ACT I, READY TO GO!
IS SAYOKO GOING FIRST?
WHERE IS SHE?
OKAY! I'LL GET HER!
SLAM
WAIT!
YOU MUSTN'T DANCE!
......
I WON'T LET YOU!

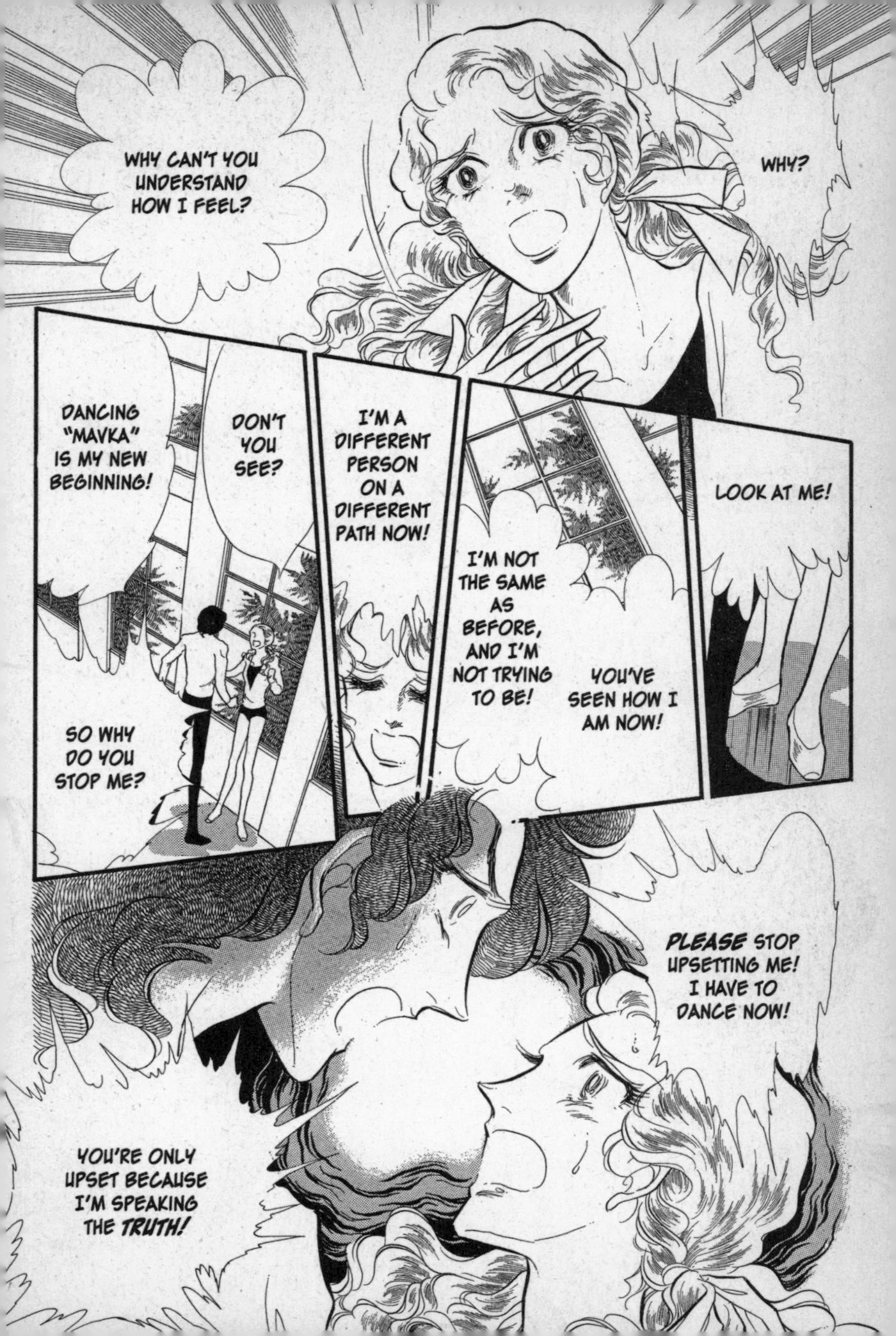
WHY?
WHY CAN'T YOU UNDERSTAND HOW I FEEL?
LOOK AT ME!
I'M NOT THE SAME AS BEFORE, AND I'M NOT TRYING TO BE!
YOU'VE SEEN HOW I AM NOW!
I'M A DIFFERENT PERSON ON A DIFFERENT PATH NOW!
DON'T YOU SEE?
DANCING "MAVKA" IS MY NEW BEGINNING!
SO WHY DO YOU STOP ME?
PLEASE STOP UPSETTING ME! I HAVE TO DANCE NOW!
YOU'RE ONLY UPSET BECAUSE I'M SPEAKING THE *TRUTH!*

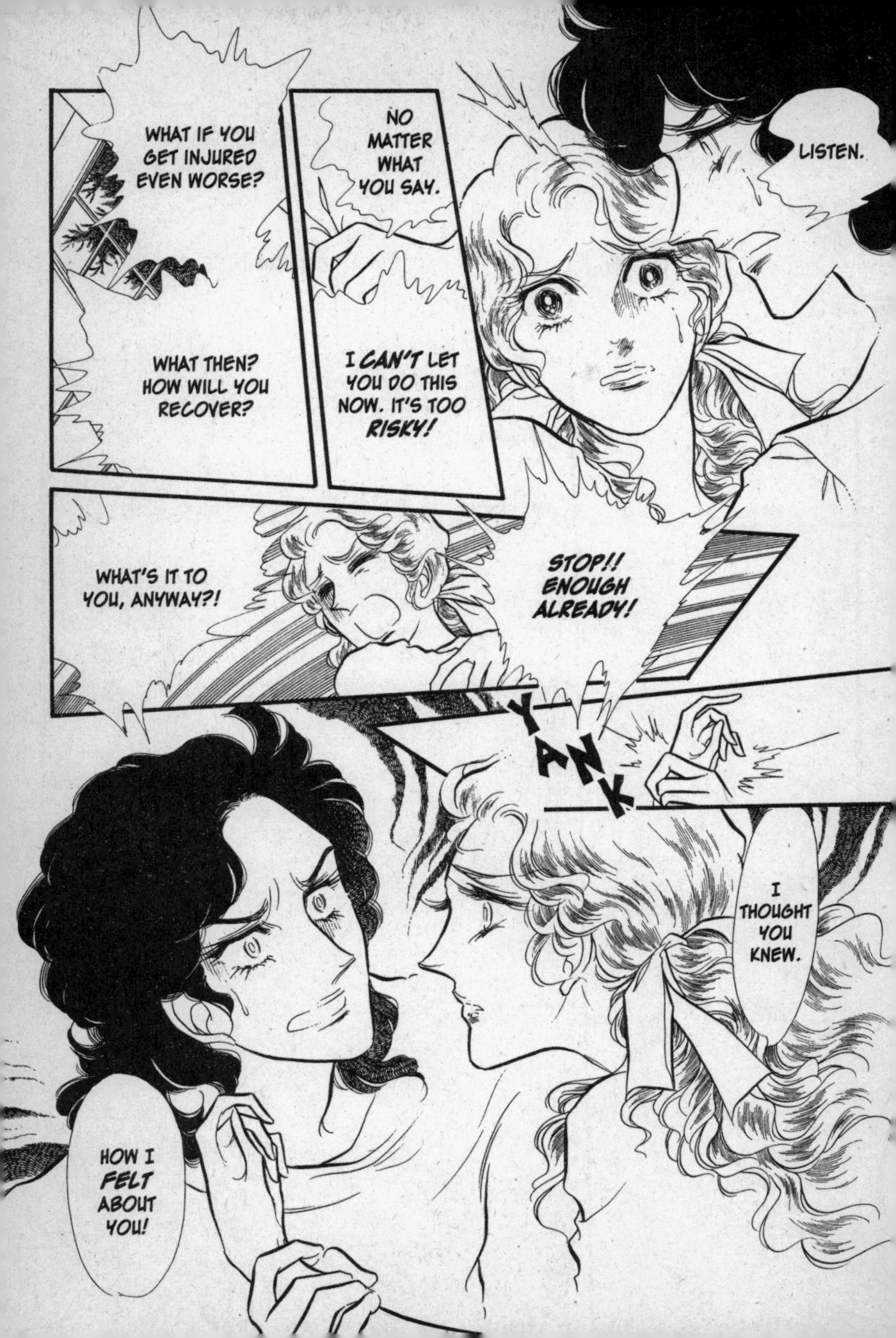
LISTEN.
NO MATTER WHAT YOU SAY.
I *CAN'T* LET YOU DO THIS NOW. IT'S TOO *RISKY!*
WHAT IF YOU GET INJURED EVEN WORSE?
WHAT THEN? HOW WILL YOU RECOVER?
STOP!! ENOUGH ALREADY!
WHAT'S IT TO YOU, ANYWAY?!
YANK
I THOUGHT YOU KNEW.
HOW I *FELT* ABOUT YOU!

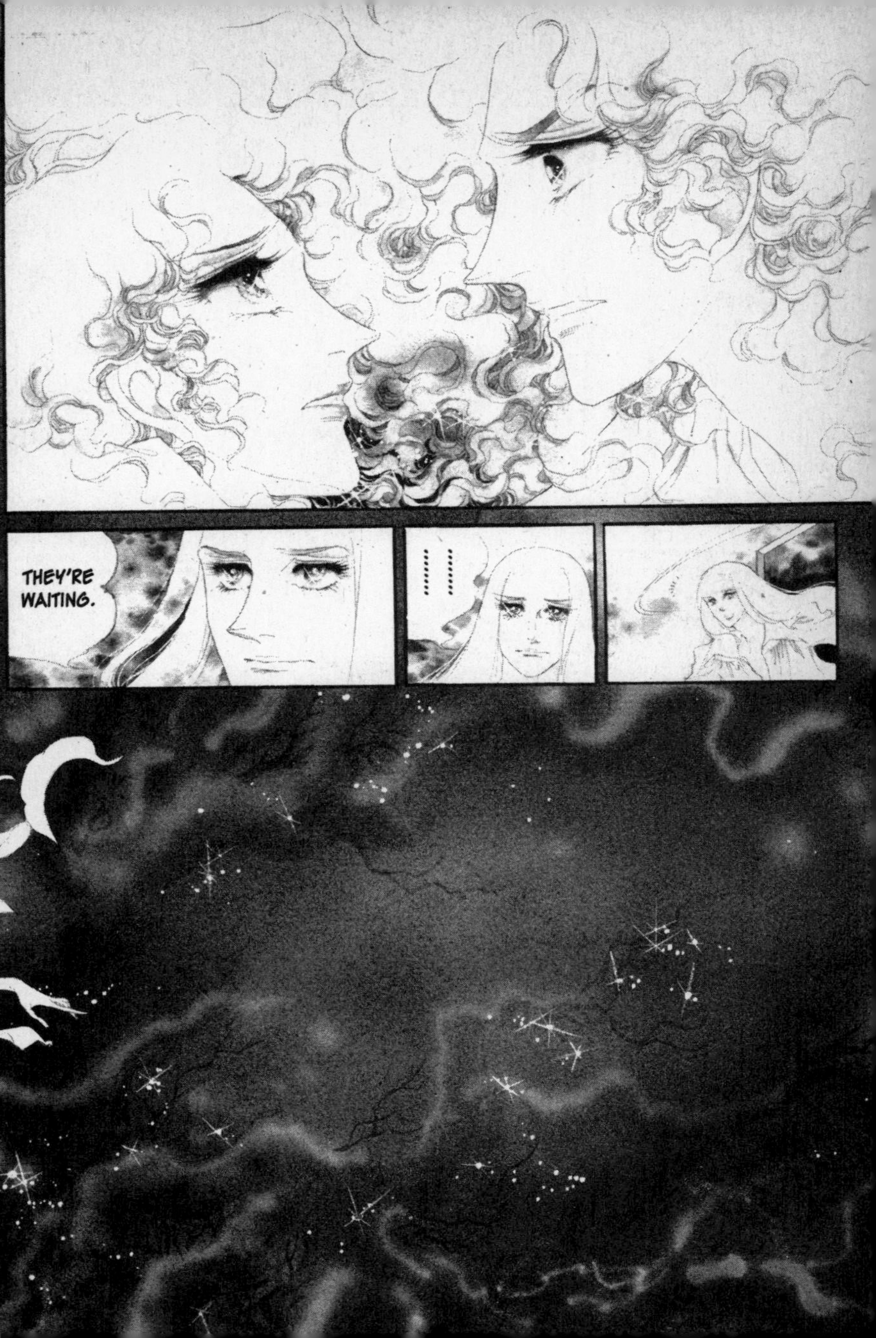
THEY'RE WAITING.
......

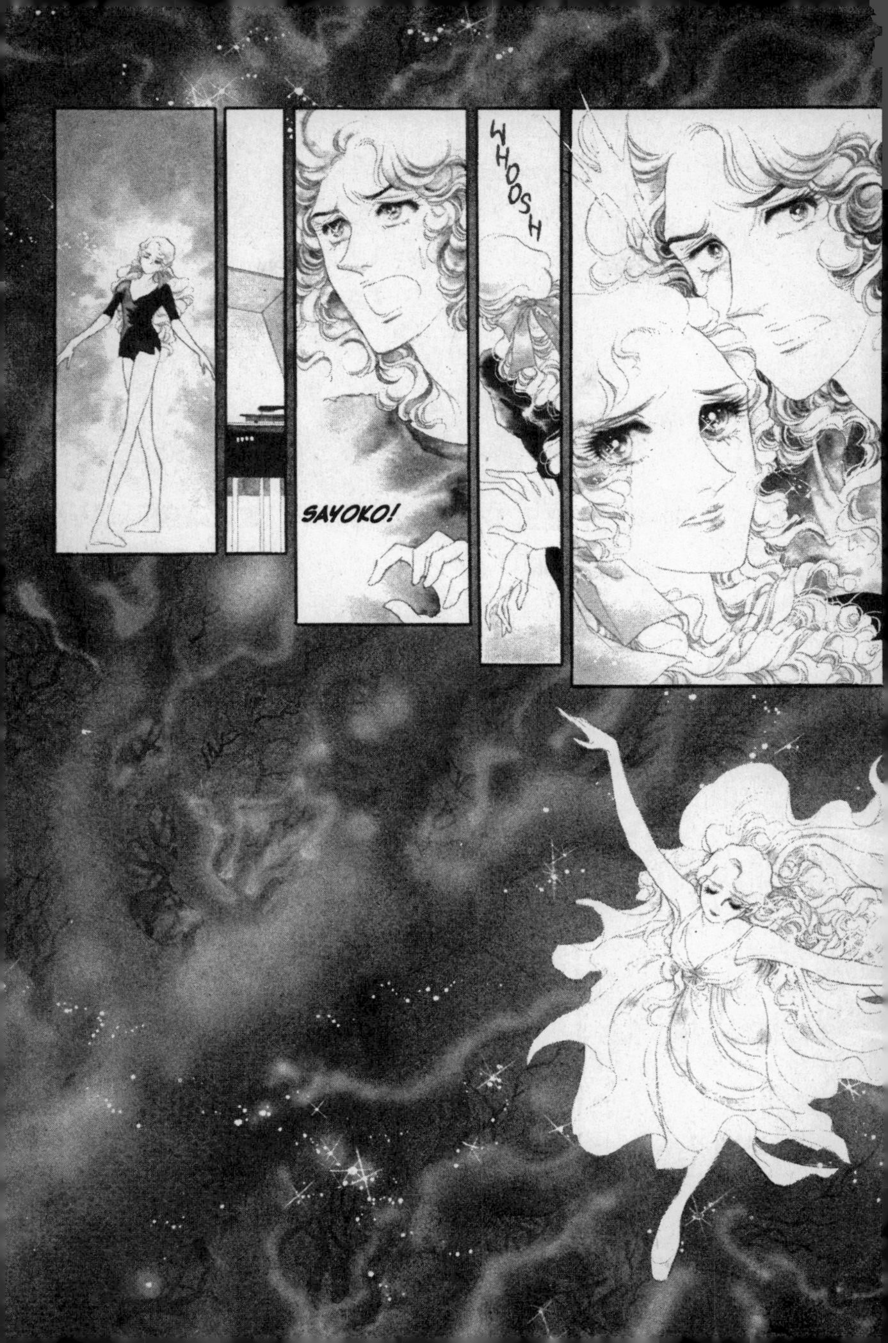
WHOOSH
SAYOKO!

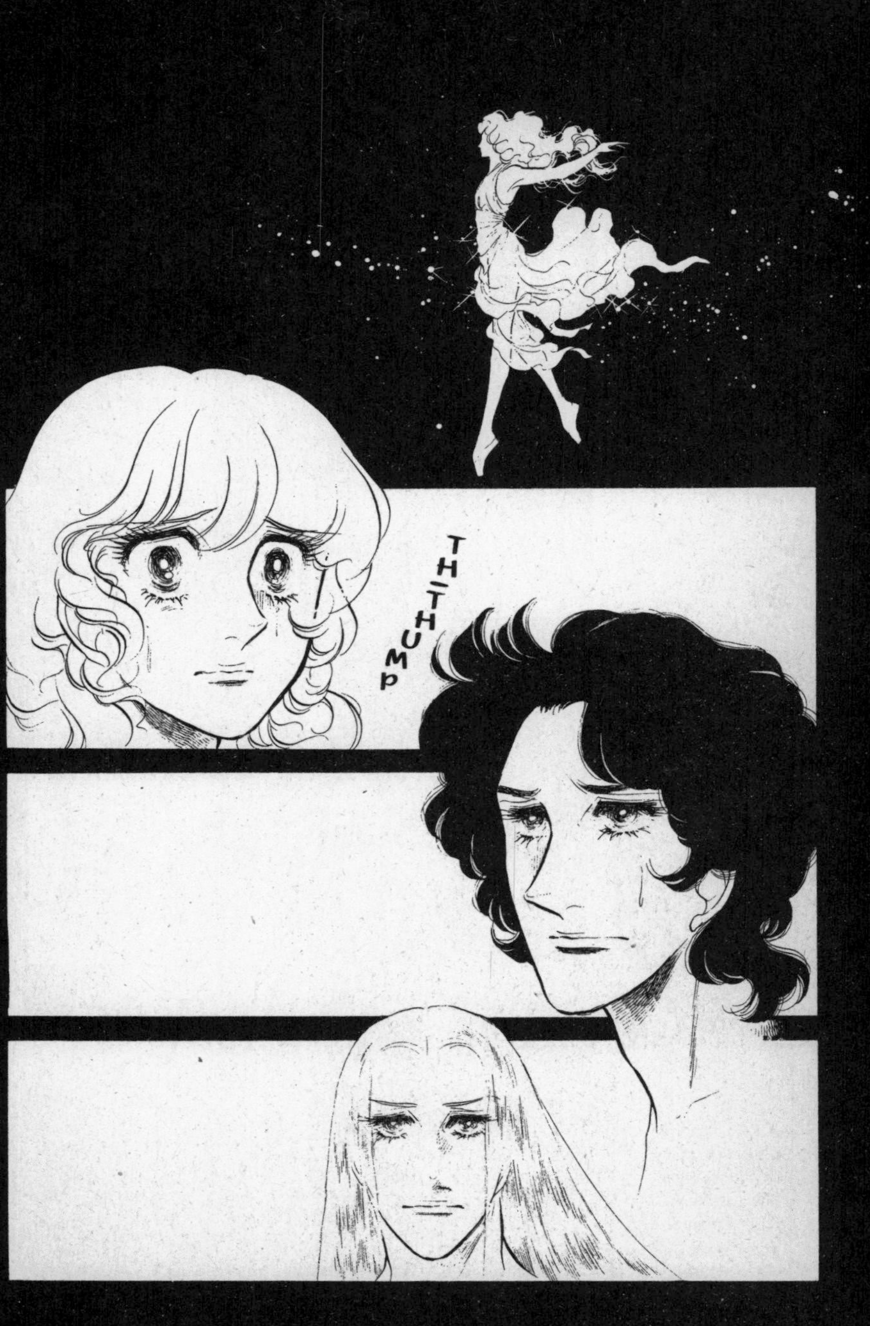
THTHTHUMp

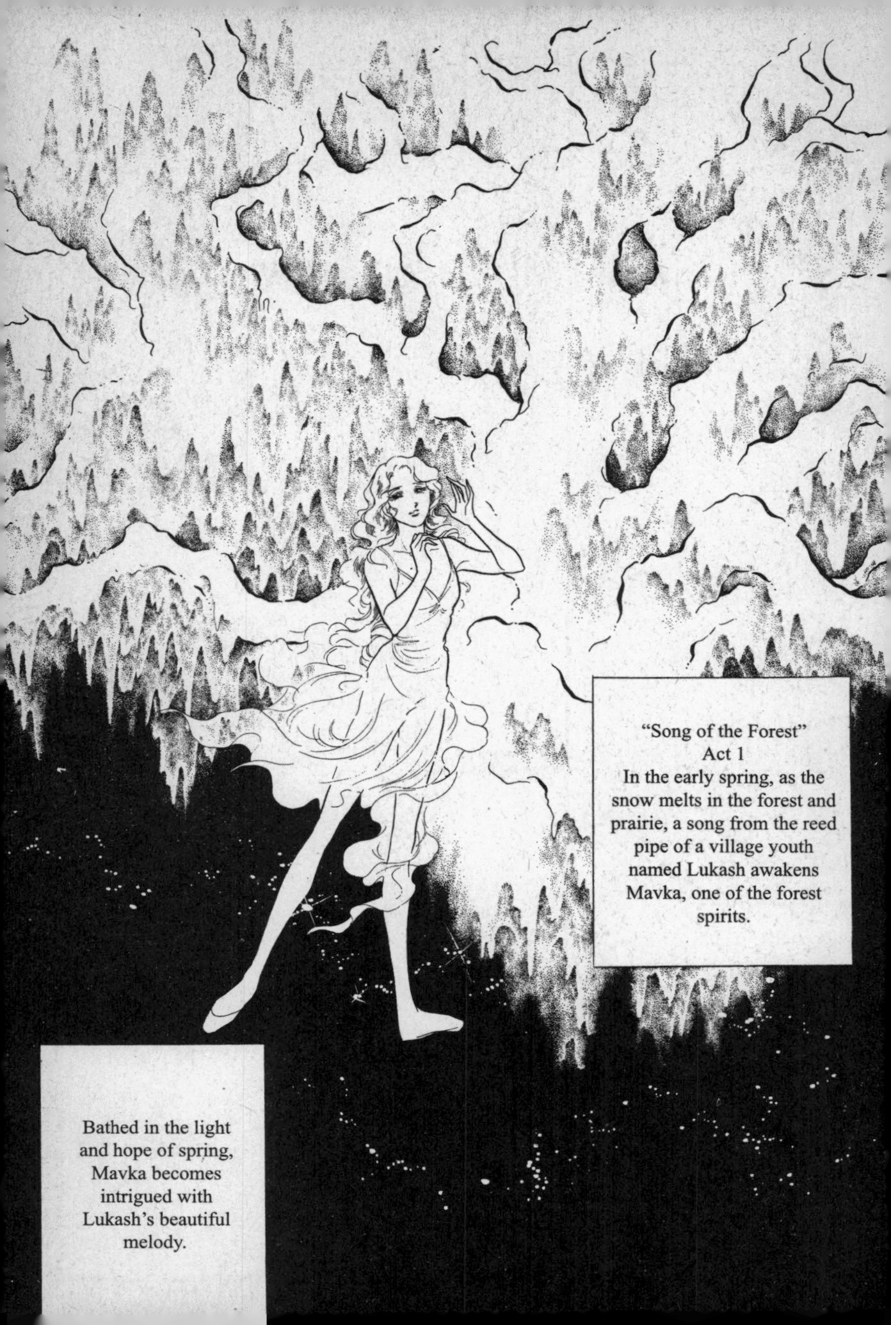
"Song of the Forest"
Act 1
In the early spring, as the snow melts in the forest and prairie, a song from the reed pipe of a village youth named Lukash awakens Mavka, one of the forest spirits.
Bathed in the light and hope of spring, Mavka becomes intrigued with Lukash's beautiful melody.

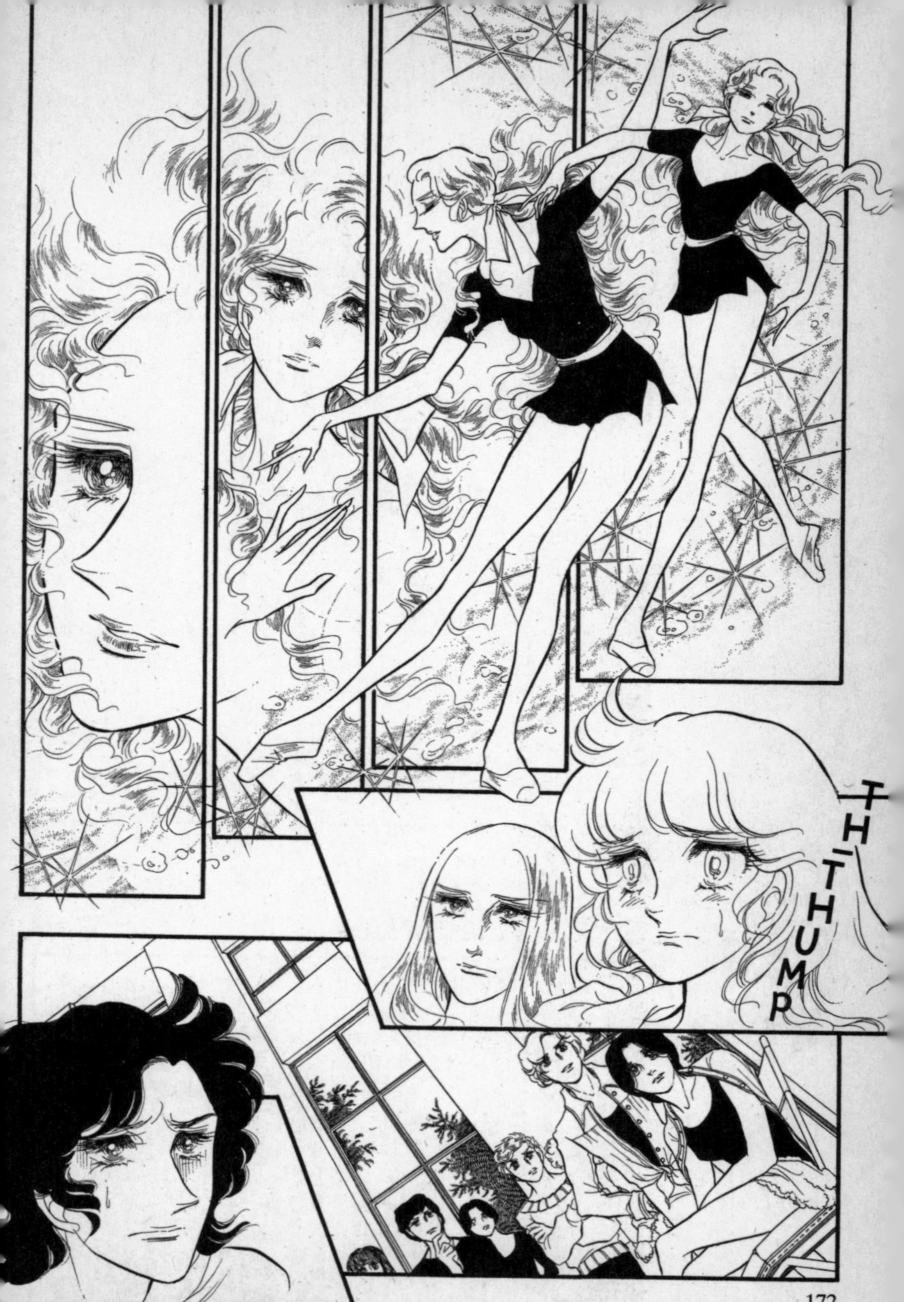
TH-THUMP

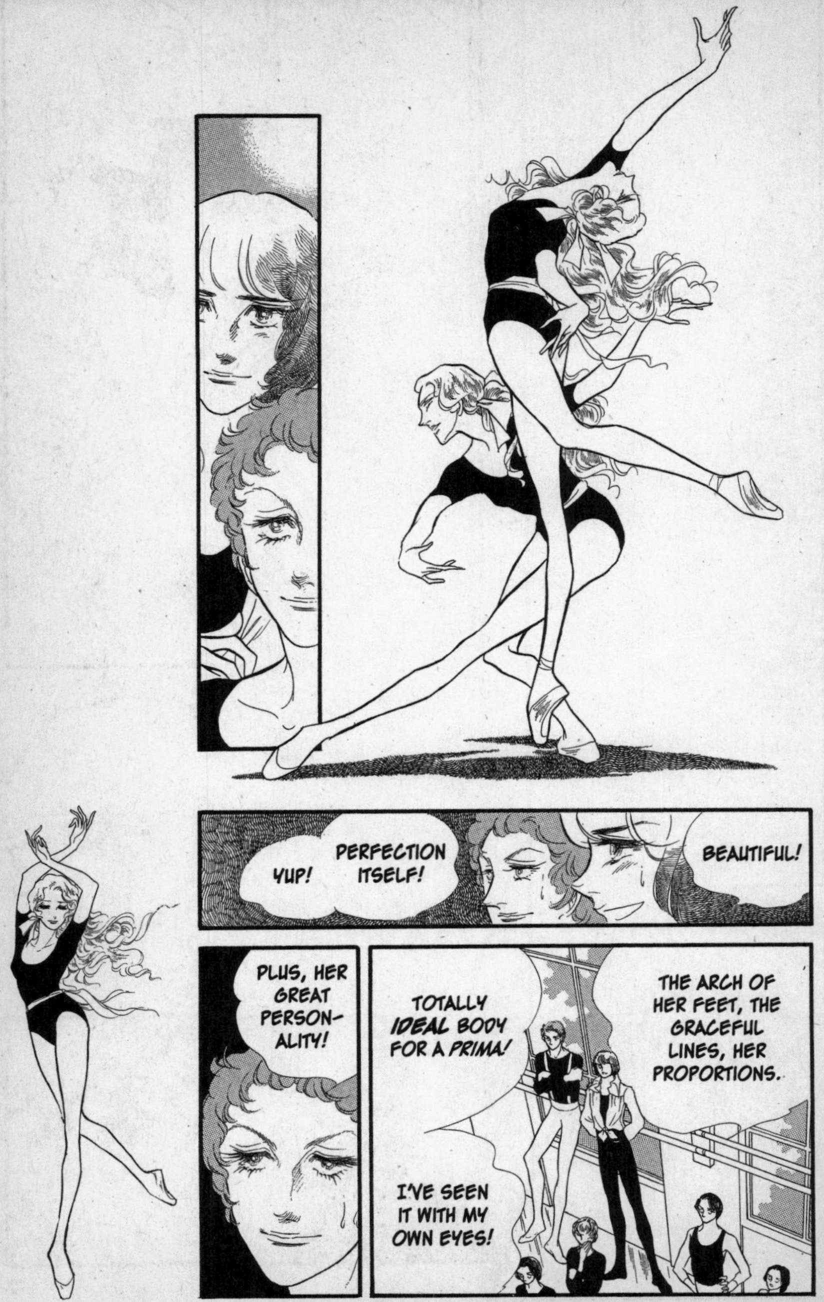
BEAUTIFUL!
PERFECTION ITSELF!
YUP!
THE ARCH OF HER FEET, THE GRACEFUL LINES, HER PROPORTIONS.
TOTALLY *IDEAL* BODY FOR A *PRIMA!*
I'VE SEEN IT WITH MY OWN EYES!
PLUS, HER GREAT PERSON-ALITY!

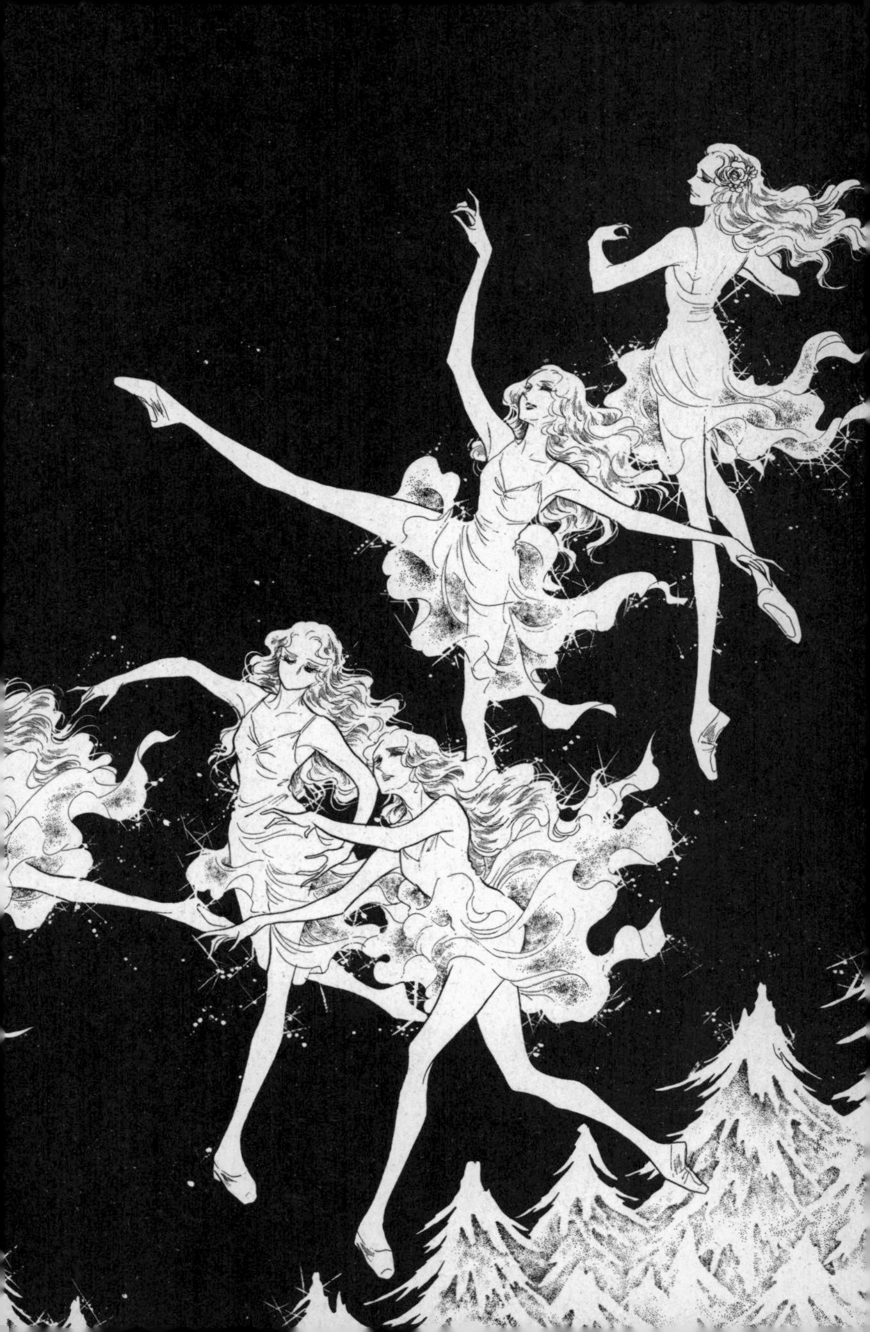

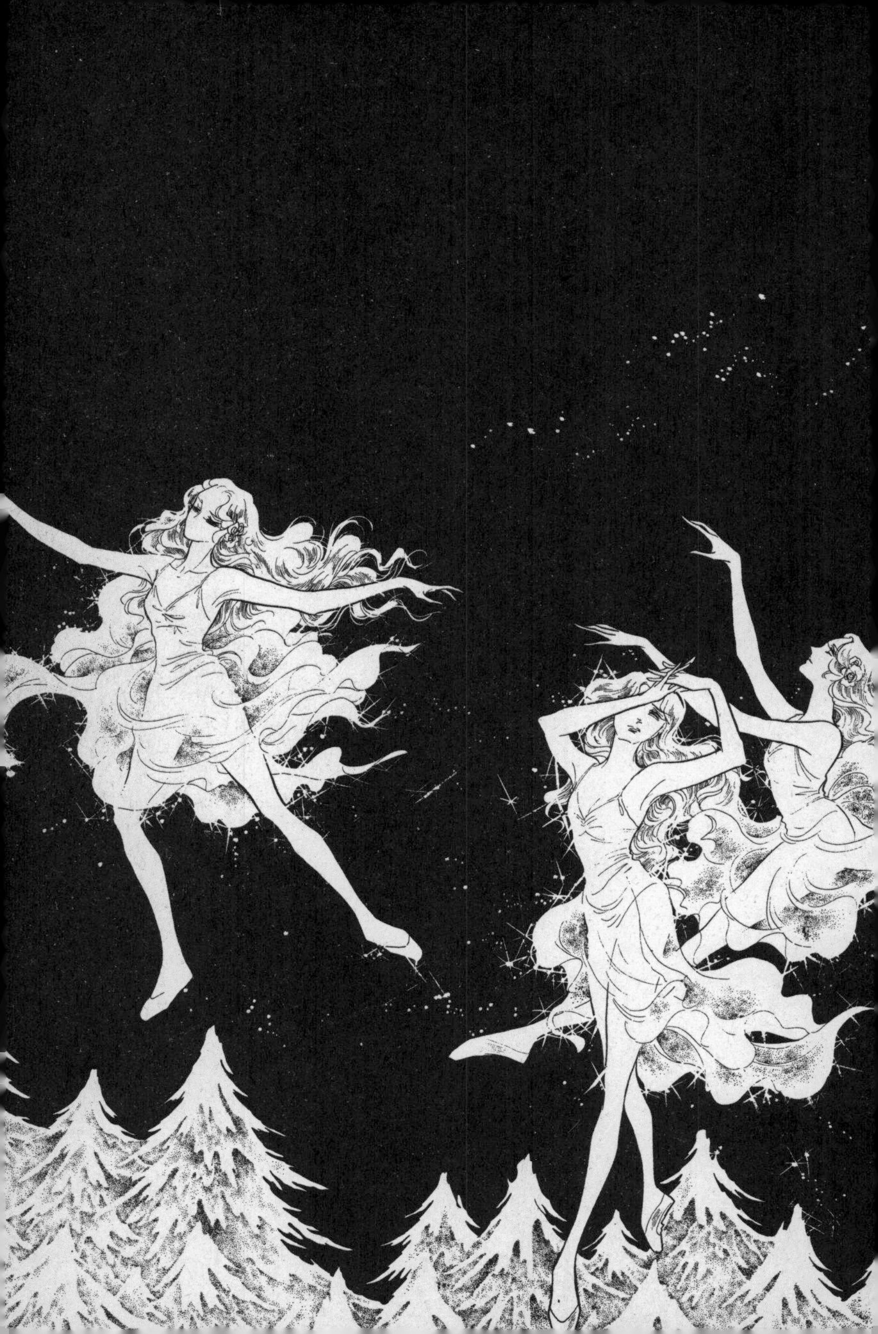

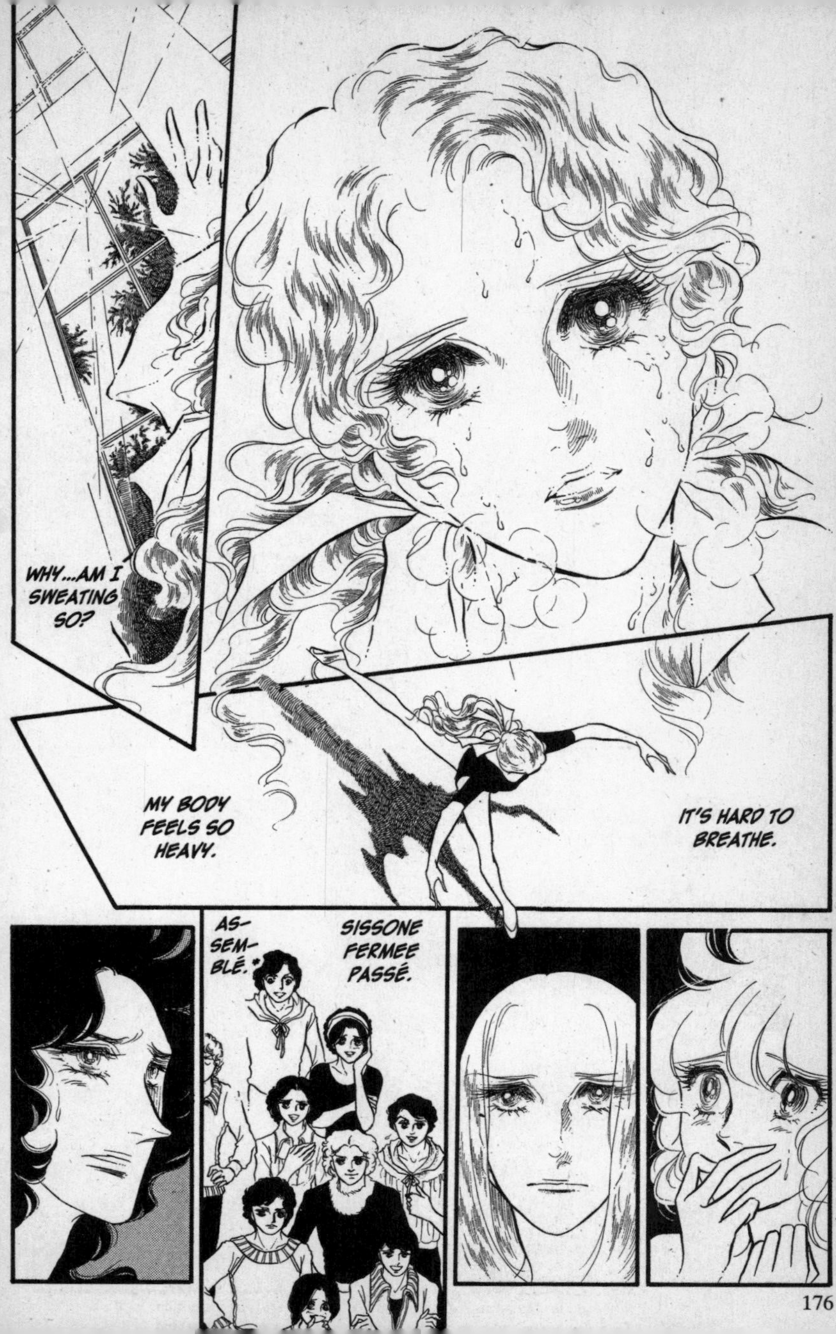
WHY...AM I SWEATING SO?
IT'S HARD TO BREATHE.
MY BODY FEELS SO HEAVY.
SISSONE FERMEE PASSÉ.
AS-SEM-BLÉ.*

**Assemblé*: A *pas* (step) in which the dancer pushes off the floor with the supporting leg, and lands on both legs simultaneously.

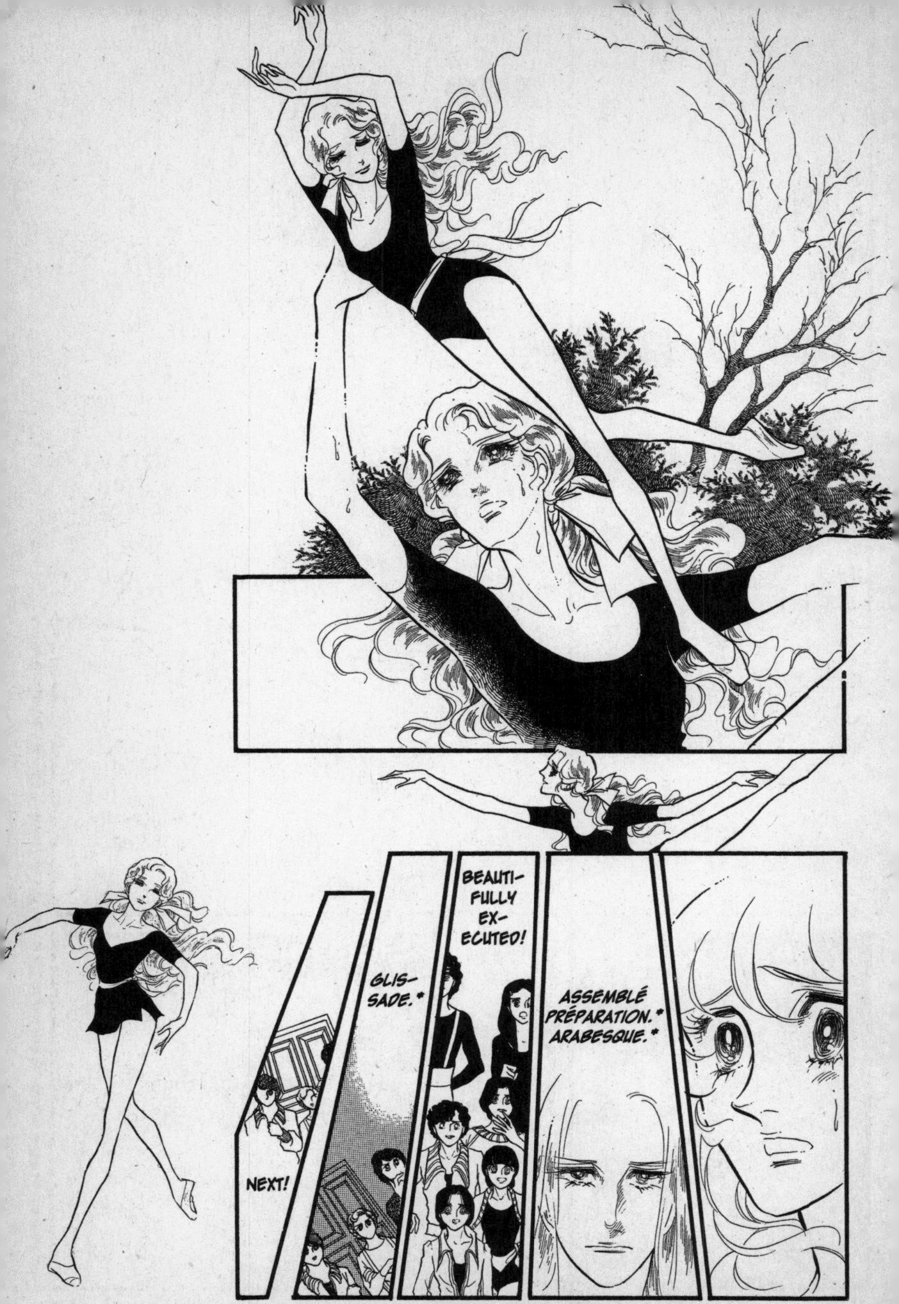
ASSEMBLÉ PRÉPARATION.* ARABESQUE.*
BEAUTI-FULLY EX-ECUTED!
GLIS-SADE.*
NEXT!

**Préparation*:* Preparing for a step or turn. **Glissade*:* A gliding step.

**Arabesque*:* A position on one leg, with the other leg extended behind.

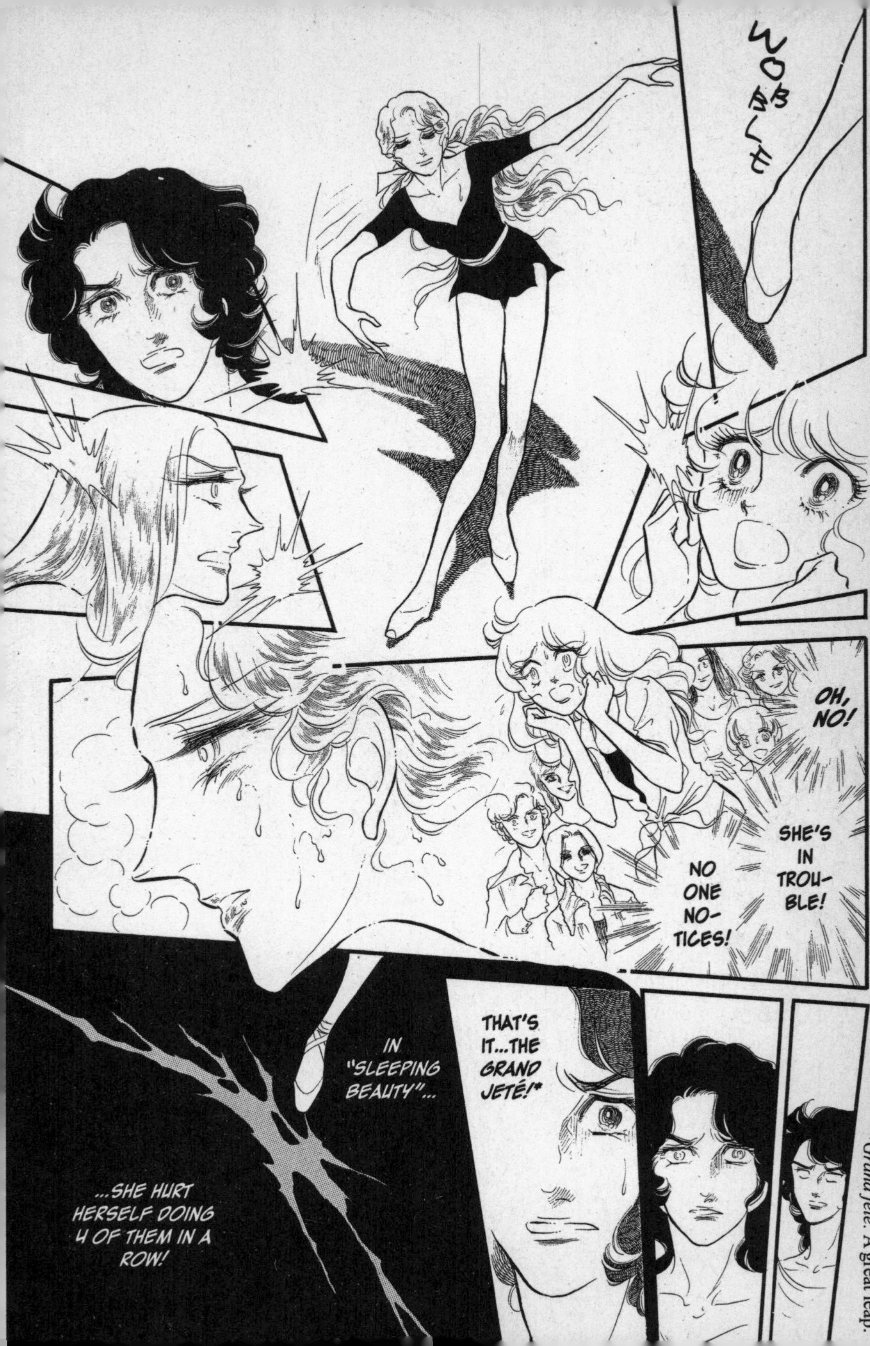
WOBBLE
OH, NO!
SHE'S IN TROU-BLE!
NO ONE NO-TICES!
THAT'S IT...THE GRAND JETÉ!*
IN "SLEEPING BEAUTY"...
...SHE HURT HERSELF DOING 4 OF THEM IN A ROW!

*Grand jeté: A great leap.

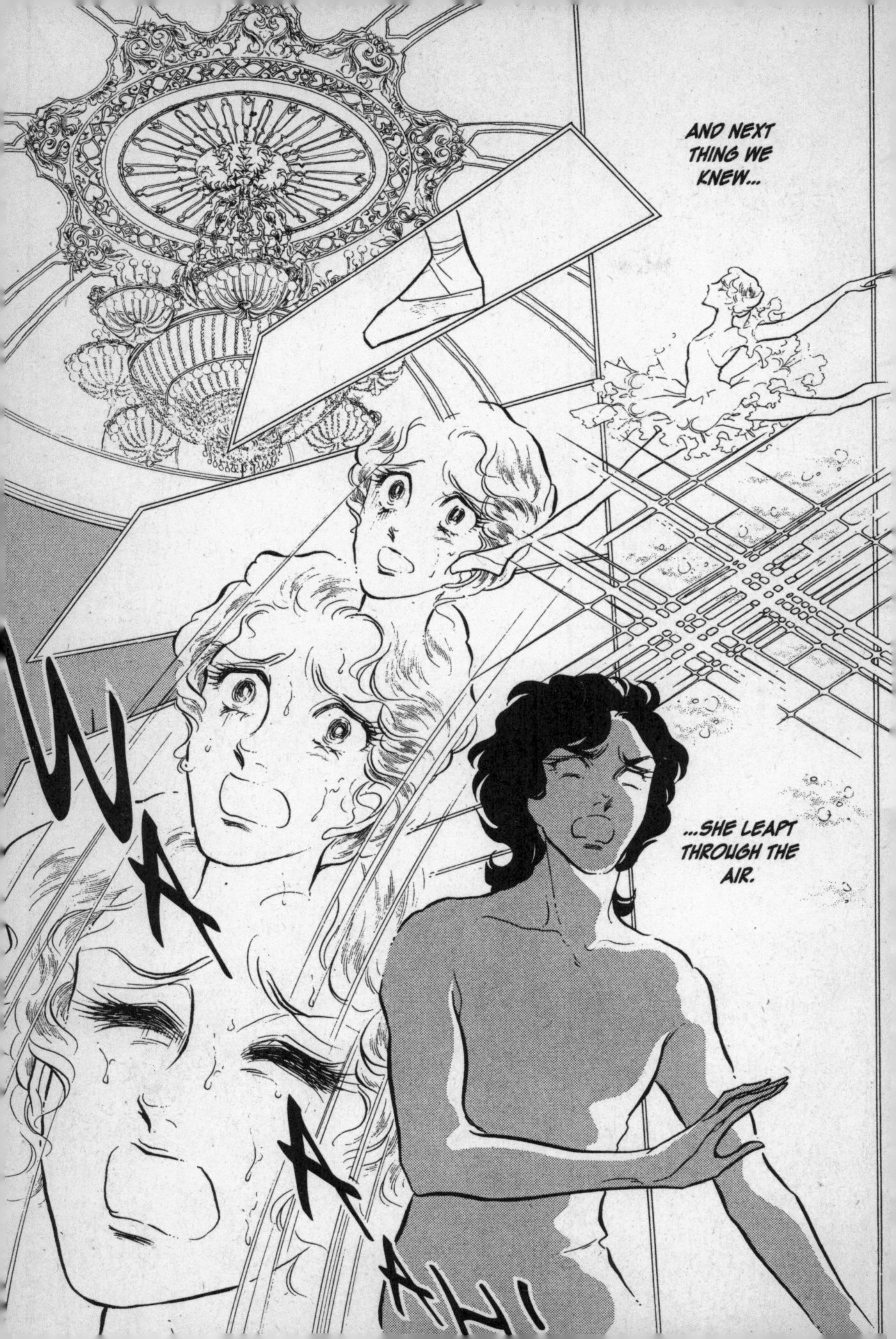
AND NEXT THING WE KNEW...
...SHE LEAPT THROUGH THE AIR.
WAAAH!

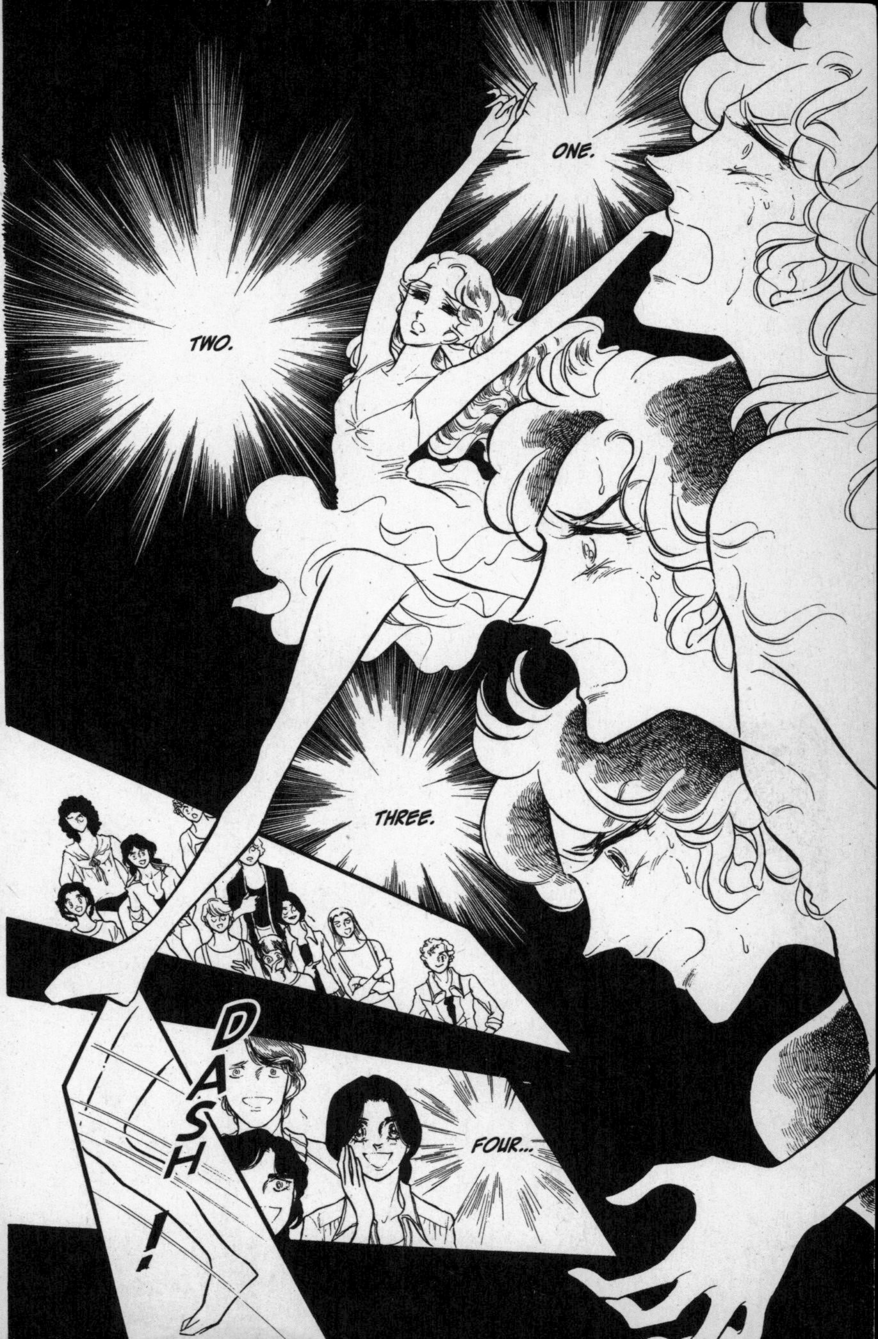
ONE.
TWO.
THREE.
DASH!
FOUR...

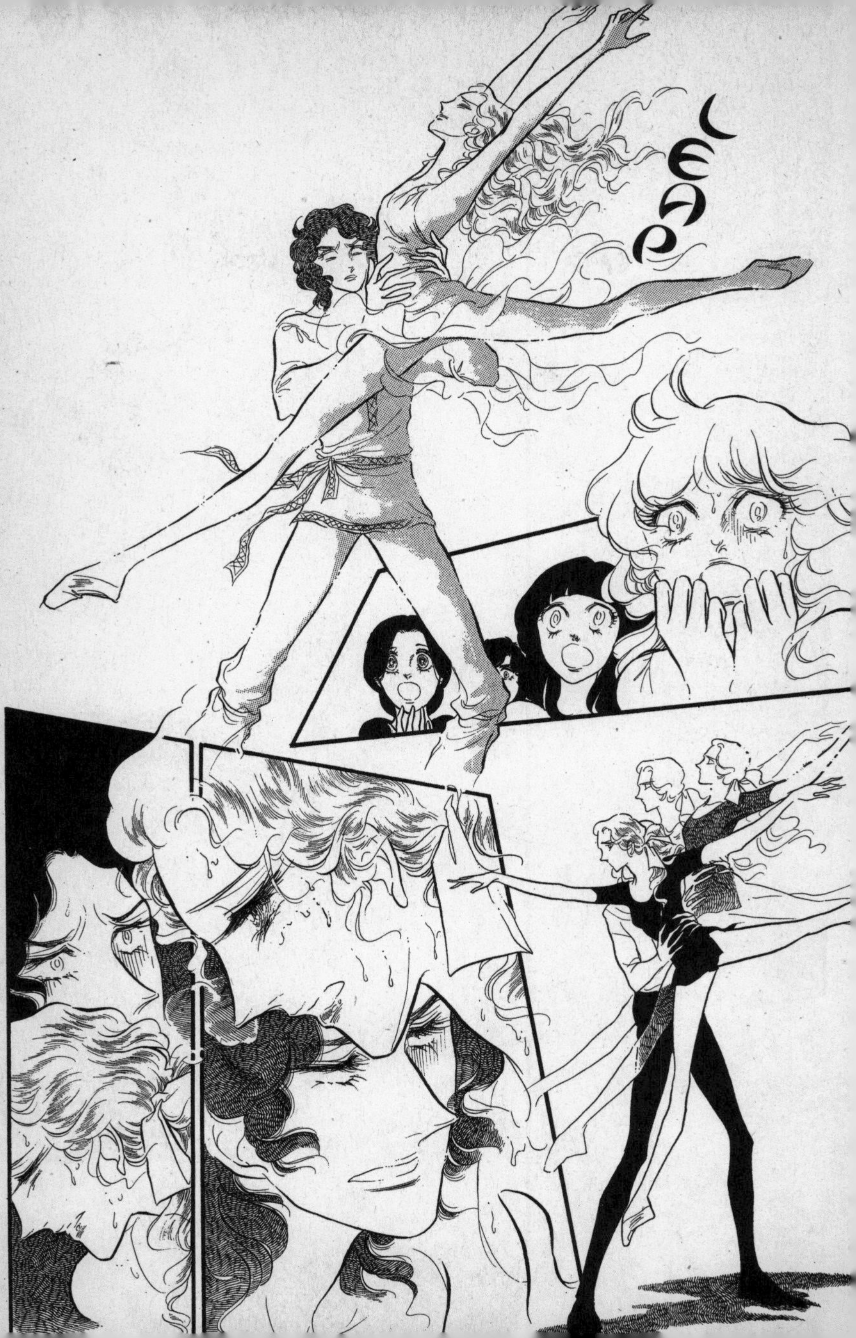
LEAP

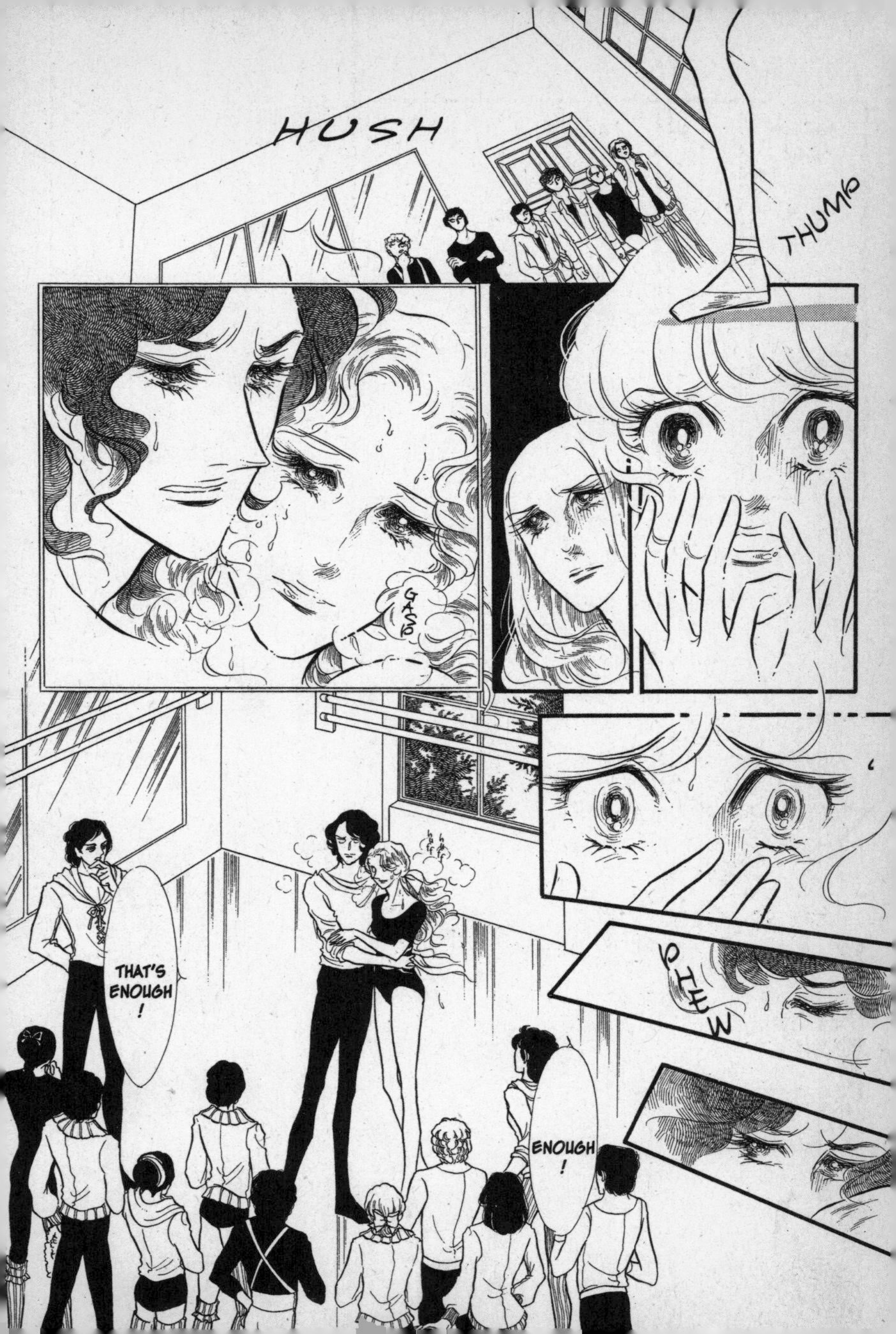
THUMP
HUSH
GASP
PHEW
ENOUGH!
THAT'S ENOUGH!

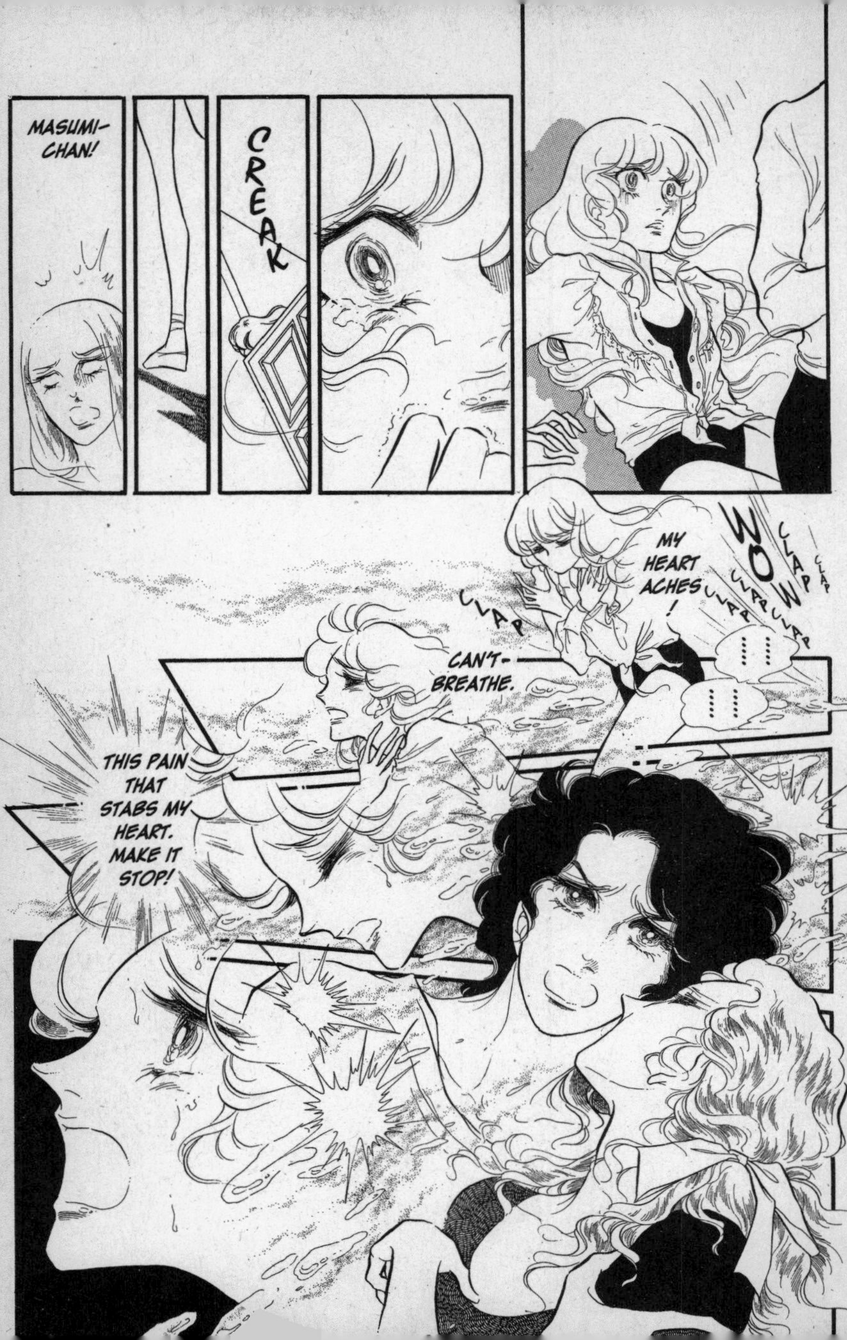
CREAK
MASUMI-CHAN!
WOW
CLAP CLAP
CLAPCLAPCLAP
MY HEART ACHES!
......
......
CLAP
CAN'T-BREATHE.
THIS PAIN THAT STABS MY HEART. MAKE IT STOP!

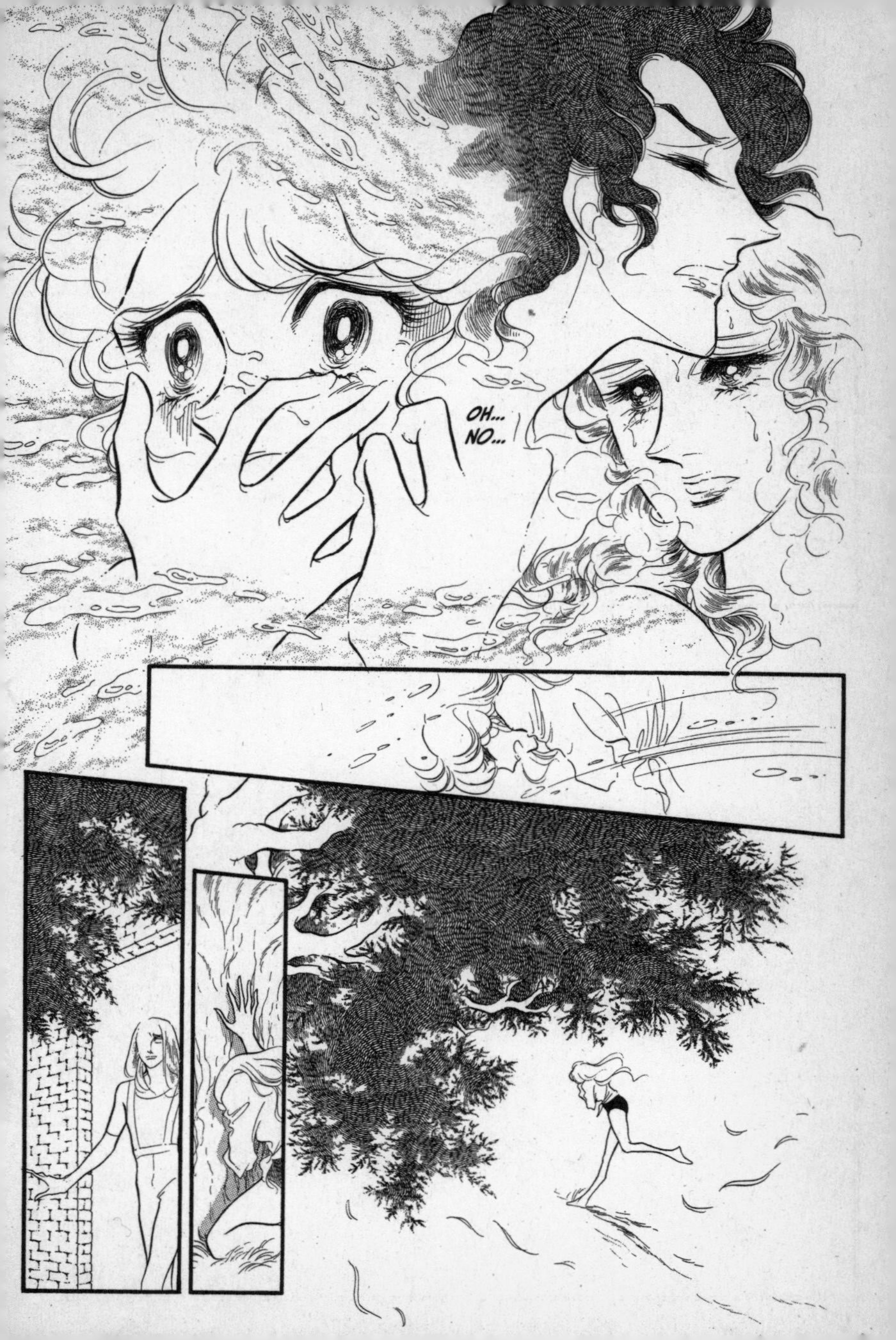
OH... NO...

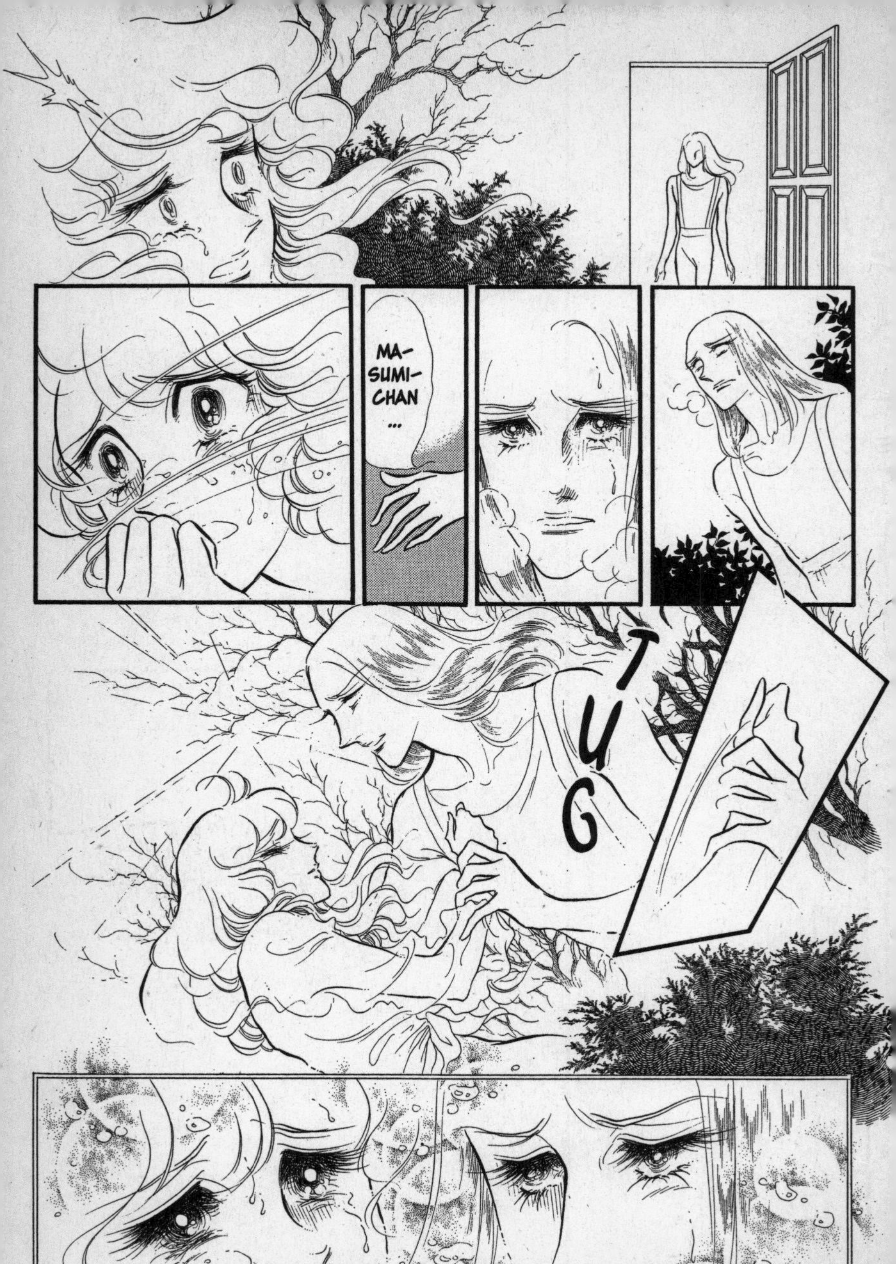
MA-
SUMI-
CHAN
...
TUG

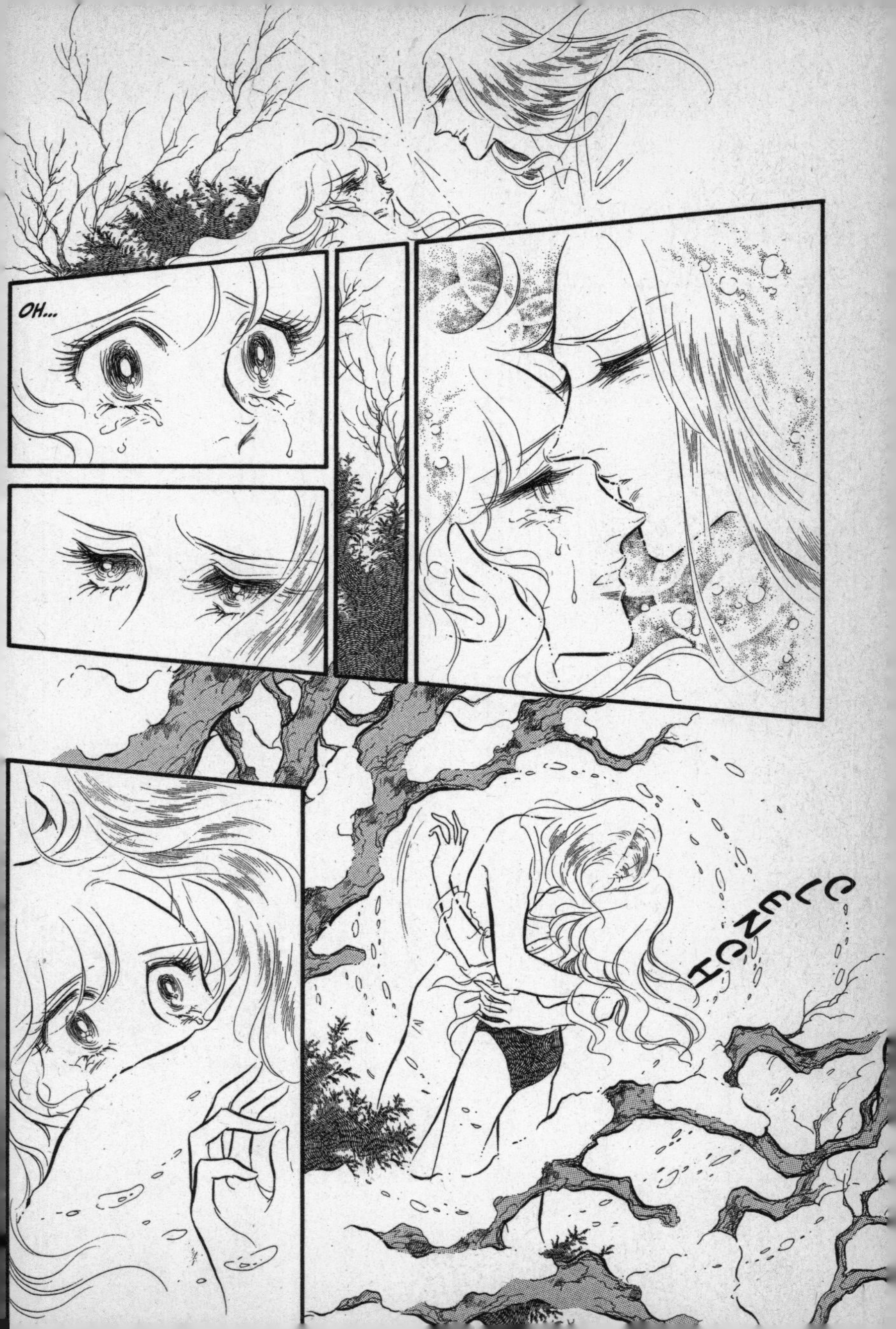
OH...
CLENCH

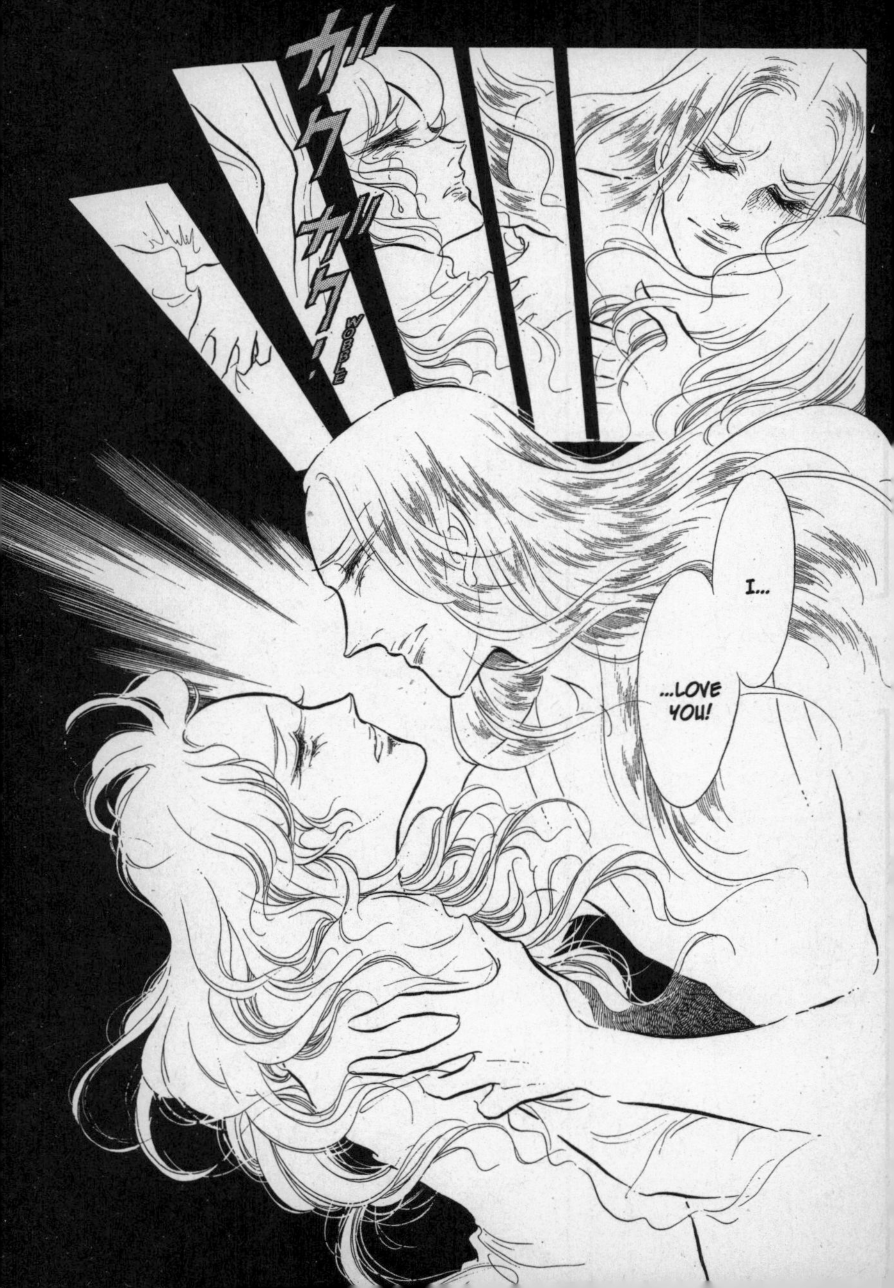
ガクガク！
WOBBLE
I...
...LOVE YOU!

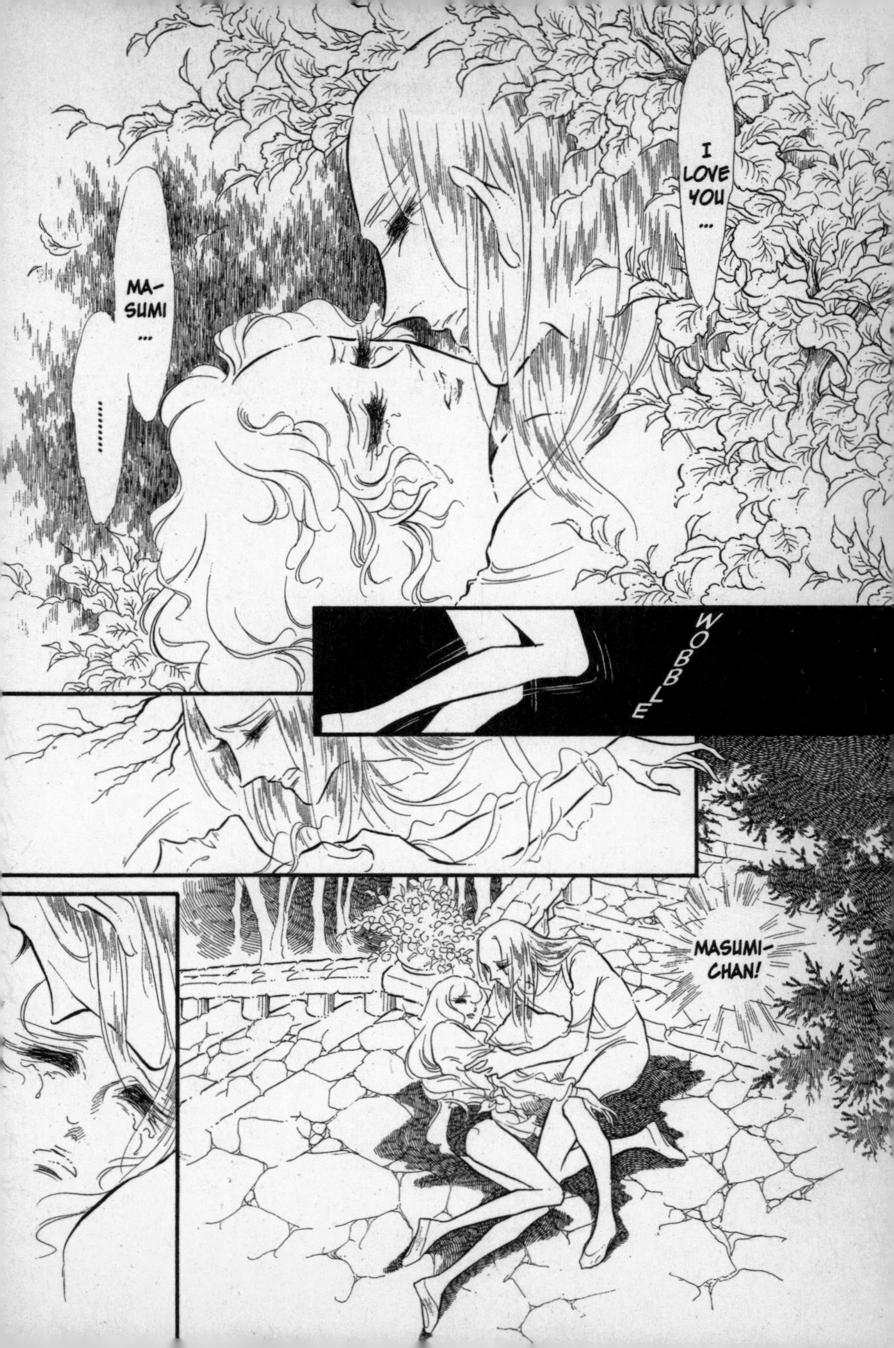
I LOVE YOU ...
MA-SUMI ...
....
WOBBLE
MASUMI-CHAN!

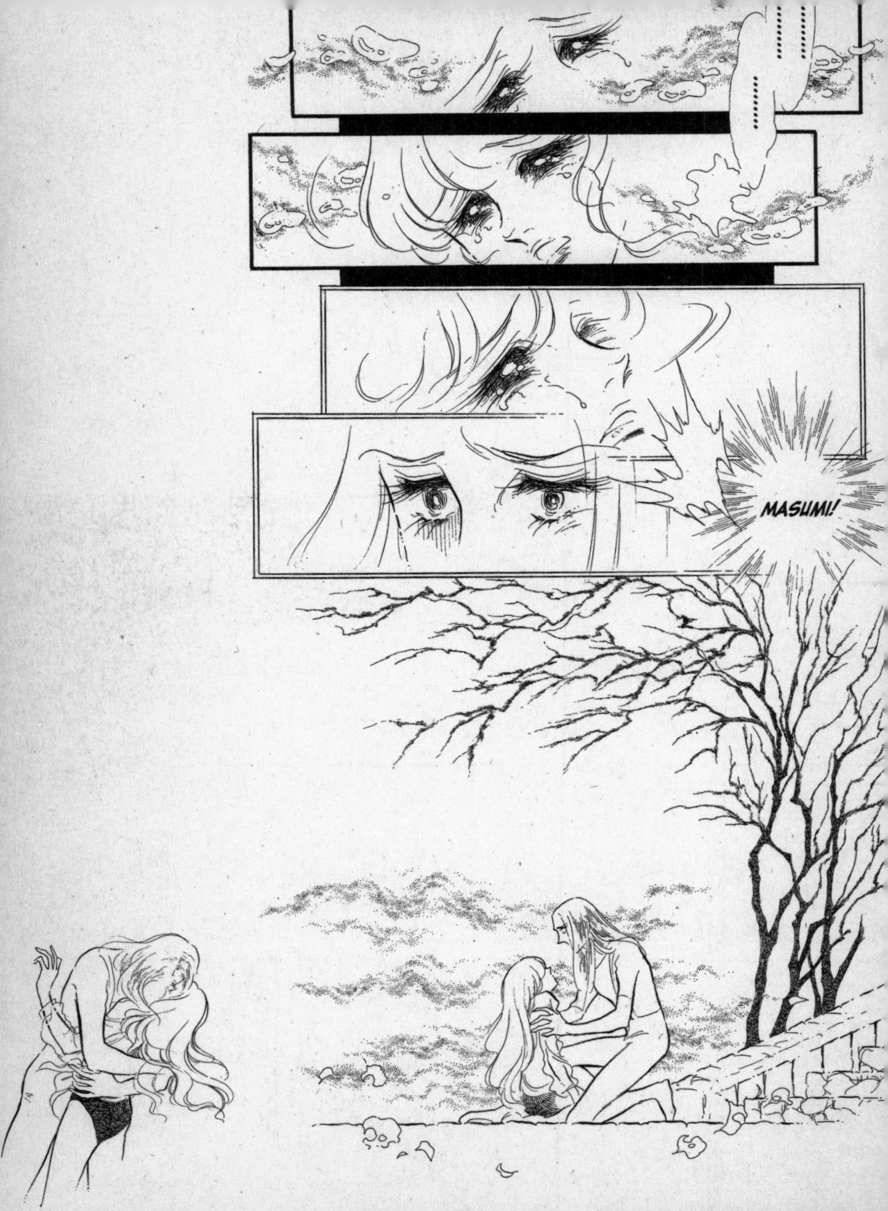
MASUMI!

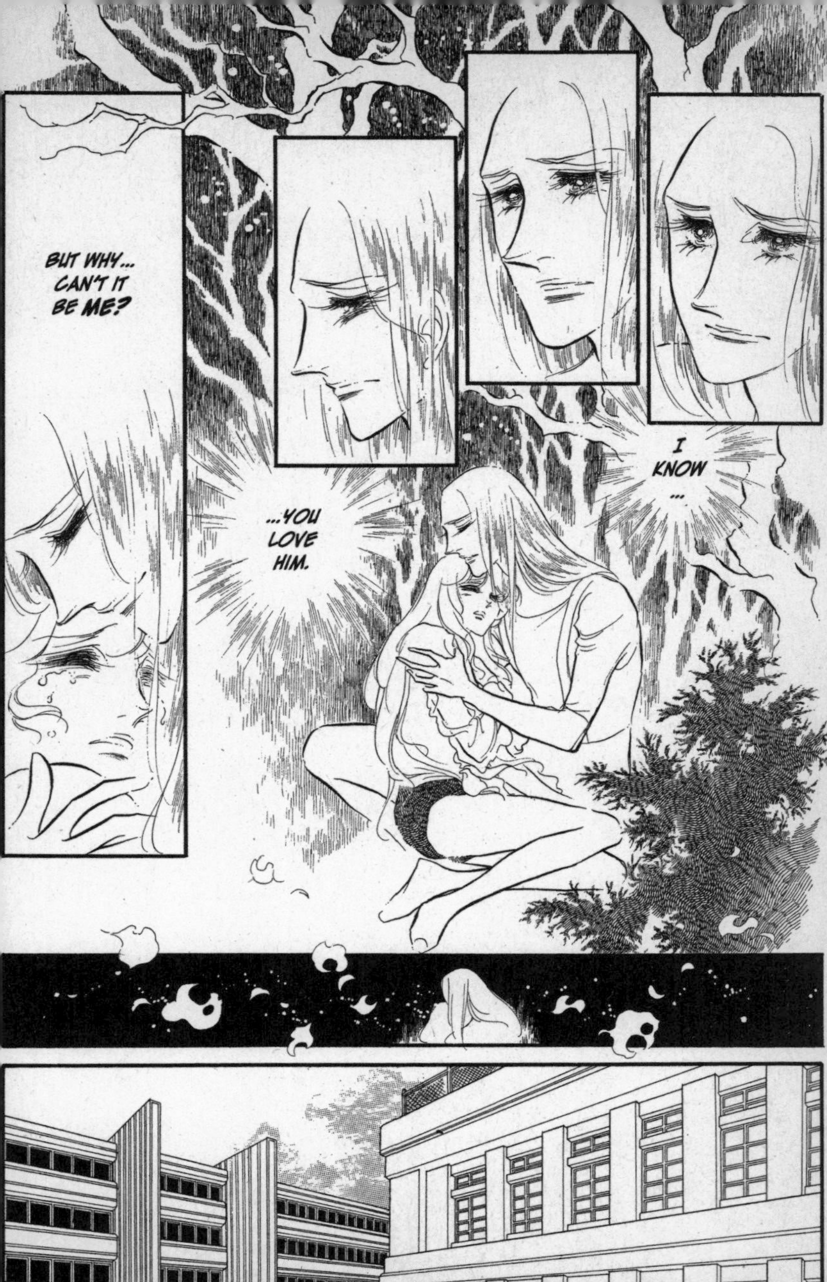
I KNOW ...
...YOU LOVE HIM.
BUT WHY... CAN'T IT BE ME?

Continued in Swan Vol. 7

Maya Lynn Perry
Translation & Adaptation

Vanessa Satone
Lettering

Larry Berry
Design

Jim Chadwick
Editor

SWAN Volume 6 © 1976 Kyoko Ariyoshi. All rights reserved. First published in Japan in 1992 by AKITA PUBLISHING CO., LTD., Tokyo

SWAN Volume 6, published by WildStorm Productions, an imprint of DC Comics, 888 Prospect St. #240, La Jolla, CA 92037, English Translation © 2006, All Rights Reserved. English translation rights in U.S.A. arranged with AKITA PUBLISHING CO., LTD., Tokyo, through Tuttle-Mori Agency, Inc., Tokyo. The stories, characters, and incidents mentioned in this magazine are entirely fictional. Printed on recyclable paper. WildStorm does not read or accept unsolicited submissions of ideas, stories or artwork. Printed in Canada.

ISBN: 1-4012-0866-5
ISBN-13: 978-1-4012-0866-0

FLIP IT!!

All the pages in this book were created—and are printed here—in Japanese RIGHT-to-LEFT format. No artwork has been reversed or altered, so you can read the stories the way the creators meant for them to be read.

JAPANESE NAMES

Authentic Japanese name order is family name first, given name second. With previous volumes, CMX has honored authentic Japanese order. By popular request, we have converted to Western format (given name first, family name second) moving forward with this volume.

RIGHT TO LEFT?!

Traditional Japanese manga starts at the upper right-hand corner, and moves right-to-left as it goes down the page. Follow this guide for an easy understanding.

Catch the latest at
cmxmanga.com!